PROFILES OF A LOST WORLD

Hirsz Abramowicz in the early 1930s.
Courtesy of the YIVO Archives.

PROFILES OF A LOST WORLD

Memoirs of East European Jewish Life before World War II

HIRSZ ABRAMOWICZ

translated by
Eva Zeitlin Dobkin

edited by
Dina Abramowicz and
Jeffrey Shandler

with introductions by
David E. Fishman and
Dina Abramowicz

Published in cooperation with
YIVO Institute for Jewish Research

 WAYNE STATE UNIVERSITY PRESS   DETROIT

Raphael Patai Series in Jewish Folklore and Anthropology
*A complete listing of the books in this series
can be found at the back of this volume.*
General Editor
Dan Ben-Amos
University of Pennsylvania
Advisory Editors
Jane S. Gerber
City University of New York
Barbara Kirshenblatt-Gimblett
New York University
Aliza Shenhar
University of Haifa
Amnon Shiloah
Hebrew University
Harvey E. Goldberg
Hebrew University
Samuel G. Armistead
University of California, Davis
Guy H. Haskell
Emory University

Published with the assistance of the Lucius N. Littauer Foundation
Copyright © 1999 by YIVO Institute for Jewish Research,
New York, New York 10019. All rights reserved.
No part of this book may be reproduced without formal permission.
Manufactured in the United States of America.
03 02 01 00 99   5 4 3 2 1

Library of Congress Cataloging-in-Publication Data

Abramowicz, Hirsz, 1881–1960.
   [Farshvundene geshtaltn. English]
   Profiles of a lost world : memoirs of East European Jewish life
before World War II / Hirsz Abramowicz ; translated by Eva Zeitlin
Dobkin ; edited by Dina Abramowicz and Jeffrey Shandler ; with
introductions by David E. Fishman and Dina Abramowicz.
   p. cm. — (Raphael Patai series in Jewish folklore and
anthropology)
   Published in cooperation with Yivo Institute for Jewish Research.
   Includes bibliographical references and index.
   ISBN 0-8143-2784-2 (alk. paper)
   1. Jews—Lithuania—Vilnius—History—20th century. 2. Jews—
Lithuania—Vilnius—Biography. 3. Vilnius (Lithuania)—Biography.
4. Vilnius (Lithuania)—Ethnic relations. I. Abramowicz, Dina.
II. Shandler, Jeffrey. III. Dobkin, Eva Zeitlin. IV. Yivo
Institute for Jewish Research. V. Title. VI. Series
DS135.L52V5519313   1999
947.93—dc21   98-27168

Book design by Joanne Elkin Kinney

CONTENTS

ACKNOWLEDGMENTS   7
INTRODUCTION   9
    David E. Fishman
MY FATHER'S LIFE AND WORK   18
    Dina Abramowicz
NOTE FROM THE EDITORS   36

I. LITHUANIAN JEWISH TRADITIONS   39
    1. Rural Jewish Occupations in Lithuania   41
    2. A Lithuanian *Shtetl*   77
    3. The Diet of Lithuanian Jews   99
    4. Healing the Mentally Ill   109

II. REFORM AND UPHEAVAL BEFORE WORLD WAR I   115
    1. Joshua Steinberg   117
    2. Samuel Gozhanski   124
    3. Chaim Fialkov   126
    4. Hirsh Lekert and His Times   132
    5. Anna Lifshits   143
    6. In Tsarist Jails   147
    7. Jewish Gymnasia without Quotas   158
    8. I. L. Peretz Visits the Jewish Writers in Odessa   162
    9. Chaim Weizmann and Kolia Tepper Debate   169

III. WORLD WAR I AND ITS AFTERMATH
     IN AND AROUND VILNA   175
   1. I Join the Militia   177
   2. The Germans in World War I   182
   3. April 1919   209

IV. JEWISH VOCATIONAL EDUCATION BETWEEN THE WORLD WARS   219
   1. The Vilna "Help Through Work" Society   221
   2. Jewish Agricultural School in Wieluciany   229
   3. The Białystok Vocational School   240
   4. Matthias Schreiber   243

V. PROFILES OF VILNA JEWRY BEFORE WORLD WAR II   249
   1. Mark Antokolsky   251
   2. Khaykl Lunski   260
   3. Samuel Hurwicz   265
   4. Eliezer Kruk   269
   5. B. Kahan-Wirgili   276
   6. Joseph Jaszunski   280
   7. Joseph Czernichow (Danieli)   285
   8. Gershon Malakiewicz   289
   9. Chief Rabbi Isaac Rubinstein   292
   10. Dr. Cemach Szabad   297
   11. Dr. Jacob Wygodzki   301
   12. A. Weiter   306
   13. Zalmen Reisen   313
   14. Moshe Shalit   321

GLOSSARY   327
ENDNOTES   333
PLACE-NAMES   357
PERIODICALS MENTIONED IN THE TEXT   359
BIBLIOGRAPHY   361
INDEX   367

ACKNOWLEDGMENTS

The editors are grateful to the following individuals for helping to make possible the publication of this book: Dr. Allan Nadler, former Director of Research at YIVO, for recommending YIVO's sponsorship of this project and securing the funding necessary to prepare the manuscript for publication; YIVO Chairman Bruce Slovin and the entire YIVO Board of Directors, for their encouragement and generous support of this project from its inception; Tom L. Freudenheim, former Executive Director of YIVO, for seeing the book through the various stages of publication; Arthur B. Evans, Director of Wayne State University Press, and Dr. Dan Ben-Amos, Editor of the Raphael Patai Series in Jewish Folklore and Anthropology, for their enthusiasm and ongoing support; the late Dr. Raphael Patai, founder and former editor of the Series in Jewish Folklore and Anthropology, for reading the manuscript and recommending the book for publication; Dr. Barbara Kirshenblatt-Gimblett of New York University and Dr. Samuel Kassow of Trinity College, for their invaluable editorial input and scholarly endorsement.

We are also indebted to the archivists and librarians at YIVO for their scholarship and steadfast assistance with research: Chief Archivist Marek Web, Music Archivist Chana Mlotek, Curator of Photographic Collections Krysia Fisher, Head Librarian Zachary Baker, and Consulting Librarian Dr. Bella Hass Weinberg all contributed materially and intellectually to the making of this book. Portia Auguste-Smith, Shaindel Fogelman, and Herbert Lazarus deserve warm thanks for their assistance with manuscript preparation. Paul Glasser proofread the manuscript numerous times with skill and care. From the firm of Paul, Weiss, Rifkind, Wharton & Garrison,

ACKNOWLEDGMENTS

YIVO Board Member Max Gitter and his associates Lynn Bayard and Olivier Sultan generously contributed their time and legal expertise. Finally, we wish to thank Andrea Raab Sherman, former Director of Publications at YIVO, for her dedicated supervision of this project through its publication. Publication of this book was made possible in part thanks to the generous support of the Lucius N. Littauer Foundation.

INTRODUCTION

David E. Fishman

Hirsz Abramowicz's *Profiles of a Lost World* straddles the boundaries between genres, subjects, and eras. It is largely a memoir in the form of biographical sketches of East European Jewish personalities from the three generations prior to World War II. At the same time, it is a work of scholarship, with several important historical and ethnographic studies based on documentary and field research. The book's primary focus is the vibrant city of Vilna, which Jews referred to as "the Jerusalem of Lithuania," yet it also devotes considerable attention to the Lithuanian countryside, with its agriculturally based economy and more traditional way of life.

The key distinction among the various chapters of this book is neither their genres nor subjects, but the circumstances of their composition. A small but significant number of these essays were written by Abramowicz, a prominent writer and educator in prewar Vilna, for publication in some of the various newspapers, literary journals, and almanacs that were part of Poland's thriving Yiddish literary world.[1] The majority of its chapters, however, were written in New York, in the decade immediately following World War II, by a refugee who had lost his wife, relatives, and friends in the Holocaust.

The divide between pre- and post-Holocaust writing remains almost invisible on the pages of *Profiles of a Lost World*. Only the most attentive reader of the bibliographic notes will realize that one of its ethnographic studies was first published in 1937 in a Warsaw-based historical journal, while the one that follows it was written for a memorial book on Lithuanian Jewry issued in New York in 1951. Abramowicz brought the essays together in a collection published in Yiddish in Buenos Aires in 1958 under the title *Farshvundene geshtaltn: zikhroynes un siluetn* (Vanished Figures: Memoirs and Silhouettes).

The seamlessness of Abramowicz's prose is the author's greatest achievement. His impetus for composing *Profiles of a Lost World* was commemorative—to recall the array of personalities, landscapes, institutions and even foods that made up the community he knew before World War II. Yet he consciously struggled to maintain the sober, analytic, and balanced tone he had established in his prewar reportage and studies. Indeed, the Holocaust is only briefly mentioned on the pages of this book.

Abramowicz displayed an ability to strike a balance between his personal voice as a Jew from Vilna, who knew intimately the people and places he describes, and the voice of a historian and ethnographer, ever mindful of larger forces and broader contexts. He was able to combine the memoirist's attention to detail and pithy anecdote with the more detached perspective of a social scientist. Although the book was written with much love and pain, its salient features are emotional restraint and intellectuality, which are hallmarks of the *litvak,* the Lithuanian Jew. The product of these creative tensions is an inviting introduction to the world of East European Jewry during the half-century before the Holocaust.

Perhaps the overarching contribution of *Profiles of a Lost World* for today's reader is Abramowicz's ability to convey a sense of the local and regional nature of East European Jewish life. This was a world in which where one came from spoke volumes about who one was. Each city and district possessed its own collective myths, legends, self-images, forms of speech, foods, religious customs, communal structures, and political inclinations. Abramowicz's book reconstructs the richly textured subculture of one region, Lithuania, and one city, Vilna, as it flourished in the late nineteenth to the mid-twentieth centuries.[2]

Several elements contributed to the formation of a distinct Lithuanian Jewish subculture and identity, and it is worth recalling them here, as Abramowicz assumed that his readers would be familiar with them.

Political factors played an early formative role: between the thirteenth and mid-sixteenth centuries, the Grand Duchy of Lithuania was a strong, sovereign state—indeed, it was the largest single state in Eastern Europe. Spanning from the Baltic Sea in the north to the Black Sea in the south, it incorporated most of what is today Belarus and Ukraine, including the city of Kiev. The Grand Duchy's capital was Vilna, a city established in 1323 and named for the Wilia River, along whose banks it is situated. The Lithuanians, who ruled over a multiethnic, largely Eastern Orthodox population, were the last pagans on European soil. They spoke a non-Slavic language that retained grammatical features similar to Sanskrit.

Geography proved to be destiny. As Lithuania's neighbors to the east and west grew more powerful, it was subjected to varying degrees of Polish and Russian influence and domination over the course of seven centuries. In 1386, the Lithuanian Grand Duke Jagiełło (Lithuanian: Jogaila) married the heiress to the Polish throne and converted to Christianity. As a result, Lithuania joined the Roman Catholic world. Jagiełło and his descendants ruled Poland and Lithuania in tandem until 1572. Although the two states maintained official separation, the alliance rapidly became a union. In 1569, the Union of Lublin created a single executive and single parliament for the Polish-Lithuanian Commonwealth, and the southern half of Lithuania was formally transferred to Polish administration. In its aftermath, the Lithuanian aristocracy became increasingly Polonized, although the official language of state documents remained a form of Belorussian, written in the Cyrillic alphabet.

Eventually, Lithuania was annexed by tsarist Russia (in the partitions of Poland in 1772, 1793, and 1795), and the Grand Duchy was abolished. With the end of independence, the pendulum of influence over the region swung eastward. Russian governors and ministries displaced the Polish-Lithuanian noblemen and landowners, and the Orthodox Church enjoyed increasing official support. Tsarist rule over what was called "the Northwest Provinces" lasted 120 years, until World War I. Jews, however, continued to refer to the region as *Lite,* and Jewish residents of the Belorussian cities of Grodno, Brześć, and Minsk, not to mention the Jews of Vilna and Kovno, were considered *litvakes.*

Jewish settlement in the region dates back to Lithuania's "Golden Age" (i.e., the period before the union of 1569), an era when Lithuania was a frontier colony of Polish Jewry. The first decree codifying the legal status of the Jews of the Grand Duchy—the 1388 charter by Duke Vitaut to the Jews of Brześć—was modeled after an earlier Polish charter. The first prominent rabbis to serve in the region—such as Rabbi Solomon Luria (1510–74), author of the mammoth treatise *Yam shel Shlomo* (The Sea of Solomon)—were temporary migrants from Poland. As late as the sixteenth century, the leaders of Lithuanian Jewish communities used to gather for annual meetings not in Lithuania, but in Poland, at the fair in Lublin.

The differences between Polish and Lithuanian Jews, and an increasing awareness of them, grew from the second half of the sixteenth century. The establishment of the Council of Lithuanian Jewish Communities (*Va'ad Medinat Lita*), was an important consolidating factor. The council was a powerful body that enjoyed officially sanctioned jurisdiction over Jewry's internal affairs: it assessed and levied taxes on its constituent communities, represented the interests of Lithuanian Jewry before the authorities, and passed ordinances governing social, economic, and religious matters. It both cooperated and clashed with the analogous council of Polish-Jewish communities, called the Council of Four Lands (*Va'ad Arba Aratsot*). Tensions between the two councils persisted, especially over matters of tax apportionment, and this reinforced the sense of regional difference until both bodies were abolished by Polish parliamentary decree in 1764.

In the sixteenth century, the distinct Lithuanian dialect of Yiddish came into being, which also influenced the local pronunciation of Hebrew prayers and texts. Certain patterns of speech became telltale signs of Lithuanian Jews: their pronunciation of *oy* as *ey*—e.g., *teyre* instead of *toyre* (Torah)—and of *sh* as *s*—e.g., *sabes* instead of *shabes* (Sabbath). These linguistic peculiarities became the subject of countless quips and anecdotes.

These regional differences would have been of little consequence were it not for the religious-cultural dispute of the late eighteenth century between the Hasidic movement and its rabbinite opponents, the *mitnagdim,* which was waged primarily on the territory of Jewish Lithuania. This was a clash between divergent religious tendencies—Hasidic mysticism, spontaneity, and ecstatic enthusiasm versus *mitnagdic* legalism, rabbinic scholarship, and sober restraint. The conflict assumed a distinctly regional character as Hasidism, which originated in Ukraine, spread northward and encountered its fiercest opposition in Lithuania. As a result, *litvak* and *mitnaged* became synonyms in the Jewish lexicon.

The towering leader of the *mitnagdic* camp was Rabbi Elijah of Vilna (1720–97), a Talmudic scholar of such gigantic proportions that he was given the appellation of *gaon,* an honorific title that had not been bestowed upon a rabbi for more than half a millennium. Although he did not occupy the formal post of Rabbi of the Vilna community, the Vilna Gaon was the unchallenged religious authority not only in his city, but in the entire region. As one contemporary and rival, the Hasidic master Rabbi Shneur Zalman of Lyadi, noted, "There is no one in all the land of Lithuania who will raise his voice to contradict him."[3]

The Vilna Gaon's personal model of strenuous study of rabbinic texts, analytic intellectuality, and interest in secular areas of inquiry molded the cultural ethos of Lithuanian Jewry for generations. The most tangible expressions of his legacy were in the areas of higher learning and Hebrew printing. Lithuania became the seat of the most prominent Talmudic academies in the world, beginning with the yeshiva in Wołożyn, founded by the Gaon's disciple Rabbi Hayyim. This was followed by the yeshivas established in Mir, Słobodka, Telsze, and others that flourished in the late nineteenth and early twentieth centuries. Because these scholars needed books, the Romm press, founded in Vilna in 1799, emerged as the preeminent publisher of rabbinic literature in the region and, indeed, in all of Europe. The Romm edition of the Talmud (commonly referred to as the *Vilner shas*) was the first serious attempt to produce a reliable version of the Talmudic text, and its commentaries were based on the comparison of manuscripts and early printings. It became the authoritative edition for generations of students.

The impact of the Vilna Gaon's mythic stature on Lithuanian Jewry was broad, pervasive and, at the same time, quite pliable. It molded the consciousness of generations of laymen, especially in Vilna itself, where religious study became an integral part of everyday life. A private letter sent by a resident of Vilna in 1856 reported that there were many Talmudic scholars among the city's artisans, and that a craftsman who studied only the religious code *Hayye adam* (Life of Man) was considered unlearned by his peers.[4] Mid-nineteenth-century Lithuanian *maskilim,* followers of the *Haskalah* or Jewish Enlightenment, also drew inspiration from the Vilna Gaon, due to his study of mathematics and natural science and his purported rationalism (in contrast to Hasidic "superstition"). Later, Lithuanian Zionists looked to the Vilna Gaon as their mentor on account of his occupation with biblical studies and Hebrew grammar, as well as his unsuccessful attempt to emigrate to the Land of Israel. Other modern Lithuanian Jews simply appropriated Rabbi Elijah as the symbol of their dedication to the continuity of Jewish knowledge and culture.

By the middle of the nineteenth century, the composite image of the *litvak* was fully formed and rooted in Jewish consciousness. He was smart, analytical, learned, worldly, skeptical, proud, stubborn, dynamic, and energetic. In 1866, the Hebrew and Yiddish journalist Alexander Zederbaum, a native of the Polish town of Zamość and a resident of Odessa, offered the following portrait:

> In general, our brethren in Lithuania have a great talent and thirst for knowledge. Among all classes of their communities, study and investigation are considered a duty from childhood through adulthood. They study not only Torah, but also secular wisdom found in Hebrew books, and some of them study books in foreign tongues as well.
>
> Our Lithuanian brethren have sharp minds and are clever in conducting their plans and endeavors. If they resolve to do something, they will not rest until they accomplish it. There is a folk saying: "A Polish Jew says, 'If you can't reach your goal by climbing over the obstacles, then climb under them.' But a Lithuanian Jew says, 'If you can't climb over the obstacles, then you *must* climb over them.'"
>
> All Lithuanian Jews, even the lowliest among them, are proud of their origins and look down with a certain amount of contempt at Ukrainian

and Polish Jews. So convinced are they of their superiority that they keep apart from their Polish brethren even when they migrate to other regions and lands.[5]

Zederbaum, a *maskil,* admired the *litvakes'* openness to secular science and to German and Russian culture. Beginning in the 1840s, *Haskalah* circles in Vilna and Kovno created an enlightened Jewish subculture in Lithuania. Lithuanian *maskilim* were highly literate, with extensive knowledge of biblical and rabbinic literature, and were committed to forging a synthesis between European culture and Jewish tradition. Their literary creativity ranged from Hebrew poetry to Yiddish fiction, from world history to biblical philology, and from books on modern science and technology to Russian-language textbooks. The communal lives of these *maskilim* revolved around the moderately reformed synagogue (*Taharat Ha-Kodesh*) they established in Vilna, the state-sponsored Jewish schools where they served as instructors, and the Vilna Rabbinical School where many of them either studied or taught.

Although Zederbaum's assessment that Lithuanian Jews were more enlightened than other East European Jews was widely shared, his admiration of this attribute was not. In Hasidic-dominated Poland, a popular epithet for a *litvak* was *tseylem-kop* (cross-head), based on the myth that there was a crucifix buried inside every *litvak*'s skull. This graphic image reflected the view that, beneath their learned exterior, Lithuanian Jews were apostates and hardly Jews at all in their hearts and minds.

It is one of the ironies of history that Lithuania, with its deeply rooted aristocracies of learning (first rabbinic and, later, *maskilic*), was the breeding ground for a modern, egalitarian, and activist Jewish counterculture. The Jewish socialist Bund, founded in Vilna in 1897, brought political and economic struggle into the Jewish community in the form of anti-tsarist agitation and strike activity. Bundism captured the imagination of a generation of Lithuanian Jewish youth, for whom it was a rebellion not only against the Tsar and capitalism, but also against the conservatism and passivity of their parents.

Vilna was the Bund's greatest stronghold—the headquarters of its underground leadership, the site of its secret printing presses, and the arena for its most heroic acts. In interwar Poland, Vilna was the only major city in which the Bund competed closely with the Zionists in elections to the local Jewish community council. The dialectical relationship between the city and the movement was profound: not only did the Bund transform the ethos of Jewish Vilna, but the traditions of Jewish Vilna transformed the Bund. In its early years, the movement came to champion Jewish civil and national rights in Russia and embraced the cause of Jewish cultural renaissance in Yiddish. Vilna's Bundists were less sectarian than their counterparts in Warsaw and more willing to work with ideological rivals for the common Jewish good.

Hirsz Abramowicz was a product of the wide reach of Vilna's *maskilic* and Bundist milieus. A graduate of the state-sponsored Jewish Teachers Institute (the successor to the Vilna Rabbinical School), he was educated and trained by the last of the *maskilim* and by intellectuals dedicated to a Russian-Jewish cultural synthesis. Abramowicz pursued his educational career in government schools for Jewish children. He was also in touch with the *Hevrat Mefitsei Haskalah,* which supervised a network of Jewish communal schools when the temporary liberalization of Russian educational policies permitted such a development.

As a young man at the turn of the century, Abramowicz was also drawn to the newly formed circles of Jewish workers and socialists in Vilna. He participated in anti-tsarist protests and even played a peripheral role in the events preceding the assassination attempt on the Russian governor general of Vilna in 1902. He became an avid reader of the new Yiddish literature, especially the work of its modernist patriarch, I. L. Peretz, and developed a lifelong commitment to Jewish economic self-help in the form of vocational education.

Many of Abramowicz's biographical profiles are of personalities from the two milieus he knew best. At the same time, the influence of the ideals of Russian Jewish liberalism and socialism permeate his book from beginning to end. Perhaps they are most evident in his studies of rural Jewish life, which exude love and admiration for the wholesome, hard-working Jews of Lithuanian *shtetlekh* and villages.

Much of *Profiles of a Lost World* is situated in the years during and immediately after World War I, when political control over Vilna changed hands nine times among the Russians, Germans, Lithuanians, Soviets, and Poles. Abramowicz vividly captures the horrors and suffering endured by Jews during World War I, which have since been overshadowed by the Holocaust. His study of the German occupation of Vilna between 1915 and 1918 remains an authoritative historical treatment. It has an eerie and surreal quality given our retrospective awareness of the subsequent German occupation a few decades later.

As German rule collapsed at the end of the war, Vilna fell under a series of rulers: the Lithuanian nationalist *Taryba* (November 1918), the Polish *Samoobrona* (January 1919), Soviet and local communist forces (January–April 1919), and the Polish army (April 1919–July 1920). The Red Army then gained control of the city and handed it over to the Lithuanians. In October 1920, Polish forces led by General Lucjan Żeligowski took over the city once again.

INTRODUCTION

The end of World War I resulted in a partition of historic Lithuania and, consequently, of Lithuanian Jewry: the northern districts constituted themselves into an independent Lithuanian state, with Kovno its capital city; the southeastern districts were incorporated into the Belorussian Soviet Socialist Republic, a part of the Soviet Union, with Minsk its capital; and the Vilna district, along with districts to its south and southwest, became part of the newly restored Poland. In the absence of diplomatic ties among these three states, each part of Lithuanian Jewry was cut off from the others, and so each followed a different course of development over the next twenty years.

The period of Polish rule over Vilna was inaugurated by a bloody pogrom in April 1919, which left scars on Polish-Jewish relations in the city for years to follow. Yet despite, or perhaps because of, this oppressive anti-Semitic environment, the interwar years were an extremely dynamic period of Jewish communal development in Poland. In the words of historian Arcadius Kahan, the Vilna community was characterized by an "excess or hypertrophy of organization," with the establishment of numerous professional and trade associations, eight major mutual aid societies, seven educational and cultural associations, four daily Yiddish newspapers, three Jewish teachers' seminaries, and three scholarly research institutions.[6] Many of these organizations appear in the pages of Abramowicz's book.

The modern Yiddish milieu with which Abramowicz identified was probably the most vibrant segment of Vilna's Jewish community in this period. As he points out, Yiddish became the dominant language of the city's Jewish communal institutions and was spoken by the Jewish intelligentsia, including Zionists, in public forums. A plurality of the city's Jewish children attended modern Yiddish schools. Vilna also became the headquarters of the YIVO Institute for Jewish Research, founded in 1925. For many—such as Zalmen Reisen, editor of the premier local daily newspaper *Vilner tog* and one of the leaders of YIVO—Yiddish was the tangible connection between past and present, and Yiddish culture represented the synthesis of Jewish tradition and a modern, progressive worldview.

When presenting the gallery of personalities closest to him from the interwar years, Abramowicz allows himself occasional expressions of personal emotion. As he recalls the institutions that he and his friends headed in their maturity, moments of sorrow and loss appear on the pages of the chronicler's biographical notes.

Abramowicz's *Profiles of a Lost World* is strikingly similar to the first work of Jewish historiography on Vilna, Samuel Joseph Fuenn's *Kiryah ne'emanah* (Faithful City), published in 1860. Fuenn, a prominent Hebrew author and one of the leaders of the Vilna *Haskalah,* similarly constructed his work, according to its subtitle, as a series of "biographical notes on Vilna's sages, scholars, writers and communal leaders." In a self-conscious effort to write about his own community according to the standards employed by professional historians, Fuenn refrained from hyperbole, adulation, and regional boosterism. He documented the lives of over 300 local figures on the basis of communal records, tombstone inscriptions, and published sources, only rarely resorting to hearsay and legend.

In a sense, Abramowicz's book is a sequel to Fuenn's, beginning where the latter left off. *Kiryah ne'emanah* depicts the Vilna of the eighteenth and early nineteenth centuries—a city of rabbis, Talmudists, Hebrew poets, and scholars of Judaica and the sciences. *Profiles of a Lost World* portrays the Vilna of the late nineteenth and early twentieth centuries—a city of Jewish revolutionaries, modern educators, communal activists, and Yiddish writers. Although Abramowicz does not analyze the cultural and historical strands connecting his city to Fuenn's, they are felt throughout the pages of his book.

There is another feature common to the opening and closing volumes of Vilna Jewry's indigenous historiography. Fuenn endeavored to transcend the partisan differences within the community—including his own personal allegiance to the *Haskalah*—by incorporating into his work the biographies of traditionalists, Hasidim, and ultra-Orthodox rabbis, with whom he had disagreed and even feuded. Abramowicz likewise included profiles of Chief Rabbi Isaac Rubinstein, the Zionist communal leader Dr. Jacob Wygodzki, and the traditionalist librarian Khaykl Lunski—all figures who belonged to segments of the community quite different from his own. Both Fuenn and Abramowicz used their histories to convey, albeit implicitly, the message that Vilna as a whole was truly greater than the sum of its often conflicting parts.

My Father's Life and Work

Dina Abramowicz

My father, Hirsz Abramowicz, was born in 1881 on an estate called Tomashevo, in the district of Troki, Vilna province, which was then part of the Russian Empire. His father's name in Yiddish was Zelig (its Hebrew equivalent being Zechariah) and his mother was Mera (Miriam). Her maiden name, Zagor, was most likely derived from the Lithuanian town Żagory.[1] It is located in northwestern Lithuania, not far from the border with Courland, and is said to be "one of the oldest settlements in Lithuania, whose history can be traced to the thirteenth century."[2]

My father was named after his great-grandfather, Hirshl Visokidvorer. His name indicates that he came from the town of Wysoki Dwór, located about thirty kilometers from Troki.[3] There is quite a bit of information about him preserved in our family lore. Hirshl Visokidvorer owned a brewery and had the exclusive right to produce alcoholic beverages in the town. He was also a leading figure in Jewish community affairs. During the reign of Tsar Nicholas I (1825–55), the Jews of Troki were threatened with expulsion as a result of a campaign by the local Karaite community. Hirshl Visokidvorer was part of a delegation that went to St. Petersburg to lobby for the repeal of the edict.[4]

One of Hirshl's sons was Abram Abramowicz, my paternal great-grandfather. He was a learned man, with enough education to be ordained as a rabbi, although he did not choose to do so. Because of his knowledge of local languages, including Russian, he once held the position of community scribe. This may have inspired his habit of recordkeeping. He even possessed a copper stamp engraved with his name. All his books (and he had quite a few of them) carried his ex libris inscription written in Hebrew and Russian, with the date according to both the Hebrew and the general calendars. He also compiled a record of family members, dated 1894.

Abram Abramowicz was a well-to-do grain merchant who dealt with local landowners and peasants. The peasants tended his fields and orchards and were paid half of the harvest for their labor. According to family lore, Grandfather was miserly and often complained to his wife that his non-Jewish business partners were cheating him. His wife, who was known for being quite virtuous and charitable, would reply, "They are stealing from you, and yet you are getting richer."[5]

Judging by family records, our roots in Lithuania went back at least as far as the first quarter of the nineteenth century. Our forebears were small-town residents who were very close to the surrounding rural population. The heads of the family were somewhat above average compared to their fellow Jews in education, economic standing, and involvement in communal activities. In his memoir "April 1919," which Father dedicated "to the blessed memory of my unforgettable father," he describes his parents' farm and recalls their charity toward neighbors and passersby, Jews and non-Jews, in this period of social and political upheaval during and after World War I.

I recall the farm from my own childhood as a big and beautiful place with Grandfather at its center. Late in the mornings he would appear in the farm yard, having already attended to his various chores, which started at daybreak. He would gather his small army of grandchildren and tell them what a good place the farm was, providing a livelihood for the family and all the other people nearby. But the farm needed good helping hands, and everybody had to pitch in, even the children. After this "propaganda" speech, he distributed our assignments. Recalling this, it is clear to me that the purpose of Grandfather's speech was more ideological than practical. He wished to inculcate in his grandchildren love and respect for his occupation and way of life. He certainly succeeded in inspiring these feelings in his son.

In a short autobiographical sketch, Father describes the elder Abramowicz as "loving Hebrew and implanting this love in his son."[6] Grandfather was a rare combination of an educated person and a farmer. This inspired a very close relationship between father and son, which Father maintained as long as his parents lived. The farm was his beloved retreat for summer vacations. During the dangerous and uncertain times of the German occupation in World War I, the farm helped feed his family in the city, which suffered from wartime food shortages. But the farm itself was also threatened during these difficult times, and Father followed all that happened in the countryside with great concern.

When the Poles seized Vilna and Lithuania broke off all diplomatic relations with its neighbor in September 1920, the city and the farm were separated by a border between two hostile countries. Despite the persistent difficulties, Father was able to visit his parents' farm at least two more times. Once, he received permission to attend his father's funeral. Grandfather's health had been undermined by the difficulties he experienced during the war, and he died on 5 April 1922. It was a loss Father felt deeply, and he returned home to Vilna a changed man. Yet contact with the farm remained very vital for him, for his mother was still there. His second visit took place during his summer vacation in 1925, and he used the opportunity to research his study, "A Lithuanian *Shtetl*."

Father's interest in Jewish agriculture lasted throughout his life. He firmly believed that agriculture was the foundation of every normal and sane society and that Jews should be involved in this occupation to the same degree as their neighbors. This would strengthen the Jews' economic and social status. Furthermore, it would help them escape rootlessness and economic dependency—conditions thrust upon them by anti-Semitic governments and competition with other social groups, such as the rising peasant class in interwar Poland. Father also saw great moral value in working the land—the ennobling ethos of being close to nature, working hard, and being able to feed oneself and others.

This love of land was one of the major traits of Father's personality. It was based not only on rational motives but also on a genuine bond with the land on which he had been raised. It was also reflected in many of his writings. In the sad story of the Jewish agricultural school in Wieluciany, he vividly recalls all the painful stages of its struggle to survive during the difficult years of 1915–21. His comprehensive description of "Rural Jewish Occupations in Lithuania" strives to memorialize the customs and occupations of "plain, hard-working people living close to nature."[7] Father's remarkable essay, "Healing the Mentally Ill," expresses his belief in the healing powers of nature. The essay describes the little-known practice of urban Jews sending their mentally ill relatives to live in the Jewish agricultural colonies of Lejpuny and Deksznie. Father happily noted that the benefits of this treatment were recognized by Polish medical authorities.

"The Diet of Lithuanian Jews," a nostalgic and sometimes humorous supplement to "Rural Jewish Occupations in Lithuania," describes the lesser-known side of rural Jewry. Their food was limited to very few basic staples. Nevertheless, it was handled with ingenuity and skill by women, with the helping hand of men; this was often a collective activity and an occasion for social events. Father wrote this essay as a tribute to his mother, who was known to family and friends as an excellent cook. Father adored both his parents, although the two were almost complete opposites. His mother was very quiet and did not demand any attention for herself. Still, she worked from morning to night without stopping and contributed a great deal to the smooth functioning of their large household. In her son's eyes, she was the model of a rural Jewish woman, whose activities he described vividly in the section on *arendarn* in "Rural Jewish Occupations in Lithuania." Father was well aware of the role of Jewish women in other fields as well. His writings include a substantial description of women's accomplishments in the development of Jewish welfare institutions in Vilna.[8]

Father's work on the farm during summer vacations was initially tied to his sympathies for Zionism, which later changed in favor of Bundism.[9] Yet he was never a card-carrying member of either movement. His memoir on the debate between Zionist leader Chaim Weizmann and the Bund's Kolia Tepper was not the work of a partisan of either side, but that of an observer documenting an event that exemplified the political and national awakening of the Jewish masses in 1903, shortly before the Kishinev pogroms.

In 1935, Father formally joined the movement known as the Freeland League. Under the leadership of Dr. I. N. Steinberg, its goal was to find an unoccupied territory suitable for settlement by Jews who, for ideological or other reasons, did not wish to go to Palestine. The settlers' main occupation was to be agriculture, and the Freeland League established agricultural colonies in Eastern Europe to prepare future colonists. Father's profiles of Joseph Czernichow and Gershon Malakiewicz reflect his interest in the leader of Vilna's branch of the movement and one of its followers. Although the Freeland League was a response to the dire situation that East European Jews faced, with Soviet communism on one side and German fascism on the other, it also offered Father a vision of a new Jewish society based on the sound foundation of agriculture.[10]

At the age of fourteen, Father was sent to the city of Vilna to receive a secular education. The city was an important Jewish intellectual center in the northwestern part of the Russian Empire, a seat of traditional learning, and the site of such great cultural institutions as the Strashun Library and the Romm family publishing house.[11] It was also the center of the Lithuanian *Haskalah,* the Jewish Enlightenment movement, which reached the city in the mid-1840s, half a century after it first emerged in Western Europe. The followers of the *Haskalah,* the *maskilim,* believed that modern, secular education would lead to an improvement of the Jews' economic condition and legal status. The *maskilim* supported the efforts of the Russian government to develop a school network for Jewish children. The curriculum and the spirit of the schools reflected the Russian government's goal of Russifying Jewish children by teaching them the Russian language and nurturing their feelings of patriotism. The attitude of most Jews toward these schools was rather negative because they neglected Jewish subjects. Nevertheless, the schools became popular in the last quarter of the nineteenth century, as they helped create a Jewish middle class that could fit into Russia's modernizing and industrializing society.

When Father came to Vilna in the mid-1890s, the city had four such schools, with a total of over a thousand students.[12] His profile of one of his teachers, Samuel Gozhanski, describes a uniformed bureaucrat who tried to fulfill his duties with exaggerated eagerness. After two years in the highest grades of elementary school, Father was admitted to the Vilna Jewish Teachers Institute. One of two such schools in the entire country, it was operated by the government to prepare teachers for its Jewish elementary schools. The institute was run in a strict disciplinary fashion, and its students were housed in a dormitory. On completion of their studies, students were required to teach in elementary schools for a certain number of years to repay the government for the expense of educating them. The education that they received met contemporary standards, with a good grounding in Russian and general studies. To teach Hebrew and Jewish subjects, the school engaged Joshua Steinberg, one of the early *maskilim,* a scholar who combined great knowledge of his subjects with old-fashioned methods of teaching and extreme loyalty to the Russian regime. Father's profiles of these two teachers reflect the attitude of the younger generation of the Jewish intelligentsia toward its mentors, whose political convictions and behavior they could no longer take seriously.

Another student who graduated from the Vilna Jewish Teachers Institute was Chaim Fialkov, an uncle of the first president of Israel, Chaim Weizmann. A man of outstanding abilities and thorough education, Fialkov helped develop new directions and programs for the *Hevrat Mefitsei Haskalah,* which ran and supported Jewish community schools throughout Russia. In 1908, this society invited Father to become the new inspector of its schools. Although he did not take the post, this was a great honor for him; he had already earned a reputation among Jewish educators for his activities and writings. In his profile of Fialkov, Father recalls meeting with the members of the prestigious society, including his encounter with Baron David Guenzburg, whose views of Jewish education surprised Father by their ultratraditionalist slant.

Father started his teaching career in 1901, immediately after graduating from the Vilna Jewish Teachers Institute. He first taught in a government elementary school in the provincial town of Merecz. Next, he was transferred to Vilna, a sign of advancement in his pedagogical career. Interested in continuing his own education, he then attended the university in Kharkov and also continued to teach—this time in a government-run Jewish school in Pavlograd. The local secretary of education, a man named Kalabanovskii, was so pleased with Father's performance that he promoted him to the position of assistant principal in Yekaterinoslav (now Dnepropetrovsk), the provincial capital. Although Father never wrote about his personal successes in life, he did mention this in order to explain Kalabanovskii's sudden hostility toward him after Father was arrested for involvement in the Bund, which the tsarist government considered seditious.

After his arrest, Father was no longer allowed to teach in government schools, but with the emergence of private Jewish education after the political upheavals of 1905, he was able to find employment in a Jewish private school in Gomel'. There, Father taught general, Russian, and Jewish history and was also in charge of one of the school's four campuses. This second period of teaching, which lasted from 1907 to 1912, was also interrupted. No amount of intervention could help him overcome the anti-Semitism and antisocialist reaction of the Russian educational bureaucracy. Father gave up teaching until 1916, when Russia retreated from its western territories during World War I and Vilna was occupied by the Germans.

Although Father's thwarted educational career was the result of Russian counterrevolutionary paranoia and anti-Semitism, his involvement in the revolutionary movement was sincere and genuine. This is not surprising for a young man whose formative years were spent in Vilna, where the Bund was founded in 1897. Father was both an observer of and a participant in the historic events that led to the execution of Hirsh Lekert. This young Jewish shoemaker shot the governor of Vilna in 1902 to protest the humiliating flogging of workers who had been punished for demonstrating against the tsarist regime. Father had the courage to protest the brutality of the police who arrested him for taking part in the demonstration, and he stood up to investigators who tried to elicit information on other participants. For the first time, his politics had an adverse impact on his teaching career. He was demoted from his position in Vilna and sent to teach in a small provincial town.

Father's second brush with tsarist authorities happened four years later in Yekaterinoslav, where he fell into a police trap set up for participants in a clandestine Bundist conference. This time his imprisonment lasted much longer, and its effects were more devastating psychologically. The close contact with criminals was a shocking experience for Father. He was especially disturbed by their spontaneous violence. Nevertheless, there were also positive moments during his time in jail. The leader of the Bundist group offered him encouragement.

Also in prison were a group of Polish railroad workers who had been organized by the Polish Socialist Party to stage antigovernment demonstrations. They were less enthusiastic about revolution than the Jewish political prisoners. Father's cellmate, a Pole who held a senior position in the railroad administration, was a like-minded intellectual. The prisoners' release due to an amnesty declared on the tsar's birthday was a joyous event.

From the start, World War I was a disaster for families with single young men of draft age. In 1914, Father was thirty-three years old, married and the father of two small children, so he was not scheduled to be drafted immediately. His brother-in-law, Matthias Schreiber, who had just graduated from the University of Warsaw with a degree in engineering, was mobilized in the first days of the war and sent to the Prussian front, before he had a chance to learn how to hold a gun in his hand. The Schreiber family was further disrupted by the departure of Mother's younger sister with her husband and their small son. They joined thousands of refugees who did not want to remain in the war zone and hoped to return as soon as the conflict was resolved. Father and Mother decided to stay, however, since their elderly parents could not be left to themselves in such uncertain and difficult times.

More than a year passed before the Russian army started to withdraw from the northwestern territories of the empire. Father describes the last days of Russia's humiliating retreat and the first days of the German occupation in his memoir titled "I Join the Militia." The feeling of relief shared by Poles and Jews, who had found Russian rule during the time of their defeat to be especially oppressive, dissipated rather quickly. The expectation of civilized behavior on the part of a central European power proved to be an illusion. The new rulers started by issuing a string of edicts designed to ensure that the local population understood the difference between the conquerors and the conquered. The spoils of war were to be the uncontested property of the former.

Father's expectation that the Germans would observe the rules of law, and that the occupied populations would cooperate among themselves in a spirit of solidarity, collapsed when confronted with reality. This short memoir, written in 1939, eighteen years after the events occurred, ends in a foreboding mood. It seems that Father not only was immersed in the sadness of things past but was overwhelmed by the premonition—which proved to be right—of worse things in the future.

Father's comprehensive account of subsequent events, titled "The Germans in World War I," was written and published much earlier, shortly after the war's end. He gathered the material for this account very carefully, as the events unfolded, using the method of "participant observation."[13] This was the same approach he applied to his study of rural Jewish occupations—in fact, both essays cover the same territory of rural Lithuania, whose urban center was Vilna. Although Father had been a resident of Vilna for many years, he managed to maintain close contact with his parents. He often

Hirsz Abramowicz's family (left to right): wife Anna, daughter Dina, the author, and daughter Tamara. Vilna, mid-1920s.
Courtesy of the YIVO Archives.

visited their farm, despite the difficulties of communication and travel during the war. Father was also in touch with relatives and acquaintances who, for various reasons, traveled between the city and the countryside. They told him endless stories of hardships and horrors that the German occupiers inflicted on the local population. His account shows that while the retreating Russian army regarded Jews as potential spies who, according to wartime laws, could be executed at a moment's notice, in such extreme situations the Germans acted as the Jews' rescuers. But the overall picture of German behavior was very negative. Their greed, lack of moral scruples, and ruthless economic exploitation were widespread, foreshadowing the treatment of conquered civilian populations during World War II (though not the practice of racial genocide). Father's account includes two incidents in which he personally experienced the German authorities' harsh treatment. Such abuses of power were everyday occurrences during the occupation.

In his essay "April 1919," Father offers an eyewitness account of the effects of World War I and its aftermath on the region. He could not resist the temptation to join his parents on the farm during his Passover vacation that year, although he knew that the undertaking would be difficult and dangerous. For this reason, he went by himself, to the great disappointment of his ten-year-old daughter. He was right to do so, as there was no transportation available. He reached his destination completely exhausted, even ill. Father tried to recover physically and mentally by turning to his beloved farm work. At the same time, he made notes on the political situation: the Soviet commissars were now the absolute rulers of the region, and they, too, freely exploited the right to requisition private property as long as the state "needed" it. Those who found it convenient to classify themselves as "dispossessed" denounced their "rich" neighbors and were compensated for the social injustice they had suffered at the "exploiters'" expense.

There was also fraternizing between the new rulers and the local population, especially the young and the poor. The Soviets were eager to win over the local population and were skilled in the use of propaganda. Nevertheless, the situation was very unstable. News that the Poles had seized Vilna came as an unexpected shock. Even worse news for the Jews were rumors that the Poles were "considering" a pogrom against Vilna's Jewish community. Father hurried back to the city.

It proved a most painful journey, not so much physically as morally, as the sudden rise of hostility toward Jews was very apparent. This anti-Semitism, new to the region, was imported from the recently established Polish Republic, which was not very fond of its national minorities, especially the Jews. Expecting the worst, Father returned home fully aware that in such times, civilian lives—especially Jewish lives—were truly expendable.

As a minority in independent Poland, Jews struggled for economic survival and civil rights in a desperately impoverished land ravaged by war. Poland had a large peasant population and smaller proletariat with aspirations that often clashed with those of their Jewish neighbors. This struggle was waged in many arenas, one of which was vocational education for the young. The problem of urban poverty had been one of the major Jewish concerns since the turn of the century. Most East European Jews who lived in cities were shopkeepers or craftsmen. The first group was not widely considered a useful and productive element of society at the time. Craftsmen were needed; however, their skills had to be improved and modernized. Russian Jewish social organizations, supported by Jewish charities abroad, had started to address this issue. Chief among these organizations were the Jewish Colonization Association (JCA) and the Society for Skilled Work (known by its Russian acronym, ORT).

Vilna had its share of Jewish poverty, and the Jewish community developed many philanthropic institutions to deal with the problem, including several for poor children. Father first encountered Jewish poverty when he was sent to Vilna to attend school. There were many poor children in all types of educational institutions in the city. Vilna's Jewish community also made pioneering efforts in the field of vocational education. As he prepared for a career as a teacher, Father became aware of this new movement. His rural background and his familiarity with physical labor influenced his interest in pursuing vocational education as a profession.

In his essay on the society known as Help Through Work, Father outlines the history of the society and its vocational school, which he was engaged to direct in 1916. The school was housed in its own modern, spacious building. It offered classes in industrial design, carpentry, house painting, and sign making for boys, and all manner of needle work for girls. The staff was carefully selected, and the student body numbered several hundred young men and women. Father supervised and coordinated all the school's activities and taught academic subjects: social sciences, history, and geography. He was quite successful in this work, with many friends among the teachers and students, and he remained at this post until the outbreak of World War II.

Although the Help Through Work school took up most of Father's six-day work week and was his principal source of income, he also managed to participate in other activities, some of which took him beyond Vilna. In 1922, the school sent him to Białystok as a delegate to the first conference of Jewish vocational schools ever held in independent Poland. In his memoir of Białystok's Jewish vocational school, Father describes the role that Jews played in the interwar economic revival of the city, which was known as Poland's "Little Manchester." He also recalls the conference's participants and agenda and recounts the unusual history of the school, which literally could not wait to reopen after it had stopped functioning during World War I.

The Vilna Jewish Technical School was another successful vocational institution described in Father's memoirs. Of all the schools that ORT supported in Eastern Europe, it was one of the most exemplary and issued the most advanced professional degrees. Polish educational authorities granted it the status of a lyceum (the equivalent of an American college). Father was on the school's board of directors, and his brother-in-law, Matthias Schreiber, was its director. Under his brilliant and dedicated leadership, the school earned its status and reputation.

Father encountered four of the people whom he portrays in this volume in the field of vocational education. Joseph Jaszunski and B. Kahan-Wirgili were both outstanding intellectuals, men of great knowledge in both general and Jewish fields. Yet they dedicated most of their efforts to the vocational education of Jewish youth. They saw this movement as both a response to economic anti-Semitism in interwar Poland and a means of strengthening the Jews' economic position in the country. Father collaborated with these men in planning two national conferences on vocational education and on many other occasions. His profiles also reveal the genuine personal friendship he enjoyed with these men.

In contrast to Jaszunski and Kahan-Wirgili, who were members of the Jewish community's social and intellectual elite, Eliezer Kruk and Samuel Hurwicz came from the poorest class. Their parents could hardly feed them and education was an unaffordable luxury. Yet, thanks to their own talents and aspirations, they were able to rise in status and recognition and become representatives of their class, which until that time had played no part in the Jewish community leadership. Father was proud of their achievements and wished to bring them to the attention of others.

Father's interest in writing started quite early, beginning in 1902, when he first submitted articles to the Russian-Jewish press. It comes as no surprise that one of the happiest episodes of his life was a literary banquet arranged by an elite group of Russian Jewish intellectuals in Odessa to honor the great Yiddish writer, I. L. Peretz, who was visiting from Warsaw. Attendance was limited to members of the writing profession, and Father received an invitation on the recommendation of a friend, the writer Mendl Levin. Recalling the event in the essay "I. L. Peretz Visits the Jewish Writers in Odessa," Father was able to name most of the participating celebrities and recount the content of their speeches, as well as to describe their behavior, gestures, and the tone of their remarks. His greatest enthusiasm was reserved for the guest of honor, Peretz, then a rising star. A romantic spirit, Peretz renewed and elevated modern Yiddish literature with his admiration for the beauty and dignity of Jewish tradition. The first version of this memoir, published in 1921, concluded with an expression of the happiness that overwhelmed the young guests who attended the banquet.

After teaching, writing was Father's second vocation. While living in Vilna, he was a permanent correspondent for two Yiddish dailies: *Frimorgn,* published in Riga, and *Di yidishe tsaytung,* published in Buenos Aires. He was proud to be a member of the Association of Yiddish Writers and Journalists in Vilna, which had been founded by S. Ansky, the famous author of *The Dybbuk*. Father's writings were numerous and quite diverse. He wrote on education, reported current events as a foreign correspondent, reviewed books and plays, and composed obituaries that actually constituted lively biographical sketches. He also wrote longer pieces, such as a series of travelogues, reminiscences of important historical events that he had witnessed, and ethnographic studies.

At the end of June 1939, Father left Vilna for a two-month vacation in Canada and the United States. He was a seasoned traveler, knew history and geography well, and liked to visit new places. In his younger years, he visited all the major centers of the Russian Empire, either as a teacher or as a conference participant. In the summer of 1914, he was ready to realize his dream of visiting Palestine and Egypt, but World War I prevented the trip. During the interwar years, his income was too modest to allow travel abroad. In the summer of 1939, he received an invitation from his older brother, Irving Adler (formerly Itskhok Yankev Abramovich), who had emigrated to Canada at the beginning of the century. When visiting his parents soon after World War I, Irving tried to persuade his younger brother to emigrate, but to no avail. Father would not leave his native land, nor would he abandon his extended family, which included his parents and his sisters, with their husbands and small children. With the passing years, however, Irving decided that it was time for a reunion. He offered to underwrite the trip and Father accepted. The times were uncertain, but it was a great opportunity to see the New World—New York with its three Yiddish dailies, a host of Jewish journalists and writers, as well as the many relatives and acquaintances who had made their home there. Father took the trip, but instead of a tourist he became a refugee, stranded in North America for the duration of the war. The adjustment was not easy, but he made a living by finding occasional work in editorial offices as a proofreader or a helping hand. Hardest for him was to live with the news about the worsening situation in Europe, to wait for the morning newspaper, to wake up in the middle of the night with a nightmare, to see people going about their business "as usual," as if nothing was happening.

In June 1943, the first volume of a periodical *Der litvisher yid* was published in New York. One of the articles, written by Father, contained excerpts from letters he had received from abroad. It was titled "Only Tears Can Help Us," a quotation from one of the letters. Although the return addresses were not included, one can surmise, from the veiled language, that they were written by refugees who had escaped from Nazi-occupied territories to the Soviet Union. They described the horrible devastation of their homes and the difficult life of the refugees, and they asked for help. Indeed, the entire publication was meant as a call for help.

Following a heart attack in 1942 and a year or so of recuperation, Father began to respond to the terrible truth about the finality of the Holocaust and the harsh reality of living with this knowledge. He no longer wrote about tears; instead, a new, much more meaningful response began to emerge in his work. He wrote to commemorate, to bring to life those whose existence had been brutally cut off. The second version of his memoir of the banquet honoring Peretz appeared in 1946. The happiness originally expressed in the final paragraph was replaced by despair, but the revised ending also included a solemn commandment: "We must continue to forge the golden chain in hallowed memory of these pillars of the people of Israel."

This "duty to continue" also responded to Father's inner need to commemorate on a personal level. He dedicated the second version of his memoir of Peretz "to the sacred memory of my wife Anna Abramowicz (née Schreiber), whom the Germans murdered in the extermination camp Majdanek." A short remark in the essay explains this dedication. Father went to Odessa to visit his girlfriend, who was taking university courses there. She later became his "life companion." Father and Mother were both teachers by profession, and they shared many common views and interests. Mother perished anonymously, like most of the other victims of the Holocaust. Father felt that this dedication was but a small token to her memory. He also paid tribute to Mother in the *Lerer-yisker-bukh,* a memorial book honoring teachers in the Central Yiddish School Organization (TsIShO) in Poland who had perished during the Holocaust. In addition to providing information about her life for this volume, he contributed excerpts from a letter that she had sent to him and their younger daughter, Tamara, from the Vilna Ghetto. In what proved to be her final message to them, Mother sent her love and reassured them that she was facing her fate peacefully. Father could not speak about this letter without tears.[14]

Father continued to be a prolific and versatile writer in the years after the Holocaust. The emphasis of his work in this period was on his "Images of a Lost World," the title he gave to a series published from 1949 to 1953 in the Paris Yiddish daily *Unzer shtime.* An article that appeared early in this series may be considered Father's literary manifesto for the post-Holocaust period. It was an appeal to the leaders of the Bund to start work on a biographical lexicon of its members. There were hundreds of them, Father wrote, both major and minor figures, but they all fulfilled some important function for the Jewish community, and all had their merits. It would be an injustice to them, and a loss for Jewish cultural history in general, if they were forgotten. Father relied on his excellent memory and vast knowledge of contemporary literature to demonstrate that little, if any, information about them was available in print. He even offered to contribute entries on the Vilna members of the party, because he "knew them personally, and could see them before [his] eyes, as if they were still alive."[15]

In his portraits of various noteworthy figures among Vilna Jewry, Father focused on the interrelationship of the individual and the community. An attachment to one's birthplace is a common trait, but Father was a true native son of his city and country, and his love for them was exceptionally well informed and articulate. He had an inquisitive mind and a natural interest in the environment that he knew from literature and experience.

Father spent much time in Vilna, both as a youth and as an adult, and he participated in the activities of a number of the city's organizations and institutions. He did not consider Vilna's nicknames, "Jerusalem of

Lithuania" and "City and Mother in Israel," to be mere rhetoric.[16] When he learned that Vilna had become the capital of Lithuania, Father wrote that the city is "the heart of all of Belorussian and Lithuanian Jewry." He even coined his own terms for describing Vilna's uniqueness, calling it "the city of the most intimate Jewishness in the world" and, elsewhere, "the most Yiddishist city in the world," a reference to the important role that Yiddish played in Vilna's Jewish communal life.[17] When Father asked journalist Mendl Levin what most impressed him about the "Jerusalem of Lithuania," he replied, "The faces of Vilna's Jews, Vilna streets. . . . A city made up entirely of poorly dressed intellectuals! There is something spiritual about every Jew, especially the young ones." In his profile on Moshe Shalit, Father writes: "It is to Vilna's great credit that . . . there was never any case of financial fraud, large or small, in any of the city's many Jewish organizations and institutions. I believe that this is due, in no small measure, to the Shalits, Szabads, Wygodzkis, Rubinsteins, Kruks and others who were the leaders of Vilna's Jewish communal life." Father asserted that Vilna would keep its place in history as a model of genuine Jewish life. "Vilna awaits its historian to articulate its role forthrightly and clearly," he wrote, refuting a skeptic who contended that Vilna's Jewishness had already been weakened by the inroads of assimilation during the last years before the Holocaust.[18]

Father's profiles call attention to a range of qualities among his subjects: their dignity in representing the community before governmental authorities; their civil courage, dedication, and concern for the poor; their involvement in relief organizations, schools, and cultural institutions; and their struggle to maintain the Yiddish language. At the same time, these are lively and honest portraits of people Father knew. As a biographer, Father was committed to judging people fairly and seeing them in historical context. He respected each person's freedom to follow his or her own interests and inclinations. He never held any extreme nationalistic views or was a blind follower of party lines, and he placed human values before political creeds.

Some of the profiles reflect his personal characteristics. It seems to me that the closest to his heart was his friend, collaborator and kindred spirit Moshe Shalit. A true native son of Vilna, Shalit responded to the many needs of its Jewish community, the practical, economic, and down-to-earth, as well as the cultural, artistic, and literary. Father characterized him as an idealist, humanitarian, and pragmatist. He admired Shalit's ability to combine prolific literary activity with communal and organizational work, as well as his independent spirit, human warmth, and moral integrity.

Shalit's many activities included his involvement in the Yiddish Writers and Journalists Association in Vilna, serving as its president for many years. Father describes the association as "the fortress of the spoken and written Yiddish word" and notes that it championed Yiddish even more staunchly than its sister organization in Warsaw did. In a number of his profiles, Father notes the special commitment to Yiddish of many of Vilna's leading Jewish intellectuals and activists during the interwar years. In his portrait of Zalmen Reisen, he stresses the pivotal role that this prolific scholar and educator played in transforming Vilna into a major center of secular Yiddishism by "converting" the city's Russian-speaking Jewish intelligentsia into practicing Yiddishists.

Father also stressed the important role that Reisen played in the development of Yiddish schools. As a teacher, Father was an active participant in this pioneering movement. His essay, "The Dawn of Practical Yiddishism," describes the spontaneous activities of Vilna's Jewish teachers to create schools whose language of instruction was Yiddish. During the years 1919–24, Father wrote prolifically about the problems of the developing network of Yiddish schools, participated in their national conferences, and helped compile the first Yiddish geographic atlas for use in the schools.[19]

The liberation of Vilna from Russian dominance in 1915 enabled the city's minorities to realize their national aspirations. The Jewish community was divided between advocates of Hebrew and those of Yiddish as their national language. Although Father had a good background in Hebrew language and literature, he joined the Yiddishist movement. This was a natural choice for him, as Yiddish was his first language. Moreover, it was the language of the Jewish folk masses, the ordinary, poor people, whose interests were always close to his heart.

Not all members of Vilna's Jewish intelligentsia, however, could make this linguistic change easily. This was especially the case for the women, who had been educated in Russian schools. Mother had to give up her beloved occupation as a teacher because she couldn't teach in a Yiddish school, and the Russian-language schools for Jewish children were rapidly disappearing. Although my sister and I attended Yiddish schools, our home remained Russian-speaking. Father understood that making such changes in private life could be more difficult than in the public sphere.

In addition to his strong Jewish identity, Father also had a solid general education, which fostered his interest in other cultures. Russian culture, especially its great humanitarian writers, had a particularly strong impact on Father and his generation. His private library contained the collected works of Tolstoy, Chekhov, and Korolenko. Nevertheless, Father had no illusions about the role of Jews in Russian society, and the Russian government's anti-Semitism fueled his sympathies for the revolutionary movement.

Father was very conscious of the multicultural dynamics of his native land. The relations between Jews and non-Jews in rural Lithuania before

My Father's Life and Work

World War I were harmonious, as he notes in his essay on "Rural Jewish Occupations in Lithuania." In his amusing account of how Jewish innkeepers kept a record of their transactions with peasants, there is no hint of mutual suspicion. Especially touching is his description of the attitude of non-Jewish fishermen toward their Jewish colleagues: when it was time for the Jews to recite morning prayers, the boat would come to shore, the Jews would disembark, and the other men would wait patiently until the Jews were finished with their "rosary."

But relations between Poles and Jews in Vilna and possibly other cities were already strained in the first decade of the twentieth century—the years of the first Russian revolution—due to the different political status of the two minorities in pre–World War I Russia.[20] The German occupation during World War I caused both Jews and non-Jews to suffer, and Father's account contains many examples of cruelty to peasants. After the war, the Treaty of Versailles established laws to protect minorities, and their struggle for equal rights and opportunities became a legitimate, officially recognized activity. Father became actively involved in efforts to promote coexistence and cooperation among the various groups. The first period of Polish rule of interwar Vilna was marked by a pogrom in which many Jews were killed, including the writer A. Weiter, and, later, the liquidation of the Jewish vocational school in Wieluciany. Jewish children on their way to school were attacked by juvenile street gangs. School excursions to recreation sites around the city became dangerous during the period before Polish authority was stabilized. In 1921, Father delivered a paper at a conference of teachers of all local nationalities on "The Role of Teachers in Establishing Normal Relations among Nationalities." He claimed that the difficulties were caused by a lack of mutual understanding and contact, and he advocated cultural rapprochement and cooperation. His paper outlined a number of steps that should be undertaken to achieve this goal.[21]

In 1935, Father repeated his appeal in an article, entitled "Vilna—a Multinational City," which surveys the history and cultural institutions of five nationalities—Poles, Lithuanians, Belorussians, Russians, and Jews.[22] He pointed out that until World War I these various nationalities lived peacefully as neighbors. The war changed this and yet the relations were still not as bad as they were elsewhere. They could be improved, Father contended, if each group would recognize the cultural achievements and rights of the others. He concluded with a wish for cooperation, which would eliminate antagonism, enrich the general culture and make Vilna a model city of peaceful coexistence among nationalities. Little did he know what was to come.

Father's trip to America in the fateful summer of 1939 was the fulfillment of a dream—an escape from tense, threatening Europe to the happier

33

shores of the New World. What was supposed to be a short summer vacation became a permanent stay for a refugee, whom his new home accepted rather grudgingly. The protracted formalities required to assure his legal status frightened and discouraged him. Father's economic situation became critical—how was he to make a living in this new country, for which his education, talents and experience were of no use? He did not want to become a burden. He would sooner sweep floors or work in a factory than stand in line at the doors of a charitable organization.[23]

Slowly, painfully, he found his way. Writing proved to be a great source of moral support. It helped him retain a sense of human dignity and provided him a means to express himself and communicate with the world. The Yiddish newspapers started to accept his work. This generated some income which, although meager, helped him make ends meet. Slowly, he made contacts with American organizations of Lithuanian and Polish Jews and with the members of the Vilna branch of the Workmen's Circle. Eventually he established a circle of friends, writers, journalists, and East European intellectuals who had settled here earlier and were already firmly rooted in America. He would visit them in their homes, where he could share with them his worries, concerns and ideas.

Journalism became Father's main professional activity in America. He published in many Yiddish periodicals, including those issued by *landsmanshaftn*—societies formed by Jewish immigrant groups who came from the same location in Eastern Europe. Father also continued to promote the ideals of the Freeland League, which had moved its headquarters from Europe to New York. He wrote frequently on the value of agrarianism and vocational education for Jews in the Freeland League's journal, *Oyfn shvel*.[24]

Despite a heart attack, the trauma of the Holocaust, and the hardships of immigrant life, Father continued to write, especially during the four years of his stay (1949–53) with his younger daughter, Tamara Gotman, in France. After returning to New York, he concentrated his efforts on compiling his writings to be issued in book form. He saw the volume published, and this was a source of great satisfaction in the final, sad days of his life. He died in the Workmen's Circle Home for the Aged on 29 January 1960, remembered by quite a few obituaries in the New York Yiddish and Russian press.

In the final lines of introduction to the Yiddish edition of Father's book, Dr. Max Weinreich describes the spirit of the volume and its author as genuine, honest, and suffused with a love of humankind. A reviewer of the book characterized Father as a regional writer who dealt mostly with Vilna and its vicinity.[25] Although "regional" can sometimes mean "of limited horizons," Father's regionalism was both a deep emotional attachment to his native land and a conscious, intellectual conviction. He was among the first to pay attention to local Jewish history during the interwar years in

Eastern Europe. Regional historians and writers believed that local history deserves as much attention as general history, because the former reveals aspects of life of ordinary people and helps to understand the environment in which one lives. Father insisted that such studies were even more important after the Holocaust, as these communities no longer existed.[26]

Father's memoirs reflected the life of an ethnic community in northeastern Europe that had lived there for centuries and that had succeeded in achieving both a cultural integration and the maintenance of its own traditions. The stormy history of the twentieth century wrought deep changes in the life of Lithuanian Jewry, but they showed great resiliency and resourcefulness, and they developed a remarkably rich communal and cultural life. The complete annihilation of this community is one of the cruelest episodes in human history. As a native son of the land, Father wished to be a witness and chronicler of his time and place, to win for it a place in history. Yet he also believed that history is not merely a remembrance of the past, but has lessons to teach—lessons of purposeful living, of concern for others, and of the absurdity and cruelty of extreme nationalism and war. It is my fervent hope that his wish be fulfilled, and that the memory of his warm and compassionate personality be preserved together with the records he left.

New York
October 1998

NOTE FROM THE EDITORS

Each essay in this volume appears in Hirsz Abramowicz's 1958 book *Farshvundene geshtaltn* (Vanished Figures), issued in Buenos Aires by the Central Association of Polish Jews in Argentina. These essays were all previously published in Yiddish in a variety of journals, newspapers, and anthologies. Bibliographical information on each essay's original publication, when known, is given in this volume in the endnotes.

This volume does not contain all the essays that appeared in *Farshvundene geshtaltn,* and the order in which they appear here has been reorganized chronologically and thematically. The author's original footnotes are indicated by asterisks (*) and appear at the bottom of the page. The editors have also added annotations identifying persons, events, publications, and organizations mentioned in the text; explaining terminology and customs; and providing readers with sources for more information about selected subjects raised in these essays. These notes are indicated by numbers and appear at the end of the book.

Personal names are romanized according to the spellings in original sources or, when available, the spellings of the Library of Congress or *Encyclopedia Judaica.* For small localities within the borders of interwar Poland, the Polish version of the name is used, with added versions in Lithuanian and other local languages, if available. For larger localities outside the borders of interwar Poland, the Russian versions current in standard sources are used, with the addition of more recent versions, where available. A table of geographic names at the back of the book lists Russian, Lithuanian, and Polish versions of place-names.

Note from the Editors

The two most helpful sources for the list of place-names were *Słownik Geograficzny Królestwa Polskiego i innych Krajów Słowiańskich,* edited by Filip Sulimierski, Bronisław Chlebowski, and Władysław Walewski (Warsaw: Wyd. Artystyczne i Filmowe, 1975), 14 vols., reprint of the 1880–1902 edition, and *Columbia Lippincott Gazetteer of the World,* edited by Leon E. Selzer with the Geographical Research Staff of Columbia University Press and with the cooperation of the American Geographical Society (Morningside Heights, New York: Columbia University Press, [1962]). Other proper names are rendered according to Library of Congress standards for Russian and Yiddish.

The biographies of most of the writers represented in the section "Profiles of Vilna Jewry" are included in *Leksikon fun der nayer yidisher literatur* (Biographical Dictionary of Modern Yiddish Literature), vols. 1–8 (New York: Congress for Jewish Culture, 1956–81).

I

Lithuanian Jewish Traditions

1

RURAL JEWISH OCCUPATIONS IN LITHUANIA

This essay deals with rural Jewish life from the late nineteenth century through World War I in the former province of Kovno as well as parts of Vilna, Suwałki, and Grodno provinces. There are no hard and fast boundaries in this study.[*] It includes places where Lithuanians lived in compact masses, as well as those in which there lived mixed populations of Lithuanians, Belorussians, and smaller groups of Poles. There were also small enclaves of Russians (primarily Old Believers), Tatars, and the occasional Karaites (except in Troki, where there was a colony of several hundred Karaites).[1]

Here Jews were engaged in trade and manufacturing and as artisans. The local non-Jewish population had almost no aspirations toward these occupations; they showed little sign of making economic progress. They tilled their fields in the manner of their forefathers generations before. The larger villages had small plots of land farmed by the peasants. There were also individual estates, most of them owned by impoverished Polish nobles. Some of these estates were so vast that they were larger than the bigger villages. Occasionally, these landowners embarked on more modern enterprises: dairies, apiaries, orchards, breweries, etc.

The villages were inhabited almost exclusively by peasants, but a few Jews could also be found in nearly every hamlet. The peasants could hardly

---

[*]We have reason to assume that these rural occupations are also characteristic of Belorussia and parts of Poland. Troki County, in the district of Vilna, provided the basis for the study.

get along without them. These Jews were blacksmiths, innkeepers, buyers of local products, and storekeepers. The villages were also visited by Jewish tailors, shoemakers, wheelwrights, fishermen, gardeners, carpenters, lime burners, orchard keepers, and the like. Jewish farmers who lived apart from the villages were a group unto themselves.

Jews complemented the ethnographic landscape of Lithuania. They were an integral part of the peasant community. They lived amicably with their neighbors, who found them indispensable to their own economic well-being, even though peasant households were from 80–90 percent independent, self-sustaining economic units.

Tailors

The peasant woman did her own spinning, weaving and sewing for herself and her family. Nevertheless, there were times when it was necessary to turn to a Jewish tailor (who was either a man or a woman), especially when the peasant needed holiday clothes or a sheepskin jacket, without which no peasant could get along. If the tailor lived all year round in the village, he usually had work only in the winter. In the summertime, he would find other ways to get by.

Usually, the tailor came from a town. He would visit the village for a whole week, bringing his own kosher pot for cooking potatoes, eggs and milk. He also brought some bread, in order not to resort to a "non-kosher slice."[2] He slept in the one-room house of the peasant who hired him, lying on his own coat or, at best, a sack or a pile of straw.

The peasant first passed his sheepskins to the tanner (called *baltushnik*), who was usually a Tatar. After that, the skins went to the tailor, who was generally not much of an expert. If the garment could be pulled on over the shoulders and the arms fit into the sleeves, it was considered acceptable. The remuneration for this work was very low, as was the general standard of living. Seldom did any piece of work pay more than a ruble. Usually, the peasant would pay for the tailor's work with farm products, such as eggs, potatoes, peas, and other vegetables, instead of money. The village tailor seldom had his own sewing machine; he usually worked with a needle and thimble.

The peasants would have liked the Jewish tailor to eat with them, but they knew that this was forbidden to him and so did not insist. It was rare that a Jew would eat non-kosher food in the village. Such a Jew was considered a scoundrel, a heretic—even the peasants had little respect for him. During long winter evenings, the tailors and the peasants would while away the time telling each other stories and singing songs together. It was in this manner, perhaps, that multilingual Yiddish-Lithuanian-Belorussian songs developed. Thus, too, Jewish artisans, particularly the younger generation, learned to sing village songs.

In later years, Jews started the development of light industry in Lithuania, and inexpensive materials became more available in the villages. The peasants made greater use of Jewish tailors and gradually abandoned the habit of sewing their own clothes. Fashion-conscious village women would buy gingham, flannel and cotton cloth from the Jewish dry goods store in town or the traveling Jewish peddler in the village and give it to the Jewish seamstresses. Their price for making a garment was low: ten, fifteen, or twenty kopeks. The seamstresses were not necessarily experts in their profession. They were young women from the town who learned enough about how to sew, either on their own or from their mothers, to make blouses and dresses for the village women.

Shoemakers

In the summer the peasant went barefoot. He wore homemade moccasins instead of shoes, but there were certain occasions for which he had to have boots. Later, the younger peasant grew ashamed of his moccasins and started wearing shoes and boots.

The Jewish shoemaker in the village would repair worn boots and women's shoes. He covered moccasins with leather of the cheapest kind. He would also make boots by stitching used leggings onto shoes. When the peasant wanted a pair of new shoes—a very costly item—he would visit the town shoemaker, who was considered more of a specialist. This was much too big an undertaking to be entrusted to the local shoemaker; he might ruin the job. The village shoemaker lived in even greater poverty than the other village craftsmen. He was frequently out of work, and the occasional small jobs that he did get brought him very little income. He worked on old shoes, placing one patch on top of another, nailing on a pair of soles or adding on a piece of leather to the sole of crooked shoes.

During the summer, the village shoemaker had no work at all, because everyone went barefoot. This forced the shoemaker to find other work, such as tending an orchard or working his own garden.

Blacksmiths

Most prominent among Jewish workers in the villages were the blacksmiths. Although there were also some non-Jewish smiths, they were very few in number until the end of the nineteenth century. Only after the turn of the century did their numbers increase, to the detriment of the Jewish blacksmiths.

Every blacksmith had his own hut, with a forge close by. He would shoe horses, repair wagons, forge plows, sharpen scythes, and make axes, knives, and other household utensils. He would also attach rims and spokes to wheels and iron runners to sleds. During the winter, when there was little work, the more skilled blacksmiths would forge a stockpile of horseshoes and nails. Later they started using ready-made horseshoes, as these proved to be cheaper.

Some peasants made a year-long agreement with the blacksmith. He would supply a peasant with all his household needs from the smithy, in return for which he was given potatoes, grain, and vegetables, as well as a little money. Sometimes the blacksmith was allowed to plant a few rows in the peasant's garden, where the smith's wife would grow vegetables for her own cooking. The peasants lived very amicably with the blacksmith, realizing that he was essential to their own primitive existence.

Despite this relative prosperity, blacksmiths were often compelled to take on additional work, such as gardening, orchard tending and lime burning.

Lime Burners

Lime burning was an exclusively Jewish occupation. There are many kinds of rock in the fields of the hilly regions of Lithuania; much of this is limestone. Lime was used in the foundations of houses and for plastering and whitewashing walls. Lime burners and their families would either gather the stones from the fields or buy them from the peasants. The latter would gather the stones when they cleared the fields for planting. They were particularly anxious to dispose of the limestone because they were certain that it would "burn up the fields"—that is, destroy their crops during a drought.

As a precaution against fire, the furnaces where lime was prepared were always outside the village. During the summer, a lime burner could produce from four to five furnaceloads of lime, each of which required about one hundred wagonloads of limestone. Every limestone furnace would use about seven cubic feet of wood in an operation, which lasted from four to six days and had to be maintained continuously day and night. The lime burner would stay there the entire time to tend the fire. This was considered quite an undertaking: it required a minimum investment of fifty to one hundred rubles. It would take a month or more to accumulate a supply of limestone for the furnaces.

After the lime was burned, the furnace had to cool for a few days before the lime could be taken out and sold. Neighboring peasants would buy one-eighth or one-sixteenth of a measure of lime. Whenever major construction or a government project was under way in the vicinity and there was a greater demand for lime, the lime burner could get a better price for his product.

Working with lime was injurious to one's health and very arduous. But who worried about such things as long as he earned a living? Although sores covered the hands of lime burners and their clothes were seared by the lime, there was money in it—something not easily dismissed.

Pitch Burners

Lithuania had many pine and fir forests. After a forest of pine trees was cut down, the stumps and roots that remained in the ground were dug up and brought to one place, where the Jewish pitch burner bought them. Sometimes the pitch burners themselves would dig out the roots and stumps. Then they would dig a pit in which to burn the roots slowly in a smudge flame, piping the liquid pitch into vats. This was the most widely used lubricant for the peasants' carts. Later, a commercially produced grease made of animal fat came into use, but this, too, was mixed with pitch, because it was cheaper. After extracting the pitch, the pitch burner would pour it into a large vat, load it on his cart or wagon and set out to neighboring villages to sell it to the peasants by the potful. There were also Jewish pitch dealers in towns. They would buy the grease from the pitch burner and then peddle it themselves. Some of the larger pitch burners used to cook it down until it hardened. This hardened tar would be used on fishing boats and to make asphalt. The pitch burners also had turpentine distilleries. They had to hire assistants to produce this valuable product, which was sent to the larger cities and even abroad. These products were made in a primitive manner and on a very small scale, yet this trade had its place in the Lithuanian economy.

Wheelwrights, Shinglers, and Carpenters

Wheelwrights, shinglers and carpenters lived mostly in towns, but their work frequently took them to the villages. A number of them even lived there. The wheelwrights made wagons, carts, axles, wheels, sleds and shafts. In the woods, Jews would operate a *parnye*, a steam bath for treating lumber. Here they shaped oak and ash rims for wheels and sled-runners and made wooden yokes for horse collars. The lumber was heated in the *parnye* to a high temperature under pressure, in order to make it pliable; then it was put out to dry. The rims and runners would be sold to a wheelwright or a peasant, who could then make his own cart or sled.

Jewish shinglers formed cooperatives in Lithuania, especially in the region near Uciana and Telsze. A cooperative had from six to twelve members. They worked for Jewish lumbermen in the forests or on farms where the wood was brought after it had been cut. Shingles, which were usually made of fir, had to be of a specific thickness. Shingle-making was a cooperative undertaking, with various tasks performed by different people: two would do the sawing, one the splitting, two the planing and two the grooving. During the summer, shinglers would sleep on straw in rustic lean-tos. In winter, they had huts, where they cooked their own food. Occasionally the wives of Jewish *arendarn* who leased nearby estates would cook one daily meal for the workers. The shinglers would go home to visit their families a few times a year, usually for the holidays. (They frequently worked quite a distance from their homes, sometimes as much as a hundred miles.)

The work was very strenuous—one worker was always trying to hurry the other—and the earnings were meager. But the shinglers were known to be honest, hardworking, God-fearing Jews. They certainly were not learned Jews, but on Saturdays they eagerly recited the Psalms, and they prayed three times a day. If there was a *minyan* they prayed collectively.

The development of the power-driven sawmill led to the gradual decline of these simple, hardworking shinglers. Even though the quality of their shingles was superior to that produced by the sawmill, they could not compete with the machine's output, and little by little these Jewish artisans ceased to exist.

The "aristocrats" among Jewish woodworkers were the carpenters who built houses. Although they lived in the towns, they frequently worked for the estate owners and the peasants. Carpenters made a good living. They always found jobs, because it was known that Jewish carpenters worked ably and conscientiously.

Lumbermen and Loggers

Jewish lumbermen hired foremen, who went to live with village Jews near the forests that were being cut. The foreman would divide the work among the peasants employed, collect their work and keep records. He would supervise day laborers as they felled trees, cut down large stumps, and made oaken staves. The oak logs were exported once they had been properly trimmed. Loggers tied the logs together into rafts to send them down the large rivers—the Wilia and the Niemen—or they tied the rafts together before sending them down the lower Niemen. It was hard work, especially because the workers were always in the water. But it was a special skill at which Jews were particularly adept. Kovno, Janów and, especially, Onikszty were known for their loggers. Not all the men who traveled with the rafts were Jews. They had to be thoroughly familiar with the river and would sometimes spend days, even weeks, aboard the rafts. This work paid rather well. There were other workers who untied the rafts and brought the logs to a camp or a sawmill. Riding on horseback, they would drag the logs with chains from the rivers to a sawmill or lumberyard. These workers were paid less than the loggers.

Gardeners

All Jewish villagers gardened. If it was not done by the men it was done by women and children. This work was limited almost entirely to growing cucumbers, which the peasants did not cultivate.

The gardeners usually entered into a partnership with the owner of an estate or the Jew who leased it, with whom they shared their income from the cucumbers. This partner would fertilize and plow the garden, lay out temporary furrows, and provide a horse to cart the cucumbers to market. The rest of the work was done by the gardeners. They grew seedlings, nurturing them in hothouses until they sprouted; they also had to spade the permanent furrows and plant the seedlings.

Then the work became challenging. Late spring frosts would often spoil the plants, and the gardeners would have to start all over again. Cucumbers should not be watered when the sun is shining, so the watering had to be done either before dawn or after twilight; this meant that the work called for great haste and exertion. When there was no rain the garden had to be watered twice daily, and many buckets of water had to be carried on shoulder poles over long distances. In the daytime, the garden had to be cleared of weeds, which thrived in the fertile cucumber soil. By the time the whole garden was weeded—it was sometimes as big as three to five acres—it would need to be weeded anew. If the weeds grew bigger than the cucumbers, the crop would be poor. In a word, growing cucumbers was truly backbreaking work.

But it was a joy when the cucumbers did grow, spreading their leaves over the entire bed, and then when the first blossoms and the first small cucumbers appeared. Usually the harvest occurred just before the Ninth of Av, so that the gardener could bring the first of the crop into town on that day. Every Jew wanted to recite a blessing over the first cucumber of the season. For this the grower charged a high price, as much as a kopek for each cucumber. If there was an early summer, with no frosts in May, the growers harvested the first cucumbers on the Seventeenth of Tammuz (three weeks before the Ninth of Av), but this happened only rarely.

These first cucumbers were always eagerly awaited. Later, they grew rapidly and had to be picked two or even three times a week and carried to nearby markets. The yields were fairly large. It was not unusual to harvest three to five thousand cucumbers at once. Then prices fluctuated; in order not to bring any cucumbers back from the market it was sometimes necessary to sell a hundred for a mere five kopeks. At that time no one knew how to pickle the cucumbers for export or pack them so that they could be taken to more distant markets.

Cucumbers were harvested until the high holidays, but the gardens had to be tended from April to the end of September. Jews had to compete with the Karaites from Troki, who were reputed to be good at growing cucumbers. In Kiejdany, Jews raised cucumbers on a large scale. Cabbage and carrots were also cultivated for marketing; beets, radishes, and turnips were planted almost exclusively for one's own consumption.

Orchard Keepers

Jews were less involved with raising fruit than with marketing it. Almost all estate owners had orchards, and the more prosperous peasants also had small orchards of some ten to twelve trees. Lithuanian fruit is known for its fragrance and flavor. Sweets were expensive, and fruit was the only treat that both town and country folk could afford. But young people in the villages did not have the few pennies to spend on fruit, nor did they want to "waste" money on fruit that was growing at arm's reach. As a result, rural orchards were always exposed to the danger of being picked clean on the sly.

Jews would frequently rent orchards in bloom, making a down payment or paying in full, and hope for a rich harvest. After renting an orchard, the Jew would take complete responsibility for it. Sometimes there might be a late frost or a storm would knock the fruit out of the trees. But the orchard tender, hoping for compassion from the Almighty, had to take the chance, lest someone come along later and offer a better price than he did. The peasant, for his part, was always in need of money, especially in the spring, after the winter had depleted all that he had saved.

In late June or early July, small fruits—currants, gooseberries, raspberries—appeared, followed by cherries. These orchards were hardly ever surrounded by a secure fence, and everyone around salivated at the thought of sneaking over at night to shake the fruit from the trees. Therefore, the orchard keeper had to guard his property day and night from June through September. He or a member of his family would have to be in the orchard at all times; sometimes they would have to work there together. If he had several orchards, he would hire Jewish villagers who were out of work during the summer, such as a tailor or a shoemaker, to be guards. They would sleep on straw mats in a lean-to.

The orchard keepers usually had a small kosher pot for cooking, but their diet generally consisted of a piece of dry bread and cheese, which they would wash down with cold water. Occasionally they would cook some applesauce and eat it with bread. They could not go home even for the Sabbath, for the orchard could never be left unguarded.

Guarding the orchard was not an easy task. There were always rascals on the prowl. The moment a guard would doze off, they were inside the orchard and at the trees. Sometimes whole gangs of them would seize an orchard by sheer force. At such times it was best for the guard to look the other way, especially if he did not want to be beaten. For this reason, the guards had watchdogs and, in some cases, even shotguns. The best policy, however, was to live on friendly terms with everyone (especially the local "bigwigs") and treat them liberally to fruit, so that the nights would not be interrupted by uninvited visitors.

The undersized, misshapen fruits were dealt with first. They were sold or used by the workers, or they were cut into slices and strung up to dry in the sun. At the time, this was the best known method of preserving fruit. After the small fruits had their season, others appeared: different kinds of apples (both early and late varieties) and many varieties of pears. The better-quality fruit, especially winter fruit, was taken to the larger cities and

Postcard from the pre–World War I era depicting peasants in the Vilna region. Courtesy of the YIVO Archives.

sold wholesale. Small fruit and summer fruit, which could not be kept long, were sold in the marketplaces of nearby townships or at fairs. Poorer-quality fruit was sold by the peck (at three to five kopeks); better fruit was sold by weight. The pick of the crop was usually bought by fruit dealers and sent to St. Petersburg, Moscow, Warsaw, and other major cities. The orchards yielded a meager income. Someone who knew how to keep apples through the winter, until Passover, could sell them at a high price. But few orchard keepers knew how to do this, and they could not wait that long to make their money.

A considerable number of Jewish families came from both the towns and the villages to spend the summer tending orchards. At least five or six Jewish families in every town were thus employed. Managing the larger orchards, which might have as many as several hundred trees, involved the creation of partnerships, because no one family had enough money for such a venture. Even then the partners would have to borrow money for so big an enterprise.

During the fall season, the fairs and markets were lively with rows of carts filled with fruit, spreading the welcome fragrance of apples. Jewish men and women hawked their fruit, their busy, joyous voices filling the air, and fruits occupied the first place among all kinds of merchandise with which a full house is blessed.

Dairy Workers

Nearly half of all the Jews had their own cows or goats, which provided milk for household use, but both wealthier Jews and the very poor would occasionally buy milk from the dairymen. The dairymen would buy the morning or evening milkings from the estate owner or the Jewish *arendar.* (Cows were milked twice, sometimes three times, daily). At night the milk would be kept cool on ice, to prevent it from souring. Early in the morning the dairymen would carry their milk pails to town (few dairymen could afford a horse and cart). The milk pails were usually carried on a yoke, sometimes for as far as five kilometers. Milk had to be delivered in time for early breakfast in town, so the dairymen had to make haste. In the heat of summer, the yoke would frequently chafe the dairyman's arms and shoulders, and he then had to carry the milk pails in his hands.

The dairyman would pay from nine to eleven kopeks per gallon and sell the milk at five kopeks per quart. Every dairyman would handle from ten to twelve gallons a day, so that during the season he could make as much as a ruble a day. If the milk clabbered, the dairyman had to swallow the loss. The mainstay of his business was fresh milk, but if he had any leftover supply he would make it into cheese.

There were other dairymen who would contract for a year's yield with an estate owner. They would pay the owner according to the number of milk cows in the herd. He, in turn, had to provide the feed. The dairyman, along with the women in his family and non-Jewish women whom he hired, would milk the cows, churn butter and make cheese. Pot cheese was made in a most primitive way: the milk was put up to sour and the cream was skimmed off; the clabber was put into an oven to curdle. Then it was poured into cheese sacks, and the whey was drained off from the final product. The demand for pot cheese was especially great around Shavuot, for making *blintzes*.

Usually the pot cheese was poured into triangular molds, which were then pressed under boards and rocks. Afterward, the cheese was dried and hardened in the sun; any mold was scraped off. This dry cheese, along with dried black bread, was carried to America by devout Jewish emigrants, who wanted to avoid eating non-kosher food during their long sea voyage. The cream that had been skimmed off was churned into butter by hand. The butter would be washed several times, salted, and taken to the city to be sold in the market or to a wholesaler, who would distribute it to dairy stores.

Dairy products were very inexpensive. Salted butter was twenty to twenty-two kopeks per pound; cheese was three or four kopeks per pound and, during a depression, as low as one or two kopeks. During the summer, the dairyman would bring his wares to town two or three times a week. If the estate owner was generous and did not press him too hard, the dairyman could manage to get by, but if the owner was mean and stingy, the dairyman would find it extremely difficult to eke out a living.

Millers

The estate owner, who controlled the streams on his property, would rent out his mills. These were usually situated near a dike or a pond, so that the mill wheels could be driven by water.

The miller was an aristocrat among village Jews. His good fortune was reflected in a folksong that boys in the towns sang. The refrain imitated the sound of the millstones:

Kataytl, kataytl, kataytl,	(Tumble, tumble, tumble,
Dem milner in baytl,	Into the miller's purse,
Dem milner in baytl.	Into the miller's purse.)

Some of the peasants, it is true, ground their own grain by hand with millstones. Generally, however, peasants had become accustomed to taking their bag of grain to the miller. He would grind it for them for a small fee, about five kopeks a pood.[3] In addition to this payment, the flour dust and chaff from sifted grain belonged to the miller. With these he would feed a few dairy cows (millers' cows were known for being sleek and fat) and some chickens and geese. After the harvest, the mills were besieged with customers and worked day and night as peasants patiently waited their turn.

Larger mills were also equipped to process a variety of grains: barley, oats, buckwheat and the like. Only the very big mills had rollers for milling white flour. The larger mills were run by hired managers, usually non-Jews, but most of the millers took care of their own machines. Some of the mills were equipped with round wire brushes and rollers. The brushes, which were rotated by the water wheels, were used to comb and pull newly sheared lambs' wool. In order to make the finished material stiff and closely woven, the wool had to be put through the rollers. The raw wool was treated with boiling water and pounded with rods for a period of twelve to twenty-four hours. This extra equipment provided considerable supplementary income for the millers. The peasant who had brought the wool was expected to boil the water and watch the material being treated.

Spring was by far the most difficult season for the miller. The melting snow and swollen streams broke the dams, frequently inflicting great damage on the mills. But the miller usually had some money saved and could survive the emergency.

In the years after World War I, the number of mills increased greatly. Peasants who lived on the banks of running streams built dams and even installed turbines. As a result, the smaller Jewish millers were almost entirely driven out of business. Windmills were seen much less frequently than watermills, and they played a comparatively minor role.

Fishermen

The many lakes in the region of Lithuania, as well as those in the districts of Troki, Święciany, Brasław, Postawy, and several others, were rich with a variety of fish. This mysterious living treasure has always fascinated the local population, both Jews and non-Jews.

For the peasants, fishing supplemented their income as farmers. For many Jews, it was a kind of gamble, a chance at striking it rich by making a "big catch" from the lake—that is, netting a large number of fish at one time. Although there was little chance of this, grandfathers and fathers would tell tales or would remember having heard of such "big catches."

It was said, for example, that someone had caught twenty to twenty-five wagonloads, each weighing twenty-five to thirty pood, in one operation. In the Brasław district, the lakes were owned by Count Plater.[4] In the 1880s, a Jew who leased the fishing rights to these lakes reportedly caught more than

1,000 pood of bream in the month of Adar each year for three consecutive years. As a rule such big catches consisted of small fish. These brought from eighty kopeks to a ruble per pood. Jewish fishermen looked for bream, large fish weighing as much as twenty pounds each, which brought a very good price. "The bream is clever," the fishermen would say. When the bream saw that it had no choice but to be caught in the net, it would lie on its side at the bottom of the lake to avoid the trap. There may be some question as to whether the bream is clever, but there is no doubt that it is difficult to catch, perhaps because there are fewer bream than there are other fish. In any case, the rare big catches lured many a Jew to continue to invest in fishing in the hope that, with God's help, he would get rich. However, this never came to pass.

Fishermen believed that they would "die in other men's shrouds." In other words, a fisherman was a poor man. The saying was justified, for despite whatever good luck they had, Jews who invested in fishing wound up poor due to small catches, numerous expenses, and the high cost of fishing leases. "He drowned his money in the lake," people would say of a fisherman. Nevertheless, a number of Jews made a living as fishermen. In the Troki district alone there were about forty such Jewish investors, each employing at least six or seven fishermen in the summer and as many as twenty in the winter.

The nets used during the summer were 250 to 300 fathoms (one-half kilometer) long and required four men to work them. The winter nets were larger, from 500 to 600 fathoms in length, and called for eight full-time fishermen plus twelve to fifteen additional workers. The latter came from the surrounding villages and were not paid in cash, but with a portion of the catch.

Every Jewish investor employed one or two Jews on a permanent basis. These were his trusted representatives and in many cases his managers; they were the ones who knew how to set up the net. This was a specialized skill that entailed sewing the net or repairing it with rope, tying stone weights to the bottom of the net (which drew it down toward the bottom of the lake), and attaching floating boards, which held the net up in the water, to the top. This caused the net to stand upright in the water, forming a wall to trap the fish as they were driven with stirrers (a long stick with a small block of wood nailed to one end). This was intended to frighten the fish and cause them to enter the large net trap (thirty-six fathoms long), from which they could not escape. If the net was not properly set and was crooked, it would buckle and tangle in the water, and the entire effort would be wasted. Setting up the net was usually the specialty of the older Jewish fishermen. They were paid a weekly wage of four to five rubles per week, higher than that of the other workers, who received two or three rubles. In addition, the fishermen received free bread, fish, and milk. The fish were cooked at the edge of the lake after the day's work was done. The pot used was *parev*. Sometimes the men also boiled milk or cooked an additional dish. If the catch was made near a village where a Jew lived, the Jewish fishermen ate at his home.

The Jews employed in the fishing industry were usually pious. Each man carried his prayer shawl and phylacteries. In the morning, after the net was cast, the men would return to shore, the only place where the rowboat could be secured and the net pulled up, and then the Jewish men would pray under a tree. The Christians regarded the prayers of their co-workers with reverence and never made fun of the "Jewish rosaries." In the meantime, the non-Jewish fishermen would wind the ropes onto the reel (a cylinder with a handle). When the net had been pulled up to the boat it had to be pulled the rest of the way into the boat by hand. The men who had been praying returned to help with this. The task called for great physical strength and took place in all sorts of weather, including storms, pouring rain and freezing cold. Yet the Jewish fishermen never lagged behind their non-Jewish co-workers.

Fishing was usually done during the night or at dawn. Seven or eight castings had to be drawn up every twenty-four hours. Each casting lasted at least an hour or an hour and fifteen minutes. When the fishing was done the men had to hang the net out to dry and then transfer the nets and the boats to the next lake. The Jew who managed the enterprise hired carts from the local peasants to do this. He would also decide whether it was worthwhile to remain at a lake or whether it had been sufficiently "fished out." When the investor arrived at the lake to collect the catch, the manager would have to report on the number of castings made. Often the lake was the object of curses—"A plague on it!" or "May it burn!"—when the catch was insufficient to cover the expenses. It was usually the smaller investor, who had little to begin with, who invoked such "blessings" on a lake. Such investors were obliged to return to a lake many times and would catch few fish, because "a lake likes to take a rest."

Another curse besetting the Jewish investor in fishing was the notion that fish did not "belong" to anyone—in other words, many people did not consider fish to be merchandise and wanted to get them free. This cost the Jewish investor a great deal of income, for he had to be on good terms with everyone. The landowner from whom the Jew leased the lake certainly felt privileged and expected to receive the largest and best fish. The peasants in the villages surrounding the lake also expected free fish, as did the surveyors (the official overseers of state-owned forests and lakes), the foresters, and anyone else, such as the police officer and the guard, who enjoyed fish that did not cost anything.

When a catch was made in a lake near a town, all of its poor folk would gather: the slaughterer, the synagogue caretaker, the *melamed*. The investor would complain: "Why is it that people don't go to the butcher for free meat, or to the dairyman for free milk, or to the tavern for free whiskey? Why are fish so accursed?" But after this lament, these "merchants," as they were ironically called, would each receive some fish.

At calends, when the pre-Christmas fast must begin with the eating of fish, the Jewish fish merchant had to outdo himself, providing fish to all the wealthy landowners, the police, forest officials, town scribes, village elders, and others. Otherwise, each would keep interfering with him, serving him with summonses for "illegal fishing," and preventing him from making any catches.

As the catch was weighed it was sorted into three categories: "select" (large fish), "half-select" (medium-sized fish), and "small fry." The large and medium-sized fish were packed into carts (with ice in summer) and sent to the "Friday market" in Vilna or Kovno. The small fish, suitable for dumplings, were taken by Jewish retail merchants to the nearby larger towns. The demand for these was especially great during the first nine days of Av.[5] Because Friday's catch was brought in too late to go to big cities, it was sent to the same local merchants, who would sell the larger fish to those housewives who could afford a piece of *gefilte fish* for the Sabbath meal. At the turn of the century and earlier, the "small fry" might also be sent to Vilna or Kovno, but by the 1900s these could not be sold in the larger cities and were consumed locally. Almost every town had its fish dealers. They were quite simple Jews who did not command a great deal of respect. Nevertheless, housewives would tremble before them.

Jewish investors leased the lakes either from wealthy landholders or from the government. Every landholder had a Jew with whom he did business. If the Jew was not himself engaged in fishing he would recommend another Jewish investor of his acquaintance to the landholder. In earlier times, the landowners were usually very fair in their dealings with their fishing lessees. They would not lease to others, even if offered more money. They would not go back on their word. They would often entertain the investors and serve them refreshments (fruit or things made with honey, which an observant Jew is permitted to eat in non-Jewish homes).

It was worse with lakes owned by the state. At the time, a Jew did not have the right to lease lakes officially in his own name. He would go to the auction, at which leases were sold, with a non-Jewish surrogate, in whose name the envelope containing the bid was submitted. The Jewish investors would sometimes agree among themselves not to bid against each other. To make the agreement binding, each participant would deposit a certain amount of money with a neutral party. The bidder who was awarded the lease would then distribute five- or ten-ruble bills, or even more, to Jews who had nothing to do with fishing but who wanted a couple of rubles for keeping quiet. In most cases, however, Jewish competitors could not reach an agreement. Then *"Fonye* would get stuffed with Jewish money," by raising the lease on lakes that could not be rented profitably. Often, when the auctions were over, someone who had taken part in an agreement and was dissatisfied with the outcome would denounce the other participants. A review panel would then annul the bids and start anew. Bribes were common, but the bribe taker felt obliged to do something in return.

The lease on a particular lake came to be handed down from father to son. In later years, these Jewish investors tried to outsmart each other. There no longer was any unity among them. At auctions they would raise the bids sky high, until they were no longer commercially viable. This practice resulted in the impoverishment of many investors. World War I, the German occupation, and the postwar years almost completely eliminated the Jewish investor from fishing.

In addition to these investors, there were others who were involved in fishing on a more modest scale, using smaller nets. Here, only two people were needed for the job: one drove the boat, the other lowered the net and then pulled it up. Compared with the work involved in setting a large net, putting out these small ones (ten to twenty fathoms long) was a simple task. These nets were light, made of fine cord, and were loosely woven, with large "eyes," or spaces, which would only catch larger fish. At night the net was suspended vertically in the water across the width of the lake. The fish would not notice it and would enter the eyes. They could not escape, because fish are usually wider in the middle and cannot pass all the way through the eyes. By attempting to continue moving forward, the fish would become entangled in the net (fish can't swim backward). The net consisted of two large wings, which fenced off an area in the water, and a sack, or snare, into which the fish were driven. Fish caught in the wings of the net belonged to the workers. The chances of a big catch were smaller here, but the workers still benefited from a good catch. "A lake is a card," the fisherman used to say, and just as a gambler is drawn to a card, a fisherman is drawn to the lake.

This kind of fishing was most successful during the time of year when the fish shed their roe and spawned. At one time, this work was done primarily by Jews. Later, it was taken over by Russians from Dvinsk and Brasław. Jewish fishermen, especially the younger ones, abandoned the occupation when the mass emigration to America began. They went abroad in search of better opportunities and often found work connected with fishing.

The older Jewish fishermen had their superstitions. They feared the "evil eye" could be brought on them by anyone who stood on shore to observe them fishing. If a rowboat drifted away from the water's edge without its oars, the fishermen would call the "rascal" back with the following words:

| Batsikl, batsikl, shvim nisht mer, | Boat, boat, swim no more, |
| Derlang zikh tsurik a ker. | Turn around back to shore. |

They believed with unshakable faith that the boat would return.

Fishermen, whether Jewish or non-Jewish, were not averse to drinking whiskey. They would surround someone who visited them on shore and tie a rope around him as their way of saying that he had to pay them a ransom of "half a small bottle" or enough money to buy either a "half" or a "fourth." The men would drink together, often from the scoop used to bail out the boat. Most of the Jewish investors also enjoyed having a drink, especially in the company of others. This drinking was sociable, and there was no brawling or carousing. In most small towns, fishermen were considered ignorant and were not held in high regard. During the early decades of the twentieth century, however, there were still some among them who were well-to-do members of the merchant class.

Some Jews would buy fish from the village peasants to sell at the Friday market in Vilna or Kovno. To do this they would have to travel all night regardless of the weather ("the merchandise is not the kind that can wait"). This was especially exhausting on winter nights and in the mud and slush of autumn. They always hoped for a "good market" on the eve of a holiday, especially Passover. On those occasions the marketer could set his own price. Fishmongers who traveled a considerable distance to the Friday market had no choice but to spend the Sabbath in Vilna or Kovno.

In general, fishermen believed that the fish trade was conducted in a more reliable fashion in Vilna than in Kovno, where the marketers were reputed to be "robbers." In Vilna, middlemen sold the entire catch to the retailer in a single transaction, whereas in Kovno the middleman was also the retailer, who took the best of the sales for himself. All that was left for the poor man who had worked day and night for a week catching the fish were "a few bones that had been gnawed clean," or even less. There were times when he did not even earn enough to pay for the cart he had hired to take the fish to market.

Nets made of hemp were produced by peasants in the vicinity of Dukszty, Sołoki, and Widze. Some Jews made a business of buying up these nets, which came rolled up in log-shaped sections weighing twenty to thirty pounds each. A net could require from fifteen to thirty of these sections. Every Jewish investor bought his nets from a dealer in one of the towns mentioned. Selling nets was a business of considerable scope. At the beginning of the twentieth century, however, some fishermen began using nets made of cotton, which were produced by machine in Landsberg, Prussia. They were more expensive than hemp nets, but they were stronger and more practical. Cotton nets were also imported through the mail by Jewish agents in Grajewo. Trading in large, domestically produced nets ceased altogether.

Immediately after World War I, prices for everything, including leases on properties, shot up because of inflation, and fishing began to die out as a Jewish occupation. Jewish investors in the industry were completely impoverished, and one by one they had to liquidate their businesses. Enterprising non-Jews were already arriving on the scene. In the newly created republics, they were shown considerable favoritism and were awarded the leases even when they submitted much lower bids than did Jewish businessmen. By the time governments lowered the leasing prices, the taxes were so high that there were few Jewish applicants for leases on lakes. Moreover, the lakes that Jews did lease were being fished by local peasants, who paid nothing and were exhausting the supply of fish. Unwilling and unable to do battle with the peasants, the Jews had no way to forbid them to fish in the lakes that the Jews had leased.

Currently [the 1930s], there are only a few Jewish investors in the fishing industry in the areas mentioned, and they are on the verge of going out of business. Incitement against Jewish leaseholders both in the press and on the part of government has made it impossible for them to continue. Jews who formerly worked as fishermen have almost entirely disappeared. Non-Jews do not hire them. Here and there, a Jew will buy a peasant's catch, but the fishing cooperatives have all but completely excluded Jewish dealers and have opened a number of stores supplied and operated entirely by non-Jews. The final blow to the Jewish fishing industry came with the controlled raising of carp and other fish, which is now done on all the larger estates and even by peasants. The number of Jewish women selling fish in cities has been reduced by half, and the earnings of those who still do so are minimal, often amounting to only a few groshns.

In former days, fishmonger women earned themselves a poor reputation because of their scolding, cursing, and frequent physical insults, such as slapping a customer in the face with a fish. Some would give short weight or measure, but housewives were afraid to argue with them. It was said that on the Sabbath the fishmongers were better dressed—in lambskin coats!—than anyone else and bought the best seats in the Yiddish theater. Nowadays they are rejected, indigent women, glad to earn enough to buy a piece of dry bread. With every passing month, their number declines. Their weekly earnings are between one and ten zlotys. The few Jewish middlemen still in the fish business are convinced that, in only a few years, there will be no trace of Jewish fishermen and fish merchants.

Innkeepers, Drivers, and Distillers

An old saying among wagon drivers advises, "Never avoid an inn." Evidently, inns were indispensable early in the twentieth century, especially as railroads were few and buses had not yet been invented. All land transportation was by wagon. Many dozens, even hundreds, of versts had to be traversed with the help of horses.[6] It often took many days to go from small towns and the countryside to the large city and then return. Farm products and raw materials were brought to town, and manufactured and imported products were carried back.

Each town had one or more Jewish drivers, who would accept lists from shopkeepers for all sorts of merchandise they wished to purchase. These drivers would also take personal orders for things ranging from medical prescriptions to "city" (i.e., fatty) meat for the Sabbath. They would even handle requests to borrow books for the town's *maskilim*, to obtain information, and deliver or collect messages, letters, money, and the like. Rural Jews would transport their dairy products, grain, cows, and calves. Village merchants transported hog bristles, seed, poultry and fish. Jewish gardeners brought cucumbers; orchard keepers—berries and fruit. The main roads were busiest before market days and especially as Friday drew near, when city residents demanded quite a variety of products for the Sabbath. Small-town and country folk eagerly delivered goods to the "gourmets" of Vilna. Vilna's residents acquired this reputation among the poor village Jews because the former used butter, cheese, poultry, fish, and fruit not only on the Sabbath but even on ordinary weekdays. The following anecdote, related with tongue in cheek in small-town, middle-class homes, illustrates this type of gourmet eating:

> "Mother, Khayimke is a gourmet."
> "Why? What's the matter?"
> "He's eating bread."

The city gluttons and gourmets "indulged" in bread.

Jews traveled the highways on heavily loaded carts. Often, there was no room for the driver to sit, and he was forced to travel the entire distance on foot, reins in hand. If the horse was good and could be relied on to follow the proper path, the driver might tie the reins to the shaft and walk alongside the cart with his hands free, unless a wagon approached from the opposite direction and it became necessary to steer the horse to one side. To make it easier to walk, the man would tuck in the tails of his caftan, worn during the summer, or his fur or sheepskin coat in the winter.

Rain, snow, thunder, lightning, a blizzard wind cutting across the face: the wagoner dared not stop for any of these or otherwise interrupt his journey for any length of time. First of all, his load had to be delivered to the marketplace before dawn. Second, if he "indulged" himself by stopping overnight until the storm abated, he would not arrive home in time for the Sabbath. Spending the Sabbath on the road was considered tedious and unpleasant. With such an arduous way of making a living, the one joy that the driver could look forward to was spending the Sabbath at home.

So the men rode or trudged, chilled to the bone in winter, parched and dusty or soaked through with rain or perspiration in summer. Eventually, the horse would be hungry, his mouth covered with froth (called "cream" in driver's slang), and the man's stomach was also empty. It was time to rest a little, have a bite to eat, and feed the horse. At the inn, one could get some food and even have a small drink of whiskey to "warm the soul." The inn was a sort of promised land to regular drivers and their passengers.

An inn on the highway was like a train station. True, it was rather primitive, befitting the travel conditions of the time, with little more than a modest buffet, but the inns were also hotels and stores, where one could buy a box of matches, cigarettes or cheap tobacco, a glass of beer or *kvas*. Also available were tar or grease for wheels, leather straps, nails, and "other food products," as a Russian sign on one old inn announced.

After traveling for a night or two without interruption, a driver simply had to have a nap of at least several hours, usually on a hard bench at the inn. That was certainly better than dozing off in the driver's seat of an overladen cart: he could fall off, or the cart might even capsize, driver and all.

The inn played an important role in the history of transportation. Without it, maintaining regular passenger and freight service would have been impossible. Neither the national nor local government did anything to meet the needs of people who spent most of their days traveling. The inn thus filled a vital economic need.[7]

An inn could also be a sort of first-aid station for all who passed by. At the inn, one could take care of whatever might occur on the roads: a broken axle, hub or linchpin, or a torn yoke thong. If a man became ill along the way or something harmed his horse, the innkeeper was like a brother and his wife was like a mother. Where else could one wait out a heavy downpour or a blizzard, when continuing "without a road" in pitch darkness meant risking one's life? At the inn, of course.

Jews were avid innkeepers. It is difficult to calculate how many Jewish innkeepers there were in the last decades of the nineteenth century. There were ten inns, not counting those in the villages, in a stretch of about eighty versts from Jezno to Vilna.* By the 1930s, not one remained. It may therefore be assumed that along the more important highways there were, on the

---

*Jezno, a town in Lithuania, was known from the expression "Yezne un Stoklishok!," which Jews used in place of "Jesus Maria!"

average, no fewer than one inn to every ten versts. On side roads there were considerably fewer. In addition to the inns along the highways, there were one or two in every sizable village. Those inns were always situated at the roadside, usually at each end of the village, where they would be noticeable. Although such inns served travelers en route, they were mainly village gathering places.

It should be kept in mind that in those days no cultural activity was provided for the peasant population. There were no schools; 99 percent of peasants were illiterate. There was no intellectual entertainment; there were only village parties, known as *grishkes.* There were no pleasures for the peasant other than drinking whiskey or beer to help him forget, for a while, his miserable life of toil.

This could be obtained from some "Abramka," "Moshka," or "Haimka" at the inn. In addition, the inn was spacious compared to the peasant's sooty little dwelling. At the inn, he would find kindred spirits who also longed for a glassful. At the Jew's place, one could unburden the soul. The Jew did, after all, have contact with the outside world, and one might hear some news at his inn. The Jew could give advice regarding complicated questions. Both among Jews and non-Jews in Belorussia there was a saying: "Let it be as Sarah said." In all probability, there was at one time an authoritative Jewish innkeeper by that name who had furnished good advice to the peasants. The expression also provides an indication of the relations between Jews and non-Jews of the period.

It was not always possible to make a living solely from keeping an inn, especially one on a side road or in an isolated village. In such a case, the wife ran the inn while her husband engaged in some other work, making the rounds of the villages to sell merchandise or ply a trade (as a tailor, wheelwright, fisherman, or the like). The wife had to be a "woman of valor,"[8] to serve drinks to the peasants, stay in their good graces, converse with them and even come to their aid in an emergency.

As a rule, the inns belonged to wealthy landowners who leased them to Jews. In some cases, Jews established claims so that no one else was allowed to offer to pay more to obtain their leases. Nevertheless, it did occasionally happen that a rival outbid a long-term innkeeper and "unseated" him.

Before the government monopoly on whiskey was introduced in 1897, a system known as "propination" prevailed in many localities.[9] This gave the landowner the exclusive right to brew and sell whiskey. The right to sell the whiskey would be given to one Jewish tavernkeeper only. No one else could open a tavern in that village or town. A town innkeeper with such an exclusive right was considered a privileged person. Indeed, he frequently was the "absolute ruler" of his town, a figure of influence and authority. He was often also the synagogue administrator. Sometimes such a person might even go as far as to slap the face of an "insolent" man for attempting to assume power for himself or refusing to obey a synagogue administrator.

However, among the village tavernkeepers, there were no influential men. These were simple people who did not give up one iota of traditional village Jewish life, although they lived among Christians. These Jews observed the Sabbath, when they sold no whiskey and handled no money. Gentiles did not dare to come in on that day. Everyone at the inn rested on the Sabbath "in accordance with God's command." On the Sabbath, very few wagons were on the road. Certainly there were no Jews, and non-Jews, too, had very few places to stop. Everything in the town or village was at a complete standstill.

Whiskey was the "principal commodity" at the inn, as the saying goes: "A tavern without whiskey is like a driver without a whip." The whiskey was stored in oaken casks resting on two blocks of wood in a darkened room, which had only one or two tiny windows. Below the tap fitted into the barrel there would be a copper pot to catch any drips from an ill-fitting tap. The whiskey would be drawn from the barrel into the copper pot or a similar container and then poured into bottles. Individual purchases would be dispensed in small vessels of copper or tin of various sizes: a half-quart, a quart, a half-gallon, a gallon, etc. The quart container was shaped like a cut-off cone. A siphon was often used to drain whiskey from the barrel through a special opening that was kept closed with a bung. The air was first extracted from the siphon by mouth and then the whiskey was drawn up and deposited into a container. Siphons were most often used to draw beer from barrels. Beer was also poured into small buckets. At celebrations the peasants would consume quite a few bucketsful. Beer was drunk with companions at fairs, markets, and on church holidays.

The innkeepers suffered a great deal at the hands of inspectors, who came to see that the alcohol content of the whiskey met with excise regulations (45 percent). Of course, sometimes the proof strength was sub-standard (someone might risk adding a little water). This resulted not only in police citations and fines but also in prison sentences of from six months to a year. Sometimes one could come to terms with the enemy by slipping him a ten- or—in case of a severe infraction—twenty-five-ruble note. Usually, though, the innkeeper could expect a peck of trouble, so that during the last years before the state monopoly law went into effect there was little tampering with whiskey.

Before the government monopoly, the production of whiskey lay entirely in private hands. Owners of large estates built distilleries in which they made alcoholic beverages from their produce. The cost of such produce was very low. (The purveyors of rye and potatoes used for this purpose were often Jews.) As a rule, distilleries were leased by Jews. Excise personnel were always present at the distillery to determine the amount of tax due to the government for the number of buckets of whiskey produced. Excise officials lived in great luxury. It was worth paying them large sums so that they would not record the full amount of production, thereby reducing the amount of tax levied.

Those employed in making whiskey were mainly Jewish distillers, who were responsible for the entire process. They prepared the mashes, determined the strength, and distilled the spirits. Jewish distillers were highly skilled specialists who had their professional secrets, and it was difficult to replace them. Innkeepers obtained their whiskey in barrels directly from the distilleries. Later on, there were special plants for bottling whiskey and beer, and then the tavern owners and innkeepers bought their liquor there. By the 1930s, it would probably be impossible to find a Jewish distiller anywhere in the Lithuanian and Belorussian regions. Similarly, wine making has also become an extinct occupation among Jews.

The inns located along the highways or in the towns through which the highways passed were large buildings with many rooms. In some cases, these rooms were only half-partitioned; they surrounded a big Russian stove, which was meant to heat them all. If the space was large there would also be portable heaters. Because these often emitted smoke, the walls of inns rarely stayed white. The floors in a few "deluxe" rooms would be of wood; the rest would be of clay or loose brick. Floors were rarely washed—"Dirt is going to be tracked in, in any case." Besides tables, an inn's furniture consisted of a wide or narrow couch or a hard sofa on which the traveler could take a nap. The bedding was the guest's own overcoat, fur coat, or simply "his own fist." It was good to be at an inn in winter, when bread was being baked and the oven was hot. Here the wet, bone-chilled traveler might be able to get warm and dry. There would often be sacks of rye, oats, or barley drying on the *lezhak*, a low, horizontal extension of the oven, before they were taken to be milled. Lying down on a hot sack of oats was considered a remedy for many an illness: "Hot oats draw out the pain." This applied to rheumatism, abdominal cramps, stabbing pains, aching bones, nausea, and the like: "A warm stove heals the bones." As a rule, every villager's oven had a special medical function. It was the resident physician, one that did not require payment. (The *lezhak* was utilized mainly by elderly people.)

From the inn's kitchen there was a direct entrance to the stable, which was a very large barn with several bins for wood, straw, and hay. Here, in addition to the horses, ten or more wagons could be sheltered. There were no windows, only a large double gate through which the wagons entered. The stables' roofs were often in disrepair and leaked rain and snow. With the dirt on the floor, this made the stable wet and muddy. Travelers and the innkeeper's household tracked much of the mud into the house, especially during the autumn and on rainy winter days.

No one, however, complained. That was how it had been for generations, as natural as day and night, winter and summer. In a word, it was the universal order of things. Much about the inn remained unchanged from the days of Solomon Maimon to the late nineteenth century.[10]

If the innkeeper owned any chickens, geese, a horse or a cow, they were all kept in the stable. The inn and the barn were one indivisible whole. In the summer, there were swarms of flies and plenty of other insects. Guests were often unable to sleep. Some inns were particularly notorious for their bedbugs, which would attack the traveler. There was a joke that went around:

> "Yudl's inn burned down."
> "Oh, my! But then, so did the bedbugs."

In every misfortune there is some consolation; in this case, it was revenge on the "red tricksters." On summer nights, transients often slept on their wagons in the barn or in the inn's courtyard to avoid bedbugs. While the horses ate their oats from the feed bag, the driver and his passengers tried to catch a short nap.

There were affluent inns and poor inns. In the rich ones, travelers could get a bite to eat. The poor ones did not always have much food, as the following innkeepers' joke (although it more likely originated with *maskilim*) illustrates:

> A Jew is traveling along the highway. He is hungry. He is cold. But there is an inn not far away. He'll be able to get something to eat there. Exhausted, he enters.
> "Good evening!"
> "Good evening to you!"
> "Food!"
> "What would you like?"
> "Well, some meat."
> "There isn't any."
> "A piece of fish?"
> "There isn't any."
> "A glass of milk?"
> "We don't have any. The cow isn't giving milk."
> "An egg?"
> "The hens are not laying!"
> "A roll, a slice of cheese, potatoes! Just put something on the table!"
> "Oh, my, what an appetite this man has!" says the innkeeper's wife. "He'd like to have everything!"[11]

Nevertheless, the inn offered some comfort and pleasure on long journeys. It felt good to be under the same roof with another Jew, from whom one might learn what prices were like in the city or about the condition of the road ahead, the bridge, the river (in the springtime), or the mud puddles.

On a Christian holiday, travelers would sometimes find themselves in the midst of a party at the inn. Peasant men and women would gather, and the young people would dance. A thought might occur to the more energetic Jewish traveler: it might not be a bad idea to dance a little and forget his troubles. There is a typical innkeepers' tale about a rabbi who traveled the countryside to collect food for himself from the farmers, and who was not averse to accepting money as well.

> The rabbi arrived at an inn where peasants were having a party. Soon other Jews entered the inn and saw the rabbi dancing a polka with a non-Jewish woman and saying to her, "Faster, faster!" When the rabbi noticed the newcomers, he went to greet them.
>
> "But Rabbi," said one of the guests, "is it proper for a rabbi to be dancing, and with a Christian at that?"
>
> "You must understand," replied the rabbi defensively. "It comes with the occupation."

One might wonder what connection there is between a non-Jewish woman and the occupation of a rabbi. The point is, however, that being on the road and imbibing a little gives one license to do things at an inn that one would never do under other circumstances. The village Jews, innkeepers included, were close to the local peasants and adopted some of their customs, sayings, and songs. In those days, there were no feelings of hatred or antagonism between village Jews and peasants. Each group depended on the other. The peasant needed the Jewish tailor, shoemaker, wheelwright, shopkeeper, innkeeper and, especially, the blacksmith. The Jewish villager believed that "one must live among non-Jews but die among Jews," and a popular saying among peasants advised: "When in trouble, turn to the Jew." Picketing and boycotts were as yet unknown.

The non-Jews' proximity and the paucity of young Jewish men, however, led not infrequently to conversion and mixed marriage, especially in the case of innkeepers' daughters. "Youth will have its fling," and the young Christian men would pursue Jewish village girls, some of whom did occasionally stray. On dark nights a girl might steal away from her parents and take the horses out to graze in the pasture where her Christian lover waited. If the fellow had serious intentions, a few God-fearing, well-to-do Christian women would intervene. Eventually, after many reproaches at home, the girl would run away, sometimes even taking some of her father's money. After her conversion and the wedding, the girl might return to the village with her husband and settle not far from where her parents lived. Although such instances of conversion were not infrequent, each case would arouse much concern among the entire Jewish population of the nearest town and among the neighboring rural Jews. Soon a unified effort to save the young Jewish woman would be underway. The Jews would make entreaties and go to considerable expense, but in the end the Christian clergy would usually prevail. Such events tended to damage relationships between Jews and peasants. Sometimes the struggle lasted for years. In most cases, the converted girl would come to a sorry end. The romance would soon fade and her husband would begin to remind his wife of her origins. This would progress from words to beatings and torment.

The fate of the Jewish woman who converts to Christianity is well known from Yiddish literature—for example, in Sholem Aleichem's classic work, *Tevye the Dairyman*.[12] At the time, it was impossible to return to the Jewish faith in Russia. In such a case, there was only one course of action— to find a way, with the help of someone with "connections," to spirit the woman away to America in secret. There she could assume a pious life and marry a Jewish man.

Men converted to Christianity less frequently than did women. There was even a saying among young village men: "When there is no girl, a *shikse* will do." But this usually pertained to flirting; no Jewish man wanted a Christian woman for his wife. It should also be remembered that Jewish boys who lived in the country did receive some Jewish education and were more steadfast than girls when it came to religion. "A young man is like a copper vessel: well-scoured, it's clean once more," mothers used to say of wanton youths. There were, nevertheless, occasional instances of conversion among young Jewish men, some of them even well-to-do. In all cases, the conversion was in connection with a romance.

Rural Jews, especially innkeepers, were aware of this threat to their children and endeavored to shield them from this "plague." The laws of *kashrut* were strictly observed. In conversation, parents referred to non-Jewish neighbors with deliberately cryptic names: they might be called *sherets* and *shrotse* (reptiles); the word *shvester* (sister) became *shvesterlo; foter* (father) *foterlo; muter* (mother), *muterlo,* and so on. *Khasene* (wedding) became *khaserlo; geshtorbn* (died) became *gefaln* (fell), *geboyrn* (born) became *geflamt* (flamed). There was no malice whatsoever in the practice. It was merely a device to ward off the possibility of conversion, to prevent assimilation into the surrounding sea of peasants.

There were also a few non-conformists who ignored Jewish ritual and adopted non-Jewish customs. (The expression, "worse than eating pork," implying a complete rejection of Jewishness, originated with rural Jews.) The following song describes one such rebel. While it dates from the second quarter of the nineteenth century, it is still characteristic of a later period. I came across the song, which was documented by M. Bernstein, in the collections of the YIVO Institute.[13]

> Yanke Khaymovich [Jan, son of Khayim],
> Registered on the list
> As number thirty-five,
> Should be conscripted into the army.
>
> He doesn't listen to his father and mother,
> Doesn't wear ritual fringes or phylacteries,
> Doesn't pray to God,
> Doesn't obey the Jewish community leaders.
>
> He doesn't like to eat hallah on the Sabbath
> Or *tsimmes* with goose fat;
> He won't touch it.
> To him tallow from swine tastes much better.

Uncomfortable living among Jews, such fellows would disappear and, absent from a traditional environment, they became ignorant of Jewish custom and religion. They would convert while in military service, marry non-Jewish women, and blend into Russian or Belorussian life. Sometimes, however, even they would eventually become observant Jews, emigrate to America and live among their "own people."

Jews felt that the inn itself did not corrupt the souls of either Jews or non-Jews: "It was a living like any other." The tavern, on the other hand, did not have a very good name. The word *shenkerke* (female tavernkeeper) was often a synonym for uncouthness and lack of honesty. Nevertheless, there was a saying, perhaps somewhat hypocritical—indeed, it probably originated among tavernkeepers—that "the tavern would not spoil a good person; a bad one could not be corrected even by the synagogue."

For the most part, innkeepers were very pious and honest. They seldom engaged in illegal activities, such as dealing in contraband or stolen goods. In any one administrative region, such people could literally be counted on the fingers on one hand, and people scrupulously avoided inns that were the site of shady activities.

There were some professional non-Jewish thieves. There were no Jewish horse thieves in either Lithuania or Belorussia, but a few shady Jews did trade in such "goods."[14] For the most part, they hid stolen horses, although around the turn of the century there was considerable trading in horses for export to Prussia, and stolen horses could also easily have been sent abroad. Some places earned a bad reputation for this reason. For example, a few Lithuanian towns were known for harboring horse traders, some of whom did not rule out illegal merchandise. Innkeepers might easily have played a considerable role in such trading, but they preferred not to. As a rule, Jews held horse traders in low esteem. Always referred to as "stablemen" and thought of as being rather like gypsies, they were often liars and unreliable in business.

Innkeepers and the neighboring village Jews who lived within the *t'hum shabbat* were all close with each other, almost as though they were one family. If there were ten men among them—including all males over thirteen years old—a *minyan* would gather every Sabbath in the center of the *t'hum shabbat*. Where Jews lived somewhat beyond the *t'hum shabbat* the town rabbi would be consulted. As a rule, he would not be strict about an extra mile, thus permitting the Jews in question to pray collectively and not forsake their Jewishness. In such cases, an *eyruv* was established on the road: symbolic food was hidden in the hollow of a tree and a religious fiction created.[15] The town would lend such a rural *minyan* a Torah scroll. It was kept in a free-standing closet or a drawer, and an effort was made to see that no unsuitable object, such as a utensil or discarded garment, was placed there. In exceptional cases, clean linen or other clean clothing might be stored there.

There were not many Jewish scholars among the village Jews, but there was always someone among them who was able to lead the prayers and was generally familiar with all the Sabbath and holiday rituals. Most often the *minyan* met in the home of an *arendar* or at the inn, for the inns were generally centrally situated. Because the inns had some large rooms, a separate one might be designated for the prayer service. Some of the more affluent *arendarn* had large homes. After the service, the owner of the house where the *minyan* met would usually invite all the worshippers to partake of refreshments: whiskey, small cakes, cold *tsimmes,* sometimes herring—as a rule, foods which, according to Jewish law, can be eaten without washing one's hands and with the recitation of the simple blessing that thanks the "Creator of various kinds of foods." When it came to the High Holy Days such arrangements for worship were considered insufficient. Then all rural Jews would travel to a town. If the town was nearby they would bring along their Torah scroll for the ceremonial processions on Simhat Torah, in which the entire *minyan* would participate as a group.

Many of the innkeepers and other rural Jews were uneducated; they did not understand the meaning of the words in holy books and were generally weak in Jewish knowledge. This was especially evident when they were in public—for example, during the reading of the *haftarah* in the synagogue. This furnished the towns' youngsters, who studied with private teachers or attended *heder,* much grist for ridicule. There are a large number of stories and anecdotes about the ignorance of rural Jews. Here are a few of them:

> The young son of a village Jew is called up to the Torah. He mistakenly recites the blessing thanking the "Creator of the fruit of the tree." At that point his father interjects: "Forgive him, the boy is so used to potatoes!" (The blessing over potatoes thanks the "Creator of the fruit of the earth.")

A village Jew is reading the Passover *haggadah* aloud. Instead of "Take the cup [the Hebrew word *kos,* written כּוֹס] into your hand," he cries out, "Take the foot [the Yiddish word *fus,* written פוּס] into your hand." [A fly had put a dot inside the כ and the village Jew mistook it for a פ, without realizing the absurdity created by the change.]

Also while reading the *haggadah,* the village Jew bursts into tears at the Hebrew verse *tam mah hu omer.* [The simple one (*tam*), what does he say?]
"Why are you crying?" asks his wife.
"How can I not cry when I am mentioned? What will they ask *there?*" [In Russian, *tam* means "there." The rural Jew substituted the Russian meaning for the Hebrew word and assumed that the phrase referred to his being questioned "there"—that is, in heaven.]

A country blacksmith does not know how to conduct the Passover seder. He sends his wife to look in through the window of the innkeeper, who is reputed to be something of a scholar, to see how things are being done there.
The innkeeper was very punctilious. Disagreeing about some detail with his wife, he was beating her. Having seen this, the smith's wife returns home but says nothing.
"Well, why don't you say something?" She makes no response whatever. Finally, the smith loses his patience and strikes his wife.
"Well," she says, weeping, "if you already know what to do at the seder, why did you send me to the innkeeper's?"

Rural Jews had no compunctions about using expressions that refer to bodily functions and applied them freely in their speech. For instance:

The daughter of a rural Jewish family, which has come to town for Rosh Hashanah, is cooking the meal. Her mother is praying in the women's section of the synagogue. The daughter runs in, exclaiming, "Mother, Mother, the *tsimmes* is so overcooked it looks like sh-t!" The mother is furious. "You nasty creature, you country rube! To say such a vulgar word in a holy place! I'll hit you so hard with my prayerbook you'll sh-t yourself right here!"

Townspeople also mocked the Belorussian-Yiddish expressions of the rural Jews:

Before Passover a villager would say: "Khlebets, khlebets idzi pod stolets, a matsa idzi siuda!" [Bread, bread, go under the table, and matzah, come here!] When the holiday was over he would pronounce a similar incantation, but in reverse order.

An innkeeper who went to town for the High Holy Days knew how to lead the worship but had forgotten the melody for an important prayer. As he stood silent at the lectern his wife, seated in the women's section, began singing in Belorussian to the prayer melody: "Sivaia holova, durnaia holova, shto ty stoish kak dura?" [Gray head, silly head, why do you stand here like a fool?] The man picked up the tune and proceeded smoothly to the end.

With such tales, the town Jew made fun of the village Jew.

On the other hand, the practical and industrious rural Jew had plenty of material for deriding the town scholar and the yeshiva student, the greatest fools when it came to natural phenomena. According to the rural Jew when the townsfolk arrived in the country they asked such questions as "What kind of tree do rolls grow on?" and "Which are the cows that lay eggs?" The rural Jew also mocked the town Jews' use of non-Jewish languages. He would describe a pretentious young mademoiselle attempting to speak Russian, who says to her friend in a ridiculous mixture of Polish, Russian, and Yiddish, "Idzim na toiu lavu bo tutaj zune brene" (Let's cross to the other sidewalk; the sun is burning here).

Another story tells of a yeshiva student who was trying to learn a non-Jewish language and asked a village Jew how to say *tsibele* (onion) in Polish. The village Jew replied: *cebula* (pronounced *tsebule*). Then, the talmudic student was sure he knew how to speak Polish: if *tsibele* was *tsebule,* then *benkl* (bench) is *benkule, shtivl* (boots) is *shtivule, hitl* (cap) is *hitule,* and so on.

The rural Jew also tells about the yeshiva student who, when his horse slowed down, stepped down from the wagon and whispered in the horse's ear, "Here comes a bear." (The horse was expected to be frightened by this and begin running.) In sum, rural Jews did not hold the city dweller or the small-town bigwig in very high esteem. They considered him incompetent, fit only to be a *melamed;* he was lazy and thought it beneath him to do any kind of physical work. Thus the country Jew took revenge on his detractors.

As noted above, innkeepers lived peaceably with the surrounding non-Jewish community. They extended credit to neighboring peasants. These accounts were often registered on a wall, with a piece of coal or chalk, in a semiliterate mixture of Hebrew and Yiddish. Innkeepers who were more literate might keep books, using a system similar to the accounts that were written on the wall. When an account was settled it was struck out with two long lines, one above the other.

No innkeeper earned a fortune, but at least it was possible to make ends meet. He had his own cow, a small garden, a potato patch he had planted himself, and various other domestic pleasures. His expectations were not high. When the government monopoly on whiskey went into effect, however, Jewish innkeepers were dealt a serious blow. No longer able to sell liquor, they had to find another source of income. Many innkeepers moved to small towns and became shopkeepers. The young and middle-aged emigrated to America. Before World War I, there was still a sizable number of Jewish innkeepers, but the war all but eliminated them from the landscape. The sudden prevalence of the motor bus made inns economically superfluous, and rural cooperatives deprived them of their retail function. Thus, Jewish innkeeping came to an end.

Village Merchants and Peddlers

In the villages there were also *luftmentshn,* Jews with no particular profession, who bought and sold whatever merchandise was available. They would buy up small amounts of farm produce (the peasants never produced large quantities of goods): flax and linseed in the fall; grain in the winter; berries and fresh or dried mushrooms in midsummer; fruit at the end of summer; hog bristles and horse tails and manes all the year round, as well as honey, wax, and wool.

Often these traders had a horse and wagon and would travel from village to village. There were similar petty traders in the towns as well, and the competition among them was very keen, one outbidding the other for products to sell. As a result, these merchants were always very poor. They would even welcome an occasional fare to or from town to help augment their income. When things were very slow, the merchant would also haul logs from nearby forests to the railroad station or cobblestones to pave a new road.

Some of these merchants also dealt in livestock. They would buy a sheep or a calf or some chickens from the peasants, take the animals to town to be slaughtered and sell the meat by the pound. The animals' hindquarters were sold to non-Jews at a lower price.[16] Merchants who had no horse and wagon would carry the sheep or calf into town on their shoulders. At the end of the winter there was a brisk trade in calfskins. Trading in geese was somewhat more common. Between September and December, merchants bought geese and sold them to big dealers who, in turn, sent them to Prussia. This trade developed on a large scale; it was not unusual to see whole boxcars of geese being shipped from Lithuania to Germany.

Peddlers brought goods from the town to the peasant. Usually, the peddler had a horse, but there were some who traveled on foot, carrying their wares in a basket or a case. The merchandise included soap, matches, salt, needles, thread, and other essential items. Most of the transactions with the peasants were on a barter basis: the peddler exchanged his wares for eggs, bristles, linen, wool, and other farm products. He also accepted rags that could be sold to paper mills.

During the week, the peddler spent his nights at the home of either a peasant or a rural Jew and subsisted on next to nothing: he ate baked potatoes, baked eggs (to avoid cooking in the peasant's non-kosher pot), dry bread, a piece of cheese. Sometimes he carried with him a pot in which to cook dairy food. Therefore, the Sabbath was so special: the peddler would arrive early on Friday, bringing home a chicken, a couple of eggs, some buckwheat groats, a small fish—enough for his wife to prepare to usher in the Sabbath. If the peddler lived in town he could go to the *mikvah* and then to the synagogue for Sabbath services. This was indeed a pleasure! Even the rural peddler could enjoy the delights of the Sabbath day. Some peddlers were learned and very pious men. They would carry around a holy book to read while they rested their feet and the horse grazed, or if there was nothing to do. Nearly every peddler had the book of Psalms or a small prayer book.

Household Servants

During the 1870s and 1880s, wealthier villagers employed Jewish servants. These were backward lads who were not successful at any trade or craft, and who frequently could not recite their prayers. They did the heavy chores: fetched water for the field hands, ran errands for the mistress, pastured the horses and cattle. The servant slept somewhere in a corner; in the summer he slept in the hayloft. He was paid no more than twenty to twenty-five rubles a year. The master would also feed and clothe him and occasionally give him a pair of worn boots. In his old age such a servant could only resort to begging.

Maids were recruited from poorer rural Jewish families to work for farmers or millers and in middle-class homes in the towns. At the age of sixteen or seventeen a girl would hire herself out as a maid on an annual basis. Her wage was thirty to fifty rubles a year. She would continue this work until she was twenty-five or thirty years old. If, by then, she managed to save 100 rubles as a dowry, she could marry a laborer or a man from a poor family. Orphans and very poor girls from the towns also entered domestic service, usually in the larger cities.

Most maids could neither read nor write. They worked from early morning—in the country their day began with milking the cows before dawn—until late at night. There were no laws governing working conditions for hired help; it all depended on the master or mistress. In some homes, the conditions were deplorable; in others a maid was treated as a fellow human being. The mistress would marry her off and supply her with generous gifts. But an affair between the housemaid and the master's son or a guest usually ended very sadly for the girl.

Arendarn

I conclude with the most typical rural Jewish occupation—the *arendar*, or estate manager. Indeed, the term "rural Jew" usually brought to mind either an *arendar* or an innkeeper. Polish landed gentry often owned several properties in Lithuania. They personally supervised only the estate where they lived; the others were leased to Jewish or non-Jewish managers. As Jews were more prompt in their payments than non-Jews, the owners preferred to deal with Jews. These estates ranged in area from one hundred to several hundred hectares, in some cases even more.[17]

Jews paid the rent in advance, as a rule not for more than half a year. Sometimes they also had to give the owner a share of the estate's products. His lease prevented the Jewish *arendar* from selling any hay or straw, in order to leave ample fertilizer for the fields. The *arendar* was also expected to keep a certain number of livestock for the same reason.

The Jewish *arendar* was a manager. Usually he did not till the land himself but hired tenant farmers to work for him. In exchange for their work, they received a hut to live in, produce from the estate, and a patch of land on which to raise their own vegetables. Their pay was from thirty to forty rubles per year. The tenant farmer's day lasted sixteen or seventeen hours and he barely earned enough to feed himself. This had been the case from time immemorial. The whole system—their remuneration, the long working hours—was established not by the *arendar* but by the landowners. The Jewish *arendar* suffered as well. He lived in poverty, because he had to come up with a large sum for the lease by selling farm produce, the prices for which were very low.

Other *arendarn* sublet the land to the *pulovnik* (from the Russian word *polovina,* meaning "half"), a more established peasant, with his own horse. The *pulovnik* worked the land and divided its crops evenly between himself and the *arendar.* Since *pulovniki* were negligent, it was usually more profitable for the *arendar* to work the fields with his own hired help.

Some Jewish *arendarn* were good managers. Their fields were well plowed and harrowed, and their crops were planted in time. Almost none of their land was idle. They also had considerable livestock. (Until the late 1890s they used an ox-drawn hook plow; afterwards they started using a metal plow pulled by one or two horses.) Those *arendarn* who fertilized their fields well were rewarded by the greater yield of their land. Other *arendarn,* however, had little understanding of estate management. They did not have sufficient livestock and came to rely mainly on *pulovniki.* These *arendarn* could not last long and soon went bankrupt. They were left impoverished, without recovering anything they had invested.

Everyone in the *arendar*'s household pitched in to help with the work. The women milked cows, made sour milk and cheese, and churned butter. They also took care of the garden, seeing to it that the various vegetables were planted on time, properly watered, and harvested. Usually, the women cooked for the family, the day-laborers, and the unmarried long-term workers. In addition, they had to bake bread and care for the chickens and ducks.

Of course, the children also helped out, as did the maids. Even so, there was always work waiting to be done, and the women really slaved away from dawn until far into the night, doing everything from mixing feed for the cows (chopped grass and bran in hot water, with some sliced potatoes added) to spinning wool and flax, and knitting and sewing for the entire household. Everything was women's work! In addition, these women had to look after their children. It is difficult to imagine how they managed to do all this. These women were real heroines, yet they were not appreciated as much as they deserved.

The *arendar* spent most of his time in the fields, supervising his employees. The young children pastured the horses and cattle while the workers ate their meals. The whole family was pressed into service during the hay and rye harvests. Boys and girls gathered sheaves and stacked them. They spread out the hay to dry, then raked it into small piles. Whenever there were signs of rain, the dried sheaves were quickly brought into the hayloft or granary. At such times the youngsters interrupted their studies with their tutor. Even the *arendar* had to roll up his sleeves and go to work, carrying haystacks to the wagon, helping unload them in the barn and even raking hay.

The Sabbath was the only day when the family could rest. Jewish women did not milk the cows on this day; the non-Jewish maids did the work. On the Sabbath, one could indulge in a nap after the *tsholnt*. In summer, the *arendar* and his family allowed themselves another pleasure: a walk after the midday meal. They strolled through the meadows and fields, appraising the harvest. At the same time they enjoyed God's beauteous world and the fields of maturing crops and looked forward to a year of plenty.

The *arendar*'s family ate frugally during the week. *Borscht* was the principal dish and was eaten twice daily. Among other things cooked were barley, "mock fish" (potatoes smothered in milk, cream and onions), cereal and, on rare occasions, pancakes made of sourdough, buckwheat flour or *privarek,* a flour made from a mixture of peas, barley, buckwheat and rye. For the evening meal, they ate *farfl* boiled in milk. Meat was hardly ever eaten during the week, but the Sabbath meal usually included a piece of meat that had been brought from town. At the end of the winter they would have their own meat. As this was the calving season, they would have a calf slaughtered, and the meat was salted to preserve it for an extended period. In late summer, they would also slaughter a sheep; at such times meat was not a rarity, not even on weekdays.

Townspeople frequently visited the *arendar* to buy produce or to stay overnight while traveling. Here they knew that they could always get food and lodging, staying in the hay barn during the summer. Itinerant Jewish paupers and non-Jewish beggars also came to the *arendar*. All received a substantial meal, and sometimes they were also given used clothing.

Village Jews worried a great deal about their children's education. They had to find a way to keep their children in the fold. If a town was close by, the boys would trudge daily to the *melamdim* there during the summer. But when the town was far away and several rural Jews lived close to each other, they got together and hired a *melamed* from the city. The man was usually a bachelor, or he might simply be a helpless creature not fit to do anything but teach village children. A *heder* was set up in the house of a rural Jew who had more room than the others. The children who lived nearby would go there daily, even in winter. Those who lived farther away would stay with the family that housed the *heder*. They ate and slept there, as did the teacher. The payment for such accommodation was very low. The boys were taught how to read Hebrew, the Bible and, in rare cases, the Talmud. They were taught how to compose letters in Yiddish with the help of handbooks. Sometimes they were taught a few words of Russian. The country boys rarely grew up to be great scholars, despite the admonitions of their teachers, who called them names such as "blockhead" or "lout." Nor did the teachers refrain from slapping their pupils, pulling their ears, or even whipping them with a leather strap.

Girls were taught to write and how to read some Hebrew. Rural Jews who had the means to do so hired secular instructors—people who had completed three or four grades at a gymnasium. They offered a more modern course of instruction. Children were taught Russian to prepare them to attend school in the city. Teachers were paid anywhere from thirty or forty to seventy-five rubles per term and were provided with board, lodging, and laundry. Although village Jews were reputed to be complete ignoramuses, there were exceptions. A number of Yiddish writers, natives of Lithuania, were children of rural Jews.

The Decline of Rural Occupations

There were a considerable number of Jews in the villages. No town had less than a score of rural Jewish families living nearby. When the village Jews came to town for the High Holy Days the synagogues were always packed. Compared with an ordinary Sabbath, the holidays saw an increase in synagogue attendance by at least one-third and in some places by as much as one-half. On the eve of Rosh Hashanah, the town's streets were quite noisy as the village Jews arrived with all their family members and belongings.

The number of Jews in rural areas began to decline sharply by the end of the nineteenth century. The 1890s saw many stringent measures enacted against Jewish residents of the villages. The so-called *novoseltses* (those who had lived in the villages for fewer than twenty or twenty-five years) were expelled, and the bailiffs and sheriffs made life difficult for them. It was sometimes possible to delay this eviction for a few months or even years by resorting to the "Russian *habeas corpus*"—that is, a bribe. But frequently it was impossible to arrange such delays. Strict orders from the governor or direct from St. Petersburg would bring an end to life in the countryside. Or it might be that a new oppressor would refuse to be bought off: then the villager had to gather his belongings and leave.

On the whole, the governments of Alexander III and Nicholas II pursued a policy of limiting or completely forbidding Jewish residency in villages and colonies. A Jew could remain in a village only through bribery. Such conditions naturally led to a steady influx of Jews into the towns and cities. There was never any question of a city Jew moving to a rural neighborhood. Even those who had the "right" to live in a village, because their forefathers were born and reared there, could not move from one village to another. Consequently, these Jews simply waited for the chance to move to the cities or to emigrate. Immigrants streamed from the villages to America or some other country. Virtually the entire younger generation, along with many older people, left their homes and set out for distant locations. The government liquor monopoly of 1897 forced thousands of Jewish innkeepers out of their long-established businesses. Non-Jewish laborers, blacksmiths, and even tailors began to appear in the villages, and the Jews were hardly able to withstand this competition.

World War I dealt a fatal blow to the Jewish villages. Many Jewish homes were burned down as a result of military action; in many places people barely escaped with their lives. Tsarist officials drove the Jews out of the district of Kovno. When the refugees returned to their villages they found nothing. The village population was greatly impoverished and one could hardly make a living there. Moreover, the policies of the newly created republics of Lithuania and Poland discriminated against rural Jews. There were also widespread agrarian reforms in Lithuania, which resulted in the liquidation of compact villages. Peasants struck out on their own; very few villages remained. All told, there no longer was a place for Jews in the villages.

The state began to support and develop peasant consumer cooperatives, which bought all produce. The peasant's standard of living started to climb. Jewish artisans could no longer meet the peasants' needs. These reasons, along with other, lesser ones, led to a steady decline in the rural Jewish population. By the time World War II broke out, the Jewish villager was virtually extinct in Lithuania. Thus passed a way of life rich in Jewish tradition.

2

A LITHUANIAN *SHTETL*

The *shtetl* was the economic basis of East European Jewish life; it sustained us the way the village sustained Russian, Polish, and Lithuanian peasants. Until now, there have been few attempts to study the *shtetl,* as has been done, for example, with the Russian village, which has been analyzed comprehensively. I should like to make a beginning, in the hope that it will inspire others to undertake similar endeavors. When I was in the Lithuanian *shtetl* Wysoki Dwór during the summer of 1925, it occurred to me to take advantage of the opportunity to gather documentary materials concerning its Jewish community. I developed a questionnaire and collected the information with the assistance of a local student.

1.

The town of Wysoki Dwór was situated not far from the border between Poland and Lithuania in an exceptionally beautiful and picturesque region. The closest railroad station was thirty-five kilometers away. During the first quarter of this century, thousands of hectares of forest in the area had been stripped.

The history of the town is shrouded in obscurity. There was an old graveyard where I saw the year 1742 on one of the tombstones. The dead from surrounding towns used to be brought to Wysoki Dwór for burial. Some of the older people said that this cemetery was as old as the one in Vilna. Traces of three long graves could still be seen at the edge of the burial ground. Legend had it that giants had been interred in these plots, but no one was able to tell me more than this. In Wysoki Dwór, there was also a "castle hill" near the river. At its summit there was a sunken slab where, it was said, there once stood a palace that had "sunk into the ground," but about which no other details were known.

The town had once belonged to a wealthy nobleman who leased the exclusive right to distill and sell liquor in the area to a Jew, Reb Hershl.*

He became a very powerful figure, and the entire town trembled before him. He held this license until the state liquor monopoly was established. There was only a single inn in Wysoki Dwór, while other towns had seven or eight. The innkeeper, Reb Leyzer, was the grandson of Reb Hershl and he, too, was "master" of the town. The non-Jewish residents trusted the innkeeper completely and they liked him, despite the fact that he had struck many a man for drunken carousing. When Reb Leyzer rapped on the lectern in the synagogue, silence prevailed at once. He would order the longest liturgical poems recited and the congregation would have to comply. Reb Leyzer would not tolerate any omission from the service. Many a young upstart endured his slaps without resentment; to protest would have been unthinkable.

But times changed, and about 1900 the young upstarts decided they wanted the town to have a rabbi. Up to that time there had been only a *shohet* (ritual slaughterer), one of whose tasks was to rule on questions of religious law, although Reb Leyzer was the final arbiter. The whole town was divided into two camps, one in favor of a rabbi and one opposed. After much quarreling and wrangling, the first group emerged victorious and a rabbi came to town. He was not held in very high regard, however, and was addressed with the diminutive, as *revl* (he was still a young man).[1] Nevertheless, the innkeeper's authority had been diminished. The rabbi, however, had no means of subsistence; except for collecting the tax on yeast, he received no salary or other income.[2] So, like all young husbands in a small town, he opened a small store, which only caused resentment among the rest of the shopkeepers. Nevertheless, the rabbi remained a shopkeeper, and the town came to accept the fact.

Between 1900 and 1925 the town suffered two severe fires but was rebuilt both times. Two masonry buildings even appeared in the center of the marketplace, but they were never completed. At the time of the fighting between Russia and Germany during World War I, all but two or three of the Jews fled town. Leyzer the innkeeper was among those who remained. The Cossacks would have shot them all had not the Germans suddenly arrived on the scene, enabling the Jews to escape. All those who had fled to Vilna returned several weeks later, except for one person who remained in Russia.

---

*The names have been changed.

2.

After the war of 1914–18, the number of families in Wysoki Dwór remained the same as before, although they were not all the same families. The heads of several families had died, and some families had moved to other towns. Newly established families took their places.

The town consisted of about sixty-five Jewish families and about the same number of non-Jewish ones. In all, there were 272 Jews: 139 (52 percent) males, and 133 (48 percent) females. There were 168 adults aged twenty or over (61 percent of the total Jewish population): 81 men and 87 women. Six persons were over 70 years of age (2.2 percent) and one man was 90 years old. The number of Jewish children under six was 42 (15 percent); 14 were aged six to ten; 12 were between ten and fourteen years old, and those 15 to 20 years of age numbered 36 (13 percent). From these figures one can conclude the following: families with many children were a thing of the past. The average number of people in a family was 4.5—that is, there were, on an average, 2.5 children per family. Prior to World War I, however, it had not been unusual to find Jewish families with ten to twelve children, and the average was no less than four to five.

Besides the war, the economic situation had also had an impact on the town. It had become impossible to support a family with many children. True, we counted 42 children under six and only 25 aged six to fourteen. Nevertheless, when one takes into consideration that the number of births declined sharply during the war years, it would be incorrect to conclude that "the good old days," when there were families numbering ten to twelve children, had returned after the war.

Occupations in the town were as follows: 17 shopkeepers; 17 artisans (including 5 tailors, 3 blacksmiths, 2 shoemakers); 1 quiltmaker; 2 turners (these were brothers who also did other things, including tinsmithing, haircutting, house painting, umbrella-making); 1 furrier; 1 glazier (a woman); 1 wheelwright; 1 fisherman; 4 construction workers; 2 wool carders; 1 lime kiln operator; 1 *kvas* brewer; 1 driver; 4 butchers (all in one family); 3 peddlers; 4 *luftmentshn;* 2 orchard keepers; 3 clergymen (a rabbi, a slaughterer who was also a cantor, and a synagogue caretaker who was also a *melamed*); 2 Talmudic students; 1 bathhouse manager; 1 *feldsher.* In addition, there were 7 seamstresses (4 of whom were married), a woman who made stockings, and one who dyed cloth.

The vocations of this population demonstrate, first of all, that the productive element in the town was not as small as it is often thought to be. The total number of workers comprise about 25 percent of the town's adult Jewish population. Taking into account the number of persons depending on them for support, this percentage was even greater. Few of the artisans, however, had apprentices. One young man was learning (from a non-Jew) to be a locksmith, one was apprenticed to a blacksmith, and three were apprenticed to tailors. Five young women were learning to be seamstresses. From this it is evident that trades were not being passed on to the next generation of Jews.

Significantly, the number of shopkeepers had fallen from 30 to 17 in recent years, a decline of some 40 percent. To some extent this was due to competition, unusually high taxes, and the generally limited demand for goods in the town. These stores had carried various manufactured goods, haberdashery, groceries, and pharmaceuticals. To save a few groshns the peasants would travel to towns that had more established markets, which had been in existence before the war. Every town had its designated market days. During the rest of the week, there was hardly any business in the shops. But even on market days the local shopkeepers competed with merchants who came from elsewhere to the town.

It is not possible to determine the shopkeepers' average earnings. When one considers that the gross weekly income of the small shops amounted to from three to six dollars, it is difficult to imagine how the shopkeeper was able to get along. Support from American relatives was very helpful. Four of the shopkeepers earned a little on the side as coachmen, driving passengers to and from the train station or from one town to another. Other shopkeepers would buy sheep or calves from a peasant, butcher them, and thus earn some meat for themselves.

In general, however, it is difficult to categorize small-town vocations, because in many cases one and the same person could be a shopkeeper, an artisan, a coachman, a *luftmentsh,* and so on. As for the *luftmentshn,* one thing is plain: they did not "live on air," but their business activities were often truly snatched out of thin air. Sometimes they would earn a few groshns on a market day by purchasing and reselling a chicken, some eggs, hog bristles, seeds (in winter), fruit (in autumn), grain (in summer). Once in a great while they earned some income as brokers in a "business" transaction, as matchmakers, or from some similar source. There were four or five "lumber merchants" in town, who were involved periodically in clearing trees from designated areas of nearby woods. These were genuine *luftmentshn,* most of them married men supported by their in-laws. On receiving his wife's dowry, such a man might invest the few hundred rubles in a forest. Often, these inexperienced young husbands quickly squandered the dowry.

For the most part, the town's large number of stores was attributable to these sons-in-law. Since there was nothing else for them to do, they opened up a shop. After a while, however, the proliferation of stores ceased. The wholesalers stopped extending credit, and there were a great many taxes to

Hirsz Abramowicz with his family in Wysoki Dwór. The author's mother, Miriam, is seated in the center, with the author to the right and his younger brother, Yankev, to the left. This photograph was taken in 1925, when Hirsz Abramowicz obtained permission from the Polish government to visit his family in Lithuania.
Courtesy of the YIVO Archives.

pay to keep the shops open. As a result, it was hardly worthwhile to stay in business.

3.

Not much can be said in praise of small-town workmanship. Of course, there were exceptions, but it was generally slipshod. Incidentally, there were very few towns that employed a significant number of people in any one type of work. I know of only one such town in Lithuania, and that is Janów, which was renowned for its Jewish carpenters.

As for the clergy, the same person was always both the slaughterer and the cantor. Similarly, one man would be both the synagogue caretaker and the *dardeki-melamed,* earning six or seven dollars a month.

Of the 65 Jewish families, 32 owned one or more cows. Five families each had one goat. During the German occupation, when a family was permitted to own one cow, virtually every family found it necessary to acquire one, for it was impossible to obtain milk otherwise. Later on, when milk was available everywhere at a low price, keeping a cow was not worth the trouble. First, one had to obtain permission of the local nobleman to pasture the cows; this cost from ten to fifteen dollars for the summer. Then, one had to rise at dawn to take the cow out to the field. In the afternoon, one had to go out, sometimes a considerable distance, to milk it, and in the evening one had to bring the cow home. In sum, housewives did not care to put up with this chore. Poor people kept goats, which they were able to feed by themselves or, if necessary, by gathering grass somewhere.

There were nine Jewish-owned horses in town. Such horses were used for various chores, primarily for pulling wagons. They were also used to till one's own garden and were hired out for such purposes as picking up merchandise, hauling lumber in from the woods, and the like.

No one engaged in agriculture lived in the town. One *arendar*, who had been on the land for thirty-nine years and ran a fishing business, also worked part-time in his own field. During the rye harvest, girls were expected to reap the grain that their parents had sown with the help of hired non-Jewish workers. Some Jews did light farming in gardens and on their own fields: they gathered grain and grew potatoes, beets, and cabbage.

There were no more than ten to fifteen people engaged in work of this kind. Twenty-two of the families (34 percent) raised vegetables and potatoes in gardens next to their homes, but as a rule these gardens were tended by non-Jewish servants. All the Jewish families planted their own potatoes in fields belonging to non-Jews, for which they supplied their own manure. The peasants' fields were greatly improved by this fertilizer, as a comparison between the fertile town fields and the poor fields of the countryside made clear. The local peasants were also well compensated, in coin or goods, for the use of their land. Artisans paid them with articles that they produced.

At the beginning of this century there were as many as 37 Jews living in villages and in single farmhouses (*yishuvim*)* along the roads in the region surrounding the town. Some were innkeepers, *arendarn,* or tended gardens. For the most part, they were rural craftsmen: blacksmiths, shoemakers, and tailors. Later on, only five of the 37 were left: a miller, an *arendar*, a farm worker, an individual who was supported by American relatives, and another *arendar* who also owned a sawmill. In earlier times, these rural Jews would gather on the Sabbath in a centrally located home to pray with a *minyan.* However, when the tsarist government began to banish Jews from the countryside, the number of Jews living in villages and farmhouses began to decline.[3] Several of them died; others emigrated. Still others moved

---

*In Lithuania, *yishuv* referred to an isolated house, one not in a village; cf. Polish *zaścianek,* Russian *khutor,* Belorussian *yednosel.*

into the town in order to educate their children, although there were some rural Jews who brought teachers from Vilna.* No new Jews came to take their place in the countryside. Once the so-called "agrarian reforms" were instituted in Lithuania (these laws barred Jews from farming altogether), the number of rural Jews declined considerably, so that by the 1920s they were a rarity.[4] Rural Jews were distinctively robust and folksy, rather crude, but substantial. The townsfolk habitually derided rural Jews as ignorant and looked down on them. They told numerous anecdotes about the rural Jews, but by the time this study was conducted, these had become no more than history and folklore.**

Those rural Jews who have not passed away have long since become either small-town citizens or small-town paupers.

4.

Every small-town Jew strove to live in a house of his own. There were 37 Jewish homeowners (57 percent) in Wysoki Dwór, but almost all their houses were built on land belonging to peasants, who were paid an annual leasing fee of 10 to 20 rubles. Twenty-three families (35 percent) lived in rented houses. Except for two masonry houses, all were built of wood and most consisted of two rooms. Only about ten of the houses had more than two rooms. Not a single dwelling had indoor plumbing. Furniture was usually old and neglected; there were benches instead of chairs. Many things had been ruined during the war and no new ones were acquired. The floors were scrubbed no more than once a week in the homes of the more "well-to-do," and in many of the poorer dwellings only twice a year. In all the town, only three or four homes had cuspidors. Walls were whitewashed every couple

---

*In the courtyard of the Vilna synagogue there was a broker who found employment for teachers and *heder* instructors, many of whom were barely literate. This "institute" was jocularly referred to as "Ignorance Heights."

**Here are some anecdotes concerning rural Jews: The son of a rural Jew is called on to wrap the Torah scroll after the reading is concluded. When he steps up to the *bimah*, he is asked whether he knows how this is done. He responds: "I've moved bigger logs than this."

On Yom Kippur, father and son are sitting together in the synagogue just before *neilah*. The father is snoring. When the doors to the ark were about to be opened the son wakes his parent: "Father, get up! The gates are opening." The father rouses himself anxiously and calls out: "A-yush, a-yush!" (This is the expression used to drive away pigs when a gate on the farm is left open and the neighbors' pigs find their way in.)

As his wife serves him the steaming *tsimmes* on the eve of Yom Kippur, the rural Jew asked her whether she can see him through the vapor. She replies that she cannot see him. "Well," he says, "may you live to not see me next year."

of years, sometimes less often than that. There were some homes, however, where the whitewashing was done annually, just before Passover.

All day long "just about anything" sufficed by way of food: a piece of herring, some potatoes, a glass of milk. People cooked during the day only in very few of the homes, and hardly anyone observed a set time for the midday meal. The elderly ate only twice a day, at about ten in the morning and six in the evening. Full meals were not prepared; instead, people ate soup with a piece of meat in it, or a milk-based soup and, preceding that, "something" with bread. Everywhere people said, "Why fuss about food? Just as long as you can keep body and soul together." The Sabbath, of course, was different. On Friday night there was meat, noodle soup, and *tsimmes*. Saturday's main meal consisted of chopped herring, *tsholnt* with meat and *kugl*. Because of poor nutrition and neglect, there were no overweight people in the town. The children were lean and scrawny.

Little attention was paid to the rules of hygiene. Only about 60 percent of the women made use of the *mikvah*. Both the *mikvah* and the bathhouse were very seldom cleaned. The water in the *mikvah* was changed infrequently and gave off a foul odor.

Religious spirit did not appear particularly strong in the town. It was more a matter of tradition than religion. Wysoki Dwór had the reputation of being a liberal town, and in the surrounding towns its residents were referred to as "the Wysoki Dwór elite." About 35 percent of the male population prayed every day. There was a daily *minyan* in the synagogue, but there were seldom more than twenty men present. On the Sabbath, however, everyone attended without exception, although not a Sabbath went by without some controversy in the synagogue.

I happened to be present at several of these quarrels. Once a formal complaint had been filed against a man because he had slaughtered a cow somewhere other than the designated place, and he had not obtained permission to do so. The police chief demanded 200 litai ($20) to cancel the complaints. The accused interrupted the reading of the Torah and insisted that, since everyone butchered and ate meat, they should all raise the 200 litai and deliver the money to the police on his behalf.[5] If they did not, he threatened, he would "get even" with the town. The ruckus in the synagogue continued for two hours, until the culprit became weary of standing beside the holy ark and, sadly hanging his head in shame, stepped down from the platform. Yet no one had left for home during the quarrel; they all waited patiently for the Torah reading to be resumed. On another Sabbath, this time following the Torah reading, there was a fight because a man who was observing a *yortsayt* had not been called up for an *aliyah*.[6] The disturbances in the synagogue frequently ended with police charges, and there were times when the building was closed for lengthy periods as a result. The Jewish community's own authority figures, before whom they had all once stood in awe, no longer existed.

On the Ninth of Av, youngsters would pelt people with thistles.[7] Those who protested got the worst of it. If someone caught a clump of thistles in his beard, plucked out the sharp burrs quietly, and continued to recite the *kinot,* he was left alone. But if anyone began shouting about the "good-for-nothing louts," the "rascals," he would not escape unscathed. The youngsters bombarded him from all sides, and that would set off a real fracas. The protester would lunge at the nearest young fellow and begin hitting him. Then a father, some other relative, or one of the bystanders would take sides, and things got lively, as people shouted, pushed and slapped each other. For the youngsters, the Ninth of Av became a free-for-all, a melee. There was a man in the town who was nicknamed "Shaye [is] right" (Yiddish "*Shaye gerekht*"). During an interruption of the Torah reading one Sabbath, he had made a few remarks, and some of the congregants had sarcastically called out: "Shaye is right!" This had led to the nickname, which clung to him. One Ninth of Av, he ran out of the synagogue to pursue the young rascals who had made him the target of a large number of thistles. Shaye shouted and cursed at them, as the pranksters scattered noisily and shouted back: "Shaye is right." Similar scenes were enacted every Ninth of Av, during the *kinot.* When these were finished, both young and old went off to the cemetery to remember the dead.

More recently, the younger men could be seen going bareheaded outdoors.[8] At first the townsfolk found this to be a truly startling sight. They made loud protests in the synagogue on the Sabbath about why our youth had become "worse than Gentiles," but to no avail. Nevertheless, the young folks did keep up appearances to a degree. Older people told me that the younger generation took the liberty of smoking in the woods or out in the country on the Sabbath, but they would not do so openly in town. No one even dared to carry a walking stick on the Sabbath.[9] This, at least, was a source of some satisfaction to the older generations. When parents complained that boys and girls were going off into the woods together on the Sabbath, carrying pillows, books and food with them, one pious but also very astute man commented, "Well, what they carry *into* the woods is only half of the problem. The real problem will be when they begin to carry *from* the woods.[10]

Like other Lithuanian towns Wysoki Dwór had fallen under the influence of the outside world and was obsessed with soccer. A Maccabi group of thirty young men was organized.[11] They also did gymnastic exercises, but all their free time was devoted to "dribbling the ball with their feet." Their parents sighed, "It's terrible—the ball, the ball!" These young men were not satisfied simply with playing the game. They also invited Maccabi teams from neighboring towns for matches. In such cases, the host town was responsible for covering all the guests' expenses: travel, food, and the like. After a match, the participants were often battered and bruised, but that only fueled the Maccabis' devotion to the sacred art of kicking. At one match the ball struck an elderly spectator. He shouted, "I've been killed!" and fell in a faint. A commotion ensued. The town was in an uproar; some of the people were prepared to ban the players. However, the man suffered only a scare and thought that he had gone on to his heavenly reward. The matches continued to be held.

In Lithuania, the Maccabis were closely tied to the Zionist organization. They carried out all of the Zionists' functions, including raising money for various funds. These activities were even written into the Maccabi by-laws. During soccer matches, plays were called in modern Hebrew. Other than the Zionists, there were no organized political groups in Wysoki Dwór. Until very recently, both old and young were quite passionately committed to Zionism. The young people had an abiding faith in the Land of Zion. Two of them worked on a *kvutsah,* or agricultural colony, where people were trained to become pioneers in Palestine.

The young people established a library of some 400 books, about 300 of them in Yiddish. During the summer, the library had about 30 members, and 40 to 50 during the winter. Dues were eight cents a month. The reading room and the library were used exclusively by young people. The library subscribed to two Yiddish-language newspapers and one in Hebrew. No individual had his own subscription to a newspaper except for one person in the town, who regularly received a newspaper sent to him by a relative in Palestine. The townspeople were very eager for news of the world, but no one was willing to spend money on a newspaper subscription.

In this provincial atmosphere any tendency toward left-wing revolutionary politics evaporated. This could be seen in the young married men. On the Sabbath, even those of them who were Bundists went dutifully to the synagogue with their prayer shawl bags. "There are things one has to do for one's livelihood," people joked.

Marrying off one's daughters was a very severe problem, especially for the more substantial families in town. "The boys are going crazy," mothers were heard to complain. "They are not ashamed to insist on payment of a thousand dollars." The minimum dowry was $300–400. In addition, parents had to provide wedding presents and pay for the wedding. Frequently, the groom had to be outfitted with all his clothing. For the small-town Jew of those days, this was more than he could swallow. Statistics showed that, while men outnumbered women in the town, there were fewer young men of marriageable age than there were unmarried young women.

During the years 1920–25, seven people emigrated from Wysoki Dwór to America, seven to Palestine, one to Uruguay, and two to Mexico. Seventy percent of the emigrants were young men. This only made the problem of getting married worse. Both in theory and in practice, there was no way to marry off a daughter. "But," the townsfolk would say, "is that any excuse? We make weddings with miracles!" Financial support from relatives in America proved very helpful in such cases. For the average individual in town, merely maintaining one's existence also entailed a miracle. How a man and his family managed to get along here is one of the sociological mysteries in the history of the Jewish people. My statistical method was unable to establish any solution.

More recently, wedding celebrations have been modest. Fifty or sixty years ago (in the 1870s), a wedding would go on for three or four days, or at least for two days. Relatives would come from all the surrounding towns. There would be a band of five or six musicians, one of whom played the hammer dulcimer. Whoever requested a dance number paid for it. Someone would treat the celebrants to a quadrille, another would pay for a waltz or a lancers. Food and drink were provided by the bride's parents who, as a rule, bore the wedding expenses. For each relative of the bride or groom, the band would play a song or a special tune or fanfare, for which the musicians would receive a few coins. The *badkhn* would greet each person with a quip: "Hannah is quite a *kochana* [sweetheart]." "For Reb Khayim we'll drink a *lekhayim* [toast]." "For Reb Yidl we'll play on the fiddle." "Reb Moyshe will pay for a large *koyse* [glass of spirits]."

As most private homes were too small to accommodate everyone, many weddings were celebrated in barns. Everyone in town was expected to be at the wedding dinner. After the meal, the *badkhn* would announce the wedding gifts, again accompanying the name of each person who gave a gift with a clever remark. Among these gifts were cups, spoons, sugar bowls, and, primarily, money in amounts of from one to five rubles. In this way, some 150 to 200 rubles were amassed and were handed to the groom. Giving wedding gifts to poor newlyweds was one way of fulfilling the religious obligation of providing for indigent brides.

The next morning an event known as *rumpl* was held at the groom's home. Refreshments were set out—cake, whiskey, preserves, and other sweets—and several performers entertained the company. One person might go dancing across the table in his stocking feet; another would dance *kazatskes;* a third might perform peasant drinking songs. Several of the dancers might enact amusing sketches of peasants in conversation. Whiskey flowed like water and there was much merriment. Later, the main meal of the day was served by the bride's family.

In more recent years people had quiet weddings, without musicians or the presence of numerous relatives. Often, a couple simply went off to the city to get married. Upon their return they would invite the people closest to them for the traditional *sheva berachot,* and that would suffice—no more wedding gifts, no more dancing, no more *badkhn* or any of the other trappings of the weddings of the past. War had cast a pall over the merriment of Jewish celebrations, which once had brought a ray of light into the Jews' life of constant worry.

5.

At one time there were quite a number of rural Jews around Wysoki Dwór. On the High Holy Days, they and their families all gathered in the town. Even though they could convene a *minyan* in the countryside, they did not wish to remain among Christians on these holy days. On such occasions, the population of the town increased by a fourth, even a third. Each rural Jew went to the home of a relative or a good friend. Despite the crowded conditions that this created, the guests were treated in a most hospitable manner and were put up in the best part of the house. The rural Jews would arrive in large wagons driven by teams of horses. As they entered the town they were greeted first by the adults and then by the children, who stared at the visitors with great curiosity. Children in the town were especially envious of the children from the countryside, because they had the opportunity to ride on horses.

In general, the town was very hospitable. After prayers, particularly on the holidays of Passover, Shavuot, and Sukkot, a guest would be invited "to recite a blessing," that is, to partake of refreshments. Sometimes the guest would "recite a blessing" at four or five different homes, in order not to hurt anyone's feelings. Refreshments might include cookies, preserves, fried *kreplekh,* strudel, compote, honey cake, or other typical Jewish treats. Of course, there was plenty of whiskey.

Only a few traces of this former way of life remain. Besides the changing times, the emigration of local Jews has had a particularly significant impact on the village. No longer do residents compete over a visitor, pulling him in every direction. Nevertheless, the older generation still displays a friendliness toward visitors that is no longer found in the big city. Every man in the town used to consider it his duty to approach a visitor and welcome him, inquire after the health of his wife and children. The talk would turn to politics: "What will happen? Where will the borders be drawn?" (a question of the greatest interest to people at the time). "How are the Jews in the various countries of the world getting along?" and similar topics. When asked how they were getting along, they gave a stock reply: "There's no longer any need to ask about us," "There's nothing left to say," or "We are as useless as a broken vessel." It must be said that a considerable number of families truly were "broken vessels."

Until the war began, the stream of emigration was so great that some entire families left for America. Moreover, there was not a single family remaining in town that had not sent some member to the United States, Canada, or Africa. Consequently, the small-town Jews' attention was directed entirely toward what was happening "over there," as they waited for letters and money.

Of the town's 65 families, 55 (85 percent) received goods and financial assistance from abroad. Of these, seven (17 percent) subsisted entirely on "money from America." Only ten families (15 percent) did not receive any help, for various reasons, although they, too, had relatives across the sea. Were it not for this assistance, Wysoki Dwór, like many other Lithuanian towns, could not have continued to exist. American relatives provided the wherewithal for clothing, shoes and, above all, dowries. Over time this assistance diminished. Nevertheless, it remained a considerable part of the family budget. In order to live comfortably in town, a family of five or six members required about $25 a month. Ten dollars made for a meager existence, and even six or seven dollars was not an insignificant sum, because goods were inexpensive. In July 1925, I recorded the following prices in American money: a kilo of bread was two-and-a-half cents; a kilo of meat, nine or ten cents; a kilo of butter, twenty-five cents; a bucket of cherries, ten cents.

6.

Wysoki Dwór possessed those basic community institutions without which no Jewish community could function: a synagogue (a rather large wooden building), as well as a bathhouse and a *mikvah*.

The bathhouse was heated about once every three or four weeks. The place was unsanitary, with rotting window frames and flooring and walls covered with mold. The water in the *mikvah* was changed very seldom, despite the fact that it stood at the very edge of the river and had a pipe through which water could be brought in. Sometimes the bathhouse could not be heated because there was no wood, or because something went wrong with the stove, and nothing was done about it until a hue and cry was raised in the synagogue.

Although the bathhouse was perhaps used more by the town's non-Jewish population than by its Jews, it typically never occurred to anyone to request that the community share the cost of its upkeep. Financially, the bathhouse was a purely Jewish institution.

There was also a small house for travelers, where the poor could find a night's lodging. Located close to the synagogue, this house contained several broken-down beds made of planks and a few soiled straw mattresses.

For several years, there were scarcely any paupers. Later when the population of Lithuania became impoverished, a great many paupers, sometimes entire families, came from other towns. At the end of the nineteenth century there was a whole extended family of paupers, headed by a man known as Bezruchka (which means "missing a hand"). No one knew his actual name. He married off his many children to other paupers and then took them into his home to "support" them. He used his horse to drive his sons-in-law, his daughters-in-law, and their brood around to various towns so that they could be fed by the inhabitants. When the Bezruchka family had grown quite large, the elder Bezruchka "divided" Lithuania into regions and allocated each region, with its towns and villages, to a single son or son-in-law. During the 1920s, all traces of the Bezruchka family disappeared, but new paupers arrived and went begging throughout the town. There were set amounts to give to a pauper, an itinerant preacher, a Talmudic student, and so on. The donation was no more than ten or fifteen Lithuanian cents. It must be said that town dwellers gave a proportionally greater amount for charity than did city residents. In addition to collections for Zionist causes, townsfolk often raised funds for impoverished families and widows.

In Wysoki Dwór, medical care was in the hands of a *feldsher*, who was known as "Professor." There was also a genuine doctor who lived near the town, but most often both Jews and non-Jews turned to the "Professor." He gave advice along with medicines he made by himself, even though there had been a pharmacy in the town for some twenty years. In his youth, the *feldsher* had worked in a military hospital. He was somewhat acquainted with Russian literature and had some quasi-intellectual inclinations. In time, he became a fixture in the town and was involved in all its community affairs. The town considered him a provocateur, the sort of person who creates controversy, so they called him "the spy." The town also accused him of being greedy and of overcharging his customers.

This *feldsher* represents a psychological enigma. He had a higher level of education than anyone else around him, yet he never made any attempt to raise the town to his level. On the contrary, he was always immersed in its affairs and managed to provoke quarrels over trivial matters. Perhaps this was a unique type of revenge by someone who felt he was sentenced to remain in this environment for the remainder of his life.

In addition to medical remedies, the older generation also believed in incantations and, in certain situations (such as cases of dog bite and infected sores), in exorcising the evil eye. For example, to cure an abscess it was customary to draw through it a piece of string over which an incantation had been recited. In case of epilepsy or insanity, a Tatar was called on to perform the exorcism (there was a Tatar colony in a nearby town).[12]

There were times when someone needed to seek medical help elsewhere and lacked the money for travel expenses. Inevitably, the money "appeared," and the patient was sent to the city to be cured. As a rule, the townsfolk responded to every need. No one was permitted to fall by the wayside—for, after all, all Jews are friends.

The burial society consisted of thirteen persons. They looked after the cemetery. Yet, here too, there were occasional incidents of a typically "Jewish" nature. The burial of a corpse might be delayed a day or two, pending payment of burial expenses.[13] The society was very secretive, and no one knew how they spent their funds. Every attempt to penetrate the group failed.

7.

The town never had a real school until 1919, when it was under Polish domination. At this time, EKOPO, the Jewish Relief Committee for War Victims, extended its activities to include all the Jewish towns in the province of Vilna, and thus a school was established in Wysoki Dwór.[14] A committee along the lines of a community council was organized in the town. One of its duties was to distribute the aid provided by EKOPO. Although the council had a secretary who was something of an intellectual, its methods of accounting and of conducting business in general were quite primitive. The younger generation was represented on the council, and there often were disputes and counteraccusations at its meetings. The different factions would go to Vilna to appeal to EKOPO, or they would request more or less influential compatriots to prevail upon EKOPO for one thing or another.

The school generated considerable controversy. The rabbi demanded that there be a *melamed;* the younger people wanted a secular teacher. After various disputes, a compromise was arrived at: both a *melamed* and a secular teacher would be provided. EKOPO certified a man who taught Hebrew and a woman who taught general subjects in Yiddish. Having had no prior experience with a Jewish school the townsfolk could not accept the idea that the children were taken on walks (for nature study), that there was singing and dancing (for physical exercise), and that, on the whole, time was "wasted on useless things."

It was not possible for the school to exist solely on the funds provided by EKOPO, so the parents were obliged to pay tuition. Although the fee was nominal, there was little inclination to pay it. But the school became very precious to the children, and they attended willingly. The school's weak financial situation, as well as the antagonistic attitude of the rabbi and some of the parents, threatened it with collapse. It might have weathered the crisis were it not for the Bolshevik invasion of 1920. When Wysoki Dwór was taken over by the Lithuanians and its ties with Vilna were severed, the school was closed.

In 1925, education in the town was a mix of the medieval and the modern. Only a few years earlier there had been three *dardeki-melamdim* and one *gemara-melamed.* Only one *melamed,* who was also the synagogue caretaker, remained. Everyone knew that he was ineffectual. The five- and six-year-old children, who were put in his care until they reached the age of ten, barely succeeded in mastering a little Hebrew and a smattering of Bible knowledge. But people made excuses, saying that a child must be sent to *heder.* The *melamed* beat the children and gave each one a nickname: Yakum the Bomb, the Philosopher, and the like. The method of instruction consisted of learning to read letters, then syllables, then whole words, and so on.[15] A group of five or six of the more intellectual families hired a private teacher who, as might be expected, was a Hebraist. He taught all subjects: Bible, Hebrew, natural science, even Lithuanian.

I had occasion to meet one of the *heder* teachers, a former scholar who spent all his time in a small house of study. His method was to strike terror in the hearts of the children. The six- or seven-year-old children spent from nine o'clock in the morning until sundown (in summer) in *heder.* The teacher let them go home for only a single hour during the day. They had to stay in the classroom even when another class was being taught. They were forbidden to speak to each other. This teacher often punished the children by ostracizing them, forbidding all of their classmates to utter a single word to those being punished; it was a sort of boycott. This punishment had a dreadful effect on the children. They cried a great deal, would not eat, and could not sleep. One seven-year-old girl became ill. One mother, whose child had been struck by the teacher, went to see him and created a scene: "If you are going to hit anything, hit your own head against the wall," she shouted. Still, even this teacher was kept on in the village for two entire terms. "But children really did accomplish something in Bible and Hebrew," several fathers told me. For this, the modern small-town Jew was ready to sacrifice even his own child.

The town had a Lithuanian progymnasium, where eight Jewish girls were among the students (12 percent of the enrollment). Boys were not sent there. ("What can one do with a girl?" the small-town Jew would say.) Six sons of prosperous families studied at Hebrew gymnasia in large cities. One boy was enrolled in a Russian gymnasium in Kovno. The town had one student at the yeshiva in Słobodka. There were five boys studying Gemara in the town itself.

The most difficult question to answer was, how would the children earn a living? In this respect, the psychology of the town remained unchanged.

True, the *halutz* movement had had an impact on this town as it had elsewhere, but many a prejudice remained. There was no rush to the trades. People were ready to perform the most back-breaking labor in Palestine, but very few had the courage to undertake physical work in the diaspora.

8.

When there was an inheritance to divide, intense feuds took place—among brothers-in-law but also, at times, among brothers and sisters. Sometimes the participants became sworn enemies. There was one man in the town who, after thirty years of marriage, still could not forget that his in-laws (who were long since dead) had not, as he reckoned it, provided him with a dowry. (The joke in the town was that he had a good memory and was still "itching" for a dowry.) All his complaints were directed at his brother-in-law, who had inherited his father-in-law's house. The "plaintiff," insisting that he had been wronged (albeit thirty years earlier), demanded a part of the house. In some instances, the adults on the two sides of a dispute did not speak to each other, but their children, who were cousins, remained best friends and frequently visited each other in the "feuding" homes.

There were also cases where, immediately following the burial of an elderly father, a conflict arose over an old hut, bare to the walls, that the deceased had owned. There were curses, oaths, and even worse things said, until the rabbi or some other neutral party intervened and brought about a compromise of sorts. Peace did not endure in such disagreements, however, and enmity rankled.

The town blacksmith's widow was a blind woman, about eighty years old. From her husband she had inherited a smithy and a house with two wings. She rented out one wing and lived in the other with her grandson and granddaughter (their father, her son, was deceased). She managed to support them with money she was sent by her children living in America. During the years 1920–23, when the dollar was highly valued in Lithuania and times seemed to be improving for Americans, many a townsman was envious of the widow. She was even able to have a chicken for the Sabbath meal and to eat meat on weekdays. She drank her tea not with saccharin but with real sugar. "If only every poor person could do likewise." But, over time, the support from America was reduced and came less often. To marry off her granddaughter, the old widow deeded her house to the girl's husband. The widow used what savings she had for a dowry. She evicted her tenant from his rooms, saying that she needed them for the young couple.

Then the blind woman's former daughter-in-law (the young bride's mother), who was newly widowed by her second husband, moved into the house. A year passed and the once fortunate grandmother, who had given her part of the house to her granddaughter, no longer had so much as a corner for herself. With the consent of the other residents, the granddaughter's husband began driving out the old woman: "You can't stay in my house!"

The old woman ran around town and complained to people that she was being abandoned, terrorized in her own home (which formally was no longer hers)—this despite the fact that she was living on assistance from her children in America and was even sharing some of the money with her grandchildren. They wanted no part of the "shrew" (for to be old was, after all, to be a shrew). On many a morning the town would come running: the son-in-law was driving the old woman from the house again. People would upbraid the young man, and peace was restored. This would last only a few days, and then, once again, the blind woman would be drowning in her tears and lamenting her truly bitter fate.

Yet there were also instances of the opposite kind. There was an old woman whose children were all grown and had large families, yet each wanted her to live in his home. Each of the woman's fifteen grandchildren came to her to ask: "Mother, what do you need?" But she had no needs. She had a good word for everyone and at times even had something to give. The entire family lived in harmony.

In this town the love of children was exceptionally strong and, to a degree, patriarchal in nature. Long after a father had seen his children married, he continued to be close to them, helping them and frequently sending them parcels if they moved to another town.

9.

On the whole, the relationship between Jews and Christians in the town was very peaceful. Christians knew that Jews were the ones to engage in trade, sew clothing, build wagons, make horseshoes, make hats, and so on. True, Christians would also mutter that Jews were thus and such; that in the summer, Jews would be busy doing who knows what, when there was so much to be done in the fields—familiar complaints. Nevertheless, when he had a disagreement with a Jew, the Christian went to a rabbi to complain. When the Christian had a contract to sign with a Jew and money was at issue—once again, he went to the rabbi.

Nevertheless, the town's Christian intellectuals, who were extremely chauvinistic and bourgeois, interfered in these matters. Let us do business, too, keep shops, establish cooperatives—they argued—that way, we will force out Jewish businesses. They did, indeed, establish a cooperative. In the Jewish stores, however, one could bargain and make one's choices without any fuss. As a result, the cooperative did not create much competition.

Matters became worse whenever an anti-Semitic priest came to town and exploited his opportunity to sway the masses from the church pulpit, inciting them against the town's Jews. There was nothing that could be done about the priest, but his attacks did not result in action. From one Sunday to the next his congregants forgot his inflammatory remarks.

To get along with lower- and mid-level government officials, Jews employed the help of a bottle of whiskey or a "secret contribution." Things were bad when there was a "white crow"—that is, an official who was incorruptible. Such was the case in a nearby town, where it was impossible to do anything at all without winding up with a citation: this is forbidden; that isn't allowed; this had not been reported; that is not recorded; here it's not sanitary; there the flag was not displayed on an official holiday; this person made a sale later on Sunday than is permissible. In short, there was enough for dozens of citations daily, and people there really suffered greatly. Fortunately, the turnover in subordinate officials was frequent, and this provided an occasional opportunity to breathe a little easier.

Nevertheless, if an "intellectual" happened to become a government official, things went badly. A former priest became the director of the town's progymnasium. He was an ideological anti-Semite who believed that the "fatherland" needed to be rescued from Jewish hands. He went after a Jew who had lived on a certain piece of land for forty-five years. The land belonged to a Russian Orthodox congregation and had earlier been the property of the Catholic Church. Despite the fact that the Jew had a government contract for the use of the land, which he worked himself, the director succeeded in persuading the ministry to transfer the property to a Catholic women's alliance. The Jew was ousted from all but a fraction of the land, as well as from all the buildings that he had erected there over the course of half a century.

The director would order goods from Jews, but when they came to collect a debt he would take a gun and chase them away or he would set his dog on them. On one occasion a Jewish furrier made some hats for the school's students. When he asked for his payment, the director incited the students to attack the furrier. Whenever the local priest was away, the director would substitute for him and inveigh against the Jews from the pulpit. In private life he was no recluse (although he was a bachelor); he liked to enjoy himself and was hardly an enemy of women. He persecuted any teacher whom he suspected of liberalism. Reports of his behavior finally reached the Lithuanian *Sejm* and he was removed from the town. He wreaked havoc on the local economy, for example, with cooperatives that kept people from patronizing Jewish businesses. Nevertheless, he obtained another post, and it was rumored that this gentlemanly teacher-priest became a candidate for a ministerial appointment.

Still, the relationship between Jews and Christians was not bad. There was not yet any fear of pogroms or of any other anti-Semitic excesses. There was, however, a fear that the Christian Democrats would make deliberate attempts to "educate" the populace in this matter.[16]

Two of the town's councilmen were Jews, both of them storekeepers. People in difficult circumstances turned to them for advice. There was even a Jewish secretary on the council. Under the Germans he was virtually in charge of the entire district. When the town came under Polish rule he became secretary to the district chief officer and would ride into town on a pair of government-owned horses. When the Lithuanians came to power, this young man studied Lithuanian and attained such mastery of the language that no Lithuanian could keep up with him. As a result, he was chosen to be the secretary of the community. Later, he became a teacher of German in a Lithuanian progymnasium until, finally, he resigned from all his posts, passed the entrance examinations and was accepted at the Lithuanian university.

10.

Anything that differed at all from the town's customary way of life would arouse the closest attention. A man had only to eat his meals at a regular hour to earn the appellation of "Count" or "Prince." A family that kept its home clean, changed the linen every week and showed some measure of self-respect was soon dubbed "Royal Family." If a man returned from the city wearing a cape he was immediately called "Havelock."[17] Indeed, it must be granted that the town was most observant and often summed up the entire nature of an individual in a single expression. I offer several examples. "Leybe the Head" was a blind man with a large head. He sat at home and constantly gossiped about everyone. "Sholem the Jacket" was a diminutive Jew who always wore a quilted jacket. Although he was in his seventies, everyone addressed him as "Little Sholem the Jacket." He had reached the point where he no longer even felt insulted.

An entire family of brothers were conspicuous for their long noses (which, it seems, is no rarity among Jews). In communal matters they were steadfast in support of each other. Everyone referred to them as "the Noses."

"Kaiser" was a poor Jewish peddler whose eyes were crossed. He had a sharp, stern look. The way the townsfolk understood it, only a monarch could have that sort of look. The man's son was called the "Heir Apparent," his wife was the "Empress" and their daughter was the "Princess." Even the non-Jews called the man *Cesarz* (which is Polish for "Emperor"). No nickname could have been more ironic.

One Jew in the town had built a glass-enclosed balcony on his house. A shoemaker who rented the balcony was a great wag and a liar. In time, his given name was forgotten, for it had been replaced by the nickname "the Balcony." Whenever a customer was angry with the shoemaker for not having work ready on time, he would say, "A plague take the Balcony!" A tailor and his wife, who together weighed no more than four-and-a-half pood, were called "the Guards," and their dwarfish, bow-legged children were known as "the Cossacks."

Young husbands were especially ready targets of nicknames. If his in-laws inadvertently made a careless remark about him, that was enough for it to stick to the young man for the rest of his life. One man said he had finally found a *tsatske*—a "gem"—of a bridegroom. His son-in-law remained "Tsatske" ever after. Another fellow who wore spectacles was known as "Professor."

One son-in-law received a handsome dowry of 15,000 ostmarks. His name became "High-Priced." In an opposite case, the son-in-law was nicknamed "the Bargain." A very quiet, immature son-in-law was dubbed "the Donkey." One who kept his mouth slightly ajar was called "the Crow." A son-in-law who wore a half-length caftan was known as "Half-a-rabbi."

Everyone in town knew what went on in everyone else's private quarters. For example, on the advice of the *feldsher*, a man drained the milk from his wife's breasts just after she had given birth; he was known thereafter as "the Sucker." Another man, whose wife, as luck would have it, gave birth to a child three months after the wedding, was called "the Fast Worker." (It so happened that he was very dynamic and industrious and nothing was too difficult for him.)

The first tailor to give up measuring with a string and to begin using a centimeter stick became "the Centimeter." Then there were such nicknames as "Canary"—a tailor who sang as he worked; "Little Sparrow"—a diminutive shoemaker with a high-pitched voice; "Pig"—a man who could imitate a hog's squeal. "Itshe the Chatterbox" was a stammerer. There were other names: "Little Swallow," "Fox," "the Little Foxes," and so on. Few escaped a nickname during their lifetimes.

Those individuals whom everyone respected were not given nicknames. True, there were not many such people in the town, where the tendency to make fun of people was very strong, and a newcomer was observed from every angle until some special trait that could be characterized by a single word was discovered. The town also had a great capacity for humor. There were some very sharp-witted people and several true wags and raconteurs. There were also wise men and philosophers among them, typical small-town Jewish thinkers.

One such rural philosopher was Avrom-Khayim. In his youth, he was a merry fellow. He sang, played the fiddle, and performed such remarkable *hopkes* and *kazatskes* that they came to be known as "Avrom Khayim's dances." At Jewish celebrations he would lead all the lancers, quadrilles, waltzes, "the Blue Danube," and all the others. He was well versed in Jewish knowledge. But he was inclined to be boastful; everything that was his was superior, exceptional. His children were wonderful. His horse was clever, for it could open the stable door by itself. His dog was the best of all dogs. Avrom-Khayim lived on the estate of a wealthy landowner, where he managed a small turpentine refinery and several hectares of farm land. He did not pay any rent, but every so often he would arrange an evening's entertainment for the landowner and thus pay the rent with his fiddle and dances. In the small village where he lived, the Christians treated him with respect. His demeanor was proud: he was known as "*pan* Abraham."

Avrom-Khayim was strict with his children and they, in turn, had little love for him. In time, the children all went their own ways, and Avrom-Khayim and his second wife were left alone. The children who had emigrated to America sent him some money. By that time he was about seventy-five years old but was still strong. "A little sip of whiskey keeps me going," he would say. He really could not do without several small glassesful daily. All day long he sat studying the Torah and thinking about the way of the world. To him, God was Providence: "But what is Providence? We do not know. Perhaps it is very small, but we need it." Avrom-Khayim would always provide a fable. Here is one of them:

> Once, in Vilna [to the small-town Jew, Vilna was the alpha and omega of the world], Avrom-Khayim saw several boys driving a herd of forty to fifty large oxen. The oxen went where the youngsters' whips guided them. If even one of the oxen were to become enraged and toss his horns just once, the boys would have been done for. But the ox thinks that the boy possesses great power, so the ox goes along like a sheep. That is how it is with Divine Providence, too.

In addition to fables, Avrom-Khayim had an endless store of tales and ideas. He was a man full of wisdom who had his own distinctive philosophy of life. Despite his severity and even stinginess, he was most hospitable. It was interesting to spend time with the old man and listen to his countless tales and yarns. Jewish men such as Avrom-Khayim were really the "last of the Mohicans." A treasury of stories, sayings, thoughts, and ideas disappeared with them.

To conclude, I must say that, despite all its blemishes, my town had a great deal of vitality and health. It was, however, badly neglected. The *shtetl* was a great source of uniqueness, originality, and folk creativity. At the same time, it also posed considerable problems for Jews, which Jewish society as a whole had to solve.

3

THE DIET OF LITHUANIAN JEWS

Although the greater part of the Lithuanian Jew's existence was taken up by the difficult task of making a living, life's spiritual aspect occupied an important place throughout his entire life. For the material side, there was less time. Even so, the soul cannot exist without the body. It was necessary to eat, of course, but one did not give it much thought. Thus, there was seldom a regular time for meals. A person ate when there was time, when a chance came along, or else one grabbed a bite "in the meantime." Not that everyone always had something to eat—this was a problem for a considerable number of Jewish families.

The diet of Lithuanian Jews was very plain. It was based on two main products: black bread and potatoes. A third element was *zoyers,* a "sour soup" of beets (*borscht*), cabbage, or sorrel. A Lithuanian Jew, who was often inclined to make jokes about himself, told me a tale concerning a rural Jew who ate a holiday meal on the morning before the Yom Kippur fast: chicken, dumplings, and *tsimmes.* When his wife inquired as to whether he had enjoyed the meal, the man replied: "Certainly, but without some sour soup, I'm hardly my usual self." The rural Jew was the butt of many a Lithuanian joke. Before World War I, the number of rural Jews in Lithuania was quite significant statistically, and they imparted a certain special quality to Lithuanian Jewry. All Lithuanian Jews enjoyed sour soup, however, perhaps because it was the least expensive, most accessible appetizer, and the only one, except for herring, that the Lithuanian Jew could afford.

Sour soup was eaten at the main meal. In Lithuania, this was the equivalent of both breakfast and lunch. Scant attention was paid to the names of meals, nor was there much insistence that any schedule be strictly adhered to: "It doesn't matter, so long as one eats and there is something to eat."

Still, this meal was central to "nourishing one's sinful body." Sour soup was eaten with bread and potatoes. In the spring, the soup was made of sorrel mixed with some thin sour cream or sour milk. During the height of summer, beet leaves were cooked with the sorrel, which gave the soup a naturally sour taste. Many housewives made their own *kvas* by stirring rye flour into warm water, salting this mix and keeping it in a warm place for a day or two until it turned sour. Beet leaves were cooked in this mixture. Toward the end of summer the whole beet was used, minced fine and added to the beet leaves. A really good housekeeper produced a tasty sour soup—"Like wine," women would often brag. Others made a soup which was "not so special," or, worse yet, "without any taste whatever," even "nauseating." Of the latter kind, however, there was little: tradition, experience and the suggestions of neighbors all contributed to creating a nourishing dish.

The same might be said of the pickled beets and sauerkraut that were put up for the winter months. Ninety percent of housewives put up a supply of these two products. Cabbage was usually shredded several weeks after Sukkot. By then, there would have been a light frost, and the cabbage would have to be taken in from the garden. There it had been allowed to "age"—that is, not grow any larger but become firmer and tighter for pickling. The same procedure was followed with beets.

All green leaves were removed and all spots where worms had left holes were cut away before the cabbage was sliced. It was especially important to check that a cabbage worm was not hidden somewhere inside, for that would make the entire batch unfit to eat. In Jewish homes, it was usually the custom for women to invite their friends and neighbors over to help shred the cabbage. This was done with knives. For a large family, several large barrels might be put up. The work was not easy, but there was fun while it was being done. There was singing, and the children were given the cabbage stems to eat. Experienced housewives would salt the shredded cabbage, sprinkle it with caraway seeds, and then they would "knead" the shredded mass. The cabbage would be put into the barrels in layers, which were beaten with a wooden mallet (the kind used in splitting wood) until the juice of the cabbage appeared. In between the layers of cabbage were placed apples, carrots, beets (for color), and cranberries. The work of "beating" the cabbage was done by men. The filled casks were left in the house for five or six days to begin the fermentation process. The barrels had to be pierced with a stick to release the foul smelling gas generated. Then the barrels were rolled down into the cellar or pantry. Poor people had to keep their barrels in the vestibule. The cabbage had to last the entire winter. It was also eaten raw, especially with baked potato, or with bread when there was nothing else to serve with bread.

Beets were used less in the wintertime. Nevertheless, in nearly every home there were "steeped" beets. The beets were scraped, placed in water and kept in a warm place (not far from the stove) until they fermented. Beets were put up for Passover in strict accordance with the precepts for the holiday, using a new barrel covered with a white tablecloth, on top of which a heavier cloth would be placed. The resulting brine, called *rosl,* was enjoyed all through the Passover holiday.

During the winter, when there was not much milk to be had and most of the food consumed was *pareve,* beets were peeled and cooked in *rosl,* creating a "ready-made dish." Minced raw onion was added to this, and it was eaten with potatoes, either baked or boiled in their skins. Connoisseurs declared this a delicacy.

The potato was of greatest importance in the nutrition of the Lithuanian Jew. Sometimes potatoes would be eaten two or three times a day, prepared in various ways: scraped and boiled (with onion and pepper), baked, or simply washed and boiled in the skin. Potatoes would be baked when the large "Russian" oven was being heated. The potatoes would be piled onto the grate, not too close to the glowing coals, so that they would not burn. Or they might be pushed into a front part of the oven, located on either side of the hearth, and covered with hot ash containing glowing bits of coal. After baking, the potatoes were placed in a basket made of straw woven through with wood. This was covered with a cloth, to permit the potatoes to steam. The skin separated from the rest of the potato, and this made peeling easier. Often this baked potato was the only food available for a "quick bite" to quell one's hunger pangs. It should also be noted that it was permissible to eat the potato without having to wash one's hands, and that one was only required to say the brief blessing for "the fruit of the earth" before eating. This advantage of the potato was enjoyed every day of the week. (So goes the Yiddish folksong, "Potatoes on Sunday, potatoes on Monday.")[1]

In Lithuania the potato was like manna, lending itself to various modes of preparation. It was used to create many a dish, often one "fit for a king," by the standards of the Lithuanian Jew. Baked *bondes* were extremely popular. Peeled potatoes were shredded on a metal grater. The grated mass was then placed in a cloth and the liquid squeezed out. Some rye or buckwheat flour was added, if there was any in the house. Next, the mixture was kneaded a little and was placed on green cabbage leaves or on oak leaves, the widest of all tree leaves in Lithuania. The *bondes* were then placed in a very hot oven, "almost hot enough to bake bread in." After an hour on the bottom of the oven, the *bondes* were ready. They were eaten either with milk or with sour soup (instead of bread). Small *bondes* were given to children between meals to assuage their hunger. Children were also given *bondes* to take along to *heder* for a snack. Most of the time, *bondes* were eaten cold. For a special snack, however, a gourmet—beware of the legendary Lithuanian gourmets!—preferred a hot *bonde,* especially with sour cream or a pat of butter (something only the more prosperous families could afford).

In the homes of such families *bondes* were also used to make "gypsies." This name referred to *bondes* that had been covered with crushed poppy seeds (the name "gypsy" referred to their dark color), which was then covered with a layer of grated potato. "Gypsies" were baked in the same manner as regular *bondes,* except that after being removed from the oven they were each cut into four to six pieces, which were then layered in a deep copper pan that had been buttered. Each layer was covered with sour cream and butter. The pan was then placed in the oven for a couple of hours. There was a variation of this recipe: the raw batter was formed into pancakes, which were placed into the buttered pan and topped with sour cream and butter. The pan was placed in the hot oven for a longer period of time. Regular potato pancakes were often made, cooked either in poppy-seed oil or goose fat.

The "king" of all potato dishes was the *teygekhts*. The grated potato was combined with a bit of flour, minced onion, and some butter. This was placed in a pan, which was put into the oven, sometimes when it was being used to bake bread. The grated potato batter was also used for making small dumplings, which were eaten with dairy soups. In the winter, large dumplings (sometimes called "bombs") were made out of potato batter. Often these dumplings were filled with whole oats, minced onion and goose fat or chicken fat and were then cooked in a porridge of oats for several hours. These dumplings certainly brought more pleasure than did real bombs. Poor families sometimes added grated potato to the batter when making rye bread. This reduced the nutritional value of the bread, but it did fill the stomachs of hungry children.

It is difficult to enumerate all the combinations involving potatoes made by Lithuanian Jews. Potatoes were the principal ingredient in all sorts of soup. A *krupnik,* for example, was a soup made of potatoes and grains—barley, buckwheat or any other grain.

One national dish was called "mock fish," probably so named by some village agronomist with a sense of humor in order to create more appetite for it. Mock fish consisted mainly of scraped, sliced potatoes (in Lithuania potatoes were scraped, rather than peeled, so that less would go to waste). There were plenty of onions in mock fish, seasoned with a little pepper. During the winter, fat was added; in summer, a little butter, sour cream, or sweet cream was used.

Mock fish was often served as a one-dish supper. Friends would be invited to help with a monotonous chore, such as plucking feathers. All participants would eat supper together, which usually consisted of mock fish, which was so popular with all the Jews of Lithuania. Sauerkraut would also be served.

While engaged in plucking feathers, people would tell wondrous tales, which either had come down through tradition or were new ones that someone had heard somewhere or had read in a storybook. The guests might include Christian women and girls from the neighborhood. They would sing songs in Yiddish, Lithuanian, Polish, Belorussian, and Russian. Most of these were folksongs about unrequited love. Among the Yiddish songs that became increasingly popular in the 1880s and early 1890s were Eliakum Zunser's "Di sokhe" (the Hook Plow), "Der tsion-marsh" (the Zionist March), "Shtey oyf, mayn folk" (Arise, My People), as well as others.[2]

At the time, feather plucking was an established tradition in every Jewish family. The feathers, which came from geese and sometimes from ducks, were collected in sacks or pillowcases. In poorer homes, the feathers of chickens and roosters were also collected. Every daughter (and in those days it was rare for a Jewish family to have only one daughter) had to be provided with pillows and featherbeds. The girl closest to marriageable age made a special effort to acquire as many feathers as possible, so that she might be in a position to be proud of her bedding. After plucking feathers for three or four hours, everyone present had great appetite for the peppery mock fish.

As a rule, no small-town Jew failed to plant potatoes for himself, whether he had a small plot or a garden, located beside his house or a bit farther away. Often the soil was turned over and the planting was done with the help of a Christian, but the Jew did the hoeing and harvesting himself. By the Seventeenth of Tammuz or, at the latest, by the Ninth of Av, he would start to dig around the new potato plants, which had been planted by hand after they had sprouting tubers. The larger potatoes would be taken out, then the soil would be put back around the plants so they would continue to grow. This procedure would be repeated periodically until close to Rosh Hashanah.

Those Jews who did not have their own gardens, or whose gardens were too small to yield enough potatoes to last through the winter, would plant them on land belonging to Christians. These arrangements entailed various kinds of exchanges. Artisans such as blacksmiths, shoemakers, tailors, wheelwrights, and tinsmiths paid with the work of their hands. Storekeepers paid with merchandise; tavernkeepers, with spirits and beer.

In addition, "Jewish waste" was a useful commodity to the peasant. In the course of a winter, a considerable amount of manure would collect from Jewish-owned cows, horses, and even goats (the Jewish national animal in Lithuanian towns). The waste was collected during the winter and was used to improve the rather poor Lithuanian soil. This was due to the fact that the peasants rarely possessed much in the way of livestock, the basis of all forms of agriculture.

Thus, the Jew furnished the plants, the fertilizer, and several coins. The peasant provided his field and his labor, and the yield was shared equally or in accordance with a prior arrangement. The poorest Jew made it his business to see to it that he would have at least 35 poods of potatoes. In order not to wind up running short of potatoes, however, a family of six or seven members (which a few decades ago was not considered a large family) required 75 to 100 poods for the winter. Every Jewish dwelling had a cellar, in which the potatoes were stored after they were harvested. With some 75 poods of potatoes in the cellar, even a poor man could face the oncoming winter and the possibility—God forbid—of not having any bread.

In many instances the poorer Jews would get through the winter on potatoes and sauerkraut; bread was a rare treat. Yet it must be said that the majority of Jews in Lithuania succeeded in preparing for winter by laying in potatoes, several poods of carrots, beets, turnips, onions, and other vegetables. That left only the necessity of earning a little money for bread. If one owned a goat about to kid or a cow about to calve, one could hope to have milk in Shevat or Tevet. And if, "with the help of God," the calf could be used for the family itself, then there would be some meat, too, which was certainly cause for rejoicing.

Because of their potato-based diet, there were some children with rickets, the "English disease," but their number was not large. The excellent nutrition naturally available in two dietary staples, rye bread and sauerkraut, served to ward off many a disease.

The favorite accompaniment to baked or boiled potatoes was herring, which was also the preferred food to be eaten with bread. In Lithuania, herring was a national dish. A herring could be eaten uncooked, "straight from the barrel," once the thin outer skin was pulled off; in some instances, only the scales were removed. Some people even dipped a potato into the pickling brine in the herring barrel and maintained that it was a true delicacy. Herring might also be baked, cooked in a sweet or sweet-and-sour sauce, fried, or chopped with onions, and so on. In many homes, potatoes, sour soup, black rye bread and herring were the only foods eaten on weekdays.

During the 1880s and 1890s, nearly every Jewish family baked its own bread. It was all one kind of bread: black rye, made from kernels that had been milled once. The entire kernel of grain was used, including the outer membrane, the starch and the germ. This was genuine whole-grain bread. In a mixing trough, a small amount of flour was combined with some warm salt water and allowed to stand overnight. The trough was covered with cloth and, over that, a fur pelt or pillow. The warmth caused the dough to begin fermenting. At dawn the sour dough was kneaded by hand for about three-quarters of an hour, flour and water being added gradually during the process. After it was kneaded, the dough was returned to the trough, covered, and allowed to stand in a warm place for four or five hours until it had risen. Then the dough was shaped into loaves, each weighing fifteen to twenty-five pounds. In winter, the oven paddle was sprinkled with flour so that the dough would not stick to the floor of the hot oven. In summer, some housewives, especially those who lived near a river or a lake, would gather fragrant reeds and place them under the loaves of dough; in autumn, oak leaves would be used. Some families gathered enough leaves to last through the winter. Depending on their size, the loaves would need to bake for four to six hours. Housewives who did not want the tops of the loaves to appear black would sift some rye flour through a fine-meshed sieve, which yielded a fine flour. This was mixed with water and the resulting paste, which was paler than the whole-rye flour, would be spread over the tops of the loaves before they were set in the oven. This mixture, known as *kharmushke,* gave the bread a "Jewish" appearance, in contrast to the non-Jews' bread, which was "black as coal." The non-Jews would often grind grain on their own millstones, which "singed" the kernels. Non-Jews considered the coating of loaves with *kharmushke* an unnecessary luxury.

The sourdough from which black bread was made was called *roshtshine.* It was often used in baking pancakes, known as *roshtshine latkes.* Water was mixed with some of the risen dough, along with some rye or, preferably, some buckwheat flour, which reduced the sourness of the taste. The pancakes made with this batter had a pleasantly sourish taste and "fairly begged" to be eaten with sour cream or soft, salted butter.* Eating pancakes was a special treat for the children, who scarcely ever ate sweets, rich cookies, or *babka,* except during Shavuot.

An even greater treat were buckwheat pancakes, which were dipped in hot, melted butter. In well-to-do homes, pancakes were made of wheat flour for extra special guests. But that, as they say, was not for the likes of ordinary men.

Workingmen often had nothing but black bread and sour milk to eat, yet this provided the strength for performing their difficult tasks. There was

---

*Russian gastronomes have a saying: "A carp likes to be roasted in cream." The Yiddish version is "a pancake looks for butter."

no knowledge of vitamins in those years. Nevertheless, the body must have known it was receiving a considerable amount of vitamins from these foods.

It is no wonder that the aroma of fresh baked rye bread smelled like perfume. People could do even the most strenuous work having eaten only plain rye bread with sour soup or with barley soup laced with a little milk. That was breakfast.

The midday meal, eaten at about three o'clock in the afternoon, consisted of a light bite, such as sour milk with a little sour cream (known as *podśmietanka,* this was a lower grade of sour cream, between thick sour cream and sour milk). Alternatives were a piece of bread and some cheese, or some more sour soup. In summer, it was a cold sour soup made of beet leaves and small beets. Connoisseurs added some diced onion and cucumber. When they were in season cucumbers were a very popular food among Jews; non-Jews were less partial to them. Jewish people ate cucumbers both fresh, with bread and salt, and pickled. Well-established householders would put up cucumbers in brine for the winter. Those who lived on farms and were responsible for large households pickled cucumbers in large barrels. Oak leaves, which helped preserve the pickles, and dill were added to the brine. The casks were then hermetically sealed and rolled into the lake, not far from shore, where they remained through the winter. Just before Passover the barrels would be retrieved from the water. The cucumbers would be sour but firm. At Passover meals they were served with meat or simply as something to eat in place of fruit.

Supper consisted of a dairy soup made with milk, especially a soup made with *farfl.* Flour would be combined with water, then the mixture was kneaded well. The dough would be cut into thick slices which were then reduced to bits with a chopping knife. This *farfl* was made of a dark meal that was a ground mixture of peas, barley, rye, and buckwheat. It had a distinctive flavor and was used mainly in summer, when there was a good supply of sweet milk. When new potatoes appeared, they were scraped and added to the *farfl.* In wealthier homes, *farfl* were made of wheat flour. In winter, supper consisted of oven-baked potatoes with chicken fat, or baked or boiled potatoes served with sauerkraut.

Peas, lentils, and beans were among the best-liked foods. Lithuanian Jews not only found them tasty but also regarded them as a source of strength needed to do their work. During the week, peas were used to make soup. They were cooked separately for a long time until they became thick. Then pearl barley was added to create "strong" soup. Fat, especially goose fat, was also added to this soup. Beans were prepared in a similar fashion, after they had been cooked for a long time in the oven. Lentils were cooked with *farfl.* On Friday mornings it was traditional among all Lithuanian Jews to prepare a special dish of peas, which were eaten with *rosl.* Before they were cooked, the peas were carefully inspected. They would be poured out onto the table and any with worm holes or other impurities were separated out. This work was done quite willingly by children, but when there was free time most of the family members would sit around the table and pick over peas, so that there might be a supply on hand to put into the pot when there was no time to ready them. Peas and beans mixed with barley were also used in preparing *tsholnt*.

The Sabbath required one to make special preparations. Not infrequently, this was extremely onerous for the poor Jew lacking the necessary ruble on the eve of the Sabbath. Even with a single ruble it was possible to "make the Sabbath" for a household. On Friday evening and the Sabbath day, meat was usually eaten. All week long one settled for "almost anything," but it would not do to "disgrace" the Sabbath.

The contrast between dishes served on weekdays and those for the Sabbath was striking. For the Sabbath, all sorts of good things were prepared. One might explain this phenomenon as being a way to compensate the half-starved body, which needed the nourishing food it had not tasted all week. But it was really done to honor the Sabbath Queen. The Sabbath was no small matter. It seemed that not only were these small-town and village Jews observing the Sabbath, but that all of nature was in tune with the Sabbath. And since that was the case, how could one greet so important a guest as the Holy Sabbath with only *borscht* or barley soup? That would be a profanation.

Even in the poorest of homes a small *hallah* would be baked. Woe to the family that did not even have ten or fifteen kopeks needed to buy flour and yeast! For such a family, the community would have to step in. The family might do without food during the week; this was scarcely a novelty, and did not particularly move the neighbors. They could not, however, permit a Jewish family to go hungry on the Sabbath. It may be assumed, then, that in every Jewish home there was some sort of *hallah* on the Sabbath. Yet the Sabbath is still no Sabbath unless there is a piece of fish, or some meat, or both.

From the time of the major fall holidays through the winter months, meat might also be indulged in on weekdays. This was the season for sheep, chickens, and ducks. Quite a number of the village Jews would buy a calf or a lamb and take it to the ritual slaughterer. Part of the animal would be sold, and the remainder–the head, lungs, liver, feet and other small parts—were kept, providing more than enough for the Sabbath. There were, of course, some who could even afford to purchase or reserve a whole side of meat for their own use. During the winter, it would be a calf. Wealthier families would salt meat and store it frozen for use during the winter months.

Sometimes such meat would have an odor, but during the cooking the smell would dissipate without doing harm to anyone. Perhaps people were healthier in those days. Or, it could be that the air and the hard work, along with the black bread and sauerkraut, had the effect of keeping the digestive system in order and able to tolerate all sorts of food.

There is not much to add concerning special dishes for the Sabbath or for holidays. The traditional fish, meat, *tsimmes,* noodles, dumplings, cakes, and tortes were generally similar in established Jewish communities throughout the diaspora. It remains but to mention the *retshishnik,* made of toasted buckwheat meal. This was a sort of baked pudding which was served sliced into glistening pieces. In the homes of the well-to-do, it was made with poultry fat; poorer folks used poppy-seed oil. On wintry Friday nights, after a nap, one would take the *retshishnik* out of the oven and partake of it with special pleasure.

4

HEALING THE MENTALLY ILL

Woodlands dominate the landscape between Vilna and Białystok. Some areas contain trees of various species; others consist entirely of pines growing in sandy soil. It is poor soil, but the woods lend the scene a special magic—dreamy, airy, peaceful. By now, probably, these woods are no more. The accursed Germans have completed their destruction, which they began during World War I.

Buckwheat was the only crop that could be sown in these sandy fields. Summer rye and other grains yielded very small harvests. Potatoes would grow only if the fields were well fertilized. It was some of these spartan fields that the government of Tsar Nicholas I found possible to spare for the Jews.[1] More than a century ago, Nicholas I began an experiment of settling Jews in the Vilna-Grodno region. Some twenty-five Jewish colonies were established there. Despite the unfriendly bureaucratic methods of the tsarist administrators, a considerable number of the colonists remained bound to their sandy soil, where they reaped meager harvests and also raised some cattle and poultry.

The sandy fields did not provide enough for a living. The Jewish colonists had to supplement their incomes by working as drivers, peddlers, or working in some cottage industry, such as spinning, dyeing cloth, making harnesses, and the like. Still, they lived in poverty. It was impossible to develop their cottage industries to any considerable extent. They lacked money, raw materials and, most of all, community support. Shortly before World War I the Jewish Colonization Association took note of the colonists and sent some agronomists to work with them.[2] They were given credit to help them plant orchards, sow cover crops (such as lupine and clover) to improve the soil, buy some good dairy cows, and so on. But before any of this could be done, the people still depended on supplementary occupations.

One such source of income was taking care of the mentally ill for a small fee, which even families of modest means who had the misfortune to have such relatives could afford. In several towns, such as Butrymańce, Vilna province, Tatars were engaged to "heal" the Jewish mentally ill. This consisted of charms, smoking herbs, and chanting mysterious incantations. For a small fee, the patient would be left in the home of some poor folks, who were responsible for feeding the patient and taking him to the Tatars for the "cure." There was no particular supervision of the mentally ill. They would walk around the town freely. Various anecdotes are told about the mentally ill. For example, one went into a fabric store, where he began perusing the shelves and corners. The shopkeepers asked him, "What are you looking for, sir? What do you need?"

"Do you have a wagonload of cracklings?" the inquisitive visitor asked.

"A wagonload of cracklings?" the shopkeepers asked in surprise.

To which he replied, "You are mad, and there is nothing I can say to you." He shut the door hurriedly and left in a huff. He was, of course, a patient of one of the Tatars.

The healing of the mentally ill became a source of income in some of the Jewish colonies. Jews from Vilna, Grodno, Białystok, and their environs sent their mentally ill relatives to Lejpuny, Deksznie, and other colonies close to the railroad station at Olkieniki, en route to Grodno-Białystok.

The healthy air of the colonies, which were surrounded by pine woods, buckwheat fields, and wide plains, seemed to have a salutary effect on nervous, disturbed people. The Jewish colonists themselves—very calm, almost phlegmatic, but for the most part good-natured, hard workers—also inspired the trust of those who wanted to leave their sick relatives in the colonies. The food the colonists supplied to the invalids was simple but wholesome and not irritating: milk, potatoes, *borscht,* cabbage soup, black bread with butter, and various milk-based soups, all quite nutritious. Families could trust the Jewish colonists not to strike the mentally ill or torture them, even if they became violent. The colonists would only bind their hands if the invalids' actions posed a threat to themselves or those about them. The colonists often brought the invalids with them out to the fields and gave them a task (or, more precisely, a semblance of a task—pulling up weeds, gathering sorrel, etc.) so that they might feel that they were doing something useful. This, naturally, helped strengthen the invalids' disturbed nerves. In all likelihood, no less than half of them would leave the colonies refreshed and healthier.

When the Germans occupied Lithuania and Belorussia in 1915, they proceeded, as was their custom, to reduce the number of "eaters." The first victims were the mentally ill. At the time, the Germans still employed excuses: it would be better for the invalids to be somewhere near the Baltic Sea, where they would receive better medical attention, and so on. The medical division of the German Tenth Army removed all the mentally ill from Jewish hospitals as well as from the Jewish colonies and sent them somewhere near Libava, Courland. There they were put to death in a "scientific" manner—by injection. It was not until a considerable time later that this first German mass murder became known. With this the murderous Germans took their first steps in the practice of extermination.[3]

Almost all of the early colonists remained where they were, and they survived the severity of the occupation with great difficulty. During this time, their agricultural output even appeared to have developed somewhat. Those who owned a piece of land were able to exist on the grain and vegetables that they harvested from their gardens. But then came the years of inflation and looting by the Polish Legionnaries. The Jewish colonies stood at the brink of an abyss.

Even so, after the war was over they resumed the fundamentals of their way of life, earning a little from the spartan soil and a little from all sorts of supplementary occupations. In Deksznie, the "business" of caring for the mentally ill was revived, and since there was no scarcity of mental illness at the end of the war, the population of Deksznie and Lejpuny grew considerably.

Up to that time, medical scientists had paid no attention to the methods of treatment (if they may be called that) in the Jewish towns. Then the prominent Jewish psychiatrist, Dr. Abraham Wirszubski of Vilna, became interested in the results of caring for the mentally ill in private homes in Deksznie and described them in a Polish medical journal.[4] Subsequently, the hospital department of the municipality of Vilna also became interested in Deksznie.

A commission that included Dr. Wirszubski (who was then the director of Vilna's Jewish hospital) studied the condition of the invalids and the effect that rural life had on them. The commission concluded that the experiment in home therapy should be supported and that supervision of both the caretakers and the patients could improve their situation considerably.

The city authorities of Vilna appointed a psychiatrist and a nurse to be in charge of the invalids being treated in private homes. All colonists who wished to care for the mentally ill were required to notify the doctor. Their homes were then inspected to see that they offered the conditions necessary for proper care. The pay for each patient averaged forty zlotys per month. The colonists considered it a special "privilege" to care for two or three patients. This enabled an entire family to improve its situation by purchasing a cow, a horse, or some farming equipment, or by repairing the house, and the like.

The results of this type of healing demonstrated considerable success. A year or two before the start of World War II, I once visited the colony at Deksznie late in the fall. A former student at the Vilna vocational school called Help Through Work, of which I was the director, came to see me there with his mother to invite me to his wedding. His fiancée was the daughter of a Deksznie colonist who owned a house and ten hectares of land. Her aged father still lived there, but the daughter was in charge. She looked after an invalid (in Deksznie the term "insane person" was avoided) in their home. As my former student was a carpenter, he hoped that with his plane and saw, as well as the plow, horses (which would also be useful for working as a driver in winter), and the "patient," they would be able to eke out a living. It was important, however, to show his future in-laws that he was not alone, that he would have people coming to visit him from as far away as Vilna. Unable to refuse this ingenuous request, I went to the wedding. When I arrived at the bride's home in Deksznie, I met a man named Hamburg, who was the local *wójt,* or village headman.* He told me about the town's needs, which included credit, economic improvement, and a Jewish school, among other things.

The wedding was celebrated in a traditional manner. The wedding canopy was set up outdoors, in the rain and mud. Some of the patients wandered over to the canopy. If one of them shouted or called out suddenly, he was quickly calmed by being addressed gently, for everyone knew all the invalids by name.

The wedding meal was turned into a sort of public banquet. Young people who lived in the nearby countryside assembled and began to make speeches. They revealed their longing for a better life. With a certain amount of umbrage, they pointed out that the large cities nearby—Vilna, Grodno, and Białystok—exploited their communities as a hospital for their mentally ill but forgot that other people also lived there. Realizing that no one from the outside world came to them, the young people in Deksznie organized activities on their own. Whenever there was a lecture or some kind of entertainment in Olkieniki, the nearest town, they would walk there. They also strove to improve the town's humble status by reorganizing its economy on a new basis, so that the younger generation would not leave. They complained that the Jewish Colonization Association was not sufficiently

---

*He was the only Jewish *wójt* (village headman) in Poland. He was elected to this office by both Jews and non-Jews.

involved in the problems of the Jewish rural communities. These young people also established a library, collected agricultural literature, wanted to have an agronomist to instruct them, and so on. I found the speeches that these young men and women made to be refreshing. If there was such desire to renew life on a healthier basis in such a remote place, then there was hope that their aspirations would eventually be fulfilled.

Also attending the wedding feast were the physician from the Vilna municipal administration (a non-Jewish woman) and the nurse. The doctor told me that, in the course of a year, some two hundred invalids underwent the Deksznie "home cure." Quite a number of them recovered their health.

Late that night, when everyone had retired, I found myself quite unable to fall asleep. In the darkness, I could hear an occasional shout or scream from a patient who suffered from nightmares. The local residents were accustomed to this and slept undisturbed. To me, however, it seemed like a struggle between Ormuzd and Ahriman, a struggle for the most precious of man's possessions—a sound mind, to which the Jewish colony called Deksznie had contributed its share.[5]

II

Reform and Upheaval before World War I

1

Joshua Steinberg

Biographical information about the great scholar and *maskil* Joshua Steinberg is very scarce. In particular, little is known about his younger years. He left no memoirs, nor have others written much about his colorful life. He lived through three-fourths of the nineteenth century and the first decade of the twentieth. Quite a few people recalled him unfavorably, referring to him as a hack, a Jewish "functionary" who curried the favor of three tsarist governments. I knew Steinberg for four years, when he was already an old man. He held the position of Inspector at the Jewish Teachers Institute and was my professor in Hebrew language and Bible.[1] Negative assessments of Steinberg tend not to consider him in historical context. His was an era when *maskilim*—whose ranks include Isaac Baer Levinsohn, Adam Ha-Kohen Lebensohn, Samuel Joseph Fuenn, Abraham Baer Gottlober, and many others—were loyal to the government.[2]

Steinberg was a student in the first graduating class of the Vilna Rabbinical School. The objective of this school, and a similar one in Zhitomir, was to prepare teachers for the state-supported Jewish schools, as well as to provide rabbis with a secular education so that they might serve as *rabiners*, official representatives of Jewish communities to the government. This rabbinical training required ten or eleven years of study, about three more than that for the teachers.

Very little is known about how Joshua Steinberg came to be chosen as the first *rabiner* of Białystok. In Białystok, as in other cities, vital records were kept by traditionally educated rabbis until about 1860. When the first graduates of the Vilna Rabbinical School appeared on the scene, however, the government decreed that official rabbis must all be graduates of the school. Apparently the graduates of the first few classes were snatched up immediately, especially those who were as gifted as Steinberg.

A. Sh. Hershberg, the historian of Białystok, devoted about ten lines to Steinberg and confessed that he had virtually no information about him.[3] Steinberg served as *rabiner* in Białystok during 1861. His sermons on the Torah aroused considerable interest in progressive circles of *maskilim.* In a report from Białystok printed in *Ha-Maggid,* Eliezer David Lieberman relates that when Tsar Alexander II visited Białystok in October 1861 he was welcomed by a delegation that included the newly-appointed *rabiner* Joshua Steinberg, M. Zabludovski, I. B. Volkovysky, and other town notables.[4] Steinberg presented the tsar with bread and salt, as well as a small carved box containing a Hebrew poem and its Russian translation.[5] Steinberg wrote the poem, which enumerated grossly exaggerated virtues of the tsar and offered him florid praise in the style prevalent among *maskilim* at the time.

Shortly thereafter, the larger and more famous city of Vilna engaged Steinberg to be its *rabiner.* There, he married the daughter of the Hebrew poet Adam Ha-Kohen Lebensohn, a noted *maskil.* Steinberg held the post of Vilna's official rabbi for seven to eight years. Thanks to his efforts, several Russian elementary schools for Jews were opened there during the 1860s. Steinberg was also appointed an instructor of Aramaic and Hebrew at the Vilna Rabbinical School. It is difficult to say how and where Steinberg acquired these languages, in addition to the European ones that he knew. Apparently, he not only had been a very diligent student since childhood, but also possessed an exceptional memory.

It is known that he learned Russian from the Synodical translation of the Bible, and throughout his life he used its archaic sentence structure and distinctive biblical expressions when he spoke. This provided excellent grist for jokes by his students at the Vilna Rabbinical School and later at the Vilna Teachers Institute, where he taught the Bible and Hebrew after the rabbinical school closed. They even wrote down his expressions and composed imaginary conversations between Steinberg and Asher Wohl, lecturer in Jewish history and translator of Jewish prayers into Russian.[6] Wohl had been educated in Europe and was trained in the German school of Judaic studies. He knew modern Russian, but used the flowery language of Jewish prayers in his spoken Russian.

When I knew them, both Steinberg and Wohl were quite elderly. Wohl retired in 1898. I knew him only for a year. His hands trembled, and he moved quite slowly, like a very old man. Steinberg, on the other hand, still carried himself erect, although he walked with a limp. His hair was completely white, his face clean shaven. He wore the official blue frock coat, which had gilded buttons decorated with eagles. Later on, he dressed in the uniform of a senior government official, except that it had no epaulets, as did the uniforms of the Christian teachers. His cap, with its cockade and blue satin band, was stiff, like its wearer. The cap peaked at the front, perhaps the better to show off the cockade.

When he wanted to call his students' attention to something, or when he wanted to silence his young charges—who, typically, would rather converse with each other than listen to a discourse on the wonders of grammar— Steinberg would rap on his desk with the palm of his hand. The students could not understand why this made such a metallic sound. It seemed as if he had fingers of steel, or else they had become so stiff that Steinberg no longer felt any sensation in them.

Steinberg's name was known to all Jewish externs.[7] Many of these impoverished young autodidacts learned Russian from his Hebrew-Russian and Russian-Hebrew dictionaries and from his grammar of the Hebrew language, written in Russian, of which they often memorized entire pages.[8] How they managed to acquire a knowledge of spoken and written Russian in this way remains a secret. Usually, however, they were far from fluent. This is because Steinberg believed that knowledge of all grammatical forms of a language was of supreme importance; appreciation of its purity and beauty was secondary.

I had a very good command of contemporary Hebrew language and literature for someone of my time, but despite this Steinberg did not see fit to give me better than a "3+"—an average grade. One of my classmates was scarcely able to read a book like Mapu's *Ahavat Zion,* but he knew all the nuances of the mobile and quiescent *sheva.*[9] He always received a "5"—the highest grade— from Steinberg. Only in my last two classes with Steinberg did he "recognize" me. Then he not only gave me "5's," he also placed me in charge of the institute's rather modest collection of Hebrew books, which was traditionally entrusted to the student who best knew Hebrew.

Steinberg taught us the Bible, but very seldom went beyond simply translating the texts of Isaiah and Jeremiah into Russian. He did the translating himself, and it was from this that we learned. Only rarely did he share with us his great knowledge of the older literatures in the dozen languages he knew or of modern methods of Bible study. Perhaps we appeared so ignorant to him that he was reluctant to unfold before us all the depth and beauty of the Prophets. Whenever he did so, we simply marveled at his philological revelations and historical parallels.

The turn of the century was not conducive to immersing oneself in Hebrew. The sentiments of Judah Leib Gordon's deeply pessimistic poem, *For Whom Do I Toil?,* were still valid.[10] People were taken with the idea of revolution, and Russian language and literature had captured the hearts and minds of most young Jews. Steinberg, however, seemed like an old

Portrait of Joshua Steinberg, Inspector of the Vilna Jewish Teachers Institute, in the official uniform of a government employee, ca. 1900.
Courtesy of the YIVO Archives.

Polish aristocrat. His appearance was not Jewish, and if it were not for his Synodical Russian and traces of a Jewish accent he would not have been taken for a Jew. He belonged to the earliest type of *maskilim,* who saw everything that the Russian government did concerning education for Jews as entirely just. The tsar was the divinely anointed monarch, and it was the Jews' duty to pray for him.

Steinberg also demonstrated his loyalty to the tsarist regime by serving as a censor of Yiddish and Hebrew books. He was a very strict censor. If a book contained anything that might somehow be interpreted as even hinting at criticism of the regime, he took it out. The playwright Peretz Hirschbein recounted several half-comical stories about Steinberg the censor, which would scarcely be believed if they were told by anyone else.[11] It was rumored that the great learned philologist once let himself be influenced by a gratuity in the form of a twenty-five-ruble note—or even, perhaps, only a ten. This was difficult to believe, but Hirschbein and several other contemporary Yiddish and Hebrew writers confirmed the rumor.

Steinberg could not abide the new directions that literature was taking. He considered naturalism to be pornography, symbolism to be veiled sedition. Hirschbein related that Steinberg was a bitter foe of some of the younger writers, such as Hirschbein himself and Zalman Shneour, not for their "sedition" but for their pornography and immorality.[12] Hirschbein wrote a drama, titled *Miriam,* in the fourth act of which the heroine is seduced by her lover. Steinberg deleted the act, claiming that the play would suffice without it. When Hirschbein came to Steinberg to request that he approve the fourth act (for publication in Fayvl Margolin's anthology, *Ha-Zeman*), Steinberg reviled the author, calling him a young rake. The censor stamped his feet and even raised his fist.[13]

Hirschbein related:

> I tried to show him, citing examples from Russian literature, that when famous writers portrayed life realistically in all its facets they did not hesitate to show what was tragic or criminal. I showed Steinberg passages from Gor'kii, Andreev, Tolstoi—but that only incensed him further: "What do I care about Russian writers! If I were their censor I would tear their scribblings to bits. But where Jewish literature is concerned, as long as I am censor I will not permit some scribbling youngster to undermine Jewish morality." Nevertheless, before the month was over, some more skillful hand than mine convinced Steinberg that Jewish morality is staunchly defended in *Miriam,* and he permitted its final act to be printed.

In one scene a mother says, "It is foolish for mothers to mourn their little ones when they die." When Hirschbein humbly asked Steinberg what he found wrong with this innocent line, which he had deleted, the censor stormed: "What do you mean? Aren't you saying that mothers are foolish? And suppose the tsarina were to mourn the crown prince if, God forbid, he were to die—wouldn't that be foolish as well? This is sedition!" He stamped his feet.

There is a famous poem by M. Dolitski called "In the Snakes' Nest," which contains the words, "In the snakes' nest, the people are suffering." The cantor A. Bernstein, a composer who lived in Vilna, set the poem to music and brought the text to Steinberg.[14] The censor deleted the words "in the snakes' nest" on the ground that they could be construed as referring to Russia. In their stead he wrote "There, in the land of Persia and Media."

Steinberg married several times. With his first wife he had several talented children, including a beautiful, intelligent daughter and the well-known composer Maksimilian Ovseevich Steinberg, the protégé and son-in-law of Nikolai Rimsky-Korsakov.[15] Maksimilian Steinberg adopted the Russian Orthodox religion and was lost to the Jewish people. Once, when the composer attempted to calm his father during his censorial rages, the elder Steinberg turned on his son with his fists. Steinberg's daughter sought to defend her father before the Vilna community, saying that he was trying to reclaim his spoiled children by treating them strictly and only had their well-being in mind.

Very late in life, Steinberg, having been widowed, married a young Jewish woman from Courland. When he was seventy years old, Steinberg's wife gave birth to a beautiful little girl. Like most Jews from Courland, Steinberg's young wife spoke Russian very poorly. This, however, was the language of choice among the intellectual elite of Vilna. Steinberg, of course, was one of these intellectuals, who spoke Russian both at formal occasions and at home. Once, at a large gathering in the home of the noted Shmarya Levin, Mrs. Steinberg called out, "Where is my ancient Jewish husband?"[16] It was not her intention to make a joke. In Russian, Hebrew is called *drevne-evreiskii iazyk*—literally, "ancient Jewish language." Mrs. Steinberg meant to say, "Where is my Hebraist?" What came out, however, was different and somewhat symbolic. Everyone burst into laughter, her ancient Jewish husband most of all.

This woman was Steinberg's third or fourth wife. It was very moving to watch the old Hebraist catering to his young wife and "spoiling" his little daughter, whose father was old enough to have been her grandfather or, indeed, her great-grandfather. Such marriages, however, were not at all uncommon among widowed *maskilim*. The strong spirit with which most of the great *maskilim* were endowed helped them retain their youthful vigor, as did their modest, reserved way of life. Joshua Steinberg was one such person, strong in spirit.

One of his sons-in-law was Isaac Pirozhnikov, the noted choirmaster, conductor of the Teachers Institute orchestra, and concert performer. Later, he became the music critic of the *Jewish Daily Forward,* the New York Yiddish newspaper. While in Vilna, Pirozhnikov also established an art press.[17]

During the 1890s, Steinberg was appointed to evaluate the yeshiva of Wołożyn. He called for the administration of the yeshiva to add at least one course in elementary Russian and one in arithmetic to its curriculum. There was talk that he also played a part in closing the yeshiva for a short period because of the spread of revolutionary ideas there.[18]

Joshua Steinberg's scholarly work, particularly in the field of Semitic and Oriental languages, was highly regarded by philologists. For us, his students, his philological elucidation often illuminated obscure passages in the Bible. We wondered where the old man found all the time and energy to write and compile his lexicographic works, thick dictionaries, and grammars. I recall his handsomely printed anthology of aphorisms from various thinkers (including a number of his own), published under the title *Mishlei Yehoshua* (Proverbs of Joshua).[19] This excellent volume, however, which included precise translations into Russian, did not find many readers. At the time, I was in charge of the Hebrew library at the Institute the book showed little sign of use.

I never heard Steinberg, Wohl, or any other professor who taught Jewish subjects utter a word of Yiddish. Indeed, at that time students showed very little interest in Jewish literature written in Yiddish. Only a few read Mendele, Peretz, or Pinsky.[20] Students had to obtain permission to bring a book into the institute. It must be said that Steinberg readily granted such permission for books in Yiddish or Hebrew.

To us, Steinberg's inner world was completely alien or, to put it better, unknown. He did not allow us to get close to him. It was not until years later that some of us realized what a great scholar we had had in this teacher, the former *rabiner* of Białystok. Perhaps we did not understand how this learned man might enhance our Judaic knowledge. In accordance with the regulations of the Ministry of Education, Steinberg had to retire at the age of seventy-five. He died four years later, in 1908, having lived to be almost eighty. His funeral was attended by all of Vilna's Jewish intellectuals, as well as by the remnants of the old *maskilim*.

Steinberg's Hebrew-Russian grammars, with their outlandishly contrived translation exercises, have long been forgotten. His dictionaries, however, which detailed the etymology of Hebrew words, are still useful for scholars. Had Steinberg converted from Judaism, as did his fellow townsman and contemporary, Daniel Chwolson, he, too, might have become a professor of Semitic languages and cultures at some Russian university, for there were not many orientalists of Steinberg's stature in Russia.[21] To his credit, it must be said that he did not choose to make this change.

2

SAMUEL GOZHANSKI

When I knew Samuel Isakovich Gozhanski I was a boy of about twelve or thirteen, and in my eyes he was already quite an elderly man.[1] He was a teacher in the government-run Jewish school in Vilna where I had come to study along with two friends from the countryside. We had had lessons together at home with a tutor. In Vilna, we lived together in a single room.

Gozhanski taught the preparatory class, which had some forty children about seven to eight years old. Gozhanski was always immaculate and very neatly attired, wearing a small bow instead of a tie over his pressed white shirt and a hard, stiff hat. As a teacher in the government school, he also wore a peculiar blue frock coat, its two tails pinned up in the back, with a velvet collar and gold buttons. Presumably, this garment was intended to imbue students with awe for their teacher, for government teachers were the only Jews required to wear what was known as a "button." True, it was adorned only with buttons, not with cockades or epaulets or any of the other insignia that graced the uniforms of even the most modest non-Jewish officials.

In the government Jewish schools all classes, even those in religion, were conducted in Russian, as were prayers, which a designated student recited each day both before and after lessons. The prayers began with the words *Preblagii bozhe* (Most gracious God). The children, especially those in the preparatory class, knew not a word of Russian. There was a rule that in the preparatory class (and in that class alone) one might, in an emergency, translate something into Yiddish for a child who did not understand it in Russian. Gozhanski and the other teachers, however, almost never applied this rule. Every effort, however difficult, was made to avoid the use of Yiddish. Moreover, the pedagogical authorities told elementary school students to refrain from speaking Yiddish among themselves outside the school as well.

Gozhanski taught only a year or so at the school. After that he was assigned to teach in another city. He was not my teacher but was frequently on duty during recess periods. He made sure the children did not become too boisterous. His face was very serious. He had dark eyes, and on his forehead, just above the nose, were two vertical creases which intensified his stern expression. Even so, the children in his class made excellent progress. He wasted no time and made every effort to ensure that his pupils understood him. When talking to them he used a staccato tone, hammering out each syllable, which greatly impressed the youngsters. When Gozhanski also furrowed his brow, intensifying his stern appearance, the students "quaked in their boots." Nevertheless, all his students regarded Gozhanski with great respect, if not with affection. Whenever he substituted for a colleague in the upper classes, the students regarded it as something of a treat. His explanations were so clear that it was no trouble to understand and remember them. He was a teacher both by training and because of his natural gifts. Thus it was perhaps no accident that he was known as "Teacher" in the underground political circles of the period.

One day two friends and I walked out of the school conversing loudly in Yiddish, our mother tongue, unaware that Gozhanski was walking behind us. Apparently, I was the last one he heard speaking, for Gozhanski walked straight toward me, stopped our group and said (in Russian) in his staccato tone, "Go back to school and report to Il'ia Isakovich [Lazarev, the school administrator] that you and your friends were speaking Yiddish outdoors." I had no choice. My two friends and I returned to the school. But Ilia Isakovich had already gone, and there the matter ended. From a historical point of view, the fact that Jewish children in the most pro-Yiddish city in the world were forbidden to speak the language in public is noteworthy. So, too, is the fact that the enforcing agent was none other than Gozhanski, who was later one of the founders of the Bund.

It must be said that, at the time, Yiddish was just beginning to be recognized as a cultural language. It was decidedly not the vernacular of the Jewish intelligentsia. Their commitment to Yiddish grew out of working with the masses and with the members of the Bund in particular. Years later, many of Gozhanski's former students took pleasure in reading Yiddish articles signed "Lonu" (Gozhanski's pseudonym), which appeared in various illegal publications. The Yiddish he used in these articles was correct for that time. Several years later Gozhanski was arrested, and he and his wife (née Klis) were banished to Siberia. His later activities, however, are beyond the scope of this personal account.

3

Chaim Fialkov

Chaim Fialkov was Chaim Weizmann's mother's brother. Uncle and nephew were almost the same age, and they resembled each other like two drops of water. They both had the same long face with sharp, chiseled features and the same small, pitch-black goatee. Each had large, dark eyes and a high, scholarly forehead. They were similar even in stature, tall and slender. Nevertheless, Fialkov was much the calmer and more deliberate of the two, and his demeanor was more modest.

The Weizmann family had its roots in the town of Motol, near Pińsk. All the younger members of the family were steeped in Hebrew. They studied the language assiduously and read Hebrew books. The walls of the room where the children did their lessons were covered with huge charts showing the conjugation of the model Hebrew verb *pakad* (count). They studied advanced Hebrew grammars, the easiest of which was a reader titled *Maslul*.[1]

Well-versed in Hebrew, Chaim Fialkov arrived in Vilna and prepared to take the competitive examinations for admission to the Vilna Teachers Institute. About 200 sixteen- and seventeen-year-olds applied; no more than twenty, sometimes even fewer, were admitted. Fialkov was accepted as one of the "top applicants with the highest marks in every subject."

The philologist and lexicographer, Joshua Steinberg, was the nominal inspector of the institute, but all power lay in the hands of the director, a non-Jew with the rank of "civilian general." Nevertheless, Steinberg had jurisdiction over instruction in Hebrew grammar, Bible, and Jewish history. In his opinion, proof of one's knowledge of Hebrew consisted of a perfect command (in Russian) of Hebrew grammar. Fortunately, Fialkov not only knew Hebrew well, but was also versed in all the particulars of its grammar. As a result, Steinberg befriended him and entrusted him with the school's Hebrew library, which consisted of a limited number of books, including all of Steinberg's own works.

Fialkov had better command of Hebrew than anyone else at the institute. He also distinguished himself in other subjects. After he completed the course of study with honors, the educational authorities made Fialkov a teacher in the government Jewish school in Nikolayev, in the province of Kherson.

The school's administrator was a very dedicated teacher named Getselter. He strove to make the children proficient in Russian and their other general courses, as well as in Jewish subjects, which were sadly neglected in most government schools. Getselter, also a graduate of the Vilna Institute, had taught himself a variety of skills, including carpentry, locksmithing, and tailoring, and he introduced vocational courses in his school.

Fialkov was a young idealist and devoted himself to his pedagogical task. He organized all of the school's Hebrew courses and provided Getselter with valuable assistance in his efforts to teach practical skills to Jewish youth. Fialkov also taught Russian and Hebrew in a community school for girls. (In southern Russia the government permitted the establishment of such schools, although this was not yet the case in the northwestern part of the country.)

Fialkov soon won the affection of the children and their parents because of his devotion to the youngsters and the excellent progress they showed in Hebrew language and literature and Jewish history under his tutelage. Fialkov even went so far as to ignore the official curricula, which were very limited. In the semi- (or perhaps fully) assimilated city of Nikolayev, he instilled a love of Jewish history and Hebrew in its young people.

When I was in New York I met a woman, Liza Bercovich, who had been one of Fialkov's students in Nikolayev. She provided me with details of his pedagogical efforts in the school she had attended. Her account was a veritable paean to this gifted pedagogue, who had had such a profoundly positive influence on the entire Jewish population of Nikolayev.

As a result of his arduous teaching efforts, Fialkov strained his vocal cords. He became very hoarse and was forced to stop teaching. Fialkov went to Switzerland to heal his throat. While there he took university courses in philosophy, psychology and, especially, anything related to didactics and pedagogy. During the few years he was abroad, he acquired a breadth and depth of theoretical knowledge in the humanities while also acquainting himself with practical systems of education such as those of Pestalozzi and Montessori.[2]

The St. Petersburg organization *Hevrat Mefitsei Haskalah* (Society for the Dissemination of Enlightenment among the Jews of Russia, also known by the Russian acronym OP) either partially subsidized or fully maintained several Jewish community schools, particularly in southern Russia (including the Caucasus).[3] The society was conducting a search for a qualified inspector to visit these schools, report on them to the OP's Central Committee and also instruct the teachers in the use of new pedagogical methods. No one was more qualified for this position than Fialkov. He was familiar with both practical teaching techniques and all pedagogical theories. Moreover, he was at home in Jewish studies, most certainly in Hebrew. He immediately assumed a leading position among Jewish intellectuals and activists in St. Petersburg.

Not surprisingly, the OP schools waited impatiently for Chaim Fialkov's visits so that, with his experience, intelligence and tact, they might solve difficult problems, resolve disagreements and receive practical guidance in how to improve the quality of instruction. Local activists in cities and towns that still had no communal schools invited Fialkov to come and help them organize a school. He would assist them in obtaining the necessary pedagogical personnel permits, and the like.

In contrast to the situation in southern Russia, there were as yet no communal schools in the northwestern corner of the country. The official in charge of education in the northwestern provinces had refused all requests for permission to establish such schools. He was particularly resistant to opening schools for girls, especially, in Vilna. The *Mefitsei Haskalah* sent Fialkov to Vilna to lobby both in official circles and in the Jewish community for this permission.

The Department of Education in Vilna was the most reactionary in all of Russia. Obtaining permission to establish a communal school there would, in effect, establish an official precedent for establishing communal schools in the entire northwestern region. And this is what eventually occurred. In accordance with the OP plan, Vera Matveevna Kuperstein moved to Vilna to work with Fialkov.[4] At their initiative, the only Jew with the title of Privy Counselor in the Ministry of Justice, a man named Galpern, came to Vilna from St. Petersburg. Thanks to his gold-braided uniform and his "civilian general" calling card, Galpern was able to influence Vilna's Director of Education and obtain his permission to open a large school for girls on Konska Street, which came to be known as the Kuperstein School. Fialkov and a group of local activists developed the curriculum for other similar public schools. It included a significant number of hours devoted to Hebrew, Bible, and Jewish history.

Late in 1907, Fialkov firmly declined to continue serving as itinerant school inspector for the *Mefitsei Haskalah,* both for reasons of health and because of his leading role in the organization. This led to a search for someone to succeed him. For political reasons, I had been removed from my pedagogic duties in the province of Yekaterinoslav, part of the Odessa educational district, so I was no longer able to find employment there. At the time, there were numerous opportunities to find work in the field of education. In the larger cities of the Pale of Settlement, a number of private gymnasia had opened under government license. As a result, I was engaged by Dr. A. Ratner's gymnasium in Gomel' as a full-time teacher of history (world, Russian, and Jewish) in the upper grades and to act as administrator of one of the school's three separate buildings, which housed four classes.[5]

Several months later, at the beginning of 1908, I received a letter from the St. Petersburg committee of the *Mefitsei Haskalah* asking me to come there as soon as possible to discuss taking over Fialkov's administrative position in the OP schools. The invitation was signed by S. Kamenetsky, general secretary, and Fialkov himself.

I came to St. Petersburg, and Fialkov described the work to me in some detail. He allowed me to read his reports, which were written in the finest Russian. In them, Fialkov demonstrated his extensive knowledge of all matters concerning the community schools and their environment. Some of his reports contained much humorous illustrative material, similar to Sholem Aleichem's fictitious accounts of Kasrilevke or Mendele's about Kabtsansk.[6]

Then I met with the principal members of the committee. They included the scrap metal dealer Miron Naumovich Kreinin, a wise and understanding man who had received an excellent Jewish and general education. Kreinin, the de facto head of the committee, was both a practical man and, ideologically, the right man in the right place. Although not a pedagogue himself, he was well versed in all matters pertaining to the school system and to Jewish education generally. The second mainstay of the committee was an attorney and a native of St. Petersburg, Grigory Abramovich Goldberg. Goldberg represented the secular European element, so to speak, on the committee. Another similarly inclined committee member was Doctor (Iakov?) Zalkind, a prominent physician who held a very broad view of Jewish life. Fialkov and Kamenetsky, the secretary of the committee, advised me to present myself before the official chairman of the *Mefitsei Haskalah,* Baron David Guenzburg.[7] It would be a courteous gesture, they said, even if without practical significance. I took their advice and called on Guenzburg. By that time the barons Guenzburg were in a state of material decline, although outwardly all the splendor of the renowned millionaire family was still maintained. David Guenzburg was then the eldest and most eminent representative of his family. As is well known, he was one of the more scholarly orientalists. He published quite a number of monographs in the field of Jewish history in the eastern countries. He also wrote articles for the Russian-language Jewish periodical *Voskhod.*

When I arrived, the servants conducted me into one of Guenzburg's large reading rooms, where the baron sat at a large desk. David Guenzburg, who had previously been informed that I would be coming in connection with a business matter, received me very courteously. He asked me several personal questions and then requested that I lay out before him my "credo" of Jewish education. In broad strokes, I outlined the tasks confronting the *Mefitsei Haskalah* school system, how it was meant to differ from the government's Jewish schools and run-of-the-mill private schools, which offered only a smattering of Jewish studies. It was imperative to inculcate an integral sense of Jewishness in the children, based on a knowledge of the Hebrew language and Jewish history. It was important to introduce the study of the Bible from the original text and to follow other principles then prevalent among nationalist Jewish intellectuals.

When I mentioned study of the Bible, Guenzburg interrupted me, "Yes, that is all very fine. But tell me, kind sir, how will the present and future generations educated in *Mefitsei Haskalah* schools differ from the Karaites, who accept only the Bible and reject all the other sources of our deep-rooted Jewishness? No, not only the Bible must be taught in our schools. The Talmud must be introduced, and a considerable number of hours assigned to it. Our Jewishness is not 'Judaism,' for everything that ends in 'ism' is worthless. Socialism, Zionism, Bundism, other 'isms'—none of these is the way, nor is it in the spirit of the people of Israel. Even the concept of Judaism is faulty. Jewishness—that is good." In the same vein, Guenzburg elaborated on his theory of teaching the Talmud in Jewish elementary schools, so as to avoid being like the Karaites.

For the first time in my life, I saw before me a deeply orthodox Jew with extensive secular erudition, a man who had grown up in the totally non-Jewish environment of St. Petersburg and had all the convictions of a *rosh-yeshiva* in Wołożyn. Although I was aware that the baron's opinion was not applicable to the circles of the *Mefitsei Haskalah,* I did not want to cause him grief by explaining the impossibility of initiating such a curriculum in the elementary schools. At the conclusion of our conversation, Guenzburg wished me success and we parted in friendly fashion.

The end of the school year was not far off, and the Ratner gymnasium in Gomel' declined to release me. It was therefore agreed that I would begin the task of traveling to the various schools at the start of the following school year. Fialkov continued to carry out some of the administrative functions of the position until I was to take over. For family reasons, however, I was unable to begin working for the *Mefitsei Haskalah* school system, and I continued at the gymnasium in Gomel'. Fialkov maintained his close connection with the *Mefitsei Haskalah* schools, except during the years he was abroad completing his studies in pedagogy.

World War I produced a stream of Jewish refugees from the western provinces of Russia, presenting the *Mefitsei Haskalah* with the very pressing problem of establishing orphanages for young refugees. The teaching methods and curricula of these institutions had to be altered in order to accommodate Yiddish, the refugees' vernacular. Fialkov, too, was obliged to bow to the demands of the period. (It should be said, however, that similar orphanages were also established where Hebrew was the language of instruction.)

Fialkov's name will certainly occupy a prominent place in the history of Jewish education in tsarist Russia.

4

HIRSH LEKERT
AND
HIS TIMES

In 1901, the tsar's minister of the interior, Viacheslav von Plehve, decided to send the former mayor of St. Petersburg, Victor von Wahl, to Vilna to be its governor.[1] A relative of Baltic aristocracy, von Wahl was a notorious alcoholic, a libertine, and, moreover, a political cynic. While he was in office in St. Petersburg, a strike broke out in the large La Ferme tobacco factory. When thousands of women who worked in the factory complained about their starvation wages, he advised them to augment their earnings by walking the streets.

More than once von Wahl was discovered drunk, lying under the table of a St. Petersburg or Moscow restaurant frequented by the aristocracy. Before serving as governor of Vilna, von Wahl occupied the high position of director of the Smolny Institute, an exclusive school for women of the aristocracy. This was typical of the mentality of the tsarist regime. No one was better suited to educate the future ladies-in-waiting in the image of Virubova, the mistress of Rasputin.

Von Wahl arrived in Vilna in the autumn of 1901. The Bund greeted him with a protest demonstration. The governor summoned Police Chief Nazimov and other high police officials. He railed at them for permitting "such acts" and for their inability to discover the perpetrators and anti-government "criminals." He would no longer tolerate any such thing.

Von Wahl also called in the representatives of the Jewish community and chastised them about their "wanton and godless young people." One of the Jewish representatives was Shepsl Klachko. Formerly an official rabbi in Vilna, he now was advisor on Jewish affairs to the governor. Hoping to win favor with von Wahl, Klachko declared that the Jews had no connection with the revolutionaries. There were some rascally Jewish youths who would, he said, be "calmed down" with a whipping. Word of this exchange became known in the city. The next issue of *Klasn-kamf* (Class Struggle) printed a feature in which Klachko and Governor von Wahl were depicted, armed with switches and shouting, "How do you do!" to each other as they stood to bless the new moon.

I knew Klachko personally; he was head of the Vilna religious community and also one of the city's more affluent, "respectable" Jews. He appeared to be a well-fed man, had a carefully combed beard and wore gold-rimmed spectacles. His manner of speaking was authoritative and assured. Klachko obviously did not doubt that truth dripped from his words, and he believed that the government would be kinder to the Jews were it not for the young "rascals." Nevertheless, I cannot believe that von Wahl needed Klachko's advice to resort to whippings, assuming that Klachko actually offered it to him. German barons—von Minn, von Riman, Rennenkampf, and other "pacificators"—used these practices without benefit of Jewish counsel in 1905 and 1906, when they liquidated the first Russian Revolution.

In any event, the police started rumors that there would be whippings if the "Jewish scoundrels" dared to demonstrate in the streets on May Day. This posed a difficult dilemma for Vilna's Bundists. On the one hand, the local organization had been considerably weakened by numerous arrests, leaving them with few active and responsible members. A demonstration would result in many further losses. The severe oppression that would inevitably come with such a demonstration would frighten the masses. There was a danger that the movement would be weakened even further.

On the other hand, there was the argument in favor of a demonstration: should it not be held, the insolence of the local satraps would increase, constituting a victory for the government's politics of terror, and the labor movement would lose its dynamism. Revolutionaries ought not to be intimidated by oppression. The resolution to organize a demonstration was passed by a small majority.

The participation of Polish and Lithuanian workers in a general strike on May Day was out of the question. Deliberate revolutionary activity on their part was still negligible. Nevertheless, their leaders did promise to attend the demonstration after work. That was very important, because a demonstration by Jewish workers alone would not suggest, to either the general population or the government, a mass movement that was international in nature.

Therefore, the demonstration was called for seven o'clock in the evening, when the non-Jewish workers would be returning from work. Very few Jewish laborers went to work on May Day. By police order, the gates to all houses were kept locked, and building watchmen were to stand guard, cudgels in hand, beside their gates. Cossacks and police hid in courtyards, ready to disperse any gathering in the streets. There was very little traffic. "Respectable" people, fearing for their safety, made every effort to avoid being seen outdoors.

In the evening, close to seven o'clock, the streets began to fill up with young Jewish men and women in holiday garb. Most of the side streets leading to German Street, which had been designated as the center of the May Day demonstration, were closed by police patrols. Nevertheless, small groups of people managed to steal into German Street by way of Rudnitskaia, Broad, Trokskaia, and Dominican Streets, which could not be sealed off completely.

Seven o'clock passed, then seven-thirty, then seven forty-five. Everyone was waiting for the Polish workers, but they did not arrive. This caused some nervousness among the Jewish workers. From the organizers came word that the demonstration had been canceled. This order, however, which was being passed from mouth to mouth, failed to reach some of those assembled. When a small group of non-Jewish workers appeared outside Shirvint's Pharmacy, the Jewish flag bearers and those who were to accompany them stepped off the sidewalk into the street.

Under their coats they had hidden banners and sections of poles for displaying them, which were to be screwed together. The demonstrators had practiced assembling the flags in seconds, creating a fluttering display of slogans. When the crowd saw the red banners appear it was electrified. Loud cheers rang out: "Long live May Day! Down with autocracy!" At the same moment, however, hordes of policemen and Cossacks spilled out of the courtyards. Police Chief Nazimov, riding in a convoy of police officials, issued a brief command to all "armed forces": "Beat the scoundrels!" By then, the order was practically superfluous, for the Cossacks, the policemen, and the building guards, armed with cudgels, were already at work. Like wild animals, they leapt at the flag bearers and all the young men and women in the street. The bloodied flagbearers fell to the ground, their banners torn to shreds.

The demonstrators were chased through the streets and beaten mercilessly. Many were bleeding from head wounds, others suffered injured and dislocated limbs. Most of the demonstrators scattered, only the wounded being left behind. More than thirty Jewish workers were arrested, but only two or three non-Jews.

All those arrested were whipped again at the police station and subjected to the notorious Russian practice of being struck in the teeth. On his way to the theater, Governor von Wahl stopped at the police station to see the captured insurgents with his own eyes. His first question was, "Who are the flagbearers?" Botvinik and Feinberg, both badly beaten, were pointed out. Von Wahl ordered them confined in a separate cell and given one hundred lashes, while all others were to receive fifty.

The same evening as this large demonstration on German Street, a smaller but equally impressive one, in which I participated, took place at the Vilna municipal theater, where Sudermann's *Heimat* was being performed.[2] By agreement with a committee from the Bund, some members of the intelligentsia decided to distribute May Day notices inside the theater. The performance was a benefit for a famous actor, and it was known that von Wahl would be at the theater in the governor's box. The audience consisted in the main of senior government officials and their wives. That same day, small slips of paper bearing the message (in Russian), "May Day is the workers' holiday! Down with autocracy!" were dropped into corner postal boxes and into private mailboxes. Some were also enclosed in envelopes and addressed to the more important officials. The aforementioned members of the intelligentsia also received some of these notices.

The group, consisting of about ten men, seated themselves in different sections of the theater gallery among their comrades. They had decided in advance that, at the beginning of the second act, some would toss the proclamations into the audience, others would throw them into the governor's box. Immediately after the first intermission, when the curtain was raised and all eyes were fixed on the stage, a shower of snow-white notices fluttered down on the audience. Several fell into von Wahl's box. The audience stirred as the ladies and gentlemen stooped to pick up the papers, believing that they carried greetings to the actors. Discovering the slogan, "Down with autocracy!" they angrily tossed the papers back onto the floor. A few rose hurriedly to leave the theater. Von Wahl was infuriated. He summoned the chief of police at once and whispered a command. The men who had tossed the proclamations had disappeared immediately, while the police were in a state of confusion and did nothing to find the "criminals." A few minutes later, however, the exit from the gallery was blocked and several policemen were stationed at the door.

The performance was not interrupted. We sat and waited to see what would happen, keeping our eyes on the stage. The guardians of the law, however, had their eyes on us. From time to time a member of our group was tapped on the shoulder and escorted to the staircase, where he was searched.

If his face and dress suggested that he might be one of the intelligentsia, he was ordered to step to the side and wait. He was not to return to the theater, nor was he to leave. Finally, it was my turn.

"Hey, you!" said a policeman's voice beside me. I stood up and said angrily, "I'll ask you not to address me that way!" But the policeman pushed me so hard that I fell. "Don't you dare hit me!" I shouted. Just then Snitko, the chief officer of the first police district, approached. He was famous for the beating he administered with his own hands to people under arrest, especially laborers apprehended for "politics." Snitko asked me to identify myself. I answered that I was a teacher in a government school. To this he replied, "I'll teach you!" But I was not harassed after that, except that I was searched. All my pockets were turned inside out. I was thoroughly frisked, then ordered to stand with the other suspects. We protested against being detained, since nothing was found on any one of us, but the police continued to follow their procedures. Our names and addresses were recorded and an order was issued on the spot that our residences be searched. The steps were crowded with police.

Among those who had been detained were a number of people who had nothing to do with the affair. They stood there, pale and frightened. Snitko turned to one of them and asked, "How did you get in with these bastards?" The man began to cry. "Really, what could I have to do with these fellows! You know me, Mr. Commissioner!" Snitko took pity on this acquaintance and commanded that he be let go. The man was so grateful he kissed Snitko's hand. Snitko pushed him aside contemptuously, saying, "Go to the devil!"

After combing the entire gallery the police held some thirteen or fourteen people, three of them women. Nearly half of them were actually in no way involved in the affair. When the theater audience had departed we were led downstairs to the street, which by then was empty. The policemen surrounded us with swords drawn and led us to the police station, where the demonstrators from German Street were already being held. We were put into a stuffy cell already filled with drunkards, street hooligans, and recently arrested offenders, whom the police had yet to take off to prison. Our new "comrades" cleared a bench for us, but there was not room enough for all of us to sit. We reckoned that we could make the best use of the one bench at our disposal by taking turns sleeping on it, each taking a nap of twenty minutes and then getting up. Anyone who did not get up promptly was simply pulled off by his feet, and then someone else lay down.

And so we passed the night. At six o'clock in the morning, people were let out one by one to the yard to relieve themselves. The overseer of the detention house was an elderly policeman, decorated for his military service under Tsar Nicholas. He beat and tormented the prisoners, giving a shove to anyone slow to return from the yard. We tried talking to this "grandfather," as we addressed him, about easing up on us. At first he would not listen, but we found a way to his heart with some cigarettes and silver coins. He became somewhat kinder to us, stopped calling us *zhidy* and the like.

At eight o'clock, we saw through the window that an armed fire brigade had entered the police station yard. We became very alarmed. Later we learned that this terrible wagon had been paraded through the main streets of the city in order to frighten the populace. At nine o'clock, Snitko and four or five policemen rushed into our cell and began to search everyone. In the cell with us was a young student, the son of a wealthy tobacco manufacturer, who had nothing to do with the affair. The young man turned pale and lost his composure completely. Snitko knew him personally and, apparently, had profited not a little from the father's business. With trepidation, the student asked what would become of us. Snitko replied, "You personally will not be touched." The student asked for a cigarette. Snitko immediately held out his cigarette case: "Help yourself."

When the search ended, Governor von Wahl burst into the cell, accompanied by several high police officials. Von Wahl was short, fat, and had a red face. He addressed us straight-away: "Thank you for the May Day greetings. My greetings are coming soon." Then, noticing the student, von Wahl snarled at him, "I'll show you how to rebel!"

A few minutes later we could hear terrible howls. They had begun to punish the demonstrators who had been arrested on the streets. They were being held in another corridor. We could not see what was taking place there, but we could hear, and our blood froze. Until then we could not believe that such treatment was possible, and yet it was happening. Some of us wrung our hands, tore at our hair, wept. Others seemed to have been turned to stone.

We felt helpless and powerless. We later learned that von Wahl himself had been present at the beginning of the exercise, but that he then rode off. The firemen were administering the torture. They would burst into a cell and forcibly drag out a victim. Then one of them would sit on the victim's head, another on his legs, and the third would start beating him with all his might. Anyone who fainted would be doused with water and the punishment would continue.

One of the members of the intelligentsia was not beaten. Instead, he was forced to watch as his comrades were tortured. A policeman with a lance stood to each side of the "spectator," to make certain his head did not droop or turn away. The municipal doctor, Mikhailov, was present as a representative of the medical profession. The entire "job" lasted exactly an hour, although it seemed like an eternity. About twenty men and one woman were beaten at that time, we were later told. They had been struck and beaten until they bled, and many were ill afterwards. No one from our cell had been involved.

The shattering news spread with lightning speed through the city. At about ten or eleven o'clock, the relatives of those arrested began to arrive in the courtyard of the police station, their faces desperate and teary. The police drove them away at once. A short time later, however, acquaintances of ours who had come to find out what had happened were allowed to approach our windows for the price of a few coins. There was no limit to their despair. Some asked what to do, how to react. We were the least able to provide them with answers.

People began to bring us food. We lowered pieces of cord from the second floor, packages of food and cigarettes were tied on down below, and we pulled them up. Although many of us had not eaten anything for an entire twenty-four hours, we hardly touched the food that first day. We gave most of it to the guards, to ensure that they would not prevent us from conversing with our visitors. For the sake of appearances, the guards chased them away from the yard, but a short time later they would be there again to talk and deliver packages to us.

We were transferred to a larger cell, where there were no strangers. This made us feel better. The cell was damp, but sawdust was brought in and scattered over the floor. The infamous waste bucket gave off a very strong odor, fouling the air, but we soon found a remedy for that as well. A pharmacist who was in our group asked his pharmacy to send us large quantities of potassium permanganate. We poured heaps of that into the bucket, eliminating the odor almost instantly.

On the third day, several suspicious characters, allegedly other prisoners, were sent in to snoop about and gather information. However, we realized immediately what they were after. They did not feel at ease with us and asked to be put in a different cell. Of course, their request was granted. At the same time, we did what we could to see to it that the few outsiders who had fallen in with us by chance would conduct themselves properly at our hearing and not offer any new information. Our efforts were successful, although several of them continued to assert that they would have been better off if they had been struck by lightning instead of attending the theater that accursed evening.

On about the fourth day, a commander of a gendarmerie company came into our cell, searched us, and went away. A short time later each of us was called out separately to him. We could see through a hole in the door that many pairs of eyes were trying to recognize us, especially those of a non-Jewish woman who approached the door several times. The commander enacted the following comedy with this woman, apparently either a hired informer or a volunteer, who had been in the theater gallery when the proclamations had been tossed. The hearing took place in the living quarters of a junior police official, located in the station house. The woman was to all appearances the housekeeper. Each time one of us was brought in, the woman would leave the room, but during the course of the hearing she would walk through several times, pretending to look for her keys or something else. The commander would say, "Forgive us, my dear; we are disturbing you. Well, we won't be long. We'll vacate this room soon." The "housekeeper" would give some covert signal to indicate whether or not the person brought in was one of those who had tossed the notices. She would then smile and reply to the "welcome guest," "That's all right, that's all right. You are not disturbing me."

When I was brought in the commander stood up, bowed politely and offered me a chair. He asked how I felt and held out his cigarette case. "How did you, Mr. Abramowicz, fall in with this bunch? And why would you choose to sit in the gallery?" I replied that I went to the theater often and that, since I had only limited means, I could not afford expensive seats, so I had no choice but to go up to the gallery. The commander faltered: "Well, I certainly did not mean to blame you for that or to correct you. You are an intelligent person and certainly know what you have to do. When I was a student in St. Petersburg I always sat in the gallery." That said, he began a long account of the "happy years of his youth." He also asked the "housekeeper" to bring me a glass of tea. I maintained a reserved attitude in the face of his friendliness, refused the cigarettes and the tea, and stated that I wanted to be released at once because I had no idea why I was being held.

"Oh, yes, Mr. Abramowicz, do you, perhaps, know who threw that trash in the theater? It was so foolish. Do they really expect to frighten the government with little pieces of paper? I understand that you probably did not do it, but we cannot release anyone until we know who the guilty party is. As soon as we know, we'll let all the innocent people go." I replied that I knew nothing, whereupon he dismissed me quite coldly and gave orders that someone else be sent in.

The hearing lasted for several days. Similar conversations were held with almost everyone. Apparently, the woman singled out three people as suspects, and about eight days later all of us, except these three, were set free. Later on, they (Alfes, Rekhes, and his wife) were sent to Siberia for several years, despite the fact that the people who actually tossed the notices had disappeared from the gallery before the police realized what was happening.

For me, the story had something of a sequel. In those days, a teacher employed in a government school had to be clear of even the slightest suspicion of involvement in political activity. Learning of my arrest, the supervisor of education ordered a full investigation. After my release the director of public schools summoned me. I walked into a large hall in which were seated all the school inspectors, headed by the director, an old man in his seventies, with a long white beard and the face of a patriarch. The "patriarch" began a long interrogation about what had taken place in the theater, how, and why. I explained that the police had addressed me rudely and shoved me. The director apparently wanted to know how the sacrilegious slips of paper could have been scattered throughout the theater from the gallery. The old man took two packs of cards, placed a small table atop a large one and a chair on top of that. Then he himself climbed up onto the chair and tossed the cards from on high. The cards fell at the feet of the simulated theater audience, the inspectors. The latter agreed that anything tossed from up above would fall below. No guilt on my part was established in the hearing. On the matter of my having been insulted by the police, the director proposed that I write it up in a report and present it to him. Nothing came of it, except that half a year later, it was found "expedient" to transfer me to a small provincial town in order to remove me from "harmful influences."

The entire Jewish population was very disturbed about the punishment inflicted on the German Street demonstrators. Although the bourgeoisie maintained that "the loafers deserve a whipping," they saw it as an anti-Semitic act, since the brutality was inflicted almost exclusively on Jewish workers. One couldn't be sure of one's own skin; if one is Jewish, anything can happen. Among the community's more-or-less democratic elements, hatred of the government increased. Many doctors resolved not to greet Dr. Mikhailov. An especially strong desire for revenge prevailed among Vilna's working-class Jews. They were all convinced that this terrible mark of shame must be washed away with blood. The Bund had always been opposed to acts of terror, which weaken the activity of the masses and place the burden of the struggle on the individual. In this instance, however, the masses categorically refused to consider the organization's position and wanted one thing only: to settle the account with von Wahl.

A terrorist act must happen spontaneously. Many workers, singly or in groups, racked their brains over how to carry out an attempt on von Wahl's life. They began to observe when and where the governor went out. Opposite his residence there was a small park with benches. The police noticed that several people were sitting there for a very long time. They were arrested, the police guard in the park was augmented, and several of the benches were removed. A plan was proposed to carry out the assault in the cathedral on 6 May, when prayers would be offered in honor of Tsar Nicholas II on his name day. The governor and all the more important officials were expected to be present. All secondary school students were also required to attend. Someone would dress as a student and could thus easily enter the cathedral,

A funeral for revolutionaries who were the victims of tsarist oppression. Vilna, 1905. Courtesy of the YIVO Archives.

approach von Wahl and shoot him. The necessary clothing was sought, but for reasons unknown, the plan fell through. Instead, the attempt on von Wahl's life took place with almost no preparation, as he was leaving the circus at about eleven o'clock at night.

This attack occurred on the same day, 6 May. Despite the fact that the governor was accompanied by many guards, a shoemaker named Lekert fired two shots at the governor, wounding him slightly in the leg. The governor fell; he was lifted up immediately and brought to his home. Lekert was arrested on the spot. He was brutally beaten and then taken to prison under heavy guard. Suddenly, everyone felt satisfied but also, at the same time, disappointed, because the attempt had not succeeded. The Jewish bourgeoisie complained, "Why a Jew?" Everyone—not only in Jewish circles, but even among the bureaucracy—was talking about what had happened. Indeed, von Wahl's replacement, Vice-Governor Baliasny, found it necessary to send a top-secret dispatch to St. Petersburg that "Vilna is agitated." But St. Petersburg, especially Minister of the Interior von Plehve, insisted that Lekert be tried in accordance with wartime law. When the telegraphic agency distributed this report, everyone understood that a death sentence was a foregone conclusion and that the trial would be a farce. Still, there was a glimmer of hope.

The court, however, issued a briefly worded sentence: death by hanging. The appeal was denied. On the evening of 28 May, the military authorities notified the *rabiner* to be ready that night. The *rabiner* was ill, but his refusal to be present during the execution would have been considered an anti-government action. Someone was found to represent the *rabiner*. That same night, several regiments from the local garrison were stationed on the large, sandy military fields in Snipiszki, where a gallows had been erected. Lekert's corpse was thrown into a grave that had been prepared in advance and covered with sand.* Several regiments were marched across the area in order to erase any trace of the grave.

The impact of Lekert's death was profound. People could not sleep for nights. It must be borne in mind that death sentences were very rare at the time. The telegraphic agency's report that the sentence had been carried out informed all of Russia. Almost simultaneously it was announced that, by order of the tsar, von Wahl received a decoration and, somewhat later, a higher office. Without a doubt, the entire affair added considerable fuel to the fire that erupted in 1905.

---

*During the brief period of Soviet rule in Vilna, attempts were made to locate the grave, but they were unsuccessful.

5

ANNA LIFSHITS

Anna Lifshits, the heroine of the mutiny on the battleship *Potemkin* in the port of Odessa in 1905, is all but forgotten.[1] Her name is mentioned in some of the memoirs published by revolutionaries who were active in the first decade of this century. Her file in the archives of the former Russian police department must be quite extensive, but this is not available to us. I should like to record here what I remember about her from 1902, when she was in Vilna. We lived in the same building at Zawalna 66. It was a new building, consisting of about fifty apartments, with entrances from the street. Each apartment had a small hallway with a small spare room, which was usually rented to an unmarried man or woman.

I first met Anna in the company of two of my acquaintances: Arye Brumberg ("Ari") and Leivik Zakheim ("Dmitri"). Brumberg had been a student at the same government school I attended, but was several years ahead of me there, being three or four years older. At the time, he and Zakheim were studying at the chemical-technical school in Vilna, and both were members of the Bund. Although I belonged to one of its small propaganda groups, I was not officially a member of the organization. I did perform certain tasks that the Bund assigned to students who were enthralled by the new revolutionary spirit of the times. I was eager to absorb as much knowledge as possible, studying sociology, philosophy, history and languages with youthful fervor.

As my command of German was not perfect, Brumberg and Zakheim recommended their friend Anna Lifshits as a tutor to help me improve my style and pronunciation. I believe Anna had just come from Berne,

Switzerland, where she was a student at the university. At the time, Brumberg, Zakheim, and Anna were all active in the Bund. They would give me illegal literature and proclamations. Several copies of *Posledniia Izvestiia,* which was published regularly by the foreign central committee of the Bund, were sent to my address from abroad. I was assigned two small groups of workers, whom I was to instruct secretly, on a regular basis, in political economy and cultural history and to provide general enlightenment. There were ten to twelve people in each group. We would meet once a week, usually on Saturday afternoons, somewhere on Novgorod Street in the workers' district or in an attic room in some other poor Jewish neighborhood, and there the "enlightener" would give his lessons and lead discussions.

The propagandists and lecturers met once every week or two to discuss and coordinate their educational work, present reports, and so on. During the summer months, these meetings were held in the Zverinets, Zakrety, or Belmont Woods. During the winter, we met in the home of a working-class member of the organization or, not infrequently, in a bourgeois home where there were "sympathetic" young people, usually students. One such home was that of the leather manufacturer Surovich, on Łukiszki Street. During the summer, when the hosts were away from the city, small illegal gatherings of Bundist activists would take place in their apartment.

Many bourgeois families went to country homes and spas in the summer. Rather than leave their city residences at the mercy of Vilna's notorious thieves, the owners had some young person stay there, usually a university student, who was in most cases under the Bund's influence. These young people did not have to pay rent. Bundist groups often met in these empty apartments. I, too, stayed in one of the many "free" summer residences that were available in Vilna when I came there during summer vacations. It was the home of Fayvl Bentselevich Getz, a government-appointed authority on Jewish affairs, who worked for the director of education.

During the winter of 1901–1902, I often met with Brumberg, Zakheim and Anna Lifshits to discuss underground literature, especially the *Posledniia Izvestiia.* We talked a great deal about Russian periodicals that were filled with covert revolutionary propaganda and about Bernsteinism ("revisionism"), which was detested by the young members of the Social-Democratic Party.[2]

We read Plekhanov's anti-populist book, which repudiated the members of the Russian Populist Party (*Narodniki*) who followed Mikhailovskii.[3] We talked of the terrorist movement. Anna defended resorting to the use of terror in certain instances. She was also convinced of the need for an armed uprising against the monarchy. Later, in Odessa, when she was the principal propagandist among the crew of the battleship *Potemkin,* she tried to put these ideas into practice.

We spoke Russian with each other, as was then the custom. During our German-language lessons, Anna and I spoke in German. She spoke both languages flawlessly. In those days, German was the preferred foreign language among students and they studied it assiduously. At the time, young people virtually idolized the German social-democratic movement. The Social-Democratic Party flourished with such leaders as Bebel, Liebknecht, Palmar, Singer, Mehring, and others. People wanted to (and actually did) read their works, especially Bebel's *Die Frau und der Sozialismus* (Woman and Socialism) in the original.[4]

Anna was an excellent teacher. Since I read German almost effortlessly, but gave a Yiddish cast to the construction of my sentences (both oral and written), she had me write short essays on some of the hundreds of paperback editions of the German classics. She read and corrected my work and would explain the rules of German grammar in a simple, understandable way. I would discuss the week's events, retell the contents of a book I had read, or simply converse with her. My progress in learning German really surprised me. In large part, it was due to my youthful (and, naturally, subconscious) desire to prove myself worthy in the eyes of an attractive young woman who had studied abroad.

I had lessons with Anna twice weekly, but since we were neighbors I would frequently drop by her place for a chat. Except for my German lesson we spoke to each other in Russian. I made use of my German during the German occupation in World War I, but after the winter of 1901–1902 I never studied the language further.

Anna came from a middle-class family in the Lithuanian city of Ponevezh. She looked like a typical Jewish girl: black hair, dark eyes, a pale complexion. Her eyes had the sparkle of a prodigy's. She was not pretty, but she had a sharp mind, and her eyes had a magnetic power. Therefore, it was not surprising that our two mutual friends, Ari and Dmitri, who visited her often, both fell in love with her at the same time. Their friendly relationship gave way to a pure (in every respect) love. Inevitably, such a triangle had to lead to a personal drama, a rift in their triple alliance and a conflict between the two young men. Ari emerged victorious: Anna married him. Eventually, I lost track of these friends. I later learned that Anna's union with Ari was short-lived, and they parted company.

The name of Anna Lifshits resurfaced during the summer of 1905, in connection with the mutiny on the *Potemkin,* which she helped to organize. The sailors on board the *Potemkin* tossed several hated tsarist naval officers overboard. Lieutenant Schmidt took over command of the crew. Several salvos of cannon fire were directed from the ship at the city of Odessa, where the military's anti-revolutionary forces were concentrated. The *Potemkin* sailed into the Romanian port city of Constanţa, but it was not able to remain independent for long. The mutiny was suppressed; Schmidt was arrested and sentenced to death. The sentence was carried out at Fort Ochakov on the Black Sea. Schmidt's execution and, indeed, the entire *Potemkin* event profoundly agitated all of Russia during the summer and early fall preceding the October Revolution of 1905.

When the uprising failed Anna Lifshits disappeared. I learned subsequently that she died in 1925. During the latter half of the 1930s, Ari Brumberg settled in Vilna. He had remarried and was practicing law. He was apparently no longer connected with the Bund. Between the two world wars, Leivik Zakheim was a director of the cooperative EKOPO bank in Vilna. Several years before the start of World War II he became ill and ceased to be active in the public arena. Brumberg perished in Ponary in 1941.[5] Zakheim's fate is unknown to me.

6

IN TSARIST JAILS

Most of the Jews in Ukraine, especially those in the provinces of Yekaterinoslav and Kherson, emigrated there from the Lithuanian and Belorussian regions at the beginning of the nineteenth century, when fantastic stories about Ukraine's riches were widely circulated. Over time the Jewish population of the region developed into a community distinguished from Lithuanian Jewry in both custom and dialect.

Ukrainian Jews were considerably better off economically than those in the poor districts of Lithuania and Belorussia. The peasants were richer and better fed. Ukraine's black soil nurtured all its inhabitants, including the Jews, most of whom were engaged in trade. There were fewer Jewish artisans and laborers than there were in Lithuania and Belorussia. This may explain why, at the beginning of the twentieth century, the revolutionary movement was much more limited in Ukraine than in northwestern Russia. Nevertheless, in the years just before the storm of 1905, political agitation began to be noticed among Ukrainian Jewry's youth and its small number of workers. The Bund intensified its activity, as did the various Zionist labor organizations (Sejmists, Zionist Socialists, Poalei Zion, etc.). There were also Jewish anarchist groups.

Most of the promulgators of revolutionary ideas were young people who had come to Ukraine for one reason or another. In 1904, I moved from the Vilna area to Pavlograd, a district town of Yekaterinoslav province, where I was appointed assistant principal of a Jewish government school. The principal was a Russian. A colleague of mine from Vilna, somewhat younger than I, was already teaching at the school. He and I began to distribute Yiddish literature—some fifteen to twenty copies of the Vilna newspaper, *Di folkstsaytung*. Our "masses" consisted of several tailor's apprentices, a few store clerks, university students, and other young people who had a feeling for Yiddish language and books. We also issued a sort of proclamation (in Russian) in the name of the Bund. The poet Moshe Bassin was one of our fellow activists and newspaper distributors.[1]

In 1906–1907 I was appointed assistant principal of the Jewish government school in Yekaterinoslav. At the same time, I was enrolled as a law student at the University of Kharkov. In October 1906, the Bund called a regional conference in Yekaterinoslav, and I was invited to be a guest.

I arrived at the designated address and rang the bell several times. No one answered. I rang again, louder and louder. Suddenly, the door burst open. A policeman and a military guardsman appeared before me. Their revolvers were aimed at me as they shouted, "Hands up!"

They pushed me inside. Several policemen, investigators, and secret police agents were there. They searched the place thoroughly, turned it upside down, even tore up the floor boards. Standing to one side were some seven or eight "delegates" representing various organizations in the province. Among them was the head of the conference, Nehemiah, acting calm and determined.* The police guarded the group with drawn swords. Two of the "dicks" proceeded to empty my pockets, confiscating everything inside. When they saw that we had no weapons, they told us to drop our hands. They proceeded to ask each of us for his address, occupation, and reason for coming to the place. I said that I had come to rent a room; there was a vacancy notice at the street entrance. Later on I was told that neighbors who had been standing on the street had signaled to me not to ring the bell, but I hadn't noticed this. Thanks to those signals, however, several of the delegates did succeed in escaping arrest.

The investigation continued until evening, when a heavy guard was summoned to escort us to the police station. Once outside, we were surrounded by several dozen armed Cossacks and policemen with guns at the ready. It was a chilly autumn evening. With a few shoves in the back, we were put in a cold cell with a cement floor; it was empty except for a few stools. Even the infamous *parasha* (the bucket for human waste) was missing. To relieve ourselves we had to ask the guard for permission to

---

*His last name was Fichman. He came from Kishinev (in southern Russia) or its environs. His appearance was very Jewish. He was dark skinned and had large, black, blazing eyes. The Central Committee of the Bund had assigned Nehemiah to direct its work in the region of Yekaterinoslav. He had all the attributes of a responsible worker in an underground movement. He was intelligent, well read, and a forceful speaker who spoke Yiddish well. It was, however, frequently necessary to use Russian, because in this region the vernacular of the younger generation, even those who were laborers, was Russian.

go into the corridor. The guard was not particularly polite and brushed off our requests by making insulting remarks about our mothers. We spent the entire night in the cold; there was no thought of sleeping.

Nevertheless, Nehemiah told us what he had intended to say at the conference: we should not be intimidated by the reactionaries. It was imperative to overcome and to endure. The Bund needed to attract Jewish workers, who had special cultural and national needs. Of course we had no knowledge of what awaited us—perhaps long years of imprisonment and exile. In that case, we ought to use the time to further our knowledge. In the short time we were together, Nehemiah proved to be not only a first-class political activist but also a good and devoted comrade who endeavored to keep our group together. Although he was twenty-six to twenty-eight years old, he was the oldest among us.

That same night we were transferred, under even heavier guard, to the main prison of the province. Before we entered we were searched again, but this time we were not pushed nor were our mothers insulted. Apparently, we were now being taken seriously. We were led into a large common cell holding several hundred prisoners, most of them criminals, although there were also a number of "political" detainees. Our group attempted to find cots that were next to each other, but without success. On one side of me was a criminal prisoner; on the other was a "political," a Pole.

The Polish political prisoners had been brought from Aleksandrovsk, a large railroad junction en route to the Crimea. Most of the men were middle-aged. Employed in the railroad workshops, they had gone on strike in October 1905. Perhaps one of them had held up a red flag or, in the general excitement, had called out, "Down with the autocracy!" Now, however, they appeared to regret the whole affair. My neighbor said to me, "What do you want from us? We were making a good living. We don't want to be drawn into the revolution." The rest of them said the same thing. And, indeed, they were released several weeks later.

My neighbor on the right, however, the criminal, considered himself a revolutionary. He criticized the tsar and the ministers; he said they should all be shot: they tormented the poor and showered themselves with gold. As a rule, the criminals wanted to be considered the equal of the political prisoners. Nevertheless, this did not deter my neighbor from taking a five-ruble gold piece that I had sewn into my jacket. Although I kept the coat tucked under my head, the gold piece disappeared. My neighbor must have been quite a specialist in picking pockets. To get the coin he had to remove the jacket from under my head, remove the coin from the jacket, then resew the opening and return the jacket to its place without my noticing anything. To this day I cannot understand how he was able to do it all so skillfully.

The air in the cell was so dense you could "cut it with a knife." We were permitted to use the toilet only once a day, in the morning. During the rest of the day and at night one was obliged to use the *parasha,* in the presence of everyone. Right from the start, we were attacked by vermin. Once a week the prisoners were conducted to the jail bathhouse. The day was considered a holiday; for a little while, at least, it freed us from filth and pests.

Morning and evening our food was a piece of dark bread and some hot water. At midday there was soup made of chopped cabbage, beets, turnips, and potatoes. Occasionally, it also contained barley and, several times a week, pieces of ox head. The soup was served in large tin bowls that each served ten people. In the hope of obtaining a piece of potato, a bit of barley or a bone, the prisoners would scrape the bottom of the bowl with their spoons. Not infrequently, what they found was a cow's eye. I simply could not get used to those common bowls, in which ten persons stirred the soup greedily, put their spoons into their mouths and then back into the bowl. For three or four days, I was unable to so much as take a taste of anything.

Nehemiah finally notified the officer in charge of the prisoners, the officer notified the doctor, and a special diet was ordered from the kitchen for me. The meal consisted of a chopped meat patty (containing more bread than meat) and some cooked buckwheat. In place of the soup, the doctor also prescribed a glass of boiling water with a lump of sugar.

Meanwhile, something occurred in the prison that upset both the entire administration and all the inmates. Adjacent to the prison yard there was a whiskey distillery that belonged to the excise authority. Several hundred people, many of them women, were employed there. One of the distillery buildings, a one-story structure with a nearly flat roof, stood close to the prison wall. Every morning the prisoners were let out by groups to walk for twenty to thirty minutes in the prison yard next to the distillery. From a certain point it was possible to see into the distillery courtyard.

The prison was overpopulated, for the government, having triumphed over the revolution, wanted to punish all those who had participated in the strikes. People were being arrested right and left. Because of the crowding in the prisons, the administration overlooked many things, and the guards were unable to tend to everything. This made it possible for the inmates to establish contact with the distillery workers. How this began I do not recall; perhaps through prisoners who had been released.

On their walks in the prison yard, some of the bolder prisoners took along bundles of letters which the "postmen" (who were mostly criminals) would collect while cleaning cells, corridors and other common areas. These illegal letters would be thrown over the fence into the distillery yard, and the women who worked there would see that they got to the post office. In the same manner, we would receive uncensored mail from the outside.

In time, this "post office" took on grand proportions. Entire packages would be thrown over from the outside. They contained food items, bottles of whiskey (both for the inmates and for the guards, to "soften" their hearts), as well as small saws for cutting through window bars, and various digging implements. Digging was done only at night, after a few floorboards under a cot had been removed. The soil removed was hidden under the cots or under the prisoner's pillow. Later, during their walks, the inmates surreptitiously scattered the soil in the prison yard or where building materials for prison renovation were stored. The pockets of inmates who were taken out of the prison on work details were also utilized for this purpose.

The iron prison bars had to be sawed when no one was looking. Secret surveys were conducted to find out who wanted to escape. Preference was given to those who faced a death sentence or expected to. I remember one such individual. He was involved in the murder of an official, perhaps also in expropriating private property, a widespread practice at the time. The prisoner's name was Tkachenko-Petrenko.

In stature and general appearance, Tkachenko was a giant. Even the prison guards were somewhat afraid of him. Whatever (or whomever) his hand struck was never the same again. I witnessed a demonstration of this scene during a prisoners' scheduled "walk."

One of the guards decided to intercept a package that a prisoner, out for his walk, was about to toss over the wall into the distillery yard. Tkachenko noticed this and immediately leapt at the guard, tossed him to the ground like a ball, and threw the package over the prison wall into the factory yard. The guard, unwilling to admit to his superiors that he had been bested by a prisoner, did not report the incident. Some time later, after I had been freed, I learned that Tkachenko had been hanged in prison. This courageous giant surely did not let himself be easily bound and led to the gallows.

I cannot quite recall how the escape plan was discovered. The bars in one cell had been cut. The plan called for a group of prisoners to attack a couple of guards, disarm them, tie them up, take their keys, and unlock the exit doors. Early one day a large contingent of police, Cossacks, and gendarmes suddenly burst into the larger common cells. They surrounded the prisoners and began to search their cots and personal possessions.

Naturally, they discovered the excavation and a number of weapons, along with tools for breaking and prying things open. Those found in possession of these forbidden items were confined to the dungeon. Anyone suspected of leading the "revolt" was transferred to a special penal institution. The event caused an uproar in the entire prison population, especially among those sentenced to death or serving long sentences. The prison administration also ended the distillery "postal service," thus cutting off the inmates from the outside world. In addition, a large number of arrests were made in the city.

I was sentenced to solitary confinement. Since there were not enough cells, however, each one had to house two prisoners "in solitary." The cell I was taken to was already occupied by a Polish engineer, who had been the chief of railroad workshops in Aleksandrovsk. He was accused of having encouraged the general railroad strike of October 1905 because of his attitude toward the workers. A descendant of landowners, he was generally opposed to the tsarist regime and was a very moderate liberal in his political views. He treated me with the utmost politeness. Railroad engineers received excellent salaries. His wife and other relatives in the city sent him all sorts of good things: partridge pies, the finest meats and cheeses. He would offer these to me, but I still was receiving my special prison diet of a daily meat patty and plate of barley, so I would merely taste his dishes, just to be polite.

Being in a small, separate cell had both positive and negative consequences. Sharing it with a cultured individual made it possible to maintain a minimal hygienic standard. We had almost none of the vermin that are the scourge of Russian prisons. Nor did we have to fear the various criminal types who stole everything a city person might have with him and who played nasty tricks on political prisoners. Nevertheless, constantly being cheek by jowl with a stranger in a cramped cage for humans was psychically oppressive and brought on dark moods. At one point, I fell into a deep depression. It seemed to me that I would be there forever, that I would never see my loved ones, that I was wasting my youth. I felt I was losing my mind. I began nervously pacing the three steps of our cell. Noticing my agitation, my cellmate called my name and tried to calm me. I gratefully recall his plain but logical words, which forced me back to sanity. Criminal prisoners would come by to clean the corridors and also our cells. I recall one of these men, who was about thirty years old. After the usual questions about how long he had been a prisoner, where he was from, and the like, came the inevitable question about what had brought him from the open fields of Ukraine to prison.

He told the story of his crime frankly, displaying no hint whatsoever of regret or remorse. Along with several others, he had worked for a landowner. The man reproached them for something. "We did not want to hear about it, so we grabbed him from behind, threw a rope around his neck and hanged him from a nearby tree." My cellmate and I were astounded to hear a normal person recount the cold-blooded murder so calmly. As I listened, I thought about how easy it was for anti-Semitic demagogues to incite such primitive peasants, to whom a human life is worth less than that of a bird. During the violent attacks of October 1905, pogromists in Iuzovka (in the province of Yekaterinoslav) had thrown Jewish revolutionaries, while they were still alive, into red-hot smelt furnaces.[2]

I heard many a story from the prisoners about their crimes. They were quite glad to tell them, as though such deeds were part of their way of life. Typically, most of the crimes were committed under the influence of alcohol. I do not recall any criminal prisoners in the Yekaterinoslav prison who were Jews. We did suspect one of theft, but Jews in Russia never spilt blood. There were no Jewish bandits or murderers. That was the "privilege" of non-Jews.

In those days, revolutionary sentiments were found across a wide spectrum of the population. Criminals, too, sought to play on those strings. They listened attentively to the rhetoric of the political prisoners, but they tried to use it to their own advantage, claiming that they were victims of social injustice and that their crimes were the result of such inequality. In many respects, the criminals were more radical than the political prisoners. The political terror aimed at high-level officials and, especially, at low-ranking policemen was close to the criminals' mentality of violence.

Criminal prisoners who were taken into the city on various work details gladly took our letters and deftly dropped them into mailboxes before the very eyes of the guards accompanying them. Notes without postage were usually handed off to women laborers passing by; brief gestures indicated that the messages were to be delivered. At the time, a wonderful book about the life of prisoners in penal colonies, *In the World of Outcasts,* by the poet L. Melshin (known as P. Iakubovich), had made a powerful and widespread impact in Russia.[3] There was strong sympathy for those in the penal colonies as well as for political and other kinds of prisoners. Hence almost all of our messages were delivered to the intended recipients.

The provincial prison was very crowded. Some of the prisoners were transferred to barracks surrounded by barbed-wire fences. There was no longer any point in even talking about solitary cells. Moreover, supervision of prisoners was less strict. We were permitted daily visits. Long tables stood near the prison entrance. Visitors stood along one side of the tables, the prisoners along the other, so that they saw each other and spoke face to face rather than through double layers of bars and wire mesh, as was the case in the main prison. Occasionally prisoners who wanted to escape seized an opportune moment to mix with the visitors and exit with them, while the guards looked on. All sorts of food was brought into the barracks from the outside, with almost no regulation.

My future wife, a history student, came from Odessa to see me in the hope of effecting my release. She visited the barracks almost every day. While still in Odessa, she had made an agreement with a well-known attorney and defender of political prisoners, a man named Zwilling, to take on my case. However, it never came to this. On St. Nicholas Day (6 December), which was always celebrated as a state holiday under Nicholas II, the government marked the occasion with "acts of clemency" on the part of the tsar. Amnesty was granted to several groups, among them the one that had been seized at the regional conference of the Bund. We learned of this from the newspapers, which carried lists of our names. Naturally, there was great rejoicing among those of us granted amnesty. We embraced each other, sang, and danced. That same day we were called into the office of the provincial prison, handed the belongings taken from us at the time of our arrest, and told to go wherever we chose.

The intoxicating feeling of freedom gradually subsided and life resumed its normal course. At home I found that all my possessions had been turned upside down as a result of a police search, but nothing was missing. When I returned to work at the school, the director produced an official notice from Kalabanovskii, the chief of the province's school system, barring me from resuming my duties. Kalabanovskii's wife was the provincial chair of the Soiuz Russkogo Naroda (Union of the Russian People), an organization that endorsed pogroms and was affiliated with the Black Hundreds, of which Tsar Nicholas II himself was a great friend and supporter.[4] As an important government functionary, Kalabanovskii was officially barred from belonging to any political organization, but was nonetheless a "Unionist" at heart.

He also had a personal reason to be angry at me. He had appointed me assistant principal of the school in Yekaterinoslav when the post had become vacant. It was considered quite a prize, as everyone preferred to work in a major city rather than in a provincial town. Many candidates hoped and waited for such an appointment. And suddenly, this great disappointment! His candidate was consorting with socialists, who wanted to dismiss "our beloved tsar." And so "his anger burned in him."[5] He could not forgive me for that. Although I had been granted amnesty, I had spent several months in prison. From Kalabanovskii's point of view, that was enough to disqualify me permanently for work in schools in general and in government schools in particular. I, however, did not want to submit to the educational director's order. Full amnesty restored all my rights, at least legally. On the basis of this, I appealed directly to the governor of Yekaterinoslav, von Klingenberg.

Von Klingenberg's family was well known in Russia for the worst reasons. A brother of the governor of Yekaterinoslav had been governor, first in Kovno and then in Mogilev. He had already been known as an anti-Semite in Kovno, but he revealed the full extent of his hatred of Jews and revolutionaries as the head of Mogilev province. He allowed pogroms to take place in the city of Mogilev and in other towns of the province when recruits were being enlisted for the Russo-Japanese War. The new recruits robbed Jewish stores, attacked Jews, broke into Jewish homes and ransacked them. The pogroms took place in full view of police and military personnel. They remained completely indifferent to what was happening, although they could have controlled these future "defenders of the fatherland." It was later shown that the governor had actually issued orders that, for patriotic reasons, the youthful "defenders" were not to be hindered too much in their "merrymaking" during the enlistment period. Thousands upon thousands of Jewish families were ruined during this "frolicking." The governor of Mogilev also distinguished himself as a "pacificator" during the 1905–1906 revolution. He organized punitive expeditions that flogged, tortured, and shot peasants and others suspected of revolutionary acts, without even giving them a hearing.

The Yekaterinoslav von Klingenberg, however, was somewhat of an exception. He was what was called at the time a "European." In any case, he showed no sign of being a "Pompadour" satrap. He took the petition I had prepared and said, "Please come back in three days, when I will be able to give you an answer." When I returned three days later he said to me, briefly but courteously: "I considered your case and have nothing against you. I have written the director of schools of the province of Yekaterinoslav to this effect. I believe you will have no difficulty returning to your post."

Quite against his will, Kalabanovskii was obliged to withdraw his order, and I went back to work at the school. This lasted until the end of the school year. To avoid encountering me, however, Kalabanovskii no longer visited the school, nor did he follow his usual practice of attending the graduation examinations. Instead, he got even with me during summer vacation.

While spending the vacation at my parents' home in the province of Vilna, I received an official notice from Kalabanovskii, telling me to request immediately a release from duty for personal reasons. Otherwise, he would be forced to dismiss me, in the interests of public education. Were I to let Kalabanovskii carry out his threat, any possibility of my legal employment as an educator would have been ended. Therefore I wrote a request that I be released for family reasons. I interrupted my vacation and went to Yekaterinoslav with my request in order to speak personally to Kalabanovskii and try to protest my forced withdrawal. He received me with an angry glare.

"Have you come to ask for a release from duty?"

"Yes—No. I would like to explain to you—"

"No explanations! You betrayed my trust and the good opinion I had of you. It was in my power to dismiss you, but I gave you another chance. Do it immediately." I had no alternative but to hand in my request for withdrawal.

At the time, a group of prominent community leaders in Yekaterinoslav opened a community school for girls. The *rabiner,* Brustein, was also interested in this school. At Brustein's suggestion, the school committee offered me the position of principal. I told them I doubted that Kalabanovskii would approve me. The members of the committee were confident that if a delegation of such loyal (that is, politically reliable) representatives of the Yekaterinoslav Jewish community as they were would approach him, Kalabanovskii would approve my candidacy. *Rabiner* Brustein was among the delegates. Nevertheless, Kalabanovskii not only rejected the delegation request, he also reproached them for asking him to approve such an "unreliable" candidate. Nothing helped. Kalabanovskii would not change his mind.

A few words about Brustein: he was a studious type, in his late thirties, blond, with a short beard. He had passed a special examination for a certification that qualified him for the position of *rabiner.* One day, several weeks after my release from prison, I was told unofficially that *Rabiner* Brustein wanted to see me and had asked that I call on him that evening. I went to see him. We had not met each other before. I was curious to learn why he had asked me to come. It was a confidential matter. He had been asked—he did not say by whom, but this was evident—to translate a letter addressed to me from someone in the city of Pavlograd. The letter contained passages that clearly referred to my revolutionary activity, which could have had grave consequences for both me and the letter's author. The *rabiner* was prepared to return the letter to me, so that its author might rewrite it, using the same kind of paper and retaining its present form, but omitting the dangerous sentences. The new letter would have to look entirely like the original, completely covering four sides.

The letter, written in Yiddish, was from a young colleague, a teacher in the Pavlograd government school. It had been found in my home when it was searched after my arrest. Brustein requested, for obvious reasons, that the matter not be prolonged. Not wishing to trust the letter to the mail, I left for my friend's home that same evening. Together we composed a new text that presented a friendly correspondence between two comrades. In his original letter, my friend had asked me to take care of a matter involving the Social-Democratic Organization in Yekaterinoslav. Of course, these sentences, which might have aroused suspicion, were eliminated. The rewritten letter was completely innocent. I brought it to Brustein, who was very pleased with its content. He translated it and delivered it to the police administration. After Brustein did me this favor we became friends, and when I was looking for lodgings he proposed that I come to live in his home. He was exceptionally mild and affable, a truly compassionate individual.

At the same time, revolutionaries were committing terrorist acts of expropriation. The punishment for the perpetrators was "Stolypin's neckerchief"—that is, the noose.* When the condemned persons were Jews, the *rabiner* was usually "invited" to the hanging to hear their final confession, if they so desired. Almost none of them wished to do so. Nevertheless, they often asked the *rabiner* to convey final messages to their loved ones. The area where the hangings took place was surrounded by cordons of soldiers, who in turn were surrounded by rows of Cossacks armed with lances. The leaders of this inquisition feared that the soldiers, who were peasants and sons of laborers, might turn their guns on the executioners.

Brustein shuddered as he related the details of executions he had had to attend. Soldiers would tremble as they carried out the sentences. Others whispered curses on the official representatives of the government. After these early morning events, Brustein would return home broken and ill. It would take him several days to recover. He told me that he was seriously considering resigning from his position as *rabiner* because he was required to be an official observer at these hangings. Soon afterward, I left Yekaterinoslav for good and never saw this humane *rabiner* again.

---

*This was a famous expression used by the liberal deputy Rodishchev against Russian premier Peter A. Stolypin, who instituted courts martial that resulted in an endless number of hangings.

7

Jewish Gymnasia without Quotas

The first Russian revolution against the tsarist regime was a failure. After the brief "liberal" period of October 1905, the tsar stifled the revolution with the help of the Black Hundreds, organized by the police, and with countless pogroms against Jews. Nevertheless, as happens after each great revolution and counter-revolution, some consequence of liberalism remains that cannot be taken away. One such result of the 1905 October Revolution was the liberalization of academic education and the development of private schools, especially among Jews. The quota system was broken indirectly as a consequence of the opportunity to open special secondary schools for Jewish children, with Jewish administrators and teachers.[1] Later, however, the Jewish administrators also had to engage non-Jewish directors, who were well paid.

Private Jewish gymnasia opened up in a number of cities with large Jewish populations: Vilna, Minsk, Gomel', Warsaw, Odessa, Białystok, and even St. Petersburg. The ministers of public education, Casso and Schwartz, allowed Jewish students to receive diplomas in these schools if a delegate of the local chief of the educational district was present at the examinations.

From 1907 to 1912, I worked in the Gomel' gymnasium directed by Dr. A. Ratner, both as an inspector of the lower grades and as a full-time teacher of Russian and Jewish history. The official name of the course I taught was "religion." The school had a staff of fifteen to twenty teachers and employees, both Jews and Russians. One teacher of mathematics, Anatolii Saadievich Gurovich, a graduate of Moscow University, was a very talented educator. He was active in community affairs, an excellent teacher, and in general blessed with many good qualities. His earnest nature was tempered with a sense of humor, and he also had strong Jewish national feelings. Politically he was a Bundist. Gurovich was not impressed with the idea of remaining a teacher in someone else's school for the rest of his life; his ambition was to open a school of his own.

Gurovich preferred Białystok, a bustling city where Jews had helped to develop a flourishing textile industry. The Jews of Białystok were not overly enthusiastic about the existing Jewish gymnasium. After contacting his friends in Białystok, Gurovich considered opening a private gymnasium there. He applied to the head of the Department of Education in Vilna for permission. At the time (1911–12), the authorities did not readily license Jewish schools, especially if they were to be granted the privilege of accreditation—and certainly not when the applicant was a socialist and a Bundist.

One day in February 1912 the director of Dr. Ratner's school, a civil servant named Maksimov, received an order from the head of the regional office of education to remove me at once from my position as a teacher and inspector because of my "harmful" activities in 1906 and 1907. This was after I had been working for five years at the Gomel' gymnasium. I left immediately for Vilna to find out the reasons for my removal. True, I had a record of political arrests, but I had been granted amnesty afterwards by both governors. After much effort I learned in the offices of the educational authority and the governor that I was accused of political agitation in Kharkov province and of participating in the London Social Democratic Conference: I was also charged with seizing the party treasury in Kharkov, among other things. In other words, I was quite a catch—a Social Democrat and, moreover, a thief.

The governor of Vilna had received this information about me from Chernigov. He sent this report to the director of the Department of Education in Vilna, who did what was expected of him and fired me. When I examined all the papers that a clerk at the education office handed me, however, I noticed that, on the copy of the report from Chernigov, the word "not" had been omitted when the text continued on a following page.

The governor of Chernigov had originally written: "The investigation established that the student Hirsz Abramowicz is *not* the Abramowicz who seized the treasury and who was at the London Social Democratic Conference in May 1907." (I had been a student at the University of Kharkov, where there were other students named Abramowicz.) But if one read the governor's statement without the word "not," I came out looking quite different.

Ostroumov, the director of the Department of Education in Vilna was an alcoholic or, to put it plainly, a drunk. His office was full of liquor bottles. Ostroumov was also a blatant anti-Semite. Once, when he was on an official visit to Dr. Ratner's gymnasium in Gomel', which occupied three separate buildings, he ordered that the school erect its own special building. When he was told that it was impossible financially—and that such a request would force the institution, with its six hundred students, to close—Ostroumov raised the coattails of his uniform and, tapping his pocket, said vulgarly, "Don't worry, the Jews have *gelt*," using the Yiddish word for money.

Gurovich and I had become friends. As he felt certain that I would be in Vilna for a long time, he asked me to look for an opportunity to obtain permission from the Department of Education to open a gymnasium in Białystok. His petition had been circulating in various offices for quite some time, even though the political police had cleared him without reservation. But the drunken anti-Semite Ostroumov did not want a Jew to have an easy time of it and, using various pretexts, found different ways not to sign the permission papers. It seemed obvious that he meant to postpone issuing the license for years.

Gurovich understood that, despite my complete rehabilitation, the hostile Ostroumov would persist in preventing me from continuing to work as an educator one way or another. Gurovich was sure that I would have to make frequent appearances at the department in order to revoke the judgment against me. Eventually, my case reached the minister of the interior, Biletsky. He officially informed Ostroumov that errors and negligence were committed against the Kharkov student Hirsz Abramowicz, and a notice to that effect was issued by the police department. When I returned from St. Petersburg and learned about this document, I went to Ostroumov and demanded my right to be reinstated as a teacher in Ratner's gymnasium. But he interrupted me and said, "My dear fellow, you are not going to work for me, even if you are right a hundred times. We know you too well!" I saw that I was never going to get out of this morass. I was fed up with wasting time and effort running from one office to another. I gave up on Ostroumov and got a job in a bank that the Jewish Mutual Credit Society opened at the time in Vilna.

Nevertheless, I succeeded in reviving the Gurovich case in the following way. During my frequent visits to the Vilna Department of Education and its drunken chief, I saw a short man who appeared to be Jewish and seemed to me to be a regular presence there. Sitting in the reception room together on several occasions, we became acquainted. His name was Levin. Many people in Vilna knew him on account of his diminutive stature. I learned that he visited Ostroumov privately and played cards with him, confirming the Yiddish saying that "every anti-Semite has his favorite Jew." Levin was a respectable merchant. I did not want to involve him in my political case. Nevertheless, I did tell him that a friend of mine had submitted a petition to the director about opening a gymnasium in Białystok, and that

Ostroumov had not granted him a license. Meanwhile, Gurovich was near financial ruin, for he was unable to stabilize his affairs. Gurovich believed that opening a school in Białystok would be a profitable business, because children from the city and the surrounding area would stream to a school with a good reputation. He was willing to take on a partner who could succeed in obtaining a license from the authorities. Levin became interested in the matter and prevailed on Ostroumov to give his "good friend" permission for the school, albeit temporarily without accreditation.

Around 1913 Gurovich opened the gymnasium in Białystok, which soon acquired a good reputation. The district inspectors praised the school. It goes without saying that Levin, now directly connected with Gurovich, succeeded in getting accreditation for the school from Ostroumov. Gurovich became prominent in the communal life of Białystok as his school grew. But the storm of 1914 was approaching. Białystok was on the front line in the war between Russia and Germany, and Gurovich's school had to be closed. I later heard that Gurovich became a Soviet citizen and held a high position in the statistical office of a government agency in Moscow.

8

I. L. PERETZ VISITS THE JEWISH WRITERS IN ODESSA

This article is dedicated to the sacred memory of my wife, Anna Abramowicz (née Schreiber), whom the Germans murdered in the extermination camp Majdanek.

It happened in Odessa, at the close of the Passover holiday, in 1904. I. L. Peretz had come there for the first time to see the sun-lit city and the Black Sea and to meet with its Jewish writers. It proved impossible to obtain an official permit to hold a banquet, particularly in honor of a radical writer like Peretz (such was his reputation at the time). Nevertheless, a committee was spontaneously formed to organize a reception for him.

Odessa was the citadel of Russian-Hebrew writers, but Mendele lived there as well. Mendele was, in Elhanan Leib Lewinsky's words, "sitting on a fence"—that is, he wrote in both Hebrew and Yiddish.[1] As a result, the Hebraists also showed respect for the Yiddish language, which had only just begun to interest Jewish intellectuals. It should be noted that *Der fraynd,* Russia's first Yiddish daily newspaper, which was published in St. Petersburg, was only one year old at the time. However, Peretz was known to quite a few Russian-Jewish intellectuals from the translations of his work that appeared in *Voskhod;* some even knew of him from *Der fraynd.*

Because of police regulations then in effect, the banquet in Peretz's honor had to be limited to the Odessa Jewish writers themselves, whose number, incidentally, was not at all small. I had come to Odessa to visit a friend (later to become my life companion) who was a student there. Mendl Levin, the Odessa correspondent of both *Voskhod* and *Der fraynd,* was a good friend of ours. Knowing that I had made my debut in both newspapers with an article and some correspondence, Mendl Levin saw to it that I, a young student from "the distant North," was given the opportunity to attend the banquet.

The event took place at a Jewish restaurant on Bazaar Street. This was done so that, in case the police discovered this "secret meeting," we could say that we had gathered there simply to mark the conclusion of the Passover holiday.

Some forty writers were assembled, but the start of the banquet had to be delayed; Mendele, the "lion of the fellowship," had not arrived. We learned that he was not feeling well, had a bit of a cold. Yet how could there be a writers' celebration in Odessa without Mendele? It was decided to send his favorite, Hayyim Nahman Bialik, with an "order" to fetch the "Grandfather of Yiddish literature"—provided, of course, that Mendele was not, God forbid, seriously ill.[2] And so it was. Bialik returned with the Grandfather, who arrived with an ironic smile on his face.

When the two entered, there was a cheer: "Long live Reb Mendele!" Soon, Peretz also arrived and was welcomed with resounding applause. He looked at the assembly with his wonderful brown, piercing eyes and bowed as he said, "Good evening." His eyes drew one toward him. They seemed to look right into one's soul and see something that someone else would not.

The organizers of the evening turned the chair over to Mendele, whom they seated between Ahad Ha-Am and Dr. Joseph Klausner. Near them sat Bialik, Yehoshua Hana Rawnitzki, Lewinsky, among others.[3] Mendele expressed his thanks but declined the honor, since he was not feeling very well. He said he was happy to see his "grandson" Peretz, who was on the verge of surpassing the fathers, let alone the sons. "Would that we had many such people, the more the better!" he said. Peretz must be studied, continued Mendele, for his work has several layers of meaning. Mendele then remarked that since he was sitting between Scholarship (gesturing with one hand to Dr. Klausner) and Philosophy (gesturing with the other hand to Ahad Ha-Am), he knew the two men would "take care" of Peretz. He then asked Ahad Ha-Am to chair the meeting, since he was younger and was familiar with the business of leadership.

Ahad Ha-Am spoke in Russian, very good Russian indeed, without a trace of an accent. His words gave evidence of his firm convictions and careful thinking. He spoke like a professor, even, at times, like a prosecuting attorney, accusing some writers of a lack of principle, of being no more than pinwheels fluttering in the breeze of their day or according to their employers' wish.*

---

*The speeches are quoted according to the impression they made on me at the time. I no longer recall the exact texts, but the general content is correct. In many cases,

In our literature, the intention and practice of striving toward an ideal that would be useful and of service to the people has always prevailed. The principle of art for art's sake, beauty for its own sake, and similar "creeds" has had almost no place among Jewish writers. A writer must have a God he believes in and whom he compels others to believe in. Peretz has always served his God sincerely and honestly. If we cannot, like Ruth the Moabite, say that his God is our God, we nevertheless can say forthrightly and emphatically the rest of Ruth's words: "His people are our people—all of us!" Ahad Ha-Am proclaimed expressively.[4] "We all have one goal: to uplift our people and ennoble them! We have different ways of approaching it, but we are all inspired by the same ideal. We appreciate Peretz's true talent, especially in these times, when many writers have turned away from the foundations of our literature, and lack of principle has almost become a principle.* 'Pinwheelism' seems a permanent phenomenon and the only goal. This evening in honor of our guest has united all writers, of various ideological bents, in an expression of respect and devotion not only to a talented person, but to a writer with a world view, with convictions, with an honest approach to literature and to the printed word in general." This is what Ahad Ha-Am, the world famous author, said that evening.

Bialik, a short man in a long black coat, looked like a small-town young husband about to take his first steps in business. He was rotund and looked quite prosaic until he picked up his golden pen or began to speak.** At the evening in honor of Peretz, the young Bialik astonished all the participants with his speech, which was both profound and poetic, almost prophetic. The provincial young man disappeared and a fiery mountain stood before us in the person of Bialik, the great poet. It would be difficult to convey the contents of his speech. It was rhythm, music and, if you will, even color.

The Hebrew he spoke was almost biblical. Bialik pointed out the ethical themes and human values of Peretz's Hasidic tales and other sketches. Yet Peretz, a *maskil,* is also deeply lyrical and stirs the most delicate strings of

---

expressions are given verbatim. Nevertheless, since I do not, after a lapse of forty-odd years, recall the contributions of several of the speakers, my "report" is incomplete.

*At the time, there was some commotion in the world of Jewish journalism about the spending of "pogrom money"—that is, money newspapers were collecting for the relief of the victims of the Kishinev pogrom. One hesitates to mention any names in this connection. The "guilty" are by now all "housed in dust."

**With the passing of the years, the bourgeois appearance of the young Bialik changed considerably, however. I had occasion to see him in Vilna a year before his death. His face, especially his forehead, was deeply creased. A Jewish scholar and a sharp thinker, a born leader, a great man among the people of Israel—that was the image of the sixty-year-old Bialik.

the human soul, said Bialik. He dwelt especially on the Hasidic motifs in Peretz's works, finding in them a divine spark.

"Our sages of old created three monuments: *halakhah, aggadah, and Kabbalah.* We also have all of them in modern Hebrew and Yiddish literature. Indeed, we even have them here, among us now: Here is *halakhah* (Ahad Ha-Am); *aggadah* (Mendele), and here, *Kabbalah* (Peretz). *Halakhah* and *aggadah* are restricted in time and place, although they are the foundation of our national structure. *Kabbalah,* however, opens up distant, infinite worlds to us, never-ending horizons resplendent with the divine presence."

Peretz's Hasidic tales lead us out into the magic land of "even higher and higher."[5] His works penetrate into the depths of the popular soul. Peretz's oeuvre is profoundly national, for he portrays the spirit of the people, their heroes, with so much insight and artistic intuition that no one, perhaps, has done it any better. Every vibration of the Jewish soul is reflected in Peretz's works.

Bialik's address was a masterpiece.

Mendl Levin's focus was on the folk tales that Peretz had written about simple people, like "Bontshe the Silent," who lived in basements and attics. The author speaks to revolutionaries, however, who wish to create a world without silent Bontshes, or pious cats, or skullcaps—a new, free world that is our visitor's ideal. Peretz is the great democrat of Yiddish literature.[6] Lewinsky (Reb Korev), the splendid Hebrew and Yiddish essayist, declared that he was happy to have a colleague like Peretz. The difference between them, Lewinsky said, was that Peretz's essays would endure in the literature, because whatever issued from Peretz's pen had profound and lasting value. Reb Mordkhele (Khayim Chemerinsky), the Hebrew poet and clever translator of Krylov, read aloud a rhymed piece that his audience enjoyed very much.[7]

A. Ludvipol, a well-known Hebrew essayist and journalist, spoke of Peretz the newspaperman, who sees things clearly and is always alert to what matters in Jewish life. S. Ben-Zion remarked that, along with his monumental works, Peretz also publishes some unimportant, although quite enjoyable, writing.[8] Together with the Tablets of the Covenant, there is a little sand. We have very great expectations of a talent like Peretz's. We demand only Tablets of the Covenant because Peretz is truly in a position to bring them to us. Rawnitzki emphasized that Peretz, with his profound themes and allegories, was more of a writer for the intelligentsia, but not all writers need be popular and accessible. Sometimes a writer should not only be read, but studied; Peretz should be studied and perhaps even interpreted like a sacred text.

With the gentle manner of a charming, elderly student and a young scholar, Klausner made the point that he finds in Peretz's work eternal youthfulness, eternal striving to discover new forms and to synthesize the old with the new into one vessel, which is Jewish literature. Klausner counted Peretz among those young writers possessed of a great talent that is fresh and vigorous. Peretz's talent blooms colorfully and continuously. It renews itself and bears ripe fruit that gives us not only enjoyment but also something very substantial to contemplate, delving deep into the Jewish soul. At present, said Klausner, there are two streams in Jewish literature, which he identified as "Odessa" and "Warsaw." Odessa stands for stability. Everything that is great and significant, that has lasting value, was created by the writers of Odessa. Warsaw represents the dynamic. Everything there boils and seethes, renewing the literature with innovative, ever-changing forms. In Peretz the two streams are confluent.

Alter Druyanow added that Peretz advances the idea of renewal in Jewish life.[9] In this respect, his work shares many common points with the Zionists, who also strive toward new forms for Jewish life. That is the reason that so many Zionist writers came to this reception for Peretz. Druyanow concluded on a pessimistic note, however. At the time, there were rumors that the Black Hundreds, who happened to be especially strong in Odessa, were planning a pogrom on the first anniversary of the anti-Semitic riots in Kishinev.[10] Druyanow observed that we were speaking at the banquet of lofty intellectual matters pertaining to our people, but we were not at all certain whether at any moment in the next day or so—during Easter, the Christian "holiday of love"—we would suffer a tragedy in which both body and soul would, Heaven forbid, be destroyed.

B. Frankenfeld spoke dramatically of the powerful impression that Peretz's work made on him as a reader. He compared it to a refreshing drink that revitalizes the spirit and "brings joy to both men and gods." Frankenfeld said he was one of those readers who wait impatiently for the "next delivery" from Peretz's pen. There were still other speakers, but I no longer recall their names or the nature of their remarks. Peretz's individualism was stressed, as was the influence of Stanisław Wyspiański and the great Western European symbolists on his creativity.[11] At the same time, Peretz was recognized as always being original, creative and genuinely Jewish.

In his response—which was delivered, strange as it may seem today, in Russian—Peretz began by joking that he had just been praised for not stealing the silverware (a reference to Ahad Ha-Am's comment that Peretz was an honest writer).* Yes, it's true— thus far, he had not stolen, and in all likelihood he would not do so in the future.

---

*Seven years later, in 1911, at a banquet held in his honor in St. Petersburg, Peretz protested against Simon Dubnow's speech about the duality of Hebrew and Yiddish,

He was praised for the heavens and for the earth, Peretz said, for the sun and for the cellar. Each person praised what he likes. One commentator found his work to be nationalistic, another saw it as internationalistic; one found it religious, another heretical, and so on. This was not quite right. He was a Jew, and he directed his attention wherever he saw Jews. A writer should not be the product of a political party or class. He must be sensitive to every phenomenon in the life of his people. He should react to everything that is great and beautiful in the community for which he writes. Peretz dwelt particularly on his early works, written when Jewish social organization was still in its infancy. Then, a Yiddish writer had to do everything by himself, because the field was still wild and uncultivated. The writer had to enlighten, teach, tell stories with a lesson. There were no special journalists, essayists, reporters, or critics. The writer who wanted to serve his people with his pen had to explore all these forms of literature and journalism, going off in all directions. It was not possible for him to devote himself entirely to writing only what he was inclined to, following where his soul led him. But the time for being able to do everything, know everything and write about everything had passed. Now one could feel more disposed to specialize; a writer could devote himself more to that toward which his entire being led him.

In closing, Peretz thanked the writers for their hearty reception and for the bit of pleasure that the Russian beauty known as Odessa and her Black Sea (which was actually bright and sunny) had brought him. A delegation of Jewish students and young laborers presented Peretz with a gift, a deluxe album of paintings by Isaak Levitan.[13] Levitan's pictures express the infinite loneliness and melancholy of the central Russian landscape, which has such gentleness and unique beauty. Yet there is sorrow in his pictures, with their white birches suffused with longing.

The moment provided another opportunity for Bialik to excite those assembled, this time with a comment about Levitan and Peretz. Bialik said, among other things, that we see in all of Levitan's pictures the loneliness and heartbreak of a Jewish soul on alien soil, yearning for a Jewish resolution. Yet the fruit of Levitan's great Jewish talent is in the possession of others, of strangers. Although cut off from life at an early age, he is considered one of the greatest Russian artists. However, his sadness and loneliness are Jewish.

Now we present these copies of Levitan's splendid work, with their vibrant Jewish soul, to another great talent which, fortunately, remains with

---

which Dubnow delivered in Russian. Dubnow demonstratively left the banquet. On the whole, there was no concord between these two great writers. (Dubnow once criticized Peretz's poem "Monish" and believed that Peretz employed a moralizing tone.)[12]

us and among us. May Peretz's great talent live on and blossom and warm our souls! Thus concluded Bialik, the divinely inspired poet.

The banquet continued until four o'clock in the morning and left an unforgettable impression on everyone present. I still remember it. A group of writers escorted Peretz home, and another group, led by Bialik, accompanied Mendele to his home. I went along with the latter group and heard the Grandfather speak of his first impressions of Odessa. Whenever he had a free moment he would go to gaze at the ocean, which enchanted him and spoke of the earth's creation.

When one remembers what Russian Jewry once represented, and the intellectual giants it produced, one can easily give way to despair, but we must continue to forge the golden chain in hallowed memory of these pillars of the people of Israel.[14]

9

Chaim Weizmann and Kolia Tepper Debate

This event took place in Pińsk around Passover in 1903, during a time when people still believed in discussions with their opponents—although, to be sure, the Jewish community was then quite sharply divided along political lines. For the purpose of propaganda, however, they would meet and debate. Organized discussions about Bundism, Zionism, and socialism took place in almost every city and town. At the time, each party was still enthusiastically and aggressively zealous. Not infrequently, these discussions resulted in physical clashes. Both of the two major Jewish parties—the Bundists and the Zionists—had experienced propagandists and public speakers. Sometimes rank-and-file members left one party and joined another as a result of the oratorical appeal of a speaker.

Moreover, the Jewish socialists in the Bund and Poalei Zion were eager to demonstrate their superior faithfulness to Marxism, and they accused each other of heresy (Bernsteinism or some other deviation).* General Zionists also participated in these competitions.[1] They were not afraid to denounce socialism. One such Zionist was Chaim Weizmann, whose parents, brothers, and sisters lived in Pińsk.[2]

I happened to be spending several months in Pińsk and was there on the eve of Passover. The Jewish intelligentsia of Pińsk, together with several

---

*I recall a cartoon that appeared in a Yiddish humor magazine in about 1905. Karl Marx, with his rabbinical beard and wearing a skullcap and a *tallit katan,* was standing on a chair. He was surrounded by figures representing the Bund, Poalei-Zion, Zionist Socialists, Sejmists, etc. Each was pulling on of the tassels of Marx's *tallit katan* toward himself. Marx was throwing up his hands, shouting "Help! Jews, please, help me!"

labor groups, conceived the idea of arranging a major debate in order to take advantage of Chaim Weizmann's presence in the city. Weizmann was only twenty-seven at the time, but he was already well known for his addresses at Zionist Congresses, where his polemical skill and his opposition to Theodor Herzl's diplomatic dealings attracted attention. Certainly, Weizmann was not bashful.*

Indeed, the Weizmann family, whose many members all came home for holidays, was quite conspicuous in the city. They all spoke loudly and sang songs at gatherings. The younger ones, students dressed in Russian gymnasium uniforms, had a way of enjoying life. I remember a ditty that one of them—I think it was Samuel—used to sing under his breath: "One bottle of beer, two bottles of beer, three bottles of beer and whiskey."[4] The young Weizmanns exuded confidence in their own abilities, both intellectual and physical. They were filled with a love of life.

At the same time that Chaim Weizmann was recognized as a spokesmen for a large segment of Russian Zionists, Kolia Tepper was popular in labor circles as a brilliant speaker and fanatic Bundist. Tepper, too, had recently come to Pińsk. Only a short time earlier he had been an ardent Zionist and had participated in the Zionist Congresses. He became disillusioned with Zionism, however, especially after Bernard Lazare withdrew from the movement because of the founding of the Colonial Bank. This, in Lazare's opinion, was an unmistakable indicator of the bourgeois nature of Zionism.[5] A zealous convert, Tepper trounced Zionism at political gatherings.

Thus, the time, place, and people were all favorable for a general discussion about Jewish problems within the framework of the two main political ideologies, Zionism and socialism, as represented by the two "duelists," Chaim Weizmann and Kolia Tepper. To augment their forces, the Zionists summoned Abraham (Aba) Rubenchik, a veteran Labor Zionist, from Minsk. In his later thirties, he was the eldest of the debaters.

As all such meetings were illegal, they had to be kept secret from the police. In the summer, these gatherings took place in the woods surrounding the city and in the winter, in private homes or factories. This was usually done without the knowledge of the owners, although on rare occasions a "liberal" manufacturer, usually a General Zionist, might participate in the meetings. There was one such manufacturer in Pińsk; his name, I believe,

---

*Vladimir Jabotinsky related in his memoirs that at the 1903 Congress, when he was a newcomer in the Zionist movement, he saw Weizmann for the first time.[3] Approaching the table in a cafe where Weizmann sat in heated conversation with others sitting around him, Jabotinsky asked, "I'm not disturbing you, am I?" Weizmann retorted sharply, "You are!" Jabotinsky withdrew.

was Lichtenstein. His factory was outside the city limits, where he also made his home.

Pińsk was becoming highly industrialized at the time. A large number of factories had been opened, including a match factory that employed a thousand Jewish women, a veneer factory, and a plant that made chalk (owned by Grigorii Lourie).[6] There were a number of other industries, as well as a wharf. Except for those who worked on the wharf, most of the laborers were Jews. Like every large city with a Jewish population, Pińsk had its slum, where impoverished people lived in hovels. Gomel' had its "Ditch," Vilna its "Novigorod," Belaia Tserkov (called *Shvartstume*, "Black Impurity," in Yiddish) its "Georgia."[7] In Odessa, it was the "Moldovanka" district; in another city it was known as "the Caucasus," and so on. In Pińsk, the slum was called "Linishches." Thousands of Jewish families with no today and no tomorrow lived there, hungry and squalid, in sagging, lopsided, sometimes even roofless ruins, their windows stuffed with rags. This district, whose population was one hundred percent Jewish, provided the new factories with cheap labor. The Jewish socialist parties, primarily the Bund, raised the workers' consciousness through socialist propaganda and economic strikes. Pińsk thus became one of the centers of the Jewish labor movement. Its leaders were the intelligentsia, teachers, some young people, and the more informed workers themselves.

An audience of several hundred laborers attended the debate, which took place on a Friday evening in a huge dining hall. In order to avoid arousing suspicion, they arrived one at a time or, at most, by twos. Lookouts were stationed all along the road to give directions and to sound an alarm in case the evil eye—that is, the police—should pose a threat.

The evening began at about 10:30 with a brief word from one of the local Bundists, who announced that the speakers would be Comrade Kolia of the Bund, Chaim Weizmann and Rubenchik for the Zionists. The audience, which had been buzzing like a beehive, grew silent and alert.

Tepper spoke first. He delivered a sharp attack against the Zionist ideology which, according to his judgment, was that of the Jewish petty bourgeoisie. The only choice for the Jews of Russia was to follow the nation's revolutionary movement against autocracy and toward socialism, which would lead to positive solutions to all social and national problems. Tepper also dismissed Zionist literature, which he characterized as "worthless." I will not repeat all the speakers' arguments. They were typical of their time, on the eve of the Russo-Japanese War and the first Russian revolution. Tepper's speech lasted about three hours. He held the audience captive with his oratorical power and passion. Then Weizmann approached the speaker's table with energetic steps. He had a determined look on his sharply etched face, reminiscent of an ancient Assyrian. With his black beard and tall, straight build he was more impressive than the short, nearsighted Tepper.

Weizmann began by stating that he agreed with his opponent about one thing: "Your Bundist literature and our Zionist literature—both belong under the table," implying that it all deserved to be thrown into the wastebasket. Bear in mind that at the time propaganda still had its limits. People still refrained from outright falsehood, exaggeration, or distortion of the facts. The reading public would have nothing to do with literature that was replete with lies. In general, however, the literature was dry and superficial. The living conditions of its readership and the fact that the literature was illegal had a greater effect than its content.

Weizmann dwelt on the absence of territoriality in Bundist ideology, on its disregard for the anti-Semitism of the masses, and the inability of Jews to enter into higher levels of industry, agriculture, and so on. He spoke for no less than two hours. Then Rubenchik argued that it was impossible for Jews to become proletarianized in the diaspora and put forth all the other tenets of Labor Zionist ideology.

Although the discussion lasted until well after daybreak, without interruption, it had not yet ended. On Saturday night it was resumed with even greater passion on the part of both factions, each of which would have liked to declare itself the victor.

This time, Tepper spoke last. His speech lasted for four hours. The content of his remarks is not important. That night the diminutive Tepper attained the stature of a great tribune of the people. He had a thick, black head of hair. Behind his pince-nez his eyes blazed with zeal, and if it were not for the pince-nez it might have seemed that a prophet was speaking. Perspiration dripped from his face, and the pince-nez kept sliding down his sharp nose.

I must admit that my impression was, and remains to this day, that Kolia Tepper was the best Jewish orator that I had ever heard. Even Jabotinsky, when he was at his peak, did not speak with as much expression as Tepper. Chaim Weizmann, no ordinary speaker, had style and brilliance, sarcasm and irony, but at this oratorical competition he lagged far behind Kolia Tepper. The same must be said of Rubenchik, who had the look of a scholarly recluse, although he was also a good speaker.

Each side, of course, felt that it had "won" the debate. Legends arose in Pińsk about these two remarkable evenings involving speakers of such power. The police, who finally did learn about the event after it was over, made several arrests. The speakers fled Pińsk. The debate, however, continued in small, separate groups and in private homes. Young people argued heatedly for several more evenings. There was also quite a bit of activity on Kiev Street where laborers gathered.

Soon, however, the discussions ended and were forgotten. More pressing events came to pass. The Kishinev pogrom erupted, striking the entire Jewish population like a thunderbolt and attracting the attention of a large segment of Russian progressive society as well. Stormy demonstrations were held in Pińsk that summer. The provocateur Arnadski was shot and killed.[8] Many people were arrested and banished to Siberia.

III

World War I and Its Aftermath in and around Vilna

1

I Join the Militia

In August 1915, a month before they departed from Vilna, the Russian authorities indicated that they would not oppose the organization of a municipal militia. Following an agreement between Vilna's Poles and Jews, a number of enlistment centers were opened around the city where candidates could sign up for the militia (Poles and Jews registered separately).

Dr. Cemach Szabad appealed to several young men, including me, to take it upon ourselves to recruit candidates. We did not need to do much persuading. I registered militiamen in a soup kitchen for refugees on Semionov Street, where a large number of both young and middle-aged men signed up. A considerable number of them were aware of the socio-political significance of the creation of a people's militia. Most of the candidates, however, felt that being a militiaman would offer some protection against forced labor, being dragged off to Russia, deportation, sudden capture in the streets, and the like. The lists of recruits were delivered to the city hall to be approved by a special commission. An identification was issued to each person certified. The city was divided into "circuits." I was assigned to the third circuit, based at Mickiewicz Street 4.

At the beginning of September, several militiamen, myself included, were invited to the circuit headquarters. The majority of the new "defense police" were Poles, most of them bank officers. There were few Jews in my circuit. The "commissar," an older man, spoke about the responsibilities of militiamen: being polite but firm with the public, regulating street traffic, especially for the military, etc.

I asked for the floor and spoke of the common interests of citizens, irrespective of nationality, and of how, in a time so fraught with danger, unity and mutual assistance from everyone to everyone was important. It must be admitted that my words made not the slightest impression on the others. They proceeded matter-of-factly—very much so—to the rest of the agenda. We were each issued white armbands and a club about thirty centimeters long, with a heavy knob at the top. These two objects were to symbolize our authority. We were informed that we must always be in a state of readiness and were to report promptly to specific places at the first call. My region was St. John's Street and the part of Broad Street near the post office.

By 17 September, the eve of Yom Kippur, it was quite apparent that the last of the Russian military divisions were leaving Vilna. Mistreatment of Jews by the military continued. People were captured on the street and dragged off "in unknown directions" (which meant digging trenches or performing other manual labor). Companies of hundreds—Cossacks from the Don, Kuban, and Ural regions—tramped endlessly through the streets, instilling fear in the people, Jews in particular. The batteries of heavy artillery filled the air with noise. Hardly any civilians were out in the streets. Stores were closed. It was pouring buckets and the soldiers were soaking wet, but they hurried on.

Almost no one had a thought of attending Kol Nidrei services. People were afraid to appear in the streets and many hid, sometimes even in less than dignified places, in the hope of escaping the Cossacks' whips, knouts, and abuse. Everyone was so fed up with the persecution, libelous attacks, and high inflation that nearly all of Vilna wished to be rid of the Russians, having had enough of their barbaric behavior. The city's residents expected that things could only be better under the Germans.

After midnight on the night of 17 September everything was closed tight. The streets were empty of civilians, but military divisions marched endlessly through the city in the dark. Frequently, a bottleneck would develop, and an entire column of men would come to a halt. When they were stopped on Troki Street the cavalrymen tried to rob a few stores. At a small fruit store (at Troki Street 1), the protective grates were pried open and the entire stock was stolen. The desperate cries of the owner, when she beheld her misfortune in the morning, still ring in my ears. Such robberies, however, were isolated cases. The night passed almost without any other incident, except for the fear generated by the terrible explosions when bridges and other military targets were demolished.

On Tuesday morning I was on Great Pohulanka Street. The Russians had nearly all passed through and the Germans had not yet arrived. During this interval, people rushed into the military bakery and dragged out everything

I Join the Militia

left inside. Some "lucky" people even found sacks of rye flour. All the equipment—tables, chairs, benches, iron cots—was also taken.

Some tragicomic scenes ensued as greed led some to take on impossibly large loads. Chairs, buckets, small tables, and whatever other "crown" property was available were loaded onto an iron cot. The looter then placed the bed on his head. Often, he would fall flat on the ground with all his acquisitions and then would try to gather up even more stuff. The militiamen tried in vain to influence the crowd, saying that it was illegal and wrong to take anything. The people were not very afraid of these new "police," each one with a piece of white wood dangling at his side by a little strap.

The populace was not possessed by a criminal spirit. They simply felt that there was nothing wrong with taking the property of the "Russkies," and that it was no crime at all. I even saw, to my surprise, some respectable, substantial Jews who clearly felt justified in this act of "taking." When I tried to tell them that it would be better "to leave well enough alone; it's unbecoming for Jews to do this," the response was a disgruntled murmur, the sense of which was, "It's none of your affair," or "Make believe you don't see anything," or "If it's all right for them, why not for us?"

At the time, no one was actually in power. The Germans had not yet entered the city. There were a few hours when each man did "that which was good in his eyes."[1] Here and there a few Russian soldiers who had become separated from the main body of the army still wandered about in the streets. The curious crowd surrounded them and "interviewed" them about the situation on the various fronts and even about the outcome of the world war. People stopped feeling threatened by these soldiers, who now looked so miserable it would not have been out of place to offer them a slice of bread and a glass of hot tea. Soaking wet, their overcoats rumpled, their boots muddied, their faces dejected, these Russian soldiers hardly seemed very warlike.

Toward evening the news came that scouting parties, the first of "Wilhelm's messengers," had been seen in the suburbs. All the streets filled with people coming out of their hiding places for the first time. Their mood, it must be admitted, had changed for the better. They were convinced there would now be no lawlessness, people would not be captured, there would be no pogroms. There would even be sugar!

At about ten or eleven o'clock in the morning, German troops, both foot soldiers and cavalry, began streaming in. Compared to the well-nourished horses of the Russians, the German mounts were reminiscent of Rocinante in *Don Quixote:* they were exhausted and poorly harnessed.

At this time, I was at my station near the main post office. The traffic was heavy and endless. Thousands of people stood on the street corner, watching the German troops. I had to exert a great deal of effort to keep the civilian crowds from stepping onto the pavement. If they created the slightest congestion on the streets it would impede the soldiers, and that could have been dangerous. In Polish and Yiddish, I asked the crowd to disperse. I even received some "compliments," like "*Żydowska milicja*" (Polish for "Jewish militia"), but I stood my ground.

Another militiaman was assigned to assist me; he even ordered the crowds in Russian to disperse. This militiaman suffered a counterattack: a Polish master tailor who lived down on Castle Street suddenly lifted his leg, contemptuously pressed both hands to the sole of his shoe and shouted, "This is what we think of the Russian and his language now!" Curiosity seekers surged toward the commotion, and I was barely able to keep them from interfering with the troop movement.

Somewhat later, a few German soldiers and non-commissioned officers appeared, in search of something. Next came a military car carrying several officers and soldiers, as well as a civilian. I left a replacement at the post office and ran toward the car, which had stopped before a building that was later to belong to the university. At the time, the building housed a gun shop. The hunting guns and pistols there could not have been of much value to the military, but the German plan stipulated that, when the city was taken, all weaponry businesses were to be requisitioned at once. Apparently the Germans had their own people in the city who led them to specific locations where metal goods and the like were available.

Seeing me approach, the senior officer ordered the militia to see that no civilian was permitted to come near. The gun shop was locked, but it had doors that were half glazed. Without a second thought, the soldiers shattered the glass with the butt ends of their guns and entered the shop. Two men went inside to search the place and remove everything there. A third man loaded the automobile, while a fourth watched the crowd. To me, the action seemed like an out-and-out robbery. People stood around, observing the actions of Vilna's "liberators."

The stunned and not very friendly expressions on our faces enraged the officers. They brandished their revolvers several times and upbraided me for not dispersing the crowd. When I requested a list of the objects taken, one officer threatened me with his fist. Later, I learned that similar scenes had occurred at other businesses.

Within a few hours of the Germans' arrival in Vilna, proclamations by the German military governor had been pasted up all over the city. They were replete with ringing phrases about liberating Vilna, "the pearl of the Polish crown," from the Russian yoke and the advent of a new period of freedom, among other things.

This Prussian "freedom" endured for barely an hour. Orders were immediately given to tear down the proclamations. The local population

I Join the Militia

might think that they were the cream of the crop when, in reality, they should understand that it is always "woe be unto the conquered." Other proclamations and orders appeared and replaced those taken down: It was necessary to obey the military government unquestioningly; weapons must be turned in under penalty of death; each family must turn in two quilts as well as all brass, copper, lead, and so on; curfew would be from nine in the evening to six in the morning. In general, all orders were to be carried out at once.

Militiamen were to assemble that evening to make reports and receive orders. Following my report, the commissar suggested that I write an account of the burglary of the gun shop. At the same time, he warned me that it would not do to oppose the new rulers. They were armed and we were not. He reported having heard from the German commandant of Vilna about certain demands that the new authorities were imposing on the residents: people were not only to follow orders, but to show respect for the military. We were to get out of their way by stepping down off the sidewalk into the street. When encountering German officers, we were to step to the right.[2] We were to provide the German troops with all information. The militia was to collect whatever they needed from the public.

The commissar also reported an announcement from the commandant to the effect that the civilian militia would be continued for only a short period, before being reorganized later in the year. There would be a German police force, and the militia would be used as an "auxiliary" force. It could not be autonomous, and the number of militiamen would be reduced. Some militiamen complained that German military personnel expected the militiamen to take them to brothels. One militiaman had his ears boxed. Sadly the commissar commented once again, in a murmur, that "they" were armed. In a word—it was a sad greeting; the news was not good.

At two o'clock in the morning, I was back at my post. It was raining hard. The streets were empty. In the darkness, I could hear the drunken singing of German soldiers in search of "wine, women, and song." Civilian Vilna did not sleep very well on Yom Kippur night either. Heavy, dark clouds were once again suspended in the air.

2

THE GERMANS IN WORLD WAR I

1. The Plight of the Refugees

After the fall of Kovno in 1915, the entire northwestern corner of Russia was a terrible scene of "blood and fire and pillars of smoke."[1] The Germans kept pressing the retreating Russian troops, who were making a hasty withdrawal, pausing only temporarily so as to allow the major forces to depart in some semblance of order. The local populace was forced to dig trenches. At the same time, in many places, the retreating forces ordered everyone to evacuate. The army command tried not to leave behind anything in the way of sustenance for the Germans or any houses in which they might find shelter during the winter. As a result, the Russian retreat was accompanied by the torching of farms, villages, and even entire towns.

The scene was especially terrifying at night. All around, the sky was red. Refugees, with their countless wagons packed with bundles and various household goods, trudged along with the troops. Many were herding cows, sheep, or hogs that were loudly protesting their hunger. The result was macabre music when combined with the thunder of the cannons, the crackling of gunfire, and the wailing of people, women and children in particular.

No one had the slightest idea which way to go or what to do. At first people thought that they could hide somewhere "off to the side"—in the swamps, woods, or valleys—until the danger was over. This proved to be a serious mistake, however, for it was just those out-of-the-way places, which were impassable in the best of times, that became the site of pitched battles.

There was no place free from the hail of shells and bullets. The 100,000 troops rolled on like waves, flooding everything in their path. More than one civilian met his death while hiding in some remote or deserted place.

The civilian population faced a terrible dilemma. Staying home was impossible, not only because of the threat of death, but also because the military immediately took over all buildings, and in all the chaos each soldier grabbed whatever came to hand. To leave home, however, meant not only complete loss of all one's property and stability but also an uncertain future of wandering. The hail of shells and bullets compelled most people to leave.

Thousands of wagons packed with women, children, and old people, tens of thousands more fleeing on foot, and innumerable animals clogged all the roads and frequently hindered the movement of the retreating armies. The refugees were not, of course, given any consideration, and they became the first victims of any upheaval. At night the refugees stopped in fields, meadows, or woods. They dug up potatoes and pastured their animals on the unharvested grain. To make matters worse, there were heavy rains, and diseases began to spread. It is, nevertheless, worth taking note of a curious psychological phenomenon: sickly people became oblivious to their infirmities. They kept pace with their companions and ate everything.

2. The Situation of the Jews

Jews were in a special category among the dispossessed. The air was filled with hatred, and Jews were the subject of the usual accusations of espionage and consorting with the Germans, which all non-Jews believed. Rumors circulated widely that the Cossacks would annihilate all the Jews or, at the very least, inflict the most terrible tortures on them. The actual situation offered considerable evidence to this effect. It was said that any Jew and Christian found together would be "shot at once." As a result, it became most difficult for Jews to find a night's lodging among the peasants. Jews kept to themselves in the meadows and fields. Nevertheless, it must be pointed out that some non-Jews treated Jewish refugees in the most friendly fashion.

Everywhere the military proved to be sharply anti-Semitic. For example, when the last of the Russian divisions arrived in a town, the first words addressed to the Jewish representatives by the senior army officers were, "Oh, Jews. You must be waiting for the Germans." The enlisted men, of course, never failed to shout *"Zhidy*! Spies!" and the like at every turn. Things happened differently, however, in one town, Wysoki Dwór. There, the Jews had sent a telegram to the tsar wishing him victory over the enemy. The local rabbi received a response of gratitude from the governor, in the form of an official document. It was framed and hung on a wall in the rabbi's home. When Russian officers arrived there and took possession of all the rooms, the rabbi requested that one room be left undisturbed. Of course, the officers reacted sharply to such effrontery. Their attitude changed immediately when the rabbi explained the reason for his request, and the room was left alone. The Jews were not forced to leave the town and it was not set on fire, as was originally ordered. Nevertheless, nearly all the Jews of Wysoki Dwór, the rabbi included, left the town, leaving most of their possessions behind.*

Only a few people remained in the towns. They decided to risk what the future would bring at home rather than wander off to some unfamiliar place. While en route, the refugees' tired and underfed horses often refused to go further. At such times, part of the load on the wagon would be taken out and left for the peasants. When coming on a railroad line that was still functioning some people sold their horse and wagon for "next to nothing" and traveled by train to Russia. More, however, wished to go to Vilna; there they hoped to wait out the change of government and eventually return home. The situation of those few Jews who remained in the towns was dreadful. Not only were they in constant danger of being killed by bullets and shells, but every Cossack regarded them as spies and traitors "who should be shot like dogs."

And, indeed, that happened more than once. Being robbed was only a minor matter. At every encounter, Russian soldiers routinely made inspections and confiscated the Jews' money, took away their boots, and the like; frequently they were beaten as well. No wonder that, with this ever-present insult and danger, people were eager for the transition period to end and for the "Split" (a code word for the Germans) to arrive. If truth be told, the "Split" often brought deliverance from death.

3. The Russians' Final Hours

In the final hours before departure, when none but the rear guard remained, complete abandon reigned. No earthly power, no matter how good its intentions, could control the marauders. This was especially true when Jews were involved. In one town, there was a stone cellar where everything was stored that the fleeing Jews could not take with them. There, too, the few Jews who stayed behind took refuge. It was Saturday. On one side of the town were the Germans; on the other end and in the town itself—the Russians. Shooting erupted. The Jews tried to assemble a *minyan*. A Cossack noticed this and discovered the Jews in the cellar filled with goods. There

---

*The same piece of paper saved them later on, when a contingent took them for "spies."

Postcard depicting German officers on an inspection tour through the streets of Vilna during World War I. The photograph was taken by A. Grobus, official military photographer, and published by Kahan and Co., Berlin.
Courtesy of the YIVO Archives.

was no mistaking what this signified: he had found a band of Jews who had prepared everything to welcome the Germans. The goods were hurriedly loaded onto wagons and the Jews were dragged out of the cellar and taken to the outskirts of the town to be shot. Their hands were bound. They made their final confession. Suddenly, the Germans launched a forceful attack. The Cossacks, unable to carry out their sentence, dropped everything and fled. "Relief and deliverance" had come to the Jews.[2] Under a hail of bullets they thanked God, offering prayers of thanks for having escaped an ignominious death at the hands of Cossacks.

4. The Return of the Refugees

Most of the Jewish refugees from these towns reached Vilna, where they made the rounds of social agencies, relatives, acquaintances, and the like. On the second day after the Germans' arrival, the entire mass of refugees set out for Łukiszki Square, where they were to receive permits to return to their homes. It was not possible to serve all of the tens of thousands in a single day, nor in two days. The crowd pushed and shoved. The newly created militia was unable to establish any kind of order. Some people gave up hope of ever receiving the permit and began to ride or walk back to their ruined homes without authorization.

The permits contained the stipulation that horses and goods belonging to homeless people were not to be requisitioned. The roads were jammed with the mass of German troops. Their horses were utterly exhausted from the long, swift march. On the roads, German soldiers either confiscated the returning refugees' horses or "traded" them for their own animals, which were on their last legs. True, no one suffered physical harm. When they requisitioned a driver and his wagon, he was given something to eat.

The roads and fields were strewn with military equipment abandoned by the retreating Russians: guns, bayonets, and the like, as well as soiled clothing, worn boots, large pots for cooking, water flasks, and more. In many places dead soldiers lay there as well. The towns had been torched and plundered. The fields had been trampled and dug up, except for a few potatoes. (That year there happened to be an abundance of potatoes.) On estates both large and small, only piles of bones remained of whatever livestock the owners had left behind. The Germans had consumed everything that was edible on their way to the battlefields. Houses that had not been burned down often had no windows or doors, and the furniture had been destroyed by fire. Yet those who returned were content to be back in their own corner of the world, where they had spent the greater part of their lives, although they now suffered extreme poverty. As salt was in very short supply, there was considerable speculation in salt. A handful of salt could actually be exchanged for a sack of potatoes or grain.

5. The First Measures Taken by the Occupation Forces

In these places there was as yet no sign of the new regime. Only in the larger towns were there telephone operators and a representative of the military who served as agents of the government. They were, however, too unfamiliar with local conditions to be able to accomplish anything. Indeed, in the beginning they were quite passive. Even by the time that free trade had been forbidden in the larger cities and the rationing of bread was under way, the smaller towns had no knowledge of this.

The Germans tried to organize a local militia, but they did not follow through in earnest and it never materialized. For example, they appointed several businessmen and a few of the wealthier peasants as town "elders." But these people were ignorant of their duties and, indeed, had very little desire to be involved. They were in fear of the Russians who, everyone was certain, would reappear and take revenge on anyone who had anything to do with the Germans.

Several German deserters took advantage of the temporary anarchy by declaring themselves to be "officials" and taking whatever their hearts desired, particularly from the peasants, who were unable to communicate with them. Nevertheless, there were also several instances in which Jews were able, with the help of these deserters, to take back some of their property from peasants who had stolen it.

6. The Organization of the New Authority

This situation did not last long. The Germans soon began to take charge of the situation in their own way. Gendarmes were assigned to every locality to deal with matters concerning the civilian population. In other words, they were to carry out the orders of the military authority by exploiting the people to meet the objectives and needs of the war. Shortly thereafter, *Amtsvorstehers* (chief officials) were appointed, in whose hands all power was concentrated to further the aims of German imperialist policy. The area supervised by each *Amtsvorsteher* was essentially equal to that of a former rural district (which included a population of some 10,000 people, considerably fewer than were there before the war).

The first task of the *Amtsvorsteher* was to summon all the village elders in the area and announce sternly that they were all to report to him every Sunday in the town where he was stationed.* All his orders were to be carried out precisely, without delay. In many places there were still corpses of Russian soldiers lying about. The peasants of the surrounding villages were ordered to bury them. The bodies had already deteriorated; it was impossible to touch them, and the stench was awful. Therefore the bodies were pushed with staves into mass graves, on which were planted small wooden signs bearing the inscription: Hier ruhen russische Krieger ("Here lie Russian warriors"). By contrast, corpses of German "warriors" were each buried in individual graves immediately following the battle. A board of good quality was placed over each grave, bearing the necessary biographical dates.

Before long, all trading in grain was forbidden, as was crossing from one district to another. Then it became illegal to travel from one county to another without a permit. Thus, all mobility and contact between the various areas began to cease. Only at first did the *Amtsvorsteher* permit local relief committees, both Jewish and Christian, to purchase a certain amount of grain for distribution to the poor. In most cases, the representatives of these

---

*Under the Russians, the peasants had the right, after 1861, to choose a village elder. His duties were to transmit to the peasants the regulations handed down by the government, to collect taxes, and the like.

committees were rabbis and priests, who had been granted the privilege of selling salt, sugar, and candles. These were purchased in canteens or directly from the *Kreishauptmänner,* who represented the authorities in the principal cities of each district. Some nine months passed before rationing was introduced in the towns.

When the level of public nutrition worsened, however, "allocations" were instituted—not in the form of bread, but of rye flour or whole grain. When there was no rye, oats, barley, or vetch were distributed. There were times when there was nothing to distribute—and people were given nothing. Somehow or other the townspeople found a way to get by. During the best times, the daily ration was half a pound. In the worst times, it was an eighth to a quarter of a pound.

7. The Mechanics of Extortion

In order to extract everything possible from the local population, the *Amtsvorsteher* created a separate *Wirtschaftsausschuß,* a commission in charge of everything pertaining to agriculture. A junior officer was designated to run the commission, along with several soldiers.

The procedures for taking farm produce from the peasants varied from time to time. For example, those living in the area under jurisdiction would be ordered to deliver eight to ten thousand poods of grain. It was the village elders' duty to divide this order proportionately among the villages and the individual peasants. If this method failed to yield the stipulated amount, force was used to take much more than had been asked for initially. Later on, a system of estimating the harvest was imposed. The members of the *Wirtschaftsausschuß* rode around inspecting everyone's property and specifying how much produce each one was to supply. An advance amount was to be deposited into the *Wirtschaftsausschuß* storehouse in September, with the remainder delivered during October and November. This ruling also applied to potatoes, which were to be taken directly from the field to the nearest railroad station and loaded onto box cars. The Germans did not determine the percentage of the crop that was to be delivered, but rather how much the peasant would need until the next harvest. This, of course, left room for corruption. The Germans soon learned how to take bribes in this "barbaric country," much as the Russian functionaries had. There was, however, a difference: whereas this had obligated the Russian to ease "the law" on behalf of the interested party, the German felt no such obligation whatever, and he took more. Whenever it was learned that anyone had more crops left than he was permitted, all of it, including the amount the peasant was to have kept for his own use, was confiscated. There could be no arguing about it.

The peasants soon learned not to keep their "extra" provisions visible, and they began to conceal everything. At night, they dug pits in the fields and the woods and filled them with potatoes. They made boxes and barrels, filled them with grain, and hid them beneath piles of hay or straw or, again, inside pits. The sod over these pits would be plowed or even sown with some crop or other. Sometimes young trees or shrubs were planted to hide any trace of the pits. Of course, sometimes this didn't work: a "good" neighbor had only to whisper something to the German and then he proceeded to do his part.

8. Requisitions

For a quota delivery of potatoes, peasants received almost seven marks per three poods, when the actual price was twenty to thirty times greater. No money was paid for requisitioned grain. The Germans took advantage of every opportunity to seize whatever a landowner might possess. For example, a man might request permission from the *Amtsvorsteher* to take six poods of potatoes to his son, who lives in Vilna. The *Amtsvorsteher* would not turn him down, but would advise the man to take his request to the *Kreishauptmann,* who would surely grant him permission. In a few days, the *Amtsvorsteher* would receive a telephone call: "All the man's produce, including the potatoes, are to be seized, given that he has the extra amount to send to his son."

During the final two years, the authorities were so strict that if a quota of grain was not delivered on the day it was due, the Germans would take a threshing machine to the barns, thresh the grain and take all of it. To prevent the local population from consuming even a single extra bite, millstones were confiscated from all homes. Nothing could be milled except at a designated mill and with the permission of the *Wirtschaftsausschuß*. Many mills were shut down, and all the millers' sifters used for making fine flour were confiscated. Indeed, people had to forget all about flour for the duration of the German occupation.

All other foodstuffs were brought under rigid control. During the first winter, all districts were ordered to deliver specified amounts of butter and cooking fat. Since almost no milk was produced in winter, one *Amtsvorsteher* wrote his *Kreishauptmann* that the people did not have surplus fat of any kind and were in need of it themselves. The *Amtsvorsteher* was promptly removed and sent off to the front lines with this reprimand: his function was to carry out orders, not to provide his unsolicited opinions. Later, it was ruled that everyone who owned a cow was to deliver a liter of milk to the village elder every day. Next, the amount was increased to two liters. The village elder was to deliver the milk every day to the *Wirtschaftsausschuß*, which operated dairies in every town, producing dozens of poods of cheese and butter a week. If ever it was determined that any milk had been watered down or lacked the required percentage of fat, the guilty parties were severely punished, even to the extent of confiscation of the cow. Whenever it was not possible to determine who the guilty ones were, the entire community suffered, having to pay the fines. No excuses were accepted. Anyone who reported a cow that was sick or had no milk was told, "If a cow stops giving milk, it is to be brought in to provide meat for the military." In the autumn, when the cows produced no milk for about two months, these quotas were suspended. In addition to milk there was also a "butter tax": in many places a pound a week, half a pound in winter.

No one was allowed to have more than one cow. The rest, mercilessly, were seized for meat. Special permission was required to slaughter cattle, sheep, hogs, or fowl. Most calves and young bulls were confiscated for meat. Twice yearly at least two pounds of wool was demanded for every sheep; for every hen, one egg a day. In some towns, permission was granted once a week to slaughter a cow for the residents. No wonder, then, that the people lived almost entirely deprived of milk, eggs, butter and meat. The confiscation of the cattle was a genuine hardship. During the last year of the German occupation, it was finally possible to persuade the authorities to let the people themselves provide the necessary amount of meat. Each community collected a "ransom" payment of fifteen to twenty rubles per cow, and the money was used to buy meat. There were some wealthier areas where there was still a surplus of cattle, and these were purchased for delivery to the Germans. The Germans set nominal prices for everything they took. For example, four to ten pfennigs for a liter of milk or an egg. Even these small amounts, however, usually remained in the pockets of the village elders and the *Amtsvorsteher.*

All flax, hemp, and seeds were to be turned in. If the Germans noticed that people were not delivering these products, house-to-house searches were made. Then, everything was confiscated: linen cloth, various metal utensils, woolen goods, food, and so on. House searches took place quite frequently and for a variety of reasons, particularly after an announcement was issued demanding that people turn in some item (fur pelts, copper, hog bristles, etc.).

The occupation forces saw to it that all raw materials were removed from the country, since Germany and its allies were in dire need of them. Even things which at first glance seemed to be of little value were taken.

In many places the people were instructed to gather nettles, the stems of which are covered with a thin membrane which can be made into thread. The meadows of Lithuania are full of wild grasses that produce a down-like puff when mature. Children were ordered to gather this material for the Germans.

Special "collection points" were established where various kinds of waste was to be delivered. Horses were not to have long tails or manes. Twice a year these were to be cut and the hair turned in. Dead horses or cattle were not to be buried. The carcasses were to be brought to a *Verwertungsanstalt* (conversion plant).

All berries and the fruit from every orchard was the property of the authorities, and their private sale was forbidden. Certain persons were assigned to bring all these crops to the marmalade factories, which functioned exclusively to supply the front lines. The prices paid for such crops were dirt cheap, something like a few marks for three poods.

9. Requisitioning of Horses

Horses were frequently requisitioned, causing great hardship. While there was a provision for not confiscating someone's last remaining cow, there was no such consideration when it came to horses. The policy was simply to take every horse that was healthy and could be of use to the military. Owners were to bring their horses to a specified place, where a military commission evaluated the animals. Protests were of no avail. Payment for each horse was according to category. Heartrending scenes took place on these occasions. When the peasants had to bring in the only horse in their possession, their women and children, in particular, would cling to the horse, throw their arms about its neck, and refuse to let it be taken to the commission. The Germans, however, did not care for delays. The soldiers had clubs and beat the entire family with murderous blows for defending their horses. The despair of the grieving peasant women was so great that they refused to take money for the horse. But they were forcibly dragged to the cashier, where the money was thrust on them, and then they were thrown out.

Once his only horse was gone, the peasant's livelihood was ruined. True, there were orders that the horseless were to "borrow" a neighbor's horse to plow the field. Nevertheless, anyone familiar with conditions in the countryside and the demands of agriculture will understand that this was hardly a remedy. The penalty for not turning over one's horse to the commission was severe and, in the end, the horse would be taken anyway. These mobilizations took place about twice a year. In addition, every horse was required to be registered and stamped.

10. The Exploitation of Estates and Fields

At the same time, each *Wirtschaftsausschuß* was to see to it that fields not lie fallow, but that they be worked. To this end the Germans took possession of all abandoned estates and began to cultivate them. There was a considerable number of such estates. A large number of wealthy landowners had fled to Russia. The estates remained without livestock, but this was rectified by the Germans, who devised a simple method for working these fields. They would forcibly assemble the nearby peasants and their horses to plow, harrow, and plant the fields. The pay for an entire day's work—without meals—was at most two marks. Every village was required to supply a number of peasant women to harvest, dig potatoes and pull up weeds. For this labor, the pay (again, without meals) was a nominal thirty pfennigs per day. In fact, even this negligible wage was often not paid. Anyone who did not work efficiently was beaten by the Germans with whips and clubs. The same held true when anyone did not understand their working orders, and the peasants did indeed understand the Germans very poorly. In addition to the peasants, there was another category of unpaid laborers. These were the families who lived in the war zones and were expelled from their homes. They were truly like the slaves in Egypt. They were housed in abandoned buildings and fed nothing but half a pound of bread and black coffee. Their wives and children were also required to work. They were forbidden to leave the area. These homeless people were required to do the heaviest labor. In addition to working in the fields, they were forced to gather stones, pave the roads, do the laundry for the military, and so on. Little wonder that many of them died of starvation and disease.

During the first year, the Germans distributed grain for sowing to those who had none and did not charge them much for it. No travel permits were issued in the cities within the district during the planting season, except in case of dire emergency, and that only after one went to great pains. When a request for permission to travel was received, the reply given was that the peasants and the horses were needed in the fields. The permanent farm hands who worked in the estate fields also remained with the Germans; their situation was dreadful. During the final two years, soldiers unfit for duty at the front worked in the fields along with the peasants. Soldiers, however, were allotted military food rations. Despite the fact that no modern agricultural methods were employed, the fields yielded a great deal of grain for export.

11. Management of the Fish Supply

The Germans also made efforts to control the supply of fish. In our area, fishing was a sizable branch of the economy. Most fishing enterprises were run by Jews. For the first three months of the occupation, there were no restrictions on the catching or exporting of fish. Prices were quite high, and both the fishermen and the commissioners in the cities profited considerably. After a while articles began to appear in German newspapers, which said that, since meat was scarce, more use should be made of fish. In January 1916, a decree was issued in Vilna forbidding the sale of fish anywhere but in the fish market. Extremely low prices were set, barely higher than those during peacetime. This led to an immediate reduction in the size of the catch and to illegal dealing in fish. The fishermen delivered a petition to the mayor asking for a higher profit margin, without which it did not pay to catch the fish and deliver them to the cities. The mayor did not respond favorably, but the legal price of fish was raised several months later. Nevertheless, the illegal trade in fish continued for the duration of the occupation. Very little fish was brought to the market. Moreover, the district officials refused to issue travel permits to the fishermen, insisting that their fish be sold locally. Eventually, the sale of fish to civilians was prohibited entirely. Everything had to be delivered to the sales divisions of the district authorities. The prices paid were extremely low, the highest being one mark per pound for large fish and twenty to twenty-five pfennigs for small ones. Only fish of a specified size could be caught, but this rule was not strictly enforced.

The military took the larger fish, which were processed in smokehouses. The smaller fish were sent to Vilna to be sold to the mayor, who turned them over to the Jewish commissioners. Most of the small fish would arrive without having been put on ice. They would be crushed and, of course, spoiled, so that they were of no use to anyone. In the wintertime, however, when fish deteriorate less rapidly, the fish market was crowded. Then the longest lines were of people waiting to purchase a pound or two of small fish.

On one occasion, the Germans devised a rather original way to exploit the passion for fish among the inhabitants of Vilna. Notices in Yiddish were pasted up in every Jewish neighborhood stating that on Friday, fish would be sold in the marketplace at ten pfennigs per pound and in unlimited quantities. On Friday, people streamed into the marketplace by the thousands, but there was no fish for sale. The Germans needed to shoot film footage of Vilna's Jewish population, and this was the only way it was possible to assemble a large crowd in those days.

Like the Russians before them, the Germans leased the fishing rights to lakes, both private lakes (the property of people who had fled) and those belonging to the government. An attempt was made to attract Germans to run the fishing business, and at one time all of the lakes in the Koszedary district were turned over to a German. However, as he failed to make payment and never began the fishing operation, it was turned over to Jews.

All the equipment needed for fishing came from Germany. Since fish were considered a good resource for the military, the *Militärverwaltung*

(Military Administration) of Lithuania distributed nets to the fishermen at comparatively low prices and, after a time, even on credit (provided that the debt be paid in fish). If not for the smuggling of fish into the city, it would have been impossible to carry on fishing, for the expenses were too great to be covered at the prices set by local officials. Fishermen were permitted to own one or two horses, which could not be confiscated.

12. Smuggling

In order to prevent smuggling, there were guards, including military police, field gendarmes, and special patrols, posted on every road. They were stationed at intervals of ten to fifteen versts. Near cities and towns they were stationed much closer together. The same was true on the main roads to Vilna. The guards were charged with checking everyone walking or riding by to see that they carried the necessary permits and had no forbidden goods with them. On the side of every wagon, there was to be a board on which was written the owner's full name and the place and district where he lived. During the course of the occupation, the guards' strictness sometimes varied. For a while, during a quiet period, pedestrians were often allowed to pass without permits, and small packages were not confiscated. At this time there was even a rule permitting the carrying of up to a pood in weight on one's back, but this was in effect only briefly.

Because of all the rationing, the people in cities were literally sentenced to starve to death. The prices of basic items rose astronomically, as much as fifty to sixty times their previous level. Bringing goods to the city for sale was the only way that thousands of people could earn any money and also, indirectly, stave off hunger. Illegal trade became the major occupation of a large part of the population, and every day long lines of people stretched out of town and back. They often traveled dozens of versts to the villages to purchase grain, butter, cheese and other products from the peasants. These "pack carriers" then walked back to town with their purchases on their backs. Getting a package past the guards was dangerous, so pack carriers had to walk along side paths and through fields to avoid the Germans. Nevertheless, the field gendarmerie often apprehended these "criminals" and arrested them. The penalty was loss of the goods plus a fine.

Wagons also took side roads to avoid the major guard posts. But it was not always possible to slip by all of them, as the field police patrolled areas that were suspect. If a wagon fell into their hands, not only the goods but also the horse and harness were often confiscated. Therefore, those regularly engaging in smuggling had to find a means to transport goods without risk. This means proved to be the simple one, well-tested in

Russia: the bribe, which the Germans learned to take very soon after their arrival.

The guards, too, suffered hardships, and they were starved for eggs, butter, and bacon. Regular pack carriers disposed of the guards by offering them a few eggs, some butter, or a piece of cheese. More ambitious smugglers would find it necessary to offer money in addition to food, and, occasionally, a little honey or something else. The penalty for traveling at night was severe—one's horse would be seized. After dark, however, it was easier to get past guards who could not be bribed. In fact, all large-scale smugglers transported their goods at night, having first "arranged" things with several guard posts.

Some smugglers risked traveling without having made arrangements, come what may. If they were caught and asked for a permit, they would take out a twenty- or fifty-mark note (or more if the wagon was large) and give it to the soldier. This often succeeded. But sometimes the soldier or gendarme would deliver the smuggler, his goods and the proffered bribe to the authorities. In such cases, the impending sentence was grave: the horse and the goods were taken and, in addition, there was a large fine and sometimes even imprisonment.

When a wagon was stopped, the guards first demanded to see a permit. If they suspected anything, they ordered the occupants to get down off the wagon. Then the contents of the vehicle were inspected. All packages were emptied; hay, straw, and fodder for the horses were prodded. People were often searched as well. Their pockets were felt, as were parts of their bodies underneath clothing, since linen, wool, fur, and the like were smuggled by being wrapped around the body.* Smugglers made double floors in their wagons, where they hid things such as meat, butter, cheese and all sorts of expensive raw materials. This device was short-lived, however, for it was soon recognized.

In time, people became accustomed to the situation and smuggling became an illegally-sanctioned form of trade, which was necessary to the economy of the country. The Germans themselves, on an individual basis, found it necessary. It made it possible for them to make additional purchases

---

*I was once returning with my small children from a visit to my parents, who had given me some food. In Kaplica, near Vilna, a pood of potatoes, twelve pounds of peas, and twenty-five eggs were found in my wagon. The junior officer who carried out the inspection scolded me for this "crime": "That is forbidden by law." I pointed out that I was not transporting the food to sell it. The children were afraid and cried, but that had no effect. Having confiscated the contraband, the officer issued me a receipt for what he had taken. Later on, I stood trial in Vilna. I was ordered to pay a penalty of one hundred marks. The confiscated food was never returned to me.

both for their own use and for their families in Germany, whether the goods were sent by mail or carried when the soldiers went on leave.

13. The Demoralization of the Occupiers

During the latter part of the occupation, it became evident that the Germans had become quite demoralized with regard to their duty to the Fatherland and the army. Every soldier and official under the jurisdiction of either the general military administration of Lithuania or a local military administrator was mainly concerned about himself: how to make some money to send home and how to live it up in the occupied country. With "hush money," much that was forbidden could be legitimized. Every *Amtsvorsteher* had all sorts of good things. All businessmen or land owners sent him the best that they had. The higher German officials were literally swimming in eggs, butter, honey, wheat, cooking fat, and fruit. Even their servants bragged that they had a bitter taste in their mouths from eating too much honey. The same was true of the gendarmes. In addition to natural products—which they could consume only in limited amounts, and which they were therefore able to sell to smugglers—they accepted money to make various concessions when requisitioning grain, cattle, and the like. Gendarmes, especially those who were stationed in the same place for any length of time, thus amassed considerable sums.

Many officials also had local women as servants who were also their mistresses. In the village of D———, the government official simply threw a man out of his house, into which the official and two soldiers settled. The man's wife and daughter became the mistresses of their "tenants" and bore them children. Such cases were not unusual.

When an *Amtsvorsteher* or gendarme remained in a community for some length of time and made the acquaintance of its inhabitants he would, after the manner of the Russian police chiefs and constables, pay calls on all the more affluent Jews on holidays, especially Passover, to "become acquainted with" the special holiday dishes. When the wife of one *Amtsvorsteher* came to visit him for six weeks, he took her around almost daily to call on all the landowners, as well as the wealthier peasants and Jews.* During these visits, he did not refuse offerings of cash or presents for his wife. She eventually took home a considerable amount of personal property from Lithuania.

Administration of the forests brought many official foresters (*Förster*) very large sums of money. At first, the Germans attempted to manage the

---

*Although it was largely forbidden to bring one's family from Germany, an occasional brief visit by the wife of an official might be permitted in special cases.

forestry themselves, doing the logging with the help of forced labor. When this failed to meet the tremendous demands of the Fatherland for wood, the officials were forced to turn to private lumber dealers. They were contracted to deliver specific amounts of wood or to cut down specified stands of trees and sell them to German firms. These arrangements led to the greatest swindles. The *Amtsvorsteher* or his agent was to receive delivery of the lumber. A decision would be made as to how many feet of timber had been cut, for which the dealer would pay. Beforehand, the *Amtsvorsteher* or *Förster* would make a pact with the dealer: only half or a third of the delivery would be recorded, and the two would divide the rest.

Thus, tens of thousands of acres of forest and millions of trees were cut. Indeed, during the reign of the Germans, Lithuania's greatest source of wealth, its dense forests, was reduced to a fraction of its former magnitude. Large sawmills, which operated day and night, were set up in the larger forests. Often new rail lines were built, on which the lumber was transported in freight cars to collection points at railroad stations. Tens of thousands of workers were needed to cut down the forests, and the Germans instituted forced labor for this purpose.

14. Slave Labor—Popilva

The slave labor edict hit the villages and towns in full force at the end of 1916. All men up to the age of forty were eligible for conscription, but the emphasis was on mobilizing seventeen- to twenty-five-year-olds. The local police had to compile lists of eligible men. Those registered were to report for work on their own. Anyone who did not report on time was arrested by soldiers at night, like a criminal. To begin with, the slave laborer was deprived of his *Ostpaß,* which, in effect, paralyzed him.* He could not venture outside at all; hiding in an attic was his only option. Until the men who reported were sent off to work they were locked up and placed under guard to keep them from running away. Then they were sent off to various sites, primarily to cut timber in the great forests. Others built new roads, or worked as unskilled laborers to construct buildings. Some were sent to dig trenches, and so on.

Popilva, in the vicinity of Kovno, was considered one of the worst slave-labor sites in our area. There in the great Kozłowa-Ruda forest, more than 3,000 men were assigned to cut down the trees. The men were divided into companies of from 150 to 300. One group felled the trees, another loaded

---

*This was the name given to the passports the Germans issued to everyone ten years and older. The passport carried photographs and, in Lithuania, those for Jews also had text in Yiddish.

them onto the local rail line, the third onto the main rail line, the next was assigned to the sawmills, and so on. The first slave laborers at Popilva had been French prisoners of war. When they could not endure this regimen and began dying in droves, they were replaced by the local population.

Wooden barracks were erected for the workers. They slept inside on bare planks, which were sometimes covered with sawdust. In all, there were four barracks, one of them exclusively for Jewish men. In winter, it was as cold indoors as it was outside. Although wood was available, there were no stoves and no one to tend to them. Work started at five o'clock in the morning and ended at six in the evening, with a single hour, from twelve to one, for a meal. Everyone had to wake up at four o'clock. In addition, there was often a six- or seven-verst march to the work site and back. The work was difficult and not everyone could endure it, but they were shown no mercy. Until a man fell, and whips and clubs could not get him to stand up, he was forced to labor intensively. For those doing such heavy work, the daily bread ration was a kilo for every four men. There was black coffee in the morning and for the twelve o'clock meal one liter of soup, which often consisted of rotten beets, usually used to feed cattle, or, occasionally, of turnips and dried potatoes. At night there was a spoonful of preserves and some black coffee. That was all.

The winters were very harsh. The workers' clothing and shoes quickly wore out while doing such hard labor, and they went about in tattered clothes and dilapidated footgear. The soldiers tried to determine whether a man might have ripped his boots deliberately in order to be excused from work. In such a case, the culprit was beaten severely and sent back to work anyway. When a worker's footwear fell apart completely, he was given wooden shoes. The cost of the shoes was deducted from his wages, which were thirty pfennigs per day. There were no provisions for hygiene. Occasionally the men would be taken to a "bathhouse" where there was only cold water. Instead of soap, the men were told to wash themselves with sand. For a short time, the men were allowed to walk to a nearby village on Sunday to buy bread. The privilege was withdrawn after several workers used the opportunity to run away.

Once, the workers made a protest about the lack of food and its poor quality. The lieutenant in charge merely scoffed in response. Then some of the workers decided not to report for work and tore off their identification numbers. (Each man had a number sewn onto his cap and sleeve.) The Germans regarded this action as a revolt. To identify those who participated, they inspected all the workers' clothing. Anyone who did not have his number sewn on was arrested and beaten mercilessly. Fourteen people (six Jews and eight Christians) were tried. Two of them were sentenced to death, but the sentence was commuted to sixteen years at hard labor. The rest received sentences of six months to a year in prison. Once, a man who pushed ahead in line during the distribution of soup was shot on the spot by the military guard.

The workers were forbidden to write home, and they were granted a ten-day leave only once every three or four months. A worker had to pay his own railroad fare, and he was also required to post a bail of fifty marks. Anyone who returned late from leave forfeited the money. Some men cut off their fingers or toes in order to escape this hell, but in vain. If the doctor determined that this was done intentionally, the crippled man was forced to work despite his damaged hands or feet.

More than a few men died while at work. Some were fatally crushed by falling trees, others were left crippled. Even greater numbers lost hands or feet to frostbite, became rheumatic, or contracted tuberculosis. No one was excused from work unless he was completely incapable of working or he provided someone to work in his place. In the latter case, however, both men were often forced to work.

Men escaped from Popilva at their first opportunity, without a thought as to what the next day might bring. For there was nowhere to run, and without a passport they would eventually fall into the hands of the police. The edict of forced labor under such barbaric conditions continued in force for approximately a year and a half until, apparently, neutral countries intervened.

15. The Germans' Attitude toward the Local Population

On the whole, the Germans treated the local population as if they were animals that were of use to their master but had no rights whatever themselves. The Germans spoke only in the form of commands and they made frequent use of physical force. Their penalty for a word spoken out of turn or a task not done as ordered was a beating with a club or whip. Little wonder then that when the peasants caught sight of a German they trembled. They knew they could expect an edict, a requisition, an inspection, or something similar. The villagers' failure to understand the language of the occupiers frequently led to a variety of misunderstandings, which sometimes ended in tragedy. For example, a German soldier entered a village and straight-away demanded to be provided with a wagon. A peasant working on the roof of his house tells the soldier that he is just about finished and will come right down. Because the peasant was using an ax to do his work, the soldier surmised that the peasant had just offered to split his head open. The soldier ran to get his comrades and they beat the peasant. He was arrested and charged with armed resistance against the military, for which the penalty is death. Before his trial, however, the peasant died in prison of unknown causes.

Or take another case: a soldier came into the village of Krunciki and demanded a wagon from a peasant, who said he could not give him a wagon at that moment. With the butt of his rifle, the soldier began beating the peasant and his family, who defended themselves. The soldier produced a knife and hacked off the peasant's fingers. The other family members seized the soldier, tied him up and brought him to the *Amtsvorsteher*, who they assumed would mete out the proper punishment to the soldier. As soon as the German soldiers stationed in the town learned of the incident, they became terribly enraged: "Why, if the people lose their fear of us they will kill us all! After all, there aren't that many of us here!" They were about to shoot the peasant on the spot, but one soldier succeeded—barely—in holding them off. The peasant was beaten nearly to death and imprisoned. He faced a death sentence. But because this occurred during the final year of the occupation, the peasant remained alive.

It often happened that a gendarme would shoot someone immediately, without first making an arrest, at the merest suspicion of resistance or for failure to stop in response to the order to halt. For instance: in Rudziszki, a gendarme named Stachowicz fatally shot a Christian named Urbanowicz, who was carting wood from the government forest without permission. Stachowicz also shot a young Christian from the village of Onglenik, who was herding cows and failed to hear his order to "halt." This same gendarme always carried a club, with which he would hit people at the onset, or he would set the dog that always ran beside him on his victim. Once, Stachowicz met a Jew taking rye to the mill. The gendarme asked whether it was smuggled goods. The Jew replied that he was taking a little rye to the mill to be ground. The gendarme began to yell that it was smuggled goods, and he beat the Jew with his club until it snapped from a blow to the Jew's head. Not satisfied, the gendarme released his dog, which mauled the Jew.

Another gendarme carried a chain which he would wrap around the head of anyone he suspected of concealing something. He would tighten the chain around the neck of the "accused" until the person's tongue hung out. In addition to all this, the Germans reacted to every trifle by flying into a rage, shouting and stamping their feet, striking terror into everyone.

There could be no talk of resistance. The possession of weapons was forbidden. In the village of Podworańce, a peasant was found to have hidden several guns. His only motive was the thought that someday he might have some use for the metal. True, there had been an order to turn in all weapons— but hadn't there been any number of edicts? A neighbor, angry with the peasant for some reason, reported him, and the guns were found. A military court sentenced the man to be shot to death, and Kaiser Wilhelm approved the sentence, which was carried out in Landwarów in full public view. The man's fellow inmates were forced to dig his grave, in which he was buried following the execution.

16. The Germans' Attitude toward Jews and Their Situation

The German occupation during World War I oppressed everyone more or less equally. For Jews, this was their sole consolation. Moreover, because they were able to communicate with Jews to some extent, the Germans were somewhat more lenient toward them. (On the whole, Jews were less likely to be beaten as often as the peasants were.) In fact, the Jews were of the utmost importance to the foreign occupiers, who were unable to communicate with the majority of the local population and therefore relied on Jews to be interpreters. This also accounts for the fact that some of the office personnel were young Jewish men and women who had quickly acquired a practical knowledge of German.

It often happened that the Jewish clerks of the *Amtsvorsteher* were in charge of all business in the area, and thus they could give indirect advice about getting a release from a requisition order, and so on. In such a case, the clerks learned to take advantage of their privileged situation. Since they could communicate with one another, peasants who had been wronged went to the Jewish clerks to ask them to intercede on their behalf and do something for them.

Perhaps this helped improve the image of Jews held by the Christian population in general. They could plainly see how this mighty power treated Jews like everyone else and, possibly, even somewhat better. This had the effect of planting in the peasants' mind the idea that Jews were citizens, which had been an impossible concept for the peasants during tsarist times and especially among the Poles.

Of course, there was no dearth of Jew-baiters among the Germans and, in particular, among the Poles from Poznań, who had been sent to our area because of their knowledge of German.[3] They repeated all the familiar accusations: Jews are smugglers, swindlers, scheme their way out of forced labor, and so on. As for the Germans, these views were held principally by officers who came from the Prussian Junkers.[4]

Even so, the Jews had some sense of security. Once a Christian in the town of Butrymańce attempted, with the support of a priest, to spread a blood libel. Both men were promptly arrested and severely punished. After that there was no more talk to be heard about "the use of blood."[5]

This was the single ray of light for Jews in this dark time. Economically, they were in total ruin. Legitimate trade had all but died. There was nowhere to buy merchandise and no way to transport it. The few items exempted from regulation (candles, saccharin, chicory) were of little consequence commercially, and they could be purchased only in officially designated places. Jewish artisans in the towns had no work. The only solutions were to work for the Germans or to engage in smuggling. A greater number chose the second option. Others curried favor with individual Germans by serving as office workers, delivery runners, interpreters, and hangers-on.

At the same time, some Jews found productive employment working in forests or factories, while others went into agriculture. Everyone tried to make sure that he planted potatoes and a little garden for his own use. The small-town opinion that "such work is beneath me" disappeared. In such times, even the worst kind of work was acceptable if it helped put food on the table. The poverty of the Jewish population was so great that many families in small towns simply died of hunger. The funds that came from relief organizations abroad were of some assistance, but the Germans tried to get hold of any money that passed through their hands. They wanted to decide how to distribute the money and to whom, including Christians, even though it was specifically intended for Jews. Wherever they encountered no resistance, the Germans succeeded with their plan. But in those places where the representatives of the Jewish community stood their ground, the money was divided among those for whom it had been sent.

In both cities and towns, Jewish stores were ordered to be open for business for several hours on Saturdays. This put an end to the small-town psychological fear of desecrating the Sabbath. The Germans had no regard for these religious feelings and frequently forced Jews to clean the streets, repair the pavement, and so on, on the Sabbath. At harvest time or when milkweed was out, Jewish children were forced to go to work gathering the various wild grasses that could be of use. Public school teachers and their students were sent to collect stones.

17. How the Wealthy Peasants Fared

Despite all the requisitions, the life of the peasant was easier. He was not, after all, constantly under the watchful eyes of gendarmes and other officials. He was able to conceal from the Germans a considerable portion of his crops and often even his cattle. For these he was able to get almost anything he asked from the starved city dwellers. All "higher" needs, such as clothing and luxury items, were now of scant importance to the city people; their sole interest was in food. At first, the peasant demanded Russian money for his wares, then German marks. (He never willingly accepted *Ostgelt,* or *Bons,* as it was called.)[6]

When the value of money declined—and the peasant had by that time amassed enough of it—he began to demand various articles in payment and he would receive what he asked for. The peasant began to live better than he had before. He began to consume the butter, eggs, and meat that once he would have sold. The roles of the country dweller and the city resident were reversed.

18. Schools

The attitude of the occupying power toward education is noteworthy. The Germans saw to it that there was a school, perhaps two (one for Jews and one for Christians), in every town. Wherever possible, they installed a German soldier as instructor, teaching in German. Where this was not feasible, men or women from the local population were assigned to be teachers, with a preference given to those who knew German. According to Field Marshal Paul von Hindenburg's guidelines, the language of instruction was to be the children's mother tongue. In the case of the Jewish schools, however, an effort was made to Germanize them as much as possible. The greater part of the school day was conducted in German, and in some cases it was mandated that all instruction be in German. This was done because "Yiddish was only a corrupt form of German," said the Germans, echoing our own opponents of Yiddish.[7]

The residents had to cover the expense of the schools by paying a school tax, as well as supplying whatever materials were needed, such as wood, water, etc. In many places school attendance was compulsory. Nevertheless, these schools did not establish deep roots in the life of the people. Their only virtue was that they created the need for secular schools in the towns. No longer would the *heder* suffice.

19. The Battle with Contagious Disease

The Germans had a quite unique approach to combating contagious disease. One house in each town was designated a hospital for cases of contagious disease. When, for example, someone contracted typhus (the most widespread illness, which claimed the lives of perhaps a fourth of the population and made more than half of the people ill), the person would be confined to the "hospital." The director of the "hospital" was usually the local *feldsher,* who often did not appear there for days at a time. No treatment was offered, and outsiders were strictly forbidden to enter the place. The patient was thus sentenced to die. Indeed, the people considered the "hospital" a morgue.

In the towns, "delousing centers" were established in public bathhouses. These, however, were merely a farce, for there was no hot water and no steam. In fact, a clean person entering such a place might well contract any of a variety of illnesses carried by vermin. Vaccination against smallpox was made compulsory.

The small-town residents found the Germans' emphasis on the cleanliness of outhouses very amusing. The Germans insisted that they were to be kept clean, and during inspections many people were punished for not carrying out these orders. The topic was grist for the town jokers' mills.

20. Positive Aspects

Several positive aspects of the Germans' activity should be mentioned, despite the fact that they were all the result of self-serving motives. They paid a great deal of attention to repairing and maintaining roads. New highways were built, dirt and clay surfaces were paved. All bridges were repaired, and trees were planted along many roads. Signs displaying directional information and distances (in kilometers) between places were placed on every road. Of course, all of this work was done by local residents.

German military cemetery in Vilna, established during World War I.
Courtesy of the YIVO Archives.

Fire brigades were organized in every town. All male residents were required to attend practice sessions. People were required to have a barrel of water in front of every house. In case of fire, everyone was to gather at the scene and try to contain the blaze. It must be said that fires were rare during the German occupation.

The attitude of the Germans toward their fallen comrades, who lie buried in various places in Lithuania, was also remarkable. From time to time a company of soldiers* would come to tend the graves, put up fences or stone borders, plant grass, or erect new crosses bearing precise inscriptions, some of them quite sentimental. Parents and wives who visited the graves of their loved ones frequently left moving epitaphs—"gone forever, in a foreign land." In places where there were many casualties, the Germans established large cemeteries, to which all the corpses were brought from wherever they had been interred. Such cemeteries had attractive picket fences and, in the center, a stone wall bearing the name of the burial ground. The graves were in straight rows and were mounded high, each marked with an inscribed cross. In the middle of the paths, there would be a symbolic cement monument above a grid of various types of weapons. On the walls were messages: "In memory of the great battle of Nieman in August 1915. Here they conquered and fell." On the main wall, the inscription: "Faithful unto death," and others. (There is a cemetery like this about four verst from Troki, near the village of Zazdrość.) The cemeteries were decorated with flowers or small trees. During the final year of the occupation, nearly all of the corpses were transferred to these cemeteries, where German order and sentimentality prevailed.

21. Banditry

The complete destruction of people's lives and the terrible plight of prisoners of war and slave laborers led to a considerable increase in banditry, something almost unheard of in Lithuania prior to the occupation.

When the Russian forces withdrew, a few of their soldiers, who were still armed, remained in our area. Despite all the threats that they faced, they were not ready to surrender to the Germans and be taken prisoner. One way or another, they managed to persuade some of the peasants to let them work in the fields. They did not ask for wages; all they wanted was food. Nevertheless, as soon as the Germans learned that a Russian soldier was hiding out somewhere, they would immediately arrest him. The householder who sheltered him was also punished. In time, it became impossible for Russian soldiers to remain in any one place; they were forced to hide.

---

*In the shtetls they were called "Hevra kadisha."

The situation of prisoners held in Germany was also dreadful. Those who were near the Russian border often escaped. Toward the end of 1917 and throughout 1918 the number of escapees greatly increased. During the day, they hid in the woods or in ditches and then left their hiding places at night. They would knock on the windows of houses along the road, asking for bread and for directions. At first the local people supported them, but when these wandering groups began to organize into armed bands, people responded to them with hostility and fear. Unable to pass through and find sustenance peacefully, the escapees turned to violence.

The local criminal element, whom these foreigners needed as informers, joined these bands. The locals could supply precise information as to who had money, provisions, valuable objects, and so on. The gangs attacked the wealthier peasants, landowners, and rural Jews, who lived alone by the roadside with no nearby neighbors. When these attacks first began, the band (often fifteen to twenty men) would surround the house they had targeted, so that no one could escape. A few of the men would go up to the door quietly and knock. (There were no dogs anywhere; the Germans had shot them all.) When the resident opened the door he was assured that he would not be harmed if he gave them all his money. Once the victim surrendered all his money and the group was satisfied with the amount, they took all his food and departed, warning him not to report the attack.

As time went on this "peaceful" form of robbery gave way to bloody, murderous acts of violence. The bands grew larger and they demanded more money. The risk was great, so they were going for broke, as the saying goes. At first the attacks occurred in the middle of the night. Later on, they took place in the evening. After the house was surrounded by lookouts, several of the bandits would break in. Often, rather than wait for the door to be opened, they would force it open or smash a window. They would fire a few gun shots into the air to frighten the entire family into keeping still. Everyone would be forced either to hold up their hands or to sit around a table and place their hands on it. The bandits would turn to the head of the house and announce that he must hand over a given sum of money immediately, if he and his family wished to remain alive. Frequently, however, the sum demanded was so large that, even though the victim handed over all he possessed, he was unable to satisfy the attackers. Suspecting that the victim was holding back money, the bandits would begin to torture him terribly. First, he was beaten, and if this failed to produce the desired result he was dragged, hanged, choked, stuck with needles, burned with matches, and the like. Sometimes his wife and older children were also subjected to the same treatment. The torture could go on for three or four hours. During this time, the bandits would clean everything out of the house, stuff all the better clothing, underwear, shoes, and other articles into sacks and carry them off to be shared with their waiting cohorts. If, however, the bandits realized that they would not be able to extort any more from their victim they let him go, warning that no one move from the spot for an hour or they would all be killed. In many instances, the raiders would announce that they were Bolsheviks dedicated to spreading justice by depriving the wealthy of their possessions.

If a member of the household knelt before the attackers and pleaded that the father or husband not be tortured, the robbers only intensified the beating. Many a person was shot dead when he made a movement that the bandits interpreted as defiant. Some were unable to recover from their torture and died a few days after. Sometimes, if a peasant family was large, it would offer resistance. But, if the bandits prevailed, they left no family member alive. During an attack, the bandits extinguished all lights, using only electric flashlights. Thousands of families were robbed in this fashion, an attack occurring somewhere almost every night.

The bandits stayed in the countryside with suspicious individuals, through whom they were able to purchase what they needed. During the day, they would stay in the large trenches left over from the war. In winter, they even installed small stoves in some of them. The local people knew, more or less, where the bandits were staying but were afraid to say anything. In cases where someone betrayed them to the Germans, the gangs sought revenge by killing the suspected informers or setting fire to their homes.

Once a group of bandits encountered a young Christian from the vicinity of Alksninė. whom they invited to join their band. They ridiculed him for working while their bread was so easily obtained and so plentiful. Afraid to refuse, the youth said he would think about it. The bandits warned him not to tell anyone of their offer. He did tell, however, and the bandits learned of it. One night they arrived at his father's home, tapped on the window and called the youth to come outside. "You have a long tongue," they said to him, and cut off half his tongue.[8]

In the beginning, the Germans fought against these bands. Anyone the Germans found carrying weapons was shot. But the number of gangs only increased. Moreover, on the eve of their withdrawal, the Germans were mainly concerned with saving their own skins and glad to be alive after an encounter with a group of bandits. Indeed, there were instances where bandits fell upon armed Germans and killed them.

When victims notified the gendarmerie as to where they thought the bandits had their quarters, the Germans were not particularly eager to look for them. Thus, during the final months of 1918 all such attacks went unsolved. The military administrators received dozens of reports daily from the district chiefs regarding these attacks and killings. They made no effort, however, to liquidate or combat the bandits. This kind of crime was so widespread that entire towns began to fear they would be the victims of an attack by these armed gangs. The towns organized patrols, in which the entire population participated, to walk the streets at night.

22. The Liquidation

During the final months before their withdrawal, the Germans began feverishly shipping out the grain and other crops that they had requisitioned. At the very end, however, the peasants began to stop them. Fearful of the aroused populace, the Germans slept in their clothes and kept hand grenades and loaded guns close by them. In some places, people disarmed the Germans. There were Germans who shot at the angry crowds, killing some people.

Because people were no longer afraid of the Germans, the last of the troops saw to it that they were gone as quickly as possible. At the same time, they sold all sorts of government-issued items in order to make as much money for themselves as possible. Power passed to local citizen committees, which organized their own militia. The Germans left unit by unit with their guns loaded. Any grain they did not succeed in selling or which they were not permitted to remove from the country was turned over to local committees.

3

APRIL 1919

*Dedicated to the cherished memory of my
unforgettable father, Zelig bar Avrom Abramowicz,
of blessed memory, who died on the 7th day of
Nissan in the year 5682 (19 April 1922).*

I n April 1919, life in Vilna was unbearably hard. Hunger was pervasive. It was against the law to buy or sell anything. People were afraid to bring anything into the city, because both the merchandise and the wagon would be confiscated; the horse would be kept for a week or longer. Bread was difficult to find and a bowl of plain soup was also a rarity. The Soviet authorities had hundreds of employees register the population, in order to issue ration cards, but, despite all their writing and erasing, there was only one distribution—of sugar and herring—during the entire period of three or four months.

No wonder, then, that anyone who was able to do so fled Vilna. If they did not leave permanently, they at least went to stay temporarily in a town or village, where it might be possible to find something to eat or to bring back home, and where they might recuperate. My parents were living in the countryside about sixty verst from Vilna. Having experienced the terrible winter of 1918–19 along with everyone else in the city, I decided to get away for Passover at whatever cost and recuperate a bit.

There was no use hoping to find a ride on a wagon, for there was little such traffic; I had to go on foot. I wanted to obtain a travel permit, but, noting the long lines and the general disorder, I gave up hope of succeeding and decided to start out without one. There was so much mud on the roads that my feet sank into it. Nevertheless, quite a few people were out, including women and children, going "wherever the road took them." They were starving, exhausted, practically barefoot. Everyone looked dreadful. I often saw Red Army personnel walking along the roads as well; they were mainly on the lookout for something to eat.

The railroad bridge on the Waka River, between Vilna and Landwarów, had literally been blown to bits. For the distance of a verst, there were pieces of steel and cast iron strewn about. The Bolsheviks were trying to repair the bridge, but there was little noticeable progress. In Landwarów, I was told that commissars came almost daily and pleaded with the workmen to work more efficiently, but to no avail. Despite this, an entire staff of railroad personnel was stationed in Landwarów, although they themselves did not know what their function was. They received whole sheets of paper money, called *kerenki,* and somehow managed to stay alive, although they suffered considerably from hunger.[1] Jews wandered like ghosts through the streets, having nothing to do. Soldiers were billeted in every house, and both the householders and their "lodgers" suffered the same degree of hunger.

My hope that I would find a wagon in Landwarów on which to continue my journey did not materialize. I had to summon all my strength to walk the remaining forty verst, so that I could spend Passover with my parents. Near Troki I stopped at a small village for a bite to eat. The peasants would not sell me anything, saying that they were exhausted by the stream of travelers passing through, giving them no rest day or night. They also complained bitterly that the Bolsheviks were taking their cows and even their seed. There simply would be nothing to sow in the fields. Anyone who had any grain or potatoes left had tried to "throw it into the ground"—that is, to plant it—so that the Bolsheviks wouldn't be able to take it away. Obviously, there was some danger that this sowing was for naught, but there was no alternative. If it was bound to go to waste, "at least *they* would not get hold of it."

I ate a piece of bread that I'd brought with me and continued on my way. It was raining buckets and it was difficult to find a firm path on which to walk. In some places, my feet would get stuck in the mud and it was almost impossible to pry them loose. One can only imagine the hardships endured by small children, women and the elderly on such a road.

I caught up with two Christian women, both wearing linen "shoes" on their swollen feet. Both were completely exhausted, barely able to move. We got to talking. One of them recounted her terrible experiences. She was a landowner from near Święciany. About thirty years old, she was an institute graduate and had attended Bestuzhev courses.[2] Her husband, an officer, had died in the war, leaving her with two small children and her old father. They lived close to the front between Russia and Germany. At first the Germans drove them out, but later they were allowed to manage their land as best they could. For several years, they lived there with the constant thunder of cannons and bullets. When the Germans retreated the family was attacked at night by bandits, who took everything in their home and storehouse, even the clothing they were wearing. During the raid, her father was mercilessly tortured (choked, hanged, pierced with needles) to force him to reveal where the money was hidden. But the family had none. The older child suffered severe convulsions. The bandits packed everything onto wagons and drove away. The next morning a second gang came, but they found nothing. Overnight the family had become beggars, left without any clothing or even so much as a piece of bread to assuage the children's hunger.

Neighbors collected some things for them. The militia that had been organized by the residents learned of the robbery. Several local peasants had been recognized among the bandits, and all of the stolen goods were discovered in a village. There the robbers waged a real battle with the militia, who were "unable to do anything." When the Bolsheviks arrived, the matter again came under investigation. Soon it was represented as a case in which the property of a bloodsucker, a landlord, had been confiscated, and this, of course, was not a serious crime. True, two or three of the most vicious of the attackers were arrested, but while in transit they either escaped or were deliberately let go by their guards. Meanwhile, the woman was destitute. She was obliged to leave her younger child with her father while she went to a relative, a priest, to escape death by starvation. When I met her, she had already been on the road for some ten days and no longer believed that she would ever reach her destination. The woman with her was a faithful former servant who chose to share her mistress's hungry fate.

I made every effort not to stop on the road at night and to arrive at my parents' house in time for the seder. There were about ten verst still to go. Everything I was wearing was already soaked through from the rain above and the mud below. My shoes were so wet that they were falling apart. There were sores on my feet, but I was being carried along by pure momentum. At about seven in the evening, more dead than alive, I made it to my parent's home; they were very surprised to see me. I spent several days either sitting or lying down, for I was unable to move a muscle and had terrible pain in my legs.

My parents' place was about seven verst from the Bolshevik-Lithuanian front (if it may be called that) or demarcation line. It was a small estate where my father had been living for forty-odd years, farming the land. Once before, in 1915, my parents had to abandon everything and escape the approaching wave of war. As a result they lost their cows, equipment, and furniture. When the Germans captured Vilna, however, my parents returned home. They found one of their cows at a neighbor's farm and some grain left in the barn. Little by little, they reestablished some of their farm. They were even able to feed paupers passing by and to give them some good-sized pieces of bread and a few quarts of grain to take along.

Word of their charity spread quickly among the indigent of Vilna, and none of them failed to stop at the home of the "good Jew." I have been told by many people that in other places, too, the rural Jews were the only ones who never refused food to anyone. The peasants were quite hostile toward the hungry city folk and would give people bread only in exchange for other goods. At first the peasants did not want to accept German money, especially *Ostgelt,* for food.

Once a gang of bandits attacked my parents. The bandits not only took their household goods but also beat and tortured them terribly. Their grain was not taken, because my parents had hidden it in anticipation of bad times. After the German withdrawal, a militia was organized. They were given arms and energetically set about combating the bandits. Jews and non-Jews were equally represented in the militia, providing some guarantee against outbreaks of anti-Jewish violence.

In several instances, some of the young country hotheads settled accounts with village elders who had acted as agents of the Germans, much to their own benefit. These elders were relieved of any "surplus wealth." In general, however, the militia kept order and people were afraid of them. For about a month, quiet reigned. There were no reports of burglaries or looting. A citizens' court of sorts was created to adjudicate all disputes.

When the Bolsheviks arrived they promptly did away with the militia and began instituting "revcoms" (revolutionary committees), headed by seventeen- and eighteen-year-old youths. To begin with, they arrested figures of authority in the civil militia, as well as any estate owners who had not managed to flee. Actually, the revcoms exerted little control, being merely an ornament of the "workers' and peasants' government." All power was in the hands of the military commissars. The revcoms were charged with providing information about where there was anything to requisition and who had it, and they performed this function well.

There were several military units stationed in the town, and they were in need of provisions, especially bread and meat. They confiscated bulls and young cows. From my parents, for example, they took two cows and a horse, as well as sixty pood of grain, which had been set aside for seed and hidden in the hay loft. They appropriated almost all the food that the townspeople had stored up. The landed gentry suffered the greatest losses and, in addition, were ridiculed in the process. Management of their estates was ostensibly turned over to the workers. In actuality, however, it went to the military, who did little managing.

The war between the Bolsheviks and the Lithuanians at the front was like a children's game. The Lithuanians engaged the assistance of the Germans, who were still giving the orders on the other side of the line of demarcation. These Germans received wages, food, and shelter from the

Lithuanian government, but they had little motivation to fight. Each side was afraid of the other, and the moment a shot was heard everyone beat a hasty retreat. The two sides were thus positioned opposite each other for three or four months. A few shots would occasionally be exchanged for the sake of appearances, but no casualties resulted. All told, only one German was killed. This occurred when the Bolsheviks went into a village to look for "*borscht*." Several Germans approached and one of the Bolsheviks fired, supposedly out of "fear," killing one German soldier instantly. The Germans responded with several shots and then rode off, leaving behind the dead man. The Bolsheviks moved the corpse to the town and buried it near the church.

This incident provided an opportunity to establish an almost friendly relationship between the two fronts. The Germans sent emissaries to recover the body of their dead comrade. The Bolsheviks were glad to oblige and provided a military escort for the corpse. From that time on the two sides visited each other and held "parties." On those occasions, the Germans served whiskey to their Russian antagonists and were given Russian tobacco or sugar in return. They continued to "maintain" the "front" for appearance's sake.

Despite all the hardships, the town began to adjust to the Bolsheviks. In exchange for bread, one could obtain goods from them, especially warm underclothes, shoes, and sugar. They were free with their money, paying "whatever price was asked." This attitude obviously pleased the shopkeepers, who were glad to be doing business.

The Red Army men also liked to enjoy themselves. They set up a theater, and once or twice a week there would be entertainment, including dancing. This took place in the "priest's house," to which they brought furniture and a piano taken from a local landowner, a physician. All of the young townspeople, Jewish as well as Christian, would assemble there and thoroughly enjoy themselves. Every Sunday the Bolsheviks held meetings in the same place. Special propaganda evenings were also arranged for children: someone would speak or read to them or would play music on the piano. On several occasions, the children were given gifts. It should be acknowledged that the Bolsheviks found a way to reach the youngsters, who remembered them favorably.

These provincial children, used to being told to keep quiet, began to feel that they amounted to something, that the world was theirs, too. The ideals of justice—which they heard about at their children's meetings, perhaps for the first time—became very meaningful to them. Thus it was that the Bolsheviks began to become "acclimated"—until thunder struck.

An elaborate entertainment for children was planned for the Easter holiday, and the military commander left for Vilna to obtain gifts for the youngsters. He returned hurriedly that same day with the news that Vilna had been occupied by the Poles, and that communications between Vilna and Troki, where he had turned back, had already been severed. The commissar also brought word that a pogrom was taking place in Vilna.

My parents lived about four verst from the town, and when the news about Vilna reached us we became very alarmed. At the time I had left Vilna I could not have imagined that, in the course of a few days, the Bolsheviks—who, it appeared, had become so entrenched that they had no intention of withdrawing—would be ousted. The report about the pogrom plunged us into deep despair.

The military commissar summoned all the Red Army personnel in the town and explained the state of affairs to them. He described the terrible pogrom occurring in Vilna and noted that they now faced enemies on two sides. Nevertheless, it was necessary for some of them to go to Vilna both to rescue their comrades and to save themselves from this dire situation. As he spoke, he broke into sobs. All the Jews present in the marketplace (it was the seventh day of Passover) also wept bitterly. More than a full company of soldiers, including all those who were Jewish, volunteered. The commissar kissed each one. It was later reported that the company never reached Vilna. They were repelled and scattered en route by Polish forces.

The town garrison remained in place, although everyone felt its days there were limited. Their nervousness soon became apparent, and the Jewish population also felt uneasy. Moreover, no one had accurate information. A rumor spread from one Christian to another that some Jews had fired guns from windows and were therefore later slaughtered like sheep by "our people."

I was beside myself. It was impossible to go home. I applied myself to working in the field, plowing and sowing with great diligence. It seemed to me that after all my experiences there remained only one way to calm my broken spirit, and that was through healthful, natural work in the field. The war years had also demonstrated that this was the most secure way to earn a living. All we lacked was a horse. My brother and I decided to go to persuade the Bolsheviks to give us back our horse, which they had requisitioned. It was being kept at the food warehouse, several verst from the town.

What first caught the eye there were piles of bones. Because the Bolsheviks ate meat rather than bread, they slaughtered cows that had been seized from the populace. We had a statement on paper from the commandant to the effect that if the horse was not currently needed at the food warehouse it could be returned to us. The horse had been a very good one, but after four weeks in the hands of the Bolsheviks it was in dreadful condition. Their "stable boy" was a sixteen-year-old Jewish boy from Vilna, formerly apprenticed to a tailor. He had absolutely no idea about caring for a horse. The peasants told us that the boy didn't even know how to put a bridle on a horse. He would give the animal hay but leave it without water for days. No wonder, then, that so "competent" a person had already killed more than one horse.

The commissar in charge of the food warehouse did not want to surrender our horse. But the peasant at whose place the horse was quartered said that it should be returned: "That Jew is an honest man, and it should be done, otherwise he will be ruined." The commissar softened and began to inquire as to how one could cross over to the Lithuanian side. He was from the province of Kovno and was sick and tired of the whole game. Could we, perhaps, help him get across? Of course, we were discreet and avoided giving a concrete answer. He returned the horse.

The situation of the Red Army grew worse daily and the troops had to withdraw as quickly as possible. Wagons were brought in from all the surrounding villages and the men hurried to load them. Fear gripped the town. People were apprehensive about who would come in after the *gdoylim* ("big ones," the Jews' name for the Bolsheviks).[3] Their anxiety increased when the commissar bade farewell to all the Jews, even to the rabbi, and asked forgiveness for the troubles the townsfolk had suffered during the few months of Bolshevik rule. At that moment no one was glad that the *gdoylim* were leaving.

There was only one narrow pass by which the Red Army could leave. It led through the towns of Sumiliszki, Jewje, and Szyrwinty. By this route the troops could cut through to Dvinsk. The road lay half a verst from where I was staying. We on the farm did not know exactly what was happening in the town, but we could see, even from a distance, that there was considerable movement on the road. On the day the Bolsheviks left, my brother and I were plowing. The Red Army line moved very slowly, for their horses were weak and weary. Wherever possible, the troops confiscated horses. Two riders approached us and demanded our help in getting a heavy wagon up a hill: "It won't take any more than half an hour, and then we'll let you go back." We harnessed our horse to their wagon. Taking them at their word my brother left the house without putting on a jacket or taking anything along. He no sooner drove up to the line than machine guns were loaded onto his wagon. He was not let go, and instead of being away half an hour he spent ten days in great jeopardy on the road.

The Bolsheviks did not succeed in taking everything with them. They left behind a mass of propaganda material. Several days later I was on the road by which they had departed. All along the way countless brochures were scattered. The road was completely white. Just before the troops left, the commander of the regiment and an orderly rode swiftly west of the town, in the direction of the German-Lithuanian line of demarcation. Ostensibly they went to "reconnoiter" the enemy positions but their actual intention was to surrender, which they succeeded in doing. Their example was followed by some of their enlisted comrades. These soldiers were very angry at their superiors for having stayed where they were instead of leaving as soon as they had received news of the capture of Vilna. Things almost came to the point of putting an end to the commissars, but some men said that it would not help matters and could lead to anarchy and might increase the likelihood of their being captured by the Poles. Moreover, as none of the Bolshevik troops knew the road, no one doubted that the Poles would put an end to them.

As often happens in such situations, demoralization set in. Many of the soldiers took their wagons, which had been loaded with sugar, flour, soap, and so on, off onto a side road, where they sold everything and then, in many cases, deserted. There were no robberies in the town by soldiers who had been stationed there, but other departing troops left their mark on many villages and outlying farms. They took linen, clothing, shoes, and whatever else was available, not to mention feed for their horses. We, too, expected to be visited and did not sleep a wink, but the night passed without incident. The following day, at about seven o'clock in the morning, everything appeared calm at last; the Bolsheviks were gone. Suddenly, heavy shooting erupted. I was on a small fishing boat on the lake, collecting floats from fishing nets. All at once bullets began whistling over my head. I barely managed to lie down on the bottom of the boat. One bullet pierced the hull. We later learned that the Germans, who had returned from Lithuania, had been shooting at a solitary lingering Bolshevik whom they had spotted in the distance. An airplane also appeared, flying in the direction in which the Russians had retreated. A short time later we heard the sound of an explosion; a German plane had dropped a bomb onto the Bolshevik line. We had reason to believe my brother was there.

That same day, both the Lithuanians and Germans entered the town. They were now considered the best and most desirable of occupiers. At the time, we barely dealt with the Lithuanian authorities; everything was still reckoned according to the Germans. The Jews all went out onto their porches and greeted the troops in friendly fashion. They responded with restraint. They immediately began making searches, looking for anything the Bolsheviks had left behind. A few individuals suspected of being Bolsheviks were whipped, but "mercifully." The Germans left that same day, much to the regret of the Jews. In the meantime, non-Jews began to arrive on foot from Vilna. They were scarcely willing to speak to Jews, but they told the peasants about the terrible deeds of the "*Zhidy*" and how they were dealt with.

The following fact is worth recording: about four or five days before Passover, a poor Christian from Vilna had come to my parents' door. He was given food and drink, of which he had had none all the time that he had been on the road. He was moved. He motioned my father to one side and said, "I must tell you a secret, for you are a good man. I want you to know that there will be a pogrom in Vilna on Passover. If you have any of your family there, they must leave Vilna." At the time, not much credence was given to his words. They were remembered only when his prophecy came true.[4]

The local population seemed to grow hostile, and I felt I could no longer remain in ignorance about Vilna and my family there. I made an agreement with two young men, who had sisters and brothers living there, to try to make our way to Vilna. In the hope that we would find our families alive, we took some food for them, especially bread. We placed fifteen- to twenty-pound packs on our backs and, bidding farewell to our tearful parents, we set out. By that time the Poles had already been in Vilna eight days. When we arrived in Troki we went to the nearest Jewish home. The husband of the young woman who lived there was in Vilna, and she did not know what had happened to him. There had already been some robberies in Troki, but then the command was given that order be maintained. We walked on as far as Landwarów, where we encountered a group of young women. (Men did not venture out on the streets.) They told us that the husband of the young woman in Troki had been killed. One of them told me that there had been a robbery in the house where I lived, but she did not know whether there had been any casualties. The first Jewish home we had visited had suffered a loss of life, and robbers had attacked the house where I lived. I had to prepare myself for all possibilities.

Landwarów had suffered terribly. The Bolsheviks had seized horses and cows and other things as they retreated. In the wake of what happened in Vilna, there was a series of robberies and endless harassment. Groups of armed bandits came continuously from Vilna, and anything one group did not manage to take was seized by the next. All of this was accompanied by a variety of persecutions. The rabbi and several elderly people were forced to walk all the way from Landwarów to Vilna and were severely beaten for not walking fast enough. Nor were they permitted to accept a ride upon a wagon. Most of the Jews hid. Following several days of terrible robberies by bandits, the commandant issued an order that all robbers be flogged. After that, calm prevailed.

We did not encounter a single other Jew on the roads, and people wondered at our making the journey at such a dangerous time. We endured great moral pangs all the way from Landwarów to Vilna. Everyone we passed, women in particular, made a point of directing poisonous, biting, and humiliating remarks at us. Their first words were "*żydowskie komisary*" (Jewish commissars). At one place we came across several peasants with their families. One of them said, referring to me: "I sent his father to his eternal reward. Someone ought to send him there, too." The peasant women said that they had better stop doing business with Jews because "'our people' might shoot us for that."

As we reached the Waka bridge we came upon a passenger train that was supposed to go to Vilna. We went to ask about purchasing tickets. A guard (or conductor) replied, "You can't get one." We pointed out that there were other people on board. "Those are people, but not you, scum!" he replied. Despite how tired and heartsick we were from all that we had seen and heard, we walked on. With every step, we felt the earth burning under our feet. Yet soldiers passing by did not give us any trouble. This was all the more remarkable for, as we learned later, many people had been murdered on the roads.

As we entered Vilna by way of Novgorod Street I was surprised to see several Jewish children playing outside. Frightened faces looked out from behind gates, and everyone asked in anxious whispers where we were from and whether it was finally safe to venture out on the roads. Apparently we were the first Jews to enter the city since the "events."

I was afraid to enter my home immediately. From a distance I caught sight of Dr. Cemach Szabad. This encouraged me somewhat; here was an acquaintance who was still alive, so I ought not to lose hope. I hesitated to approach him, however, lest he tell me what I dreaded hearing. I no longer recall how I made my way home. Before getting there I did meet a woman I knew, who was the first to tell me that everyone in my family was safe. No one at home could believe that I had walked through the front lines and remained alive. Everyone said I should not have dared to do it. The truth is that I might well have been killed on my way back to Vilna.

IV

Jewish Vocational Education between the World Wars

1

THE VILNA
"HELP THROUGH WORK" SOCIETY

Toward the end of the nineteenth century there was a movement among Russian Jewry to involve more Jews in productive, skilled trades. Some government-run elementary schools for Jewish pupils offered rudimentary courses in locksmithing or provided carpentry workshops where older pupils could spend several hours a week under the tutelage of an ordinary craftsman. By 1890, however, there were several vocational schools connected with the *talmud torah* of the larger cities. These strove to train more intelligent artisans, particularly among orphans who lived at the schools where they studied. The administrators of these vocational schools were usually teachers who had minimal connection with skilled trades. The schools did not employ any systematic or progressive methods of vocational education.

This situation underwent a radical change at the end of the nineteenth century when, after extensive negotiations with the Russian government, the Jewish Colonization Association (JCA) established a division to lend support to any enterprise intended to bring Jews into productive occupations. The JCA hired expert craftsmen to provide comprehensive training for both boys and girls in skilled trades.

Trade schools for boys and girls began to spring up in a number of cities. Since local community leaders had no experience in the systematic teaching of these skills, the JCA sought to hire artisans who were also familiar with pedagogical issues. Engineers and instructors with at least some training in education were employed in the trade schools for boys. The girls' schools hired trained pedagogues with experience in handicrafts, drawing, and occupations generally engaged in by women (dressmaking, embroidery, and the like).

The JCA selected an engineer named Bolotin to supervise the boys' schools and a Mrs. Ber, a well-known teacher, to oversee the schools for girls. Both appointees had a broad vision of the aims of professional training for the Jewish population. The JCA also engaged various specialists—agronomists, technicians, and others—who could offer instruction in a variety of fields and occupations. In addition, the JCA recommended young, energetic engineers to serve as administrative directors for these vocational schools.

Vilna opened a new page in the history of vocational training. Among its numerous philanthropic establishments, the city boasted one of the largest *talmud torah*s in Russia. The number of orphans housed in its dormitory frequently reached between 250 and 300. The school also accepted children who had lost only one parent. They were fed there during the day, but spent their nights at home or with relatives. In compliance with the government's education authority, a Russian public school was established in the dormitory. There, in addition to the time dedicated to "religious studies," a considerable number of hours had to be devoted to the study of Russian.

After completing the *talmud torah*'s course of study by the age of twelve or thirteen, the children were sent to learn a trade either from an artisan or in the school's own workshop. The workshop was considerably behind the times both technically and culturally. The instruction it offered was primitive, but new developments were already taking place. Thanks to several new trustees, some of whom were engineers, a special vocational school was established during the final decades of the nineteenth century. This school accepted graduates of the *talmud torah* as well as those from a variety of other schools; a former administrator of a government-run school, a man named Bronzburg, was appointed the director.

The vocational school initiated a number of improvements in both technical and general studies. It offered programs in locksmithing, metalwork and electronics. In addition, a separate building was erected close to the dormitory to house the new school. The JCA provided some of the funds for the building after setting the condition that it be headed by someone with technical training. At the beginning of the twentieth century, a young engineer named L. Frenkel was recommended for the post of director. Not only was he well trained in his profession, but he was also artistically talented and had a strong interest in Jewish antiquities. Frenkel, along with several engineers in the administration (including the chairman, Adolf Gordon), reorganized the trade school into a thoroughly modern institute for vocational training. They introduced courses in freehand drawing and mechanical drawing, theoretical subjects (physics, chemistry), and others.

Inspired by the young engineers, the Vilna Artistic Industrial Association was founded at the school. The group's aim was to guide Jewish workers in employing advanced forms of modern craftsmanship. Their work was not meant to compete with factory products but would reflect the artisans' own ideas, both as to usefulness and artistic quality. Frenkel introduced courses in drawing, painting, and sculpture, all taught by native or foreign specialists of the first order. The Association became the center of a movement to beautify Jewish-made handicrafts and to attract Jewish youth with the requisite elementary education to do such work.

Parallel efforts were made by progressive *maskilim* who were leaders of Vilna's Jewish community. They sought to alleviate the dreadful poverty in the city by providing some kind of employment. Their models were the "workhouses" established by the non-Jewish community, where various kinds of work were provided, either to be done at home or in the workhouses: knitting, sewing, braiding, woodworking, or sorting certain kinds of goods.

The leaders of Vilna's Jewish community conceived the idea of establishing a "workhouse" of their own in an expanded form. In 1900, an organization named Help Through Work was conceived, but first it was necessary to obtain a permit from the central government. However, the Ministry of the Interior found the word "work" in the name of a Jewish organization to be unacceptable. This was because at the time, the Bund was involved in intensive revolutionary activity among workers in the Pale of Settlement. Nevertheless, since the tsarina herself was patroness of all workhouses in Russia, the Jewish leaders of St. Petersburg, headed by Alexander Broido, found a way to reach the proper authorities. Permission to establish the society was granted in 1903, after three years of petitioning in various government offices.

The history of Help Through Work is connected with an unusual event in Jewish life involving the family of the famous *maskil,* Samuel Joseph Fuenn. The Jews of Vilna have always been rich in intellectual prowess, both traditional and secular. Vilna was both the city of the Gaon of Vilna and of Adam Ha-Kohen, M. A. Guensburg, Kalman Schulman, and Isaac Meir Dick, as well as the wealthy *maskilim* Matthias Strashun and S. J. Fuenn, among others.[1] The circle to which Fuenn belonged was religious but not fanatically so—although in the eyes of the strictly pious they were practically considered heretics, which they certainly were not. Fuenn was exceedingly well versed in religious texts and Jewish history, as well as in Jewish literature in Hebrew, German, and Russian. The governor general of Vilna named Fuenn to the post of "learned Jew," his special counselor on Jewish affairs. This high position notwithstanding, Fuenn did not abandon Jewish tradition. He always wore a skullcap and even had short earlocks as well as, of course, a beard.

He owned some property in Vilna, including the famous Fuenn's Bathhouse on Zarechye Street. If I am not mistaken, his wife died at a young age, leaving him with two children, a boy and a girl. The daughter fell under the influence of a devout Catholic servant, apparently due to the absence of a mother's supervision, and developed a permanent attachment to Polish nationalism and Catholicism. The son attended a government-run gymnasium and eventually became a physician. Dr. Fuenn had his own coach, horse, and driver. The doctor traveled in style, wearing a top hat on visits to his patients. His practice was based in the city's wealthier Jewish circles and also included some Poles.

Fuenn's daughter (I don't recall her name) left her father's house and disappeared. It was some time before it was discovered that she had joined a convent, where she remained secluded. Despite his connections with the authorities, all of Fuenn's attempts to obtain his daughter's release from the convent were in vain. The old man was not even permitted to see his daughter. Fuenn addressed a petition to the tsar, requesting "most humbly" that the convent allow him to see and speak with his only daughter. After waiting for a long period of time an order was finally sent from St. Petersburg to the governor general. It stipulated that the conversation between father and daughter should take place in the presence of a high official from the governor general's counsel. Since the order had come from "the supreme command," the meeting had to be arranged precisely as set forth.

The daughter met with her old father, who looked quasi-rabbinical, and she grudgingly entered into conversation with him. To his plea that she come back home and his questions as to whether she had been forced into accepting the Christian faith, she responded clearly: she would not return home and no one had coerced her into turning to the "true faith." "Jesus Christ is the son of God," she said and recited a litany of Christian dogmas in which she had been well rehearsed. The authorities could do nothing for the father: his daughter was an adult and had herself stated that she had willingly accepted the Christian religion.

Samuel Joseph Fuenn died in 1890. His will provided that his entire estate go to his son, Dr. Fuenn, with the exception of a single, symbolic, ruble left to the daughter in order to prevent her from contesting the will. Dr. Fuenn was a bachelor and had no family. At his death, therefore, his entire fortune would become the possession of his proselyte sister. To prevent this from happening, the Jewish community leaders Arye Neuschul and I. L. Goldberg urged Dr. Fuenn to bequeath his estate to the projected Help Through Work organization, the full name of which would be "The Organization for Help Through Work, named in honor of Dr. B. Fuenn and his father, Samuel Joseph Fuenn."

Dr. Fuenn complied. He named the two above-mentioned community leaders to be executors of his will along with the lumber merchant Jacob ben Jacob, son of the famous bibliographer.[2] Dr. Fuenn died in 1899. The executors purchased a building at 19 Subocz Street with part of his bequest and registered it as belonging to the Help Through Work organization.

Initially, Help Through Work, which was run by members of Vilna's bourgeoisie, envisioned its "workhouse" essentially as a philanthropic institution rather than a creative center for productive occupations. The organization placed empty boxes in some of the city's larger businesses, offices, and workshops and requested that waste paper and cloth scraps from the needle trades be deposited in them. The boxes were then collected and brought back to the workhouse, where needy Jewish women sat day after day sorting the waste materials. In accordance with the wage scale of the time (1903), the women earned up to forty kopeks a day. For three kopeks they could buy a bowl of soup and some bread at the "thrift kitchen"; for five kopeks they could also have a piece of meat. The women packed the sorted materials into sacks, which were then sold to textile or paper mills. This income did not suffice to cover the payments the women received for their work.

When the Russo-Japanese War of 1904–1905 began, the management of Help Through Work persuaded the Russian military procurement department to commission orders for overcoats and boots from the workhouse. Unemployed tailors and shoemakers were called in to do the work. The organization had great difficulty completing the order, because the workers made demands that it could not meet. It was forced to use its own funds to heat, light, and manage the shops, thus depleting money set aside for wages. The workers threatened to strike. In about 1905, Help Through Work set up a barrel-making workshop, in which nearly all the Jewish coopers of Vilna found work. Their customers were the beer brewers of Vilna and other cities. This shop was eventually shut down during World War I.

Vilna was a center for the woodworking industry. Carpenters built furniture, door and window frames for new buildings, and various other wooden items for the construction industry. The furniture, however, was not of fine quality and was copied from outdated models. As most of the carpenters did not know how to follow a technical drawing, Help Through Work established courses to teach them this important skill. It also set up a model workshop for the production of fine furniture and a warehouse for furniture built by cabinetmakers in their own establishments.

Help Through Work invited an instructor from Germany to manage the model workshop, which produced furniture for business offices and living rooms. Orders came in from the larger Russian cities, and the model workshop soon acquired a reputation as a studio for the design of artistic furniture. The visiting instructor also conducted evening courses for adults in carpentry, with drafting as the principal subject. There were also lectures on the various styles of furniture, techniques of woodworking, and the like. Furniture from Vilna soon became very popular, and the Help Through Work line was ordered from all over Russia. One of these talented carpenters, a man named I. M. Berman, compiled a sort of encyclopedia in Yiddish covering all branches of carpentry.[3]

Shoemaking was another industry in which hundreds of Jewish workers in Vilna were employed at the beginning of the twentieth century. Help Through Work offered these workers courses in pattern-making for different kinds of shoes, techniques of working with leather, and so forth. There was even a model workshop, supervised by a German instructor; this, however, was short-lived. It was discovered that the Jewish shoemakers of Vilna made more elegant shoes than the Germans, and the Vilna craftsmen had nothing to learn from their Berlin "rabbis."

The administrators of Help Through Work gradually realized that in order to interest the Jewish masses in becoming productive skilled workers, it was necessary to provide regular vocational training for young people. They opened the first school of needle trades for girls, along with a model workshop, and they also established a studio for the production of artistic embroidery and knitting.

Early in 1908, the JCA and Help Through Work convened a conference of representatives of vocational schools for Jewish girls throughout Russia.[4] Toward the end of the year a similar conference on vocational schools for boys also took place. The first conference was held in Vilna's Help Through Work facility, the second took place in the vocational school. At both conferences, papers were delivered on a variety of problems, both general and specialized, in vocational education. As a result, a decision was made to increase the number of vocational schools and to include both general and Jewish studies in their curricula. The two conferences represented a milestone in the history of vocational training for Jews.

At the turn of the century, the goal of Help Through Work was not simply to help by providing work for those who needed it most, but to help through work. In other words, it endeavored to interest a wide range of young people in becoming highly skilled artisans and, at the same time, to raise the quality of Jewish trades to the level of art. Around 1910, L. Frenkel, the former director of Vilna's largest vocational school for Jews, was invited to direct the various activities of Help Through Work. He was already well known by the community, both for his interest in Jewish vocations and for his efforts to develop the aesthetic element in Jewish trades, so that Jewish artisans could compete more equitably with non-Jews in the same trades. Previously, Frenkel had set up classes in painting for teachers at the Artistic

Industrial Society and for instructors of tailoring and shoemaking at Help Through Work.

At the beginning of the twentieth century, tailoring was considered a purely Jewish trade, but even here proper training was lacking. Most people working in the trade did not know how to cut a garment properly, and even many owners of tailoring businesses were inept when it came to cutting. They also lacked the most basic knowledge of textiles. Help Through Work offered courses to fill such needs. Most of the instructors for these courses and model workshops were Germans who had the requisite vocational and artistic training.

Taking into account the great number of Jewish tailors, Help Through Work opened the first school in all of Russia to train boys in the trade. Previously, boys would learn by apprenticing with a master, who would often make them do housework, run errands, and the like. The newly opened trade schools aimed to free the boys from the masters' domination and to make it easier to learn the trade.

At first, the school for tailors offered a one-year course. Those who completed it learned how to sew a pair of trousers and a vest, to finish buttonholes, to stitch by hand and by machine, as well as other basic elements of the trade. The apprentice could hardly accomplish that much after apprenticing for three years with a master.

General and vocational subjects were introduced in the school for tailors as well as in the other vocational departments run by Help Through Work. They established a three-year course in women's trades in conjunction with a model workshop. In the workshop, where private orders were accepted, women employed in the needle trades would come to perfect their mastery of pattern cutting, fitting, and finishing intricate fashions. This provided these women with the opportunity to become independent in their trade and to establish their own shops. A two-year course was also established to teach embroidery with multiple colored threads, which was fashionable at the time. Katya Steinbok, a well-known creative artisan from St. Petersburg, taught the course. The JCA sent Jewish artisans abroad to perfect their skills and develop new specialties. During Frenkel's term as director, courses in freehand drawing were instituted. Moshe Lejbowski, a Vilna artist, taught those courses, as well as the drawing classes in the various other Help Through Work schools.

The organization did not, however, disregard the experience of local Jewish craftsmen. The more qualified among them were brought in as consultants. Among these were Eliezer Kruk—a lathe operator, who was later to be chairman of the Vilna Jewish community council and alderman in the Vilna municipal government—and Samuel Hurwicz, a locksmith, later to be chairman of the Vilna Association of Craftsmen.

JEWISH VOCATIONAL EDUCATION

Fashion display from the Help Through Work vocational school in Vilna. Courtesy of the YIVO Archives.

Help Through Work expanded its activities into other areas of Jewish life, such as emigration. At the time, the Hebrew Immigrant Aid Society (HIAS) did not yet exist.[5] With the help of the JCA, emigration offices began to be opened in the larger cities. They offered emigrants assistance, mainly with transportation, and the scope of their activity expanded from year to year. I recall that in 1910–11 these bureaus provided some 1,500 emigrants with advice and support.

The varied activities of the remarkable organization called Help Through Work from 1908 to 1914 were renowned in Russia. Attempts to establish similar organizations were made in Minsk, Bobruisk, Gomel', and other Russian cities with large Jewish populations. Still, it was not by chance that in 1908 and 1909 the two nationwide conferences on Jewish vocational training took place in Vilna, and that they played such a significant role in the history of vocational education for Russia's seven million Jews.

2

A Jewish Agricultural School in Wieluciany

Lithuanian Jews first settled in agricultural colonies during the tsarist period, and until World War II Jewish farmers were still found in villages in Lithuania and Belorussia. Between the two world wars there were close to twenty-five villages of Jewish farmers in Lithuania and western Belorussia, which was then part of Poland, as well as isolated Jewish families who farmed in various rural areas. The Jewish Colonization Association (JCA) gave them support by helping them modernize their farming methods, plant orchards and gardens, sow new crops and improve the soil. The JCA also provided them with credit to buy farm equipment.

The younger generation of Jews also showed considerable interest in agriculture, especially during the last years before World War II. Several farms for training *halutzim* were established near Vilna. The children, who were sent there by various organizations during summer vacation, were taught about agriculture and gardening. One such experiment in agricultural training, undertaken on a larger scale, began in 1916. When the Germans occupied all of northwestern Russia during the previous September, many estates were abandoned by their owners, who fled deep into Russia. One of these estates was Wieluciany, located about thirteen kilometers from Vilna.

Previously, the Russian Ministry of Justice had established a colony for juvenile offenders on this estate, which was officially the property of a society charged with preparing the young ex-convicts for their future. The estate consisted of 250 hectares of fields, wooded areas, and a large two-story building in which the "students" were housed. There were also several large outbuildings, such as barns and stables, plus additional accommodations for the youths and housing for employees. Surrounding the residential quarters were vegetable gardens and an orchard of more than 400 trees and berry bushes. During the period of transition between Russian rule and the German occupation, the property remained in the hands of its caretakers. In October 1915, it was occupied by the German military economic administration.

Dr. Sali Levi of Breslau was the Jewish chaplain of the German Tenth Army, which occupied the entire Vilna region. An ardent German patriot, he also had a sound understanding of Jewish communal affairs and strove to be helpful to Jewish institutions. With sums he obtained from the Hilfsverein der Deutschen Juden, Dr. Levi decided to establish an institution to propagate modern agricultural methods among Jews.[1]

Psychologically, the moment was right for such an undertaking. Because of widespread unemployment and the disruption of trade and industry, agriculture was the only occupation that promised some measure of survival. Jewish youth had been neglected. The educational institutions that had existed for them under tsarist rule had been destroyed and there were no new ones to replace them.

By October 1915, Help Through Work had revived its activities and reopened its vocational schools for young people. Members of the organization's board of directors asked Dr. Levi to persuade the German high command to devote part of the Wieluciany estate to an agricultural school for Jews. The directors of Help Through Work and Dr. Levi developed a detailed plan, which the German military administration approved. They even promised that, for the first two years, students and staff would be permitted to purchase food from the commissary at minimal prices. The Germans had their own motives for doing this. They hoped that, within a few years, they would be able to obtain substantial amounts of grain, vegetables, and fruit from the farm for their commissary.

Early in April 1916, the administrators of Help Through Work published an announcement in *Letste nays,* the only Yiddish newspaper in Vilna at the time, stating that the school would accept young men fifteen to nineteen years old. One hundred and twenty youths applied, most of them former students of secondary schools. After they were given physical examinations, only half of the candidates were admitted to the newly established agricultural school.

As a result of Dr. Levi's energetic approach, nearly all the buildings and remaining agricultural equipment were turned over to the school, and supplies needed for the dormitory were also taken care of. Dr. Levi gave the opening of the school a ceremonial air, leading a procession on horseback. Behind him came the board of directors of Help Through Work. They were followed by the newly admitted students, marching in even rows and singing

Yiddish and Hebrew songs. They marched through Vilna's main streets, and this had an uplifting effect on the city's Jews.

Work in the gardens and orchards on the farm began immediately, under the supervision of veteran German reserve personnel. Dr. Levi saw to it that the "colonists" prayed daily and in general followed Jewish traditions, especially kosher dietary laws. A Jewish caretaker was hired, as well as a Jewish cook. The colonists were fed fairly well by the commissary during the first summer. The Germans also placed five milk cows and several horses at the colony's disposal.

During the 1916–17 school year, the German military administration appointed a non-commissioned officer manager of the colony. He was familiar with the theory and practice of gardening and other aspects of agriculture. During the winter months, he also taught the students German language and agricultural theory.

Despite the liberalism it showed in the beginning, the military administration wanted exclusive control of the colony. Help Through Work was limited to providing a teacher of Jewish subjects (religion and Jewish history). The students were expected to take care of their own needs. During the winter, they felled trees, gathered the logs, and sawed and split them. They kept their rooms clean, did kitchen chores and fed the livestock. Work began at six in the morning. Under the direction of the German officer, the entire daily schedule was adhered to precisely. Although the Germans kept a strong hand on the colony for two-and-a-half years, the students became attached to it and invested a great deal of hard work in it. Their health was good, for they spent most of their time out in the fresh air, working in the fields and gardens. Their bodies developed and their muscles firmed.

Saturday was a day of rest for the students except for essential tasks, such as feeding the cows, horses, and poultry.[2] If they wished, the students were allowed to go home for the Sabbath and on Jewish holidays. At Passover, Dr. Levi arranged seders for the students. A room was set aside for group worship and the necessary prayerbooks and other holy books were provided. The Vilna municipal synagogue lent the colonists a Torah scroll. Help Through Work sent a number of books from its library to the Wieluciany colony. They also purchased books and pamphlets on agriculture and the natural sciences.

At the beginning of the summer of 1918, Dr. Levi was transferred to Mainz. Before departing, he insisted that the military administration officially transfer the supervision of the colony to Help Through Work. A committee consisting of three members of the board of directors was selected and charged with direct responsibility for the affairs of the colony. The three were a lawyer named Wilensky, the artist Isaac Syrkin, and the author of this essay. Syrkin supervised the art programs in the vocational

View of the agricultural school in Wieluciany, Poland.
Courtesy of the YIVO Archives.

schools and workshops run by Help Through Work, and Wilensky was then the organization's acting chairman.

Those students who had been at the colony for several years had accomplished a great deal. They knew how to operate large pieces of farm equipment. They had been given instruction in both Jewish and general studies. Most of the food needed to feed the colonists was grown there. They only needed to buy a few products (sugar, honey, etc.) at reduced prices from the commissary.

In September and October 1918, following the Germans' defeat on the battlefield, it became evident that they would have to evacuate the entire region, and they began making the necessary preparations. The German officer who was still in charge of the colony announced that he would be leaving his post and requested that Help Through Work send a replacement at once.

The Germans began liquidating their equipment and supplies. This enabled the colony to purchase a large amount of grain, as well as some horses, cows, and tools that they needed. It was soon clear, however, that the German military withdrawal and the attendant change of government would not go smoothly. The peasants living nearby seemed restless. Therefore, some of the grain and other supplies were transferred at night to the Help Through Work vocational schools in Vilna. Finding a suitable replacement to direct the agricultural school proved almost impossible at the time. Eventually, someone was found who agreed to remain in the colony, oversee its maintenance and give the appearance of being in charge.

The peasants in the villages closest to the colony reckoned that the time had come for them to inherit everything at Wieluciany, including the land, which they would divide among themselves. They would have no trouble "taking care" of the "*zhidy.*" They would simply chase them away. The students were obviously in danger. The administration announced that only those who wished to should remain at the colony; anyone who felt threatened was urged to leave. Most of the older students did not want to desert the school and leave the fruit of all their labor to chance. They decided to stay, whatever might come to pass.

Because several units of the *Wirtschaftsausschuß* (maintenance division) had recently been stationed at Wieluciany, there was still a German guard unit, ten soldiers in all, on the grounds. Here and there bands of robbers and cutthroats had formed, consisting mainly of escaped prisoners joined by local peasants. These bands attacked travelers passing through, as well as small German detachments, isolated Jewish farmers, and wealthier land owners.

For three or four weeks in December and early January, the small guard unit and the remaining students at Wieluciany stayed awake all night. The soldiers were armed from head to toe, girded with strings of hand grenades. The robber bands did not dare risk their lives. Then the Germans abruptly left the area.

Several forces were vying for control of Vilna: the Workers' Council, anti-communist White Poles, Lithuanians, and several anarchist groups.[3] There was no authority worthy of the name. The number of robberies and assaults increased. As soon as the Germans were gone, some fifty peasants from around Wieluciany appeared at the colony and announced that it was now theirs. They angrily interrogated the caretaker and the older students: Why had the livestock and grain been transferred to Vilna? But the colonists were able to offer calming words to the peasants.

Events developed with lightning speed. For a few days the Workers' Council had control of Vilna. On 2 January 1919, the White Polish army of General Stefan Mokrzecki laid siege to the Workers' Council. Unwilling to be captured alive by the Poles, the Council members committed suicide.[4] For Jews, this was an uneasy time, as though it were just before a pogrom. The number of robberies increased. Groups of Polish volunteers roamed the streets and fired their guns at random. The students who were still at Wieluciany began to run out of food, which was now obtainable only in Vilna. Polish volunteers in General Mokrzecki's army confiscated a large load of provisions that a group of students was bringing to Wieluciany.

Mokrzecki's reign lasted less than a week. On 6 January, after a brief battle in the streets of Vilna, Bolshevik troops drove the Polish forces from the area. The anarchy gradually gave way to calm. The peasants near

Faculty and students of the agricultural school in Wieluciany, Poland, photographed on 9 November 1919. Hirsz Abramowicz is at the right end of the second row from the top.
Courtesy of the YIVO Archives.

Wieluciany were no longer quite as aggressive toward the Jewish colonists. Much greater hardships ensued, however, for the Bolsheviks tended to confiscate all food wherever they found it.

It became necessary to bring the cows and much of the grain back from Vilna to Wieluciany. This required special permission from the Revcom (revolutionary committee). When the author was finally able to meet with the committee chairman and explain the situation to him, pointing out that the cows were about to die of starvation, he simply responded, "Turn them over to the nutrition committee." This meant, of course, that they would go to feed the army. During the first days of Bolshevik rule, however, there was considerable confusion. One arm of the administration was still unaware of the other. In another office, I received a permit to move the cows "for sanitary reasons." The Revcom, however, would not allow us to return the grain to Wieluciany.

Like all the inhabitants of Vilna and the surrounding region, the colonists were always half-hungry. Even so, nearly all of the students who had left the colony returned from the city, where the food situation was even worse. With the greatest effort, we were able to smuggle limited quantities of food into the colony for the students. They also had to camouflage the granary storehouse, so that the new people in power would not confiscate the seed grain needed for planting.

Having no alternative, the administration of Help Through Work invited a Polish agronomist named Jagodziński, who had returned from internment in Russia, to head the colony. There were no Jewish candidates for this position, but a Jew was hired as manager. The school gradually resumed teaching classroom subjects. But the administration's funds were nearly exhausted. There was some hope that the new authorities would include the agricultural school in the overall school system. The food shortage was acute, but the students patiently endured this burden and hoped that better days would come. Their aim was to keep the colony in Jewish hands, whatever the cost.

On 19 April 1919, one of the final days of Passover, defiant Polish railroad workers let an armored train carrying Polish White Legionnaires under the command of General Józef Piłsudski into Vilna. After surprising the remnants of the Red Army and engaging them in street battles, the Polish Legionnaries took control of Vilna and its environs. Piłsudski's troops joined with local Polish groups to carry out pogroms against the local Jewish population.[5] Close to one hundred Jewish people were murdered in Vilna, more than four hundred were wounded, and the Legionnaries harassed countless others. The administrative headquarters of Help Through Work was damaged by gunfire. In addition, roving bands stole materials from the various vocational schools and took a large amount of grain and food that belonged to the colony.

At the Wieluciany colony, the Legionnaries made off with feed, some equipment, and whatever else they found. Although the colony had obtained a "certificate of protection" from the Polish command, which stated that nothing was to be requisitioned from the colony, this had little effect. About a week after the Legionnaries took control of the region, the Bolsheviks mounted several forceful counterattacks and pushed the Poles back several kilometers. For a few days the Wieluciany colony was under Russian control. They, too, appropriated things from the students: shoes, clothing, underwear. Battles raged all around the colony, and it was often caught between the two opposing forces. Finally, the Poles prevailed and drove the Bolsheviks out.

All of these events greatly disrupted life in the colony. Hunger became a greater problem. The cattle and horses could at least eat the newly sprouting grass, but the people suffered very much. All sorts of food began arriving from several American relief organizations, especially the American Jewish Joint Distribution Committee (JDC).[6] Primarily intended to assuage hunger in schools, children's institutions and public kitchens, these shipments also helped the colony.

Work in the fields and gardens began. Whatever grain remained in the Help Through Work buildings in the city was brought back to the colony and sown. Then there was another disruption, involving Jagodziński, the school agronomist, who had defended the students during the attacks on the colony. Local Polish peasants denounced him to the Polish military, who arrested him and subjected him to a court martial. With considerable effort, I managed to reach the chief officer of the court, a Polish colonel, and convince him that the agronomist was merely doing his duty by defending the young pupils entrusted to his care. Jagodziński was, indeed, set free.

When it finally appeared that the colony was somewhat safe from external events, the administration of Help Through Work began an energetic campaign to provide regular financial support for the school. As the first attempt in Lithuania and Belorussia to offer agricultural training to Jews, the school interested both the JDC and the JCA. The JDC provided funds for augmenting the school's inventory of tools, machinery, and livestock. The administration decided to widen the scope of the colony's activity by accepting new students. For the first time, they admitted young women, who wished to learn gardening and other light agricultural work in preparation for the *halutz* movement. One of the school's buildings was designated for these young women.

The total number of new students of both sexes was 110, which brought the total enrollment to 160. An assistant agronomist and another gardener were hired. The farm's various inventories were increased, including the addition of several horses, dairy cows and sheep. Several beehives were also purchased. The newly arrived female students and the younger boys worked in the gardens. The older male students did the more strenuous field work. In addition, the agronomists led a daily hour or two of more general discussion on seasonal topics.

The colony, however, suffered much harassment from the local peasants. Their leaders constantly sent memoranda to the higher authorities, demanding that Wieluciany be "taken out of Jewish hands" and that the land be given to the neighboring villages. The ultra-reactionary Catholic press also asserted that it was "unnatural" that property so valuable be left in the hands of Jews.

The administration of Help Through Work, assisted by Rabbi Isaac Rubinstein, employed every possible means to maintain the colony's status. They sent detailed memoranda to various government agencies in both Vilna and Warsaw. Finally, the organization was able to obtain a document from Chief Commissar Osmolowski of the Eastern Region, stating that the Wieluciany estate was temporarily entrusted to Help Through Work. The administration set about reorganizing the school to bring it up to the appropriate standard. A series of consultations with professionals resulted in a plan for a three-year course of study, which included basic agriculture, dairy farming, gardening and orchard keeping. The program also included Jewish studies. The staff of teachers and vocational instructors was revised and enlarged.

Experimental stations were set up for research on a variety of plants and grains. The colony established a connection with the meteorological institute at the University of Warsaw and set up a small weather station, furnished with the basic equipment. This station, like others throughout the region, sent reports to the central meteorological station. Now the school was nearly on a par with existing lower-level agricultural schools for the general population.

During the holiday of Sukkot, a harvest festival was held. The students prepared a variety of vegetarian dishes using their vegetables and dairy products. Guests were invited from Vilna, among them Dr. Jacob Wygodzki, chairman of Vilna's Jewish community council. In addition to the meal, the students also presented an afternoon performance of songs, dances, and sketches about colony life. Both the students and their guests enjoyed themselves greatly.

With the cooperation of the EKOPO book warehouse, the colony purchased books in Yiddish and Hebrew at low cost. They also acquired books for a special library on agricultural professions in all three local languages: Yiddish, Russian, and Polish. The JDC provided the colony with collections of plants, insects and the like for nature study.

Work in the colony's fields and gardens proceeded at a furious pace until the beginning of July 1920. As Poland and Russia were still engaged in a bloody war, the colony's general status became uncertain once more. Soon the front line was rapidly advancing toward Vilna. All the while, different military divisions came to the colony and requisitioned hay, oats and other crops at will. The Red Army advanced with great speed; the Polish forces kept retreating. The Polish regime grew progressively weaker and more demoralized. The local Jewish population, including the students at the colony, were harassed and mistreated. Recalling their earlier experiences, the students were no longer willing to remain on the grounds and be exposed to danger. Once again, it became necessary to remove everything that could be stolen: livestock, food, tools, supplies. On 13 July, most of the students were evacuated, leaving behind only a few of the older ones who didn't want to abandon the colony. Dr. Abraham Makower—a member of the school administration, whose sleeve bore a physician's Red Cross insignia—was the only liaison between the beleaguered colonists and the personnel of Help Through Work.

On 14 July, the first ranks of the Red Army penetrated Vilna. Soviet troops shot any Polish Legionnaries whom they encountered on the streets with stolen goods. The Jewish population began to breathe more freely and ventured out into the streets. On 16 July, the Red Army command issued permission to Help Through Work to return its livestock to Wieluciany. On the way there, however, Red Army soldiers requisitioned two horses and two wagons.

The Bolshevik regime lasted barely six weeks. Vilna was surrendered to the Lithuanians or, rather, was taken by them from the Russians following the Russian defeat in the battle outside Warsaw (mid-August 1920).[7] Because of all these events, the number of students at the agricultural school dwindled to fifty. The colony sustained huge losses in the fields, where grain and potatoes ready for harvesting were trampled by the passing armies.

It appeared that the Lithuanians, whose attitude toward Jews at the time was not unfavorable, would not oppress the agricultural school. In light of this, life at the colony resumed once again, albeit with a smaller number of students. Before long there was again a change of authority: Polish Legionnaries under the command of General Lucjan Żeligowski "did not agree" with the peace treaty signed with Lithuania in Suwałki, which ceded Vilna to Lithuania. On the last day of Sukkot, shots were heard near Vilna. Several hours later, bullets whistled through the city streets. Once again, Vilna was under the control of Piłsudski's Poles, under the flag of a fictitious country called "Middle Lithuania." Actually, Warsaw was in command.

Abnormal times prevailed once again at the agricultural school. Despite all the assurances given by the higher authorities, Polish soldiers committed robberies, often accompanied by assaults on the students. During the winter of 1920–21, the number of students declined to thirty and the female students left, for understandable reasons. Harassment by local Poles contributed to the eventual liquidation of the school. During the battles that took place at the colony, the cross atop the church on the grounds was damaged. But the colonists' detractors claimed that the school's administration deliberately knocked down the cross while repairing the building's roof.

In a Bolshevik archive captured by the Poles, they found a letter from the chairman of Help Through Work to the Red Army commandant of the Vilna area, requesting protection against bands roaming around the colony. In reporting on the matter, some newspapers added the word "Polish" to "bands." This was promptly seen as a deliberate affront to the "chivalrous Polish people."

In a responding memorandum, the administration of Help Through Work demonstrated the falseness of these charges, which did not abate. Seeking to bolster the school's legal status, the administration enlisted the help of Jewish delegates to the *Sejm*, Y. Gruenbaum and A. Hartglas, as well as that of Rabbi Isaac Rubinstein. They asked the Polish government to recognize the validity of the school's "charter," granted earlier by the chief commandant of the Eastern Region. The government entities involved were in no haste to act, however, and offered various excuses for not issuing the requested permission. Meanwhile, the Polish press began to print articles by Polish jurists who claimed that the colony belonged to the government.

Nonetheless, normal instruction continued during the winter of 1920–21, and the colony made preparations for the spring sowing season. Suddenly, in March, the Polish government issued an order that Help Through Work transfer the colony to the custody of the courts by 1 April. All protests and interventions were fruitless. The machines and tools purchased from the Germans with Jewish community funds had to be turned over to the Polish government. Only a very small amount of the property was saved, and it was sold to help defray the school's debt.

This was the end of the agricultural school which, for five years, had maintained its existence and, moreover, had demonstrated the ability to develop in the worst of times. Quite a few former students eventually found employment as teachers of gardening, which became a popular student activity at various types of Jewish schools. Others emigrated to Argentina, Palestine, Russia, or some other country, where they applied their practical and theoretical knowledge of agriculture to the cultivation of the land.

3

The Białystok Vocational School

After World War I, life in the new Polish Republic was gradually reestablished, even in the heavily damaged eastern sections. Despite the hardships of extensive inflation, hunger, and general impoverishment, the Jewish population set about manufacturing various kinds of merchandise. It was only natural for Białystok, known as Poland's "Little Manchester," to be among the most productive cities. Once again it became an important industrial center, which, in former times, had supplied Russia with yard goods, quilts, hats, and other cloth goods.

Not all of the city's factories were back in operation by 1922. The large German Kamichau works lay in ruins, but a number of the smaller plants were teeming with life. The American Red Cross as well as other American relief organizations, such as the American Relief Administration (ARA), had their central warehouses in Białystok.[1]

The city's Jewish Vocational School, established by the tea magnate and great Jewish philanthropist Kalman Zev Wysocki, also resumed its activities in full. All over Poland, Jewish vocational schools began to rebuild, assisted by ORT and the JCA, in preparation for a new life.[2] But a uniform plan and curriculum were needed in order to carry on the work of training Jewish young people and adults effectively in this newly established nation, which not long before had been part of three countries: Prussia, Austria, and Russia.

Białystok was chosen as the site for a convention—the first of its kind—of representatives of Jewish vocational schools from all over Poland. Both the city's location and its industrial history made it an appropriate site for such a gathering, which took place in late February 1922. Among those who came were delegates from the headquarters of organizations in

Warsaw and Lwów, and just about everyone active in vocational training institutions. There were directors of trade schools, members of local groups that supported schools for artisans, and anyone who had something to say about the problems of vocational education. More than one hundred delegates participated in the conference, which was divided into sections dealing with important topics in vocational education: technical training, curriculum, publicity, training of instructors, new occupational possibilities, and the like.

I was among the representatives of Vilna's vocational school, known as Help Through Work. This was my first visit to Białystok. Winter was ending, the snow and ice were beginning to melt and the streets of the city were covered with the dirty water, chunks of ice and frozen ruts of early spring. Białystok could not make a very favorable first impression. Even on "Nowolipie" (New Linden Street), it was quite easy to twist an ankle and fall into a puddle. Nevertheless, the streets were filled with wagons full of bundles of rags needed for the local textile manufacturing as well as finished goods. People hurried, even ran. Białystok was obviously not asleep; it was preparing feverishly to renew itself and to create new and much needed products.

Years earlier, the process of industrialization had marked the city's Jewish population with dynamism and an enterprising spirit. In Białystok, people deliberated less and did more. Its Jewish Vocational School illustrated this well. During the German occupation, the school had virtually ceased to exist. Its large building was used for various Jewish community committees, offices, public kitchens, and the like. Immediately following the occupation, a group of community activists undertook the rehabilitation of the school, which operated in several cramped buildings that were not even all on the same street. Young people thronged to apply, but there was no room for new students. It was not even possible to open the textile weaving workshops, which were essential in Białystok. The community activists, headed by Joseph Smigelski, an energetic engineer and director of the school, carried on lengthy negotiations with the Jewish community administration, hoping to persuade it to move some of its offices to other sites so that the school might regain its former home.

The talks dragged on endlessly without producing any result. Then the activists decided to present the public with a *fait accompli*. One night this group, assisted by all the students in the school's workshops, broke the locks and opened the doors to the offices in the building. They removed the Jewish community council's property and installed the school's machines, furnishings, and everything else necessary for its normal operation. The students did not go home that night; in the morning they were found at work in their "new" location.

The fruitless negotiating in Białystok was thus ended by a daring, practical measure. As a result, hundreds of young people were given the opportunity to find work as highly skilled laborers in factories, artisans' workshops and other branches of industry. The Jewish community council did not, of course, cease to function, and it found suitable quarters in another building. The school continued to evolve, as the delegates to the conference could readily observe when they visited the school. At the time, the Białystok Vocational School had the only workshop in Poland for teaching textile weaving. Young fifteen- to nineteen-year-olds stood at each loom, deftly manipulating the spools of thread under the guidance of their instructors.

In the carpentry division, young people were also busy at their workbenches, learning to use saws, planes, and chisels. The motors whirred in the locksmithing shops as the youngsters filed and sawed metal. There was the smell of work everywhere—of oil, machines, wood shavings, and resin from pine and other kinds of wood. It was up to the robust young people of Białystok to rehabilitate their city. This they did, in the hope that a vibrant Jewish life would flourish there again—and it did, for about two decades. In 1939, it was interrupted and dreadful destruction followed.

The Białystok conference on vocational education played a significant role in the life of the Jewish community of Poland at the time. It laid the cornerstone for the unrestricted development of professional training for tens of thousands of young Polish Jews. There were eventually close to 100 such schools and training facilities in Poland, supported by ORT, the JCA, and other local Jewish organizations.

4

MATTHIAS SCHREIBER

Vilna frequently set an example for the rest of the Jewish community. Such was the case when it came to providing proper vocational education for its young people. The notion of training young Jews in modern craftsmanship and mechanical trades took root in Vilna during the late nineteenth century and flourished at the beginning of the twentieth century.

Vilna's well-established trade school was evacuated to Poltava in 1915 because of the war, and it never returned. In 1918, various individual community activists began to come back to Vilna. Among them was Israel Okun, an engineer, who immediately set about organizing advanced technical courses for young people ages sixteen and older. Okun enlisted the services of the few Jewish engineers and mathematicians then employed in Vilna as teachers. Young people flocked to the courses.

Due to a lack of equipment and materials, instruction was largely theoretical until 1919, when ORT took over the classes. Under Okun's direction, the courses were transformed into a technical school, where all instruction was in Yiddish. New teachers were hired, including the noted Bundist leader Arkady Kremer and the engineer Matthias (Matvei Samoilovich) Schreiber. These three men bore the primary responsibility for administering the school, with the assistance of Kahan-Wirgili of the ORT committee. Okun left for Argentina (and later moved to Canada), and Schreiber became the school's director. He held this post until the last day of the school's existence in June 1941, when the Germans attacked the Soviet Union.

Schreiber was a prominent figure in Vilna's Jewish community in general and pioneered the field of technical education for Jewish youth. He was born to an assimilated family. His father, Samuel Schreiber, was assistant *rabiner* in Vilna and, for a time, also held the post of *rabiner.* As was then the custom, even leading figures in the Jewish community did not give their children a Jewish education. Matthias Schreiber had almost no instruction in Hebrew, let alone reading and writing Yiddish. The language spoken at home was Russian. Matthias attended a Russian gymnasium and was soon drawn into the Russian revolutionary movement, joining the Social-Revolutionary Party. When he was about to graduate from the gymnasium he was arrested. As a result, he lost the right to receive certification that he had completed his studies, which was essential for pursuing higher education. He was an excellent student, however, and admired by his teachers as a skilled mathematician. They interceded on his behalf and won him the opportunity to take a special examination.

Matthias' father performed a variety of official functions both as *rabiner* and assistant *rabiner,* and he was greatly respected by the higher city officials. As a result, the *rabiner*'s gifted son was pardoned for his "political transgression." On receiving his certification, Matthias Schreiber was admitted to the department of mathematics at the University of St. Petersburg. He studied mathematics and physics for two years, but was drawn more to technology and the practical application of mathematics to mechanics. He successfully completed the competitive examination of the St. Petersburg Institute of Technology, earning "5's" (the highest scores), and was admitted to its school of mechanics. For family reasons, he transferred his studies to Warsaw Polytechnic Institute, where he received his degree in engineering with distinction.

In the summer of 1914, Schreiber enlisted in the military. Just before he arrived at camp, World War I erupted. On the first day of mobilization, with no military training whatsoever, he was sent to the front, where he engaged in the initial maneuvers. There, it was apparently noticed that this young engineer was not yet a "real soldier," and he was sent to the rear for combat training, but because of poor health, his service was postponed for a year. The Germans were about to take Vilna, and Schreiber had no desire to remain there under their rule. Instead, he went to Nizhnii Novgorod, where he joined a battalion about to be sent to the front.

At that same time, a factory for the manufacture of military field kitchens was about to open in Nizhnii Novgorod. Schreiber was assigned to organize and run the factory (which had been built by a Jewish contractor named Sarna). Schreiber organized the factory and produced the kitchens in exemplary fashion. All the while he remained a soldier, and following the revolution of February 1917, became a member of the military council.

During this period, he also held the position of mayor of a large district in Moscow. Schreiber was consistently distinguished by his courage, his exceptional honesty, and his conscientiousness both in dealing with individuals and in civic affairs.

When it became possible to travel to his native city, where he had left his mother and a sister, Schreiber returned to Vilna and settled there. He became director of the noted Jewish gymnasium named for Sofia Markovna Gurewicz.[1] Schreiber also began lecturing and teaching the courses that later evolved into the aforementioned Jewish technical school. Because the school provided insufficient income, Schreiber also took a position as industrial engineer with a firm that installed turbines and diesel motors in factories. Eventually, the technical school demanded all of Schreiber's time. He relinquished all his private work and devoted himself entirely to running the school, the only one of its kind.

In all the larger cities of the Pale of Settlement, there were Jewish trade schools for locksmithing, electronics, blacksmithing, and carpentry. They all turned out qualified workers, but only in numbers sufficient to fill the needs of small, one- and two-person workshops. Few Jewish master craftsmen were thoroughly trained in both theoretical and practical aspects of heavy industry or major manufacturing. With the support of ORT, a committee of engineers under Schreiber's leadership developed a program for an advanced technical school, which was called the Vilna Jewish Technical School of ORT. Here theory and practice could go hand in hand in teaching young Jews to become proficient in the field of technology.

Since the school's language of instruction was Yiddish, however, there were difficulties with terminology, which was virtually non-existent in the Yiddish language. So Schreiber, an assimilated Jew, learned Yiddish and produced excellent technical handbooks and reproductions of lessons on mechanics, technology, and various branches of applied physics. The engineers in the school's departments of electronics and radio also created terminology and manuals. As a result, the ORT school published some fifteen textbooks on technology under Schreiber's direction in correct and, at the same time, strictly scientific Yiddish. Most engineers, especially those whose origins were in Poland, had very little acquaintance with Yiddish. In the ORT technical school however, they were obliged to learn the language. The director himself introduced the use of Yiddish everywhere.

Schreiber was strict with the students, of whom he demanded good work. He was even more demanding of himself, seldom leaving the school before eleven o'clock at night. He insisted on participating in every committee and examining and supervising the wide-ranging operations of the school, which had became a model beyond the Jewish community.

Despite Schreiber's insistence on academic rigor, the students truly idolized him. Whatever he said was held sacred, and even his harshest words were listened to with the greatest respect. Everyone knew Schreiber showed partiality to no one; if he kept a student from advancing to the next level, that student was being treated as he deserved. They knew that everything he did was in the best interests of the young people and of Jewish economic productivity. Because Schreiber was known to be a person of unblemished reputation, he was frequently asked to arbitrate disputes between individuals or communal organizations.

Even the Polish school authorities and higher municipal officials had great respect for Schreiber. The inspector of technical schools once told me that he held the engineer "in high regard, despite the fact that he frequently will not obey our orders. He is entirely sincere and must be forgiven things we would not forgive others."

Schreiber took part in all consultations and conferences involving ORT and all the societies for vocational education, such as the JCA and WUZET, an organization for the promotion of farming and technical education in western Poland. He delivered papers on various technical matters pertaining to Poland's vocational school system.

The Vilna Jewish Technical School frequently exhibited its students' work. The precision of instruments produced by the students in the school's workshops was simply remarkable, as were the complicated and extraordinarily detailed diagrams they drew of electrification and sewage systems projects for various cities and towns in the vicinity of Vilna. With such skills, the school's graduates were fully qualified to become assistant engineers in factories.

With help from ORT, the school established a commission to find employment for its graduates. A considerable number of students worked at power plants, water supply stations, and other technical installations of the city administration. Some graduates went to Palestine, where they contributed considerably to the country's development. There were also a few who went to Birobidzhan. In general, graduates of the technical school settled wherever there was industrial activity.

The school had two main departments: one for mechanics, the other for instruction in electrical technology. Each department had subdivisions, such as for water-supply systems, radio, hydraulics, and so on. The program took a minimum of three years to complete, in most cases, four. The number of students reached 300. Young Jews from all over Poland streamed to the school. Many of them were high school graduates, but they were expected to take entrance examinations and demonstrate aptitude in mathematics and science.

Matthias Schreiber, director of the Vilna Technicum, in his office, 1935. Courtesy of the YIVO Archives.

Young men who came from other cities in Poland were often completely assimilated and knew no Yiddish. Schreiber allowed them a specified period of time in which to acquire the language. In this respect, the Vilna technical school was unique, being the only Jewish educational institution where instruction was one hundred percent in Yiddish. (Excepted, of course, was instruction in the language, history, and geography of Poland, all mandated by law to be taught in Polish.) Every student was required to take a course in Yiddish literature, which was taught by Gershon Pludermacher.[2]

The technical school also provided a variety of occasional courses for adults who wished to learn particular trades, such as those related to water supply systems, radio, and cement masonry. Schreiber was also the director of these programs under the auspices of ORT. The Polish authorities permitted all new courses on condition that Schreiber administer them. He worked more than seemed humanly possible and ORT finally realized that this director, who toiled night and day, should be provided with an assistant or two. This and many other new plans were obviated by the approach of the bloody storm.

Under Schreiber's leadership, Vilna Jewish Technical School maintained its existence despite the various changes of regime. Both Lithuanian and Soviet authorities were readily convinced that Schreiber, the great professional and teacher, was the individual most suited to run the ORT school.

Even under the German hangmen in the Vilna Ghetto, recalls Anna Šimaite, a librarian at Vilna University, "Schreiber created an excellent technical school out of nothing and directed it, maintaining mechanical, electro-technical and blacksmithing divisions. Schreiber even organized a small library of technical literature."[3] When the Vilna Ghetto was liquidated, Schreiber and his only son (a student at the technical school in the Ghetto) were sent away to the terrible Klooga concentration camp in Estonia, where both perished of hunger and exhaustion. According to some reports, Schreiber and other physicians and engineers from Vilna were shot to death just two hours before Red Army troops entered the camp. Schreiber's wife, Valentina, perished in Majdanek. The Schreibers' daughter, Sulamit, was the sole family member to survive.[4]

V

Profiles of Vilna Jewry before World War II

1

Mark Antokolsky

The son of a poor tavernkeeper in Vilna, whose angry father often beat him for making "idols" and other figurines, was perhaps *the* most famous Russian sculptor of the classical school during the latter half of the nineteenth century.

In 1871, Tsar Alexander II visited Antokolsky's studio, which was on an upper floor, to see the sculptor's marvelous creation, *Ivan the Terrible*. Afterward, Antokolsky received a sizable stipend from the delighted monarch. This enabled the artist to perfect his techniques abroad and to visit famous museums and monuments in Western Europe. The tsar also named the artist to the civilian rank of *Deistvitelnyi statskii sovetnik* (corresponding to the military rank of major general). Overnight, as Antokolsky states in his memoirs, he became famous, not only in Russia but throughout the entire civilized world.

Antokolsky's greatest admirer and closest friend was Vladimir Stasov, the well-known art and music critic. Il'ia Repin, the famous painter, was a schoolmate of Antokolsky's and shared a room with him when they were both students at the Academy. They remained good friends for life.[1]

Among Antokolsky's commissions, both in Russia and abroad, were monuments in honor of famous persons. He submitted a design for a monument to the "Tsar Liberator," Alexander II, who, as is well known, issued a proclamation in 1861 that freed Russian peasants from serfdom (although not from poverty). Antokolsky's first idea for the monument depicted the monarch seated on a throne and surrounded by angels, cherubs, and other celestial motifs. At the time, Russia was ruled by Alexander III, who was inimical to Jews, and an orgy of anti-Semitism spread throughout the land. When Antokolsky's plan was made public, the anti-Semites on the staff of the newspaper *Novoe Vremia,* with Burenin* the chief attacker, began an ugly campaign of agitation against the project.[2] "The Jew-sculptor has made the tsar subservient to Jew-angels and other attributes of the Jewish faith." The design was rejected.

Motivated to express his gratitude to Alexander II for his patronage, Antokolsky then produced a second model: proceeding in a half-circle toward the imperial throne were Russia's liberated peasants in a variety of poses, expressing their deeply felt thanks to the tsar for their freedom. Once again, the same kind of hate campaign was directed against the sculptor. The Jew Antokolsky deliberately planned to portray the Russian people in a derogatory fashion, his opponents charged. This design was rejected as well. The artist, pained and humiliated, decided to forsake the country of his birth and went to Paris in the hope of avoiding further attacks from Russian anti-Semites.

The original models for the two monuments were still in the collection of the Vilna Jewish community's S. Ansky Museum shortly before the outbreak of World War II.[3] I saw them there on various occasions, along with other works by Antokolsky, both originals and reproductions. Repin's celebrated portrait of Antokolsky in his younger years was also on display in this museum. Antokolsky, with glowing eyes and jet black hair, a devout expression on his face, is depicted standing, draped in a prayer shawl that only half covers his head.**

While still a boy, I heard various stories about Antokolsky from Vilna Jews. It was said that he had access to the royal court and others in power. Tales about his childhood asserted that his genius was evident very early. For example, an elderly resident of Vilna told me the following: the artist's mother kept a tavern on Broad Street. Drunkards often came in and disturbed the guests with their loud and aggressive behavior. Little Motke, who was very attached to his mother and wanted to make life easier for her, drew on the tavern door a soldier, a sword at his side, pointing a gun. The drawing was so vivid and realistic that the drunkards, seeing an armed soldier on guard at the entrance, would run away.

On my way to school in the Vilna suburb of Zarechye, where I lived as a boy, I would often pass a large house, painted pink. Like all the other houses, this one had a small sign outside bearing the name of the owner: "House of M. M. Antokolsky." The house stood out from those around

---

*The same *Novoe Vremia* writers, led by the mean, vulgar anti-Semite Burenin, had driven the refined poet Nadson (of Jewish origin) to an early grave with their abusiveness and ridicule of his poetry.

**Antokolsky was religiously inclined. He did not work on the Sabbath.

it on account of its cleanliness and spacious yard. I regarded the small sign with reverence. Young and old in Vilna were proud of their illustrious fellow townsman. But how did Antokolsky, who always resided in Paris (and before that, in St. Petersburg), come to have a house in Vilna that he did not live in?

This is the story: there was an influential man in Vilna, a community leader named Yudl Opatov. Among his major businesses was the so-called "postal service." There were no railroads in and around Vilna at the time, and in their absence the "postal service" provided the means of transportation between cities and towns and, indeed, between Russia and other countries. The service was frequently leased to Jews, who were expected to supply horses, wagons, and carriages (these for people of status who were passing through). Important officials were frequently obliged to court favor with Opatov to ensure that their journey would proceed smoothly, using the best horses, especially if they needed to get to the German border.

According to the lore in Vilna, the tsar was once passing through Vilna when a difficulty arose with his team of horses and the royal carriage. Yudl Opatov immediately placed his best horses at the monarch's disposal, mounted the coachman's box himself and drove the tsar to the nearest station. The royal passenger was very pleased with his Jewish driver and conferred on him the title of "Distinguished Citizen." From then on, of course, Yudl never lacked for royal contracts or, certainly, for livelihood.

Opatov had several very beautiful daughters, and it was his ambition to marry them off to young men of good family or to celebrities. One of his sons-in-law was Yakov Parnes, a Vilna aristocrat who later became chairman of Vilna's principal Jewish charity. A second son-in-law was none other than Mark Matveyevich Antokolsky, who knew the most influential people in St. Petersburg and even had a "rank." Antokolsky was older than his exceptionally beautiful bride, Genya Opatova. But the likes of Antokolsky did not come cheaply. When Yudl Opatov became his father-in-law, he pledged a dowry which, in addition to money, included the house in Zarechye.*

---

*The house was managed by Antokolsky's sister, wife of Il'ia Lazarev, the director of a Jewish crown school. I was a student at the school for three years. Lazarev, incidentally, was an excellent mathematician, a Hebraist, and an able pedagogue. The Lazarev family were friends with the family of Samuel Schreiber, who later became assistant official rabbi of Vilna (and for a time official rabbi). The Schreiber family thus had a primary source of information about Antokolsky's life and work. When Antokolsky traveled from Paris to St. Petersburg and back by way of Vilna, he would stop at the Lazarevs' house. Often he would pour out his heart to his sister, telling her about his not-too-happy family life and his sorrows as an artist, brought on by the hatred of those who were envious or simple anti-Semites.

Opatov's daughters were not only beautiful, but had received a modern education. Their wealthy father was himself hardly a man of learning, to put it mildly. Nevertheless, he endeavored to provide his daughters with the best European governesses. They taught Opatov's daughters foreign languages and, especially, etiquette, so that they could have entry to the most exclusive non-Jewish aristocratic circles.

Genya Opatov-Antokolsky spoke perfect French, not to mention flawless Russian. She ran her Paris home in high aristocratic fashion, with periodic *jours fixes,* balls, and special receptions. Mme. Antokolsky's *jours fixes* were attended by the cream of the aristocracy and foreign diplomats. Apparently she did not take into account whether this was convenient or appealing for her husband, a modest man who certainly lacked the "requisite" manners. Genya Antokolsky was perhaps even somewhat ashamed of him, with his Jewish appearance and flawed French. It often happened that Antokolsky would arrive from his studio, tired and frustrated, to find the house in an uproar. His office was turned into a guest room for the many visitors, not all of whom even appreciated who Antokolsky was; some did not know him at all. He would wander about his own home like a stranger.

Of course, it took immense financial means, which the head of the household was expected to provide, to run a house in this manner, with regular receptions for the aristocracy. Antokolsky was obliged to work beyond his physical capacity and to accept some commissions not at all to his liking, so that his wife, the grand-dame, could compete with the finest salons of Paris.

One of his last undertakings was to sculpt the head of Catherine II for a monument in Vilna commissioned by the Russian government, for which he was paid 30,000 rubles in gold.* The monument was erected by a Russian

---

Antokolsky's niece, Mrs. Sofia Lazarev-Rakovitsky, lived in Brooklyn, New York. She told me that once, on a cold winter evening, Antokolsky unexpectedly arrived from Paris. None of the Lazarev adults were home. Sofia, eleven or twelve years old at the time, was alone and did not know how to receive her famous uncle. He, however, put her at ease, sat down beside her small stove, where a fire was burning, caressed her head, and told her about his life in Paris. Mrs. Lazarev (née Antokolsky) lived to an advanced age. She died in Riga in 1930, at the home of her daughter. She was very wise and had a sharp mind. I recall that in the Riga Yiddish daily, *Frimorgn,* many articles and interviews about her were printed because she was Antokolsky's sister. Il'ia Lazarev became, in time, professor of Hebrew and Bible studies at Vilna Teacher's Institute, taking the post previously occupied by the great philologist and lexicographer Joshua Steinberg. Lazarev died in St. Petersburg around January 1917.

*The monument was hated by Vilna's Poles, who saw it as a symbol of their subjugation resulting from the Russia tsarina's policy of conquest, which led to the partitions of Poland.

architect in 1904, after Antokolsky's death. The body of Catherine II was modeled by a Russian sculptor. When the Russians evacuated Vilna in 1915 they took with them all their monuments, including one of the hangman Muraviov, one of Pushkin, and this statue of Catherine II with the head by Antokolsky.[4] Like all of Antokolsky's works, it is notable for its classical elegance.

Antokolsky had two beautiful daughters, who were brought up by their mother in accordance with her ideas. One of them married Claude Montefiore of London. The other became the wife of the Italian diplomat, Count Sforza, who was King Victor Emmanuel's foreign minister and later held the same post under the Italian Republic. Neither Antokolsky's widow nor his daughters maintained any relationship with their relatives in Vilna.[5]

During the latter years of his life, Antokolsky became greatly impoverished and was forced to sell his wonderful collections at auction. He suffered from a severe illness of the digestive tract, which prematurely ended his life during the summer of 1902, at the age of sixty-one. It may be that he did not receive proper care at home.

The general public had not been told of Antokolsky's illness, and his death was a shock to Jews around the world. His last wish was to be buried in a Jewish cemetery in the land of his birth, for which—despite the attacks of its anti-Semites—he never ceased to yearn. Russia was doubly dear to him—the land of both his Jewish Vilna and St. Petersburg, the metropolis that educated him and brought him world renown. There he had made great friends among some of the leading Russian figures in art and literature; like most of Russia's Jewish intelligentsia, he regarded them as his own. Immediately after Antokolsky's death a struggle began between representatives of the Jewish communities of Vilna and St. Petersburg, each vying to be the resting place of the great artist's remains. St. Petersburg—home to the most respected Jewish intellectuals, financiers, and intermediaries, who had access to the most powerful circles—prevailed.

Since Mark Antokolsky wore a decoration of distinction, the Russian government also had a part in the arrangements for his funeral. The administrators of the rail system assigned a special coach, rather than a freight car, to transport Antokolsky's remains from the border town of Wierzbołowo to St. Petersburg by way of Vilna.*

---

*In this context it is worth mentioning a historical anomaly that took place in Russia exactly two years later involving the transport of the body of another famous Russian, Anton Chekhov. The great literary master died during the summer of 1904, at the age of forty-four, at the spa in Badenweiler, Germany. Chekhov held no "rank" and had been educated as a physician. For the last ten years of his life, the most creative and important years of his literary career, he had severed relations with the reactionary, anti-Semitic

I recall a hot July day in 1902. I was on vacation, visiting my parents' home on an estate about sixty kilometers from Vilna. I had an errand in Vilna and arrived there by wagon. As I passed the city's railroad station, I was astonished to see thousands of breathless, perspiring Jews flocking, almost running, toward the depot. I was unaware that Antokolsky had died, as the mail was delivered only twice weekly where my parents lived. I got down off the wagon and asked the people hurrying by: "What's all the excitement about?" No one replied. A low-ranking railroad official was walking calmly from the station. I turned and asked him why everyone was rushing. His answer was: "You know, they're taking a corpse from Paris all the way to St. Petersburg: an *evreichik* (little Jew), a general. A general, an *evreichik*."* He repeated the last two words several times, astonished and, apparently, wanting to astonish me with the contradictory concept of a "Jew" who was also a "general."

I realized at once who the "*evreichik* general" was, and I, too, proceeded to the station and tried to break through the crowd to reach the platform beside the car that was carrying the casket, but the station was packed with people, and no one was permitted onto the platform. Assembled around the railroad car were the representatives of the Vilna Jewish Community Council and Jewish intellectuals, as well as senior officials representing the governor, the police, and the ministry of education.

A eulogy was delivered in Russian by the *rabiner*, Samuel Schreiber. He said, among other things, that Vilna, the "Jerusalem of Lithuania," had been blessed with the privilege of having two geniuses: in the eighteenth century, Elijah Gaon, the genius of the Torah, and in the nineteenth century, Mark Matveyevich Antokolsky, the genius of art—a fervent Jew and fervent patriot of all that was best and most beautiful in Russian literature, art, and culture.[6]

A delegation from Vilna that included the Lazarevs, his brother-in-law and sister, went to St. Petersburg for Antokolsky's funeral, in which thousands of people participated. Among them were the most distinguished representatives of intellectual Russia, headed by Antokolsky's faithful old friend, Vladimir Stasov. Eulogies were also delivered at the cemetery.

Novoe Vremia, where his best novellas had appeared, and thereafter published his work only in radical Russian journals. For Chekhov's remains, the railroad officials only reserved space in a freight car. This aroused bitterness in every corner of progressive Russian society. The liberal press and monthly magazines were very critical of the incident. It was a paradox. The anti-Semitic Russian government had honored the Jew, Antokolsky, more than the Russian, Chekhov.

*The word *evreichik* was used by Russians reluctant to use the derogatory *zhid* in a conversation with a Jew, but begrudging him the use of the word *evrei*, which had liberal connotations. Sometimes *evreichik* was derogatory, sometimes endearing.

Samuel Schreiber, father-in-law of Hirsz Abramowicz, assistant rabbi at the office of Chief Rabbi Isaac Rubinstein.
Courtesy of the YIVO Archives.

Stasov also published a large volume of Antokolsky's correspondence with him and other important figures. Although the letters are far from perfect in style and grammar, they reflect Antokolsky's inner life and shed light on episodes in his tragic career. These letters are also excellent material for understanding Jewish intellectual life in St. Petersburg. Turgenev had this to say about Antokolsky's autobiography and the letters he wrote to the famous Russian novelist: "His [Antokolsky's] language is not Russian, but it is unique, just as each kind of flower is unique."

I saw Stasov in 1904, at the Arts Academy from which Antokolsky graduated. Stasov was at work in the academy's large library, next to the special room where the original of Antokolsky's *Ivan the Terrible* stood. (There is still a bronze replica of this statue in the famous Royal Hermitage

Museum.) Stasov was explaining the origin and significance of the academy to a group of visitors. He enumerated the great Russian masters, among them "the brilliant sculptor Antokolsky."

Stasov had the appearance of a patriarch. With his very large build, snow-white head of hair, and long white beard, he made an extraordinary impression on the visitors. Although he was already an elderly man, his eyes were bright and lively. He was the embodiment of the legendary Russian hero, Il'ia Muromets, in his later years.[7] Throughout his life he fought for the independence of the visual and musical arts. He was their greatest connoisseur and a champion of significant new talent. He had vehemently defended Antokolsky against his anti-Semitic attackers. Stasov was an uncompromising Russian intellectual of the old style, who, regardless of the circumstances, fearlessly expressed his independent opinion. His majestic presence is before my eyes even now.

Several Jewish writers offered mistaken assessments of Antokolsky. As I recall, Peretz Smolenskin called Antokolsky a "slave," because many of his works were based on "foreign" themes and very few addressed Jewish subjects.[8] This was a false accusation. It is enough to mention his busts titled *Kharef* (sharp-witted person) and *Boke* (learned person), the statue of Spinoza, the unfinished but renowned group titled *Inquisition, A Jewish Tailor* (depicted threading a needle), *Nathan the Wise, The Street Vendor, The Talmudic Argument,* among many others.

Antokolsky's Jewish critics did not take into account the great scope of his genius. His artistic soul could not have been satisfied with Jewish themes alone. Like every great artist, he experienced and felt keenly his subjects' national characteristics. *Peter the Great, Yermak Timofeyevich* (conqueror of Siberia), *Ivan the Terrible, Socrates, The Miser, Mephistopheles,* and many other works attest to his intuitive understanding of the different national characteristics and his ability to fathom universal types thoroughly.

Nor should one lose sight of the times in which Antokolsky lived: the period of the *Haskalah* and the hopes of a bright future for the Jewish people once they had been "enlightened." The short but impressive epoch of liberalism marked by the reforms of Alexander II might well have contributed to the belief that Jews, too, would benefit from the favorable turn in Russian politics. Russian literature, which was essentially humanitarian, strengthened the hopes of the Jewish intelligentsia.

Yiddish literature as we know it today hardly existed at that time; it certainly was unknown to the Jewish intelligentsia. Secular Hebrew literature, too, was still in swaddling clothes. The Jewish educated classes grew up mainly with Russian literature. Thus, Antokolsky, through his great ardor and his effort to educate himself, absorbed all that was great in Russian culture. This was his spiritual milieu. Like all the intellectuals of his time, he believed with all his heart that the liberation of the Russian people would automatically free the Jews and bring them economic, moral, and political equality.

2

Khaykl Lunski

If Vilna rightfully came to be known as the "Jerusalem of Lithuania," this was due in part to the Strashun Library. During the final decade of the nineteenth century and the first forty years of the twentieth, it was a treasure trove for research in Jewish knowledge, literature, and religious studies. The library served rabbis and preachers as well as writers, historians, and students attending Jewish secular schools.

The founder of the library, Matthias Strashun, was a great scholar and typical of Vilna's pious *maskilim*. He was also a great bibliophile who purchased and collected rare books, old manuscripts, and every publication of Jewish content. He bequeathed this treasure, which at his death consisted of some 6,000–7,000 volumes, to the Vilna Jewish community. This was supplemented with the collection of Samuel Joseph Fuenn. Other scholars and book lovers similarly willed their books to the Strashun Library. As a result, it was the richest Jewish library not only in Vilna but throughout Poland, Lithuania, and Belorussia. There one could find the rarest publications, important historical documents, and on and on.

The library had no general catalogue, only some partial records of its holdings. When the democratic Jewish community council took over the Strashun Library in the 1920s, it partially renovated its building and engaged the Russian-Jewish writer L. Rubinov (a brother-in-law of Elias Tcherikower) to create a modern general catalogue.[1] Isaac Strashun, a relative of the founder, was the official librarian of the Strashun Library. Well versed in Hebrew literature and the world of books as a whole, he performed his function very correctly but was somewhat formal with users of the library.

The most famous librarian of the Strashun Library was Khaykl Lunski, who began working there in 1895. Most writers, researchers, and scientists addressed themselves to him. He knew each sacred text, each secular book, each newspaper file. He was at home in the sea of writings on religion. He greeted everyone cheerfully. Lunski suffered from a speech defect, which became apparent primarily when he was especially enthusiastic or disturbed about something. He would "sift" his words through his teeth, speaking very rapidly, so that it was difficult to understand what he was saying. He was aware of his disability and would repeat his words several times.

Lunski's main problem was that he was in awe of anyone who had written and published something. A noted author and scholar himself, he nevertheless was unable to overcome a sense of inferiority. He would never sit in the presence of someone he considered more distinguished than himself if that individual was standing. When someone talked with Lunski, he would not stand still but would inch backward.

Whenever a writer or scholar had an idea for a project, he had to see Lunski for help with the bibliography. Lunski recalled every set of newspapers and journals the library owned. Of course, no library in the world has "everything," especially complete newspaper files; some issues were missing from the Strashun Library as well. It did not even have every issue of *Ha-Melits* or *Ha-Tsefirah,* let alone the earlier copies of *Voskhod, Razsvet* or *Russkii Evrei,* among others. With great embarrassment, as though it were his fault, Lunski would say: "We don't have that year's editions," or, "We have only a few dozen issues of that year." Or he would ask whether some other publication in another language that the library did have for the year in question would serve the researcher's purpose. In this respect, Lunski was irreplaceable, and many a writer is indebted to him for his assistance. To this day, Jewish bibliography is inadequate; researchers' questions often still cannot be answered. That was certainly the case twenty or thirty years ago, when the number of bibliographical works available could be counted on one's fingers. A librarian such as Lunski was literally a savior for those in need of bibliographical guidance. Lunski himself also engaged in bibliographic work. He began compiling a catalogue of the library alphabetized according to subject, author, and title.

One winter I had occasion to spend my free evenings at the Strashun Library while preparing a study of the Kishinev pogrom of 1903. To begin with, I needed access to the entire Jewish press of that time. Lunski would have ready for me all Yiddish, Hebrew, and Russian-Jewish newspapers, as well as any brochure or book containing even the slightest reference to that great tragedy. During the period of the Kishinev pogrom, libraries were forbidden to collect and keep illegal literature. Nevertheless, at the risk of his life, Lunski had collected and secreted illegal publications of historical value.

Lunski provided me with everything I requested and with other materials at his own initiative. He showed great interest in the progress of my work, which for months appeared in daily installments in the Vilna Yiddish newspaper *Di Tsayt.* On several occasions, Lunski suggested that I publish the account in book form. This was in 1938, when ominous clouds were already spreading across the Jewish world. During the Nazi era, all of the clippings and my manuscript for the monograph were destroyed, along with my entire archive, but I shall never forget Lunski's help in the preparation of this work.

Born in Słonim, Khaykl Lunski was the descendant of rabbis. By the age of four he was attending *heder.* He later studied at yeshivas in Słonim, Lida and, most importantly, Vilna, where he remained permanently. He read *Haskalah* literature and studied with Jewish gymnasium students, who tutored poor yeshiva students for free. In order to support himself, Lunski worked as a caretaker in the Old Synagogue (*Alte kloyz*). The courtyard of this famous Vilna synagogue was also the site of the Strashun Library.[2] Lunski made excellent use of the library's treasures, and he became very familiar with the collection, especially its religious books.

In those days, Lunski subsisted the entire day on some rye bread and the head of a herring. This he washed down with tea from a teahouse where, for a kopek or even a groshn, one could buy a small container of boiling water dispensed from a large kettle. On the whole, Lunski had few wants. Year after year, he wore the same gabardine made of glossy, silken fabric. Nevertheless, his appearance was always neat. When all the personnel of the Vilna libraries joined a professional organization of business employees, Lunski's situation was somewhat improved, although it was far from enough to provide for all the needs of a family man. By that time Lunski had two children; his wife had died early in their marriage.

Lunski was truly pious. He prayed with intense devotion three times a day. On entering the library, one might glimpse Lunski in the anteroom of the Great Synagogue, where there was a small area for afternoon and evening prayers. Lunski could dash out there and join a *minyan,* which was always present from early morning to late evening. Lunski never sat bareheaded in the library. On Fridays and Saturdays, he would not attend meetings of the Literary Society or other organizations to which he belonged. Indeed, for his sake and that of several other Orthodox members, the society stopped holding meetings on the Sabbath.*

---

*The reading room of the library was open for about three hours on Saturday afternoons. No one was allowed to use a pen or pencil, however, in keeping with the

Lunski's "domain" was the synagogue courtyard and its environs, with its dozens and dozens of houses of prayer and study, the men who went there regularly, and the unique individuals who inhabited the area. During his final years, Lunski was the only person in the neighborhood who could still relate the history of each prayer house and its rabbis, preachers, scholars, and teachers. He could also tell about the various women who sold bagels, cooked beans, and other things there.

Lunski wrote about what he saw in a simple, old-fashioned, folksy Yiddish. After World War I he published these observations in a book titled *From the Vilna Ghetto: Written during Bad Times*.[3] This small volume, published in Yiddish and Hebrew, immediately attracted attention in both literary and non-literary circles. It consisted of brief profiles of various ghetto inhabitants who perished as a result of hunger, cold, or disease, often turning rigid forever while poring over a religious book. There are very few works in Yiddish literature like this one; it is a work of art in a style reminiscent of old chronicles, although this was not the author's intention.

Lunski also published an article titled "Vilna Synagogues in the *Shulhoyf*" in Dr. Cemach Szabad's *Vilna Essays,* which appeared during World War I. During this period, he collected all the ordinances issued by German occupying forces and published them (in collaboration with Y. Broides). Lunski's article, "Hunger and High Prices in Vilna during the German Occupation," was published in Zalmen Reisen's *Chronicle of Vilna in the Years of War and Occupation*.[4]

Lunski also contributed a memoir of S. Ansky, among other essays, to Moshe Shalit's periodical, *Lebn* (Life). During the last fifteen to twenty years of his life, Lunski wrote biographies of noted rabbis and scholars: the Yesod, Reb Shmuel (the last rabbi of Vilna), the Hayye Adam, Reb Abele Posvoler, and Reb Ayzele Harif of Słonim.[5] He published dozens of these profiles in *Dos vort,* an Orthodox Yiddish newspaper published in Vilna. Several volumes of his collected biographies appeared shortly before World War II.

Early in 1938 Lunski came to me to obtain information regarding my father-in-law, Samuel Schreiber, who came from a family of *maskilim* in Słonim. At the time, I learned that Lunski was at work on a history of the Jewish community of Słonim. He was quite far along in his account; it was to have been the main work on his native city and to have served as a model for similar chronicles. He showed me a long list of illustrious people who came from Słonim and detailed biographies of some of them. I do not

---

prohibition against writing on the Sabbath. This, of course, was in the best Jewish tradition of studying a book on the afternoon of the Sabbath. Thus, Lunski and Isaac Strashun "toiled" on the Sabbath for the glory of God.

know what became of Lunski's great work. When I left Vilna in the summer of 1939, it was not yet in print. In all probability it was lost, to the great detriment of Jewish historiography.[6]

In his *Destruction of Vilna,* Sh. Kaczerginski makes no mention of what became of Lunski's book on Słonim. Kaczerginski does note that while in the Vilna Ghetto, Lunski was at work on an essay "on the tombstones in the oldest Jewish cemetery" (the reference is probably to the "Old Field," the resting place of the Vilna Gaon), which were "deteriorating more with each passing day." Lunski was also writing a study of Jewish printing presses in Vilna.[7]

His extraordinary modesty did Lunski little good in the Ghetto. Frequently ill, he remained in the Ghetto until the end, after which he was sent to Treblinka. His daughter Hana was in the Ghetto with him and accompanied him into Eternity. Lunski had confided to some of his acquaintances that he had several important documents which, no doubt, he took with him.*

Khaykl Lunski was one of the last representatives of a generation of autodidacts who lived on the cusp between the declining circles of Orthodox scholars who were followers of the *Haskalah* and modern times. And if there were any righteous men in that generation, Reb Khaykl Lunski—a pure, just man and a historian of great scholarly strength—was one of them.

---

*His only son, who lived in Paris, perished while being deported. By this son, Khaykl Lunski had a grandson who lived in Paris with his mother.

3

Samuel Hurwicz

Mendl Levin, an Odessa correspondent for *Voskhod* and *Der fraynd,* was moving from Odessa to St. Petersburg. En route he stopped in Vilna, seeing the city for the first time. When I asked him what had impressed him most about the "Jerusalem of Lithuania," he responded with enthusiasm, "The faces of Vilna's Jews, Vilna's streets. In no other city have I seen anything comparable. A city consisting entirely of modestly dressed intelligentsia! There is something spiritual about every Jew, especially the young ones!"

To some degree this transient visitor perceived what Vilna was truly like—a place of Torah, of Jewish knowledge, not only among rabbis and scholars but also among ordinary Jews—workers, petty merchants, artisans. Hungry after a day of hard work, they refreshed their spirits by going to their various houses of study and prayer, where together they pored over a chapter of the Mishnah, a portion of the *Shulhan Arukh,* or of the *En Ya'akov.*[1] During the last quarter of the nineteenth century, and certainly by the beginning of the twentieth, there were some laborers in Vilna who also read a book or newspaper in Yiddish or modern Hebrew and who were quite well informed about Jewish communal affairs. For the most part, these were specialists in their occupations, aesthetes who could appreciate "a fine piece of work." From among these people emerged Antokolsky, Il'ia Guenzburg, Bernstein-Sinaeff, and other artists of world renown.[2] The number of artists from the working class who did not have famous names was very large. However, everyone in Vilna and its environs knew of them.

For example, Vilna's Abraham Grilikhes worked as engraver for the mint of the tsarist government—and even for the Winter Palace.[3] Many probably still remember silver rubles, especially those commemorating various important events in Russian history, such as the Romanov dynasty's tercentennial. In the border of these coins were the initials "A. G." Also, Abraham Gordon, the "perennial protester" in the Bundist movement, was the finest of engravers. He could reproduce the most complicated drawings in metal.

In a class with them was the locksmith Samuel Hurwicz, the vice-chairman of the Vilna artisans' union. He was the kind of locksmith who was intrigued by the "works" of the mechanism—the more complicated, the more interesting it was to solve its "mystery". Hurwicz was an "opener of gates."[4] He could take apart any kind of lock and put it back together. Safes were his specialty—not breaking them open, of course, but opening them when they malfunctioned, replacing lost keys, and so on.

I should also mention, albeit in a negative vein, another Vilna locksmith who was likewise a great expert on locks, as well as in plumbing. He appeared to be an honest, hard worker. During the first German occupation, he worked for some Jewish institutions. He was also a learned man and came regularly to parents' meetings at the Shimen Frug School, which his children attended.[5] He was a serious, pleasant individual. Suddenly it was discovered, to everyone's great surprise, that he had been working for burglars, fashioning tools, skeleton keys, and other devices to help local thieves fulfill the commandment to "use knowledge to open doors." He was given a five-year sentence by the Polish authorities. Nevertheless, this man was an exception to the rule among the masses of honest and hardworking artisans of Vilna. In case his children are still alive somewhere, I am not mentioning his name.

Hurwicz was a small, thin man, not very strong. His hands were always black and callused from filing, welding, hammering and shaping red-hot metal. His face was often smudged with oil and soot. Nevertheless, this small, grimy man had a great appreciation of beauty, of fine antique articles, and things artistically crafted. Hurwicz had no systematic education whatever. Self-taught, he thought of ways to improve the Jewish workers' situation. Hurwicz was a great devotee of Yiddish literature. He considered Mendele Moykher-Sforim's satirical novel *The Parasite* to be a guide to all that was wrong in the Jewish trades.[6] He was a strong advocate of formal education and of professional vocational schools with good instructors to teach the students systematically, using innovative methods.

When the Vilna *talmud torah*'s workshops separated from the school and became a modern vocational school, supported by JCA and subsidized by ORT, Samuel Hurwicz became a member of the school's administration. I believe he also taught locksmithing for a short time. He was very interested in the school's development and provided practical guidelines for teaching his trade.

In the early years of the twentieth century, a group of artists that included Leontii Antokolsky (a cousin of Mark Antokolsky) and Moshe Lejbowski, intellectual industrialists such as Adolf Gordon, and several others obtained a license from the Russian authorities to establish an Industrial Art Society. Its goal was to promote aesthetic culture by offering special courses in freehand drawing, sculpture, and drafting. The society also provided courses for house painters and decorators. Samuel Hurwicz was one of the founders of this society, which acquired a considerable collection of objects and sculptures to sketch, as well as a valuable collection of art books. Lev Frenkel, an engineer who later became inspector of ORT schools in France, was the director of the Vilna vocational school and the Industrial Art Society. Later, he moved to the Help Through Work organization, which he served as director until 1915.

In the evening, Hurwicz could be found sitting in the main hall of the vocational school, turning the pages of art publications with the bruised fingers of his callused hands. He would take notes and make sketches. He treated the books and precious drawings as though they were delicate creatures. One could see a second soul entering his being as he came in contact with these works of the great world of art.[7]

In 1915, as the Germans were approaching Vilna, the vocational school was evacuated to Kremenchug. The Industrial Art Society ceased to exist. Hurwicz remained in Vilna with the rest of its Jews and endured hunger, unemployment, and all the trials of the German occupation. But Hurwicz had always believed in organized mutual assistance, and he threw himself heart and soul into organizing the Jewish artisans into a society. Joined by several other skilled workers, he was able to carry out his self-help plan and guided Jewish artisans toward becoming an active force in society.

Hurwicz was a member of Vilna's Jewish community council. He was a thoroughly consistent democrat and despised the plutocracy, which endeavored, under a variety of guises, to win back some of the positions it had lost. On the whole, he was against political machinations. He spoke with passion, emphasizing each of his thoughts with sarcasm and, on occasion, with a pointed, folksy proverb.

Hurwicz followed the careers of creative people all over the world who had come from Vilna, especially those who were Jews and had in any way distinguished themselves in art. In Berlin there was A. Kulwianski, a young sculptor, several of whose wood carvings (*The Talmudists, At Twilight, A Rabbi and his Pupil*) were copied by the hundreds by those employed at the Help Through Work shop during the German occupation. In Moscow there was Zalmen Strazh, a woodcarver from Vilna who was a talented sculptor.

He achieved artistic success with his statues and busts, and he even designed some monuments. Strazh and Hurwicz were good friends.

Hurwicz used to visit me and read aloud Strazh's enthusiastic letters describing the development of Yiddish culture in the Soviet Union. This was during the time of the New Economic Policy and the growth of Soviet Jewish institutions, technical institutes, academies, schools, and newspapers.[8] Soon thereafter, Strazh died; he was probably in his late sixties. Hurwicz read me his last letter, in which Strazh asked Hurwicz to come to Moscow. Hurwicz had not wanted to bid farewell to his Vilna. All the same, he was proud of Strazh and continued to speak of him for a long time.

A few years before the start of World War I a museum of Jewish history and ethnography was founded, initiated by L. Frenkel, Dr. Wirszubski, Moshe Shalit, Khaykl Lunski and Samuel Hurwicz. Hurwicz collected forgotten treasures—such as old books, cultural artifacts, antique ritual objects—from people he knew. In 1915, all of the valuable items were evacuated to Moscow. Only a small part of the collection was returned. After the war, Hurwicz was the most dedicated of those committed to restoring this museum, which was later reopened and named for S. Ansky. Knowing where some of the museum's collections were, Hurwicz lovingly and reverently reassembled them.

On several occasions, Hurwicz wrote articles about Jewish trades for the Vilna *Tsayt* and *Der vilner hantverker*. Toward the end of his life, he published a small volume containing both his memoirs and his ideological perspective on social issues. Hurwicz died a few years prior to World War II, thus escaping the martyr's fate of Vilna's Jews, among whom were his fellow artisans, artists, and community leaders who contributed so much to the distinctiveness of the "Jerusalem of Lithuania."

4

Eliezer Kruk

During and after World War I, craftsmen and artisans came to the fore in the East European community. Prior to 1915, this significant sector of the population had been pushed off into the shadows and had played no role in the community's public life. Until then, Jewish political activity was the domain of the elites: merchants, the educated class, and party leaders. Craftsmen were not given a voice. The socialist parties also took a condescending attitude toward artisans. They were thought of as business owners, as bourgeois, even though they might be wretchedly poor with no one to act on their behalf. In the synagogue, they could expect nothing better than a seat in the foyer. They were not seen where laborers gathered, and no one expected them there.*

World War I and the German occupation introduced great change in the social structure of the Jewish community. Wealthier classes either left the country or became poorer. Food was scarce. Although the Germans had begun the occupation by paralyzing economic life, they did not tamper with developments in the internal life of the population. This situation brought to the fore the great strengths of Jewish community life: organization and mutual assistance.

A variety of associations and cooperatives sprang up. The Jewish cooperatives of the time had traditional names: *Ahiezer* ("Kinship is Help"), *Ezras-ahim* ("Brotherly Help"), *Malbish erumim* ("Clothing the Naked").

---

*It should be said, however, that in Poland, especially during the twenty years of the country's independence, the Jewish Labor Bund did have a socialist artisans' section. It was particularly active during the latter part of the interwar period.

There were many similar alliances: united storekeepers' groups, synagogues, cooperatives, trade cooperatives and others. In the large cities, trade unions were the best organized, maintaining their own cooperatives and soup kitchens. In Vilna, for example, the kitchen at Zawalna 60, a cooperative effort involving all the workers' institutions, was famous. The foremost leader of the city's Jewish workers was B. Michalewicz, who was assigned to this special task by the Bund in August 1915.[1] During the occupation, he played an extremely important role in maintaining the morale of the entire population through cultural activities and organizing. The smaller cooperatives were short-lived. The scarcity of products and raw materials became increasingly apparent as the Germans seized everything possible. Only the larger organizations survived, in part due to their purchasing advantage.

In April 1916, the Jewish Artisans' Union was formed, through the cooperation of several community leaders, including Dr. Wygodzki, Dr. Szabad, and engineer Klebanov. Almost all the city's artisans, who worked in dozens of trades, joined. Eventually the Artisans' Union had some 3,000 members and became a genuine force in the community.

Vilna's craftsmen were distinguished for their exceptional variety: cabinet makers, turners, engravers, embroiderers (who worked with gold thread), tailors, shoemakers, sign painters, among many others. The quality of their work was high, and the Germans, seeking "Jewish souvenirs" for their families, admired their products.

From among these craftsmen, several emerged who had freed themselves from the control of the communal leaders and managed all their affairs independently. Prominent among them were Eliezer Kruk, a turner; Samuel Hurwicz, a locksmith; Lichtmacher, a printer; and M. Żabinski, an engraver.[2] Kruk became the first chairman of the artisans' organization. The son of a turner, he specialized in making walking sticks and umbrellas in his shop on a narrow Jewish alley (down Castle Street, which later became known as Gaon's Street).

Eliezer Kruk attended a Jewish elementary school run by the government, where he learned some Russian and arithmetic. He was unable to stay in school because his father, like most of the artisans, was poor and needed Eliezer's help. Eliezer learned his trade well and still found time to read books and Yiddish newspapers. Endowed with intelligence, Kruk became interested in all sorts of social problems. While still a young man, he became associated with the organization called Help Through Work, where he was a consultant on matters concerning artisans.

Kruk himself initiated the founding of the artisans' trade union. He had a knack for organizing various related craftsmen into groups in order to find the best way to distribute their products, purchase raw materials wholesale, and the like. If I am not mistaken, this trade organization also had its own communal kitchen for a time. In addition, Kruk opened a reading room for the union. He published a journal called *Der vilner hantverker*, which contained articles, written by himself and others, about new developments in the life of artisans. Kruk's journal also attracted professional writers, who demonstrated interest in the problems of Jewish artisanship and productivity.

In 1918, when the Germans seemed about to make peace, the Vilna Jewish community council held democratic elections. Thanks to their efficient organization, the artisans elected a considerable number of their prominent members to the council. Situated between the Zionists and the Orthodox on the one hand and the trade unions and labor groups on the other, the artisans became the swing vote. They could shift the council's balance of power to the right or the left. They assumed the role of a centrist party. Because of the power relationships among the principal parties, it became imperative that the chairman of the council's administration be an artisan. Fortunately, Eliezer Kruk was the right person for this important, responsible position on the council, whose members included many prominent individuals.

Although Kruk had no formal education, he was very intelligent and capable, and he spoke with convincing logic and common sense. He was one of what might be termed the "folk intelligentsia." He was at ease and well integrated with the lower middle class (the majority of the Jewish population) and defended their economic and social interests. As chairman of the community council administration, Kruk had occasion to participate in a variety of important conferences, both political and social, involving the whole Jewish community. He developed steadily as a result of this work, and people heeded his opinions, which were almost always practical in nature.

Kruk was a member of the Vilna committee of ORT and, together with Kahan-Wirgili, participated in significant consultations concerning the expansion of vocational training for the Jewish population. He was also in the administration of the central council of the Jewish artisans' unions in Poland. His position as chairman of both Vilna's Jewish community council and the artisans' association required that he participate in the most important representative bodies of the Jewish community in the city and the country.

In about 1923, the artisans' association mounted an exhibition in the Jewish community council building, displaying the products of forty or fifty trades practiced in Vilna. Naturally, the entire Jewish population welcomed this effort. It was an exceptional display, a temporary museum of Jewish industriousness, energy and creativity. Both singly and in collaboration, Jewish artisans working in various crafts created model products that delighted the eye with their beauty of form and their solid structure. Hundreds, perhaps thousands of items were on display. Carpenters constructed heavy furniture of paneled wood, either of their own design or according to illustrations in magazines. Turners exhibited all sorts of toys, artistic chess sets made of the hardest woods, boxes with various secret compartments. Tinsmiths not only made dishes and housewares but also created all sorts of artistically decorated candlesticks, candelabra, Hanukkah menorahs, lamps, and more. Engravers produced wonderful monograms, seals, and miniatures.

The furriers' display was exceptionally distinguished. They used pieces of fur to create mosaics and even a depiction of scenes of life at the North Pole: the taigas and the furry animals that live there, Eskimos and their igloos. This last item was, I believe, purchased by American fur dealers. (At the time, Vilna was one of the busiest transit centers for Russian fur products. There, the pelts were graded and prepared.)

Virtually the entire Jewish population of Vilna visited the exhibition. Schools made field trips to see it. Polish artisans, most of them inimical, came and gnashed their teeth as they saw what Jews could accomplish under even the worst of conditions and without any government support. Instead, the opposite happened: "Grabski's hearse" nestled in the Jewish quarters and wreaked havoc there.[3] It especially targeted the Jewish artisans, with the intent to wipe them out as competitors. Kruk called several press conferences. The Polish press all but ignored the exhibit. Nevertheless, delegations came from other cities to view the "Jewish work"—which, incidentally, was of such high aesthetic quality that it could have been displayed not just in Vilna, but even in Paris.

Vilna's Jewish artists also had a display at the craftsmen's show, featuring over a hundred paintings. M. Lejbowski was represented by his lively depictions of people, especially children and familiar figures of the Jewish quarter. Ber Zalkind's colorist landscapes were there, as well as Jacob Szer's caricatures and views of various Vilna neighborhoods.[4] The Help Through Work trade school displayed sample articles produced in its fifteen departments.

At this point, I would like to relate an episode concerning a Help Through Work exhibition of 1920: during the late summer and early autumn of 1920, when Lithuania briefly had control of Vilna, Help Through Work mounted an exhibition in the large municipal hall. I was in the hall on October 9; it was during Sukkot. Suddenly I heard gunfire and the pounding of horses's hooves. Apparently General Lucjan Żeligowski was driving the Lithuanians out of Vilna. As director of the Help Through Work school, I immediately sent the guards home and ordered that the hall be locked.

People expected a repetition of what had happened on the last day of Passover in 1919, when Piłsudski's Legionnaries "arranged" an official military pogrom against the Jews, killing sixty people and wounding hundreds. As I walked with a group of students, bullets shrieked overhead from time to time. The anxious atmosphere in the city made it impossible to remove the exhibit from the municipal hall. To comply with an order from the new government of Middle Lithuania (which was a legal fiction; in reality, all orders came from Warsaw), the Help Through Work exhibition was reopened to accommodate a visit by the chief of the Middle Lithuanian Government, Witold Abramowicz, a non-Jew. The visiting dignitary, however, proved to be not Abramowicz, but Żeligowski, the "Conqueror of Vilna" himself. Accompanied by the director of education, he scrutinized the objects on display as well as the diagrams and other exhibits. To those who accompanied him, especially the director of education, Żeligowski did not hesitate to say, "We must catch up with the Jews and outrun them"—this within hearing of Help Through Work administrators, who were obliged *ex officio* to greet the visitors. This was the attitude of the Polish government and its senior officials whenever they encountered anything that Jews did which was somehow noteworthy. Their actual inclination, however, was not to "outrun" the Jews but to chase them away. Such was the tenor of what their press and spokesmen said with regard to the exhibition.

The second or third election for the Vilna Jewish community council again gave the artisans the swing vote, and the same thing occurred when it came to elections to the city council. After much haggling, the Poles consented to allow the Jewish population one department head.[5] There was a total of four officials who ran the various city departments. The Jewish community council then began deliberations over whom to appoint to this post. In keeping with the balance of power of the Jewish community council, it was decided that the seat should go to the council's chairman, Eliezer Kruk. The Poles wanted to appoint the Jewish director to an apolitical division of the city administration. By their reckoning, this was the department that supervised municipally owned estates, buildings, nearby woods and other such properties. As a result, Kruk had to supervise Polish agronomists, experts in forestry, architects, surveyors, and other highly trained professionals. At the very least, he was expected to be able to read an architectural plan and take a position should differences arise. Kruk had learned to speak Polish on the street; what he spoke was a distinctive mix of Polish and Belorussian. It was, of course, far from perfect and lacked an authentic Warsaw pronunciation. But this did not intimidate Kruk. This was in the 1930s, by which time he and other intelligent Jews had begun to speak Polish more correctly than they had in the previous decade.

Kruk was not acquainted with Polish literature. He had not had time for it, although he had learned some Russian when he was young. His native intelligence and tact served as his guide. As a result, his acceptance of this important position in the municipal administration did not result in failure and, in certain respects, proved a success. He adopted the correct posture in dealings with subordinate officials and saw to it that they performed their duties as prescribed. His Jewish common sense assisted him in finding answers to all the complicated problems of the municipal administration and in maintaining the dignity of his position.

I had occasion to be in the city hall in connection with the Help Through Work trade school and saw Kruk at work in his office. He was a modest man and was not embarrassed to speak Yiddish with Jewish clients in the presence of his non-Jewish employees. There was not even a hint of servility in his demeanor toward the president of the city or other non-Jewish authorities. He was probably one of only a few Jews in Polish municipal government to speak Yiddish in an official capacity.

For the most part, the Vilna municipal council consisted of members of the National Democratic Party.[6] When councilman Boruch Lubocki attempted to speak in Yiddish at a general meeting of the council, the Poles attacked him with their fists and chairs. The other Jewish councilmen came to Lubocki's defense, narrowly averting a bloody fight. It was in this atmosphere of chauvinism and hatred toward everything Jewish that the Jewish craftsman who occupied one of the highest positions in municipal government employed Yiddish in his official dealings with Jews. To a certain extent, this displayed great civic courage. And, indeed, Kruk's subordinates were consistently respectful toward him. On more than one occasion, they were heard to say, "The man has brains!" "This artisan understands more than any government minister." In the department of city government under Kruk's administration, there was no corruption or shady business. Kruk had a clear conscience and clean hands in all his public affairs. There was not a single instance of corruption in the Vilna Jewish community council. True, there was much heated discussion, but it was a holy war.

There were those who were opposed to Kruk. Many of his colleagues could not abide the fact that Kruk was "everywhere." But, he was, in fact, the most efficient and productive public servant. The Vilna Jewish community was plagued by deficits. It was unable to subsidize schools and other important institutions. Kruk's omnipresence produced this *bon mot:* "Why are things bad in Vilna?" "Because all of Vilna hangs by one *kruk*." (*Kruk* is Yiddish for "hook.")

Kruk and his friends carried on a bitter struggle in the Polish Chamber of Commerce, whose covert intention was to restrict or completely exclude Jewish artisans from the country's socioeconomic life. Dictatorial as Piłsudski's regime was, it still maintained some semblance of democracy, to which the Jewish members clung. They fought tooth and nail, until finally a Jew was installed as vice-president of the Chamber of Commerce. I believe Kruk was also chosen for this post but was obliged to refuse it, because he already held the post of alderman. A rule was also established requiring that Jews be included on committees that administered examinations for granting licenses to engage in trades, whether as masters or as assistants. It was a fateful moment for all the Jewish artisans in Poland. The Jewish trade associations, as well as Jewish members of the *Sejm* and other community entities, fought bitterly against the reactionary "guild law," which was intended to destroy Jewish artisanship. Kruk made a great contribution to this struggle for the rights of a large sector of the Jewish population. Ultimately, something was rescued from this completely pernicious edict.

Kruk did much to raise the prestige of Jewish labor. The denigrating attitude toward the Jewish artisan disappeared. Jewish life made an appreciable leap from Mendele's *Parasite* to the moment when a Jewish craftsman stood almost at the head of such a "city and mother in Israel" as Vilna.[7]

Kruk and his entire family perished in the valley of murder that was Ponary. He had been "mobilized" into the first *Judenrat,* which was soon completely liquidated in response to allegations that Jews had shot at a German soldier. Should anyone ever write the history of Vilna's Jewish community during the twenty or thirty years before World War II, it would be incomplete without an account of the role of Jewish craftsmen in society and, in particular, the role played by Eliezer Kruk.

5

B. Kahan-Wirgili

B. Kahan-Wirgili had a great influence on young socialist Bundists during the revolutionary period beginning in 1905, when he was one of the widely read writers of the Vilna *Folkstsaytung*. I recall the passionate tone of his articles. They expressed the faith of a young enthusiast who had taken up his pen to address thousands of readers. Later, Kahan-Wirgili all but abandoned his pen to devote his time to Bundist and general Jewish communal organizations, especially those concerned with the school system, professional education and cooperative endeavors. He was one of the most prominent leaders of Jewish community activism in Poland.

Kahan-Wirgili was fanatical about the things in which he believed. During his youth, this included, besides revolutionary activity, the Yiddish language. He held that even our "loving" neighbors ought to understand Yiddish. It was said that when he rode on trains in the Pale of Settlement he would respond to conductors in Yiddish, although he had an excellent command of Russian. I learned that this was not mere legend when I came to know him personally. He frequently visited Gomel', the home of his uncle, the well-known Hebrew writer Mordecai ben Hillel Ha-Cohen. Kahan-Wirgili was very attached to his uncle, despite the fact that their views were as far apart as East and West. Like his uncle, however, Kahan-Wirgili always wrote his name in the traditional Hebraic spelling (identical with that of "Cohen") and not in the phonetic Yiddish spelling of Kahan—perhaps because he knew Hebrew well and found the phonetic spelling unattractive. When traveling between Vilna and Gomel' on the rail line between Libava and Romny, Kahan-Wirgili would speak Yiddish to the non-Jewish employees. In this respect, he was a Yiddish equivalent of Eliezer Ben Yehuda, the Hebraist who spoke Hebrew to policemen and all other non-Jews, even when he was not in Palestine. Kahan-Wirgili, however, never mimicked anyone. Such was his nature: straightforward and sincere.

Here is another example: Kahan-Wirgili felt very close to Dr. Cemach Szabad. When Szabad died in 1935, Kahan-Wirgili walked right alongside the coffin bareheaded, as a secularist sign of respect and mourning. At the time, Kahan-Wirgili was ill, suffering from the terrible cancer that took his life a short time later. Walking bareheaded in this religious funeral procession, which had been arranged by the Jewish community council, was "unacceptable" behavior. Anyone not wearing a hat would be barred from the cemetery. Kahan-Wirgili's conduct angered some in the large crowd, which included many people who were religious. Some teamsters, porters, and others among the pious men threatened Kahan-Wirgili with clenched fists. They moved toward the coffin, intending to give the "heretic" his due for insulting their religious feelings. Kahan-Wirgili's friends kept the protesters away from him but at the same time appealed to him on several accounts—his health, his safety, the desire to avoid a scandal—to leave the procession. However, he was adamant. When it appeared that he was in imminent danger of having his head split open by a stone or a stick, his friends forcibly removed Kahan-Wirgili from the cortege and took him home.

Kahan-Wirgili was consistent and uncompromising in all matters of principle. He was also very frugal and careful with public funds. Kahan-Wirgili brought the idealistic spirit and a readiness to sacrifice everything to his public service. He had almost no private life. His wife, Sofia Stupel-Kahan, a prominent advocate for improving education, died very young, leaving behind two toddlers who were brought up by her mother. Following his wife's death, Kahan-Wirgili immersed himself even deeper in communal activity. Scarcely an evening went by that he was not participating in some important meeting. He frequently left Vilna to attend conventions concerning both local and general Jewish interests, in connection with both his community work and his livelihood (as head bookkeeper and auditor of the credit unions). A first-rate planner and mathematician, he introduced his straightforward approach and practical insights wherever he went.

During the 1920s, Kahan-Wirgili was in charge of the publication department of the Central Yiddish School Organization (TsIShO), which was then headquartered in Vilna. At his request, I took it upon myself to compile and edit a geographic atlas in Yiddish with the help of E. J. Goldschmidt, a writer, and J. Zavels, an educator. The noted St. Petersburg lithographer I. Kadushin was in charge of the project's technical aspects.

Opening ceremonies at TsIShO school exhibition. Among those on the stage are Joseph Czernichow, Dr. Cemach Szabad, and B. Kahan-Wirgili, Vilna, 1930. Courtesy of the YIVO Archives.

The five of us met weekly to discuss matters pertaining to the atlas: Yiddish nomenclature, what countries and cities to include, which rivers, choice of colors, and so on. Kahan-Wirgili took an interest in all details of the work, and he was as delighted as a child when we presented him with a copy of the first atlas containing several dozen maps with the place names in Yiddish.[1]

As a member of both Vilna's Jewish community council and its municipal council, Kahan-Wirgili vigorously defended the rights of Jewish workers. On several occasions, I participated with him in large conventions that had been arranged by the JCA and ORT concerning vocational education and trade schools. Kahan-Wirgili frequently served as the chairman of plenary sessions and special committees at these conventions. He was particularly interested in matters raised by delegates from Vilna—for example, a presentation by Matthias Schreiber on the subject of textbooks in Yiddish for technical and mechanical courses. We often had occasion to consult Kahan-Wirgili on such issues, and it was remarkable to see how this man, who was not a professional educator, readily grasped problems and offered ideas on how to deal with them.

Kahan-Wirgili ardently supported vocational training for young people, and he was well versed in all aspects of the issue. His essay on the organization of vocational schools was published by ORT. Although he was very strict in communal and Bundist matters, Wirgili was easygoing and gentle when dealing with people he knew well. In private life, he always greeted personal friends and comrades cheerfully. During the latter years of his life, Kahan-Wirgili wore a beard, which added a patriarchal appearance to his tall frame. His early death as a result of the illness that tormented him for many years evoked great sadness among members of the Bund, ORT, TsIShO, and the other organizations with which he was closely associated.

6

Joseph Jaszunski

Jaszunski never attended a yeshiva, but he was truly a Jewish prodigy. He had a thorough command of all branches of Jewish and general knowledge, but he was not one to remain isolated in his study. Jaszunski participated actively in all aspects of the Jews' vibrant communal life in interwar Poland. He always had something original to say and a practical solution to propose. A supporter of the Bund, he wrote a weekly series of "Talks on Natural Science and Technology," some 700 in number, for the Bundist daily *Naye folkstsaytung*. The scope of his work was of general Jewish interest rather than being confined to party matters, yet he took from his partisanship whatever was practical, positive, and imbued with idealism.

Hoping to help young Jewish people lead skilled productive lives, Jaszunski sought to imbue them with the idealistic spirit of the pioneers who were preparing to work the land in Palestine. Although still very young, Jaszunski was a Zionist, active in party work and even served as a delegate to the Zionist congresses. In 1905, however, he became completely taken with the revolutionary movement. As chief director and planner for ORT in Poland, he tried to attract the greatest possible number of young people to the various vocational schools and courses he established, as well as to apprenticeships with private craftsmen.

To this end he adopted and modernized the ideals of Isaac Ber Levinson, Menashe of Ilye, and other prominent figures of the *Haskalah,* who claimed that Jews' traditional, unproductive vocations caused their socioeconomic degradation.[1] This became the agenda of ORT, to which Jaszunski dedicated virtually all of the last two decades of his creative life, working with

Dr. Moses Silberfarb, Leon Bramson, Dr. Aaron Syngalowski, B. Kahan-Wirgili, and others devoted to building the Jews' socioeconomic life on a sound, productive foundation.[2]

Jaszunski did not withdraw from other areas of Jewish life either. He was at the same time the associate editor of the prestigious journal *Di bikhervelt,* for which he wrote a large number of book reviews himself. These were not simple reviews, but rather enlightening articles on cultural topics. He wrote for *Literarishe bleter* and edited an eighteen-volume series on natural history titled *Natur un kultur.* His weekly "Talks on Natural Science and Technology" in the *Folkstsaytung* were famous for their scientific accuracy as well as their clarity. Jaszunski also translated H. Schmidt's *The Image of the World According to the Theory of Relativity.* In his circle, Jaszunski was one of the few early interpreters of Einstein's theory of relativity.

Jaszunski's study on the Yiddish press is a notable contribution to the history of Yiddish journalism. For several years, Jaszunski was also director of the first Yiddish real-gymnasium in Vilna. He was drafted for this position simply because there was no one more suited to run what became a famous educational institution than the well-rounded scholar Joseph Jaszunski.

Jaszunski was born in 1881 to a fairly well-to-do family in Grodno. His father provided him with the best teachers, among them the well known Hebrew writer Joseph Eliyahu Triwush, who imbued his brilliant pupil with a love of Hebrew and everything connected with Jewish life in the broad sense. On graduation from the Grodno gymnasium, Jaszunski was awarded a gold medal. At the same time, he read nearly everything of any importance in Russian, Hebrew, Yiddish and German. He then enrolled in the department of physics and mathematics at the University of St. Petersburg. On completion of his studies, he received the title of Candidate of the University of St. Petersburg.

This was not enough for Jaszunski, however; He went abroad and studied for several years at the renowned Polytechnikum of Charlottenburg. More than anything else, it was his own eager, unlimited reading and studying that brought him knowledge in a variety of areas, beginning with his own field and ending with philosophy and jurisprudence.

Jaszunski began writing during his student years. He contributed to the Russian periodicals *Voskhod, Razsvet,* and *Budushchnost'*. When the first daily Yiddish newspaper, *Der fraynd,* began publication in St. Petersburg, Jaszunski became a contributor. Using the pen name "Ben Chaim," he wrote essays on a variety of social and political themes. During the same period, he wrote articles for the famous liberal Russian journal, *Pravo,* edited by the noted Kadets Vladimir Nabokov and Iosif Gessen.[3] Jaszunski's brilliant articles on jurisprudence were even accepted by the journal of the Russian ministry of justice. From 1912 to 1914 he was the secretary of the great

Russian Brockhaus-Efron Encyclopedias and was editor of the publisher's abridged encyclopedia. When *Der fraynd* moved from St. Petersburg to Warsaw in 1909, Jaszunski became manager of the St. Petersburg bureau. In addition, Jaszunski managed to write or translate a number of books on mathematics, philosophy, and history. He translated into Russian *The General History of Philosophy* and *The Essence of Mathematics.* A complete list of Jaszunski's works would take up more space than is available here.

With the outbreak of the February revolution in Russia, Jaszunski returned to writing for the Yiddish press. At the same time, he edited a volume in Russian, *A Report on National Elections to the Founding Assembly.*[4] He was also a delegate to the preliminary parliament, which planned the elections for this founding convention. In addition, Iosif Vladimirovich Jaszunski, as he was known in Russia, was chosen to be the secretary of the newly established parliament. This first—and last—founding assembly was short-lived. Jaszunski decided to leave Russia; he returned to Poland as a "repatriated citizen" and began to work for ORT.

It was Jaszunski's idea to unite all vocational training agencies, such as the JCA and WUZET, or at least to coordinate their activities, so as to avoid duplication in any one location.[5] In this he succeeded. In February 1922, a conference of representatives of all Jewish professional schools was convened in Białystok. Assisted by Kahan-Wirgili, Jaszunski organized the assembly, assigned the speakers and developed the theses for their talks.[6]

At this time, I had the opportunity to become better acquainted with this man, so replete with knowledge and so informed about Jewish life. It was truly a joy to collaborate with him. His ability to understand was so great that, when it came to a matter about which he had limited information, one had only to point out some element or fact and he was immediately familiar with the subject, as though he had known it for a long time.

Prior to his years in Poland, Jaszunski had had little opportunity to become well acquainted with the functioning of vocational schools. At the start of his work with ORT, he made a thorough study of the relevant problems. As I was then administrator of the Help Through Work vocational school, he asked me to develop curricula for various trades and guidelines for the organization of vocational schools. I was also asked to address the Białystok convention on these subjects.

More than one hundred delegates from various districts of Poland came to the convention. Those present had been educated under a variety of cultures—Russian, Polish, German. There were representatives of the JCA, who were mostly very bureaucratic in nature, and there were modern teachers and vocational instructors with radical political leanings. With his logical approach, common sense, and tact, Jaszunski succeeded in uniting the convention along substantive principles that were generally supported by a consensus. Jaszunski presided over most of the general meetings and he also organized separate meetings for committees. Thanks to him, the convention was productive and completed the first stage in establishing Jewish vocational training in Poland on a sound foundation.

The second and final joint convention of ORT and the JCA was held in the 1930s. It boasted several dozen vocational schools and programs, which offered organized instruction in skills to several thousand young people and adults. Jaszunski also had the principal role at the second assembly, presiding over the general meeting and assigning the presentations to be given at the various sessions. I was asked to speak on "Educational Problems in Jewish Vocational Schools" and "The Role of Jewish History and Literature in Jewish Trade Schools." All lectures given under the auspices of ORT were delivered in Yiddish. The directors of the JCA schools, however, gave their talks in Polish. Nevertheless, the fact that the assimilationist JCA joined with the Yiddishist ORT was an achievement. In the years between the two conventions, there were frequent smaller consultations between ORT and JCA committees, which were led by Syngalowski and Bramson, the international chairman of ORT. The proceedings of the second convention were to have been published, but this was prevented by Hitler's advancing plague. The Berlin headquarters of ORT had to be transferred to Paris.

I followed Jaszunski as director of the Vilna Yiddish high school ("*Realgimnazye*"). He had reorganized the school to minimize the role of politics and to encourage teaching that equipped students with the kind of knowledge a European secondary school ought to provide. Jaszunski himself taught mathematics, physics, and other science courses, and he also knew what was going on in other classes. He supervised the teachers and their curricula. Although he was not a specialist in pedagogy, he intuitively understood all aspects of education, thanks to his multifaceted erudition.

Jaszunski held many conferences with parents, pointing the way toward cooperation between school and home. He was acquainted with the character of every student in the upper grades. The parents' committee, the faculty council, and the central education committee were happy to have such a well-rounded, erudite, and wise individual as director of the gymnasium.

Unfortunately, after Jaszunski had run the school for only a few years, he was stricken with a very serious eye problem and faced the threat of blindness. To avoid this he was forced to undergo a crucial operation, after which he had to lie almost motionless on his back for six months. This caused him much discomfort, and when I paid him a sick call he declared in desperation that he would almost rather be dead than endure the suffering of lying motionless in bed. He was forbidden to read. Fortunately, his faithful life companion scarcely ever left his bedside and served as his eyes. She read aloud to him from scientific books and journals and whatever else interested him.

On recovering from the illness (which apparently was due to too much rapid reading), Jaszunski gave up his post at the real gymnasium and moved to Warsaw. There he became the director of ORT in Poland and continued his literary activity. His principal efforts, of course, were concentrated on the extensive activities of ORT. To reduce the scarcity of qualified teachers for Jewish vocational schools, ORT established courses to train instructors. Vocational specialists lacked a general education, while well-schooled individuals lacked vocational experience.[7]

With the terrible advent of September 1939, when Hitler attacked Poland and Polish Jews fell into the Germans' murderous trap, all these wonderful, constructive efforts gave way to the miserable existence of the Warsaw Ghetto. Because of his experience in vocational education, Jaszunski was appointed a member of the *Judenrat,* the German-mandated Jewish Council.

The Warsaw Jewish community council and ORT worked furiously to establish all sorts of vocational courses. They made it possible to provide thousands of people with work permits, giving them the right to work and thus remain alive. The destruction of "non-productive elements" had started soon after the Ghetto was established. One can imagine how difficult it was to learn skills in damaged buildings, with hardly any tools or raw materials, an insufficient number of instructors, and the impossibility of venturing out of the Ghetto. Still, Jaszunski's great organizational talent and his conviction that the action was imperative overcame these difficulties. Dozens upon dozens of courses and cooperative workshops were organized. Thousands of people received German "permits" and were able to work.

ORT also made use of every available bit of space to plant vegetables, and Jaszunski organized people for this activity. But soon the murderers had played enough games with the doomed Jewish population and determined to destroy it, leaving no trace. The final hour arrived. Joseph Jaszunski was taken away to the gas chambers at Treblinka. There, on 18 January 1943, he perished with his wife and their youngest son.

7

JOSEPH CZERNICHOW (DANIELI)

Czernichow first attracted attention in Vilna as a young attorney in 1910. People said that a new star, a man with a golden tongue, had risen on the horizon of Vilna's Jewish community. Whenever he made an appearance, lawyers and judges came to listen, their mouths agape. His pitch-black eyes and square-cut black beard endowed his appearance and his speeches with a special oriental charm. According to my father-in-law, Samuel Schreiber, who was the assistant *rabiner* of Vilna for many years, many older attorneys (let alone the young ones) trembled when they learned that Czernichow would be their opponent in court. My father-in-law told me that Czernichow frequently conversed audibly in Yiddish with his clients and others, something that was previously unheard of in court. Usually, if people knew no other language they would speak Yiddish, but self-consciously and in a whisper.

Czernichow was one of the first Jewish intellectuals to use Yiddish in government offices. I recall the time he went into a Vilna bank with another attorney. Going from one table to a second and then to a third, he heard each Jewish bank officer speaking in Russian. Whereupon Czernichow called out to his companion, "See here, Joseph Danilovich, where did you take me? I was going to a Jewish bank in Vilna with you, but here I find myself in a bank in Tula [a thoroughly Russian city in the heart of Russia]! Are we in Vilna or are we in Tula?"

Before Czernichow had become a fixture in Vilna, World War I began. With his wife and young child, he escaped to St. Petersburg, where he became active in political and social life during the days of the February Revolution. On a mission for the new government, he moved to the city of Kharkov, his wife's birthplace, where he experienced both revolutions of 1917. He made appearances before the revolutionary tribunal, defending both Jews and non-Jews. The former were charged with the sin of having once belonged to the merchant class; with having sold something in the marketplace, usually a personal item, in order to be able to purchase bread for their hungry families; or with committing some similar transgression. With his great oratorical power and logical proofs of his clients' innocence of "counterrevolution and speculation," Czernichow snatched many a blameless person from the iron claws of the new "justice." Czernichow later described his experiences in a memoir of the revolutionary tribunal.[1] (It was rumored that his arrest in 1939 had something to do with the book, although it contained no attack on the Soviet government.)

After Russia concluded an agreement with Lithuania, and refugees from Lithuania and Belorussia were permitted to return to their homes, Czernichow moved to Kovno. He soon became very active in communal work there. During the revolutionary years, Lithuania briefly implemented what was then called national cultural autonomy, which made it possible to establish communal institutions. The focus of Czernichow's community service was his work for ORT. They established vocational schools for young Jews, encouraged Jews to take up agriculture, and so on.

Czernichow published *Arbet* (Work), a large collection of essays by community leaders and writers on vocational training.[2] The book received considerable attention in the Jewish community, and it played a significant role in promoting productivization among the younger generation.

Soon, however, different political winds began to blow in Lithuania. The dynamic Czernichow, accustomed to working in large Jewish communities, began to feel that he was isolated from the greater Jewish world, especially Poland, home of the largest and most creative Jewish community to survive all the upheaval and warfare. He moved to Vilna, where once again he had to qualify to become an attorney, this time in the Polish judicial system. He soon mastered the Polish language, took the required examination and came to the forefront of Vilna's legal profession. He accepted no civil cases (which yielded the best income) but defended needy individuals who had unintentionally come into conflict with the law.

Czernichow's major effort, however, was devoted to political cases. The reactionary Polish government actively persecuted minorities, especially those who wished to pursue their national existence unhindered, as well as communists and other left-wing activists. Czernichow participated in all major political trials, particularly those in the Belorussian territories of Poland (formerly the tsarist provinces of Vilna, Grodno, and parts of Minsk). Czernichow clashed frequently with reactionary judges, whom he did not hesitate to accuse openly of being biased and unfair. Thanks to his aggressive militancy, a number of Polish-Jewish communists were saved from Polish "justice" and, in some instances, from the gallows. This, however, did not prevent Soviet authorities from arresting him immediately on their arrival in Vilna in October 1939. In addition to his successful legal practice, Joseph Czernichow occupied the most prominent place in Vilna Jewish community life. For a long time, he was chairman of the Vilna Jewish community council, chairman of ORT, and was active in other organizations.

Czernichow joined the Folkist-Democratic Party, which advocated the productivization of the Jewish masses and secular Yiddish culture. He and Dr. Cemach Szabad became the leaders of the party. Together with author Hirsz-Dovid Nomberg they published the party's organ, *Der frayer gedank*, in 1926–27. But during the 1930s it became clear to Czernichow that the situation of East European Jewry demanded a more comprehensive program of political action. He returned to the territorialism of his youth and became one of the organizers and leaders of the Freeland League in Poland. Meetings of the Freeland League took place regularly in Czernichow's home, as did planning sessions for their summer camps. There the young pioneers, known as "Hawks," prepared to work on the soil of a new homeland, which would be appropriate for dense Jewish settlement.[3] Czernichow's indefatigable activity led to the establishment of a colony near Vilna, where those with an ideological commitment to productivization could engage in agriculture. One such individual was the "socialist revolutionary" Gershon Malakiewicz, known in Vilna as "the Convict," and who later was one of the holiest idealists in the Vilna Ghetto.

Czernichow endured many attacks from his opponents. He was aggressive by nature and engaged in endless disputes. He came up with many sharp, sarcastic witticisms concerning his antagonists. Czernichow held fast to his positions. He continued to preach productivity and agrarianism and was not intimidated by the poisonous remarks of those who disagreed with him.

It would be difficult to name an area of Jewish communal activity in which Joseph Czernichow was not engaged. All preparations for the Paris Congress for Yiddish Culture of 1937 were made in his home. At the time, most of Vilna's Yiddishist intellectuals were enthusiastic about the idea of an international organization devoted to Yiddish culture. Nevertheless, Czernichow was the only delegate from Vilna to attend the Congress, convened by the Yidisher kultur-farband (YKUF).[4]

Czernichow's home was also the site of receptions in honor of Jewish writers. About a year before the start of World War II the entire Jewish intelligentsia of Vilna, headed by Zalmen Reisen, assembled at Czernichow's home to greet Joseph Opatoshu. They discussed the situation in the United States with him. Opatoshu told them that some American Yiddish writers were not enthusiastic about YKUF; instead there was discord and opposition. The Vilna branch of YKUF, however, sincerely wished to collaborate with all creative Jewish elements around the world in support of Yiddish culture so that there would be continuous contact among thinking Jews. Among the most ardent supporters of this idea was Czernichow, along with Sh. Bastomski and Zalmen Reisen. Czernichow flew to Paris at his own expense to attend the YKUF congress. On his return, he reported to a large audience on the work accomplished in Paris. He told of the enthusiastic response to the address by H. Leivick.[5]

Czernichow loved nature. He never tired of enjoying Vilna's beautiful environs. At his initiative, a group of Jewish professionals purchased several parcels of land near the scenic banks of the Wilia River in Vilna, where they built summer homes. Czernichow owned one of these homes, with flower beds and a vegetable garden. He truly enjoyed his property and would always point out to his numerous guests how much pleasure could be had from even a small garden or field. It was not surprising that he placed so much emphasis on the idea of productivity, especially agriculture.

Czernichow's wife, Rachel, taught history in the Yiddish real gymnasium (a secondary school focusing on science) in Vilna in 1924–25. His only son, Michael, was exceptionally talented. He graduated from the Historical-Philological Department at the Sorbonne, specializing in the fields of Semitic languages and the history of the Orient. He was also a founder and active member of the Freeland League's youth movement. His brilliant articles appeared under the pen name "Astour."

Both Joseph and Michael Czernichow were indeed distinguished, not only for their writing ability but also for their public speaking. For a time, Joseph Czernichow, the Socialist Zionist, created quite a stir in the United States. He had gone there in connection with a fund-raising campaign and to debate against the Bund. His American tour was described as a triumphal march, thanks to his outstanding talent as a speaker.

Czernichow certainly deserves to be included among those who, as Daniel Charney has correctly put it, have made our generation great.[6] These people, who stood at the forefront of the Jewish community, deserve to be portrayed in all the spiritual and moral strength with which they served their people and their country.

8

Gershon Malakiewicz

During the last few years before World War II, the Freeland movement set out to train pioneers to help establish new, autonomous Jewish settlements. The work was carried out primarily by young pioneers in Vilna, who were known as Sparrows. The director of their summer camp was Michael Czernichow, the brilliant son of Joseph Czernichow. The Sparrows worked in the fields and gardens of nearby peasants as well as in their own camp. There were also some adults and even some elderly pioneers who participated in these activities. One of them was Gershon Malakiewicz, a Social-Revolutionary Party member, who in tsarist days had been exiled and had spent many years at hard labor in prison.

After the October Revolution he came to Vilna, where he formed a Social-Revolutionary group with several others. Some members of the group separated and founded a journal under the auspices of I. N. Steinberg's *Fraye shriftn,* which was published in London. Gershon Malakiewicz was one of the editors of the new journal, which, as I remember, was called *Baginen.*

Malakiewicz had no definite occupation. He carried baggage for passengers at the Vilna railroad station and took on all sorts of occasional work, no matter how hard or unpleasant. Nevertheless, he constantly strove to become engaged in agriculture. The Freeland ideal of a democratic Jewish agricultural community, based on physical work, mutual cooperation, and harmonious coexistence on the land, appealed to him strongly.

The Freeland group was looking for a farm near Vilna where their pioneers could put their ideals into practice. Reuven Szapiro, a well-to-do Bundist who was interested in Jewish organizations involved in vocational training, owned several dozen hectares of suitable land with farm buildings, located not far from Vilna. Szapiro was married to a relative of mine and had a business in Landwarów, thirty kilometers from Vilna. I used to visit his family occasionally. When I learned that Szapiro had some land which he could not make use of himself, I persuaded him to dedicate it to the goals of the Freeland League. Freeland and Szapiro signed a long-term agreement, and Czernichow, Freeland's chairman, was simply overjoyed.

The gray-haired Gershon Malakiewicz was, of course, the very first to settle on the farm and to do all the work. He was joined by a young couple, the first Freeland family. Several Sparrows who lived in the city also used to come and work on the farm. I remember a bright autumn day during the middle of Sukkot in 1938, when a group of us visited the farm: Czernichow, Fayvl Trupianski, Jeremiah Szapiro, myself, and several other friends interested in the Jewish agricultural movement.[1] Gershon was busy with the cows. He cleaned the stable, then went on to dig up potatoes in the field. Several fellow farmers were performing their tasks energetically, one with a hoe, another with a spade or a plow, and all with a true sense of satisfaction. Gershon Malakiewicz seemed to be happier than anyone else. He had found his purpose in life at last!

Gershon was always so poorly dressed that he could almost be taken for a beggar. He was half-blind and wore dark glasses (one eye had been wounded by Cossacks during an anti-tsarist demonstration), but when he was in a field or a meadow his face shone with pleasure. It seemed that Freeland had found a project that would thrive and grow in the near future. It also seemed that Gershon had found a haven. However, the black clouds that would culminate in Hitler's invasion had already begun to spread from the west. There is no need to describe the end of this experiment, which promised so much success.

Gershon Malakiewicz was forced into the Vilna Ghetto. He had no family of his own. As he did all his life, he occupied himself with assisting helpless, elderly people, and children. In his small sack, he carried kindling or a bit of food to needy families. Where or how he came by these provisions, God alone knows. In all likelihood, he deprived himself of even the very little he had for his own needs. Gershon never thought of himself or what he needed. His clothes were already in tatters.

In his *Destruction of Vilna*, Sz. Kaczerginski recounts how Gershon risked his life to rescue a hundred Jews by camouflaging their hiding place.[2] The murderers took him away to Ponary, the valley of execution, but they did not discover the people he had hidden. Gershon saved them by offering himself as a sacrifice.

A more exhaustive biography of this man, who certainly might have been one of the thirty-six righteous people of Jewish legend, has yet to be written.[3] Gershon deserves an honored place on the list of martyrs: he rose from among his people and died for them. He was one of our foremost altruists. May these few words of mine serve as a modest "amen" to the Kaddish that should, at least, be said annually over the unlocated ashes of this righteous soul.

9

Chief Rabbi Isaac Rubinstein

The mere fact that Isaac Rubinstein was appointed *rabiner* of Vilna created quite a sensation in 1909. Government-appointed *rabiners* were usually worldly men, frequently with an advanced secular education, who sometimes had scant knowledge of Scripture. In any case, people did not think highly of them as rabbis. No one came to them with questions of ritual. *Rabiners* recorded vital statistics, issued marriage licenses and divorces, swore in trial witnesses and military personnel, and performed similar formal and religious functions. A tax levied on kosher meat paid their salaries.

Of course, there were exceptions among the *rabiners,* such as the renowned Rabbi Jacob Mazeh of Moscow, who supplied all the scientific data for the defense of Mendl Beilis, or Rabbi M. Eisenstadt of St. Petersburg, or Dr. Shmarya Levin, among others. Indeed, Rabbi Isaac Rubinstein's predecessor was none other than the famous Hebrew journalist and scholar, Dr. J. L. Kantor.[1] The elected leaders of Vilna's Jewish community and a considerable number of the city's orthodox Jews, however, wanted a *rabiner* who was truly devout. They wanted someone who had a traditional ordination and was also an educated man who could meet the government requirements for the position.

There was a movement in the synagogues to appoint a rabbi with these qualifications. Then, to everyone's surprise, came the choice of an unknown rabbi from the Crimean town of Genichesk, Isaac Rubinstein, who was no more than twenty-nine years old. That so young a man should occupy the post of *rabiner* in the Jerusalem of Lithuania was nothing short of revolutionary, judging by the annals of government rabbinical appointees in Vilna. Among those who previously held this office were such men as the philologist and Orientalist Joshua Steinberg and the distinguished scholar Samuel Joseph Fuenn.

Isaac Rubinstein, however, was a prodigy from the Lithuanian town of Datnów, where his father was the rabbi. Isaac had acquired his rabbinical training and the spirit of Lithuanian scholarship in the region's yeshivas and from his father's family. While still a very young man, Isaac became the rabbi of Genichesk, where he was soon known for his remarkable erudition, his talent as a speaker and his excellent knowledge of Russian. In the course of one year, Rubinstein passed the final examination at the classical gymnasium, which qualified him to be a *rabiner* as well as a traditional rabbi.

Rubinstein did not officiate at circumcisions and weddings. He regarded the rabbinate not as a source of income but as a social mission. On arriving in Vilna, he immediately reorganized his office and turned it over to his assistant. He delivered inspiring sermons about both current events and eternal Jewish ethical values. Usually he spoke in the Great Synagogue on one Sabbath and in the Taharat Ha-Kodesh Synagogue the next week. His tall, stately appearance, unusually fine features and blazing eyes were very impressive, especially when he spoke about justice and fairness. All the Vilna authorities, even the most anti-Semitic among them, held him in high esteem. This was a man neither to be ignored nor underestimated.

I recall an episode during the summer of 1915, when World War I was raging, a time of false charges and edicts against the Jews. Jewish newspapers were shut down. Speaking Yiddish in public places was forbidden (ostensibly because of its resemblance to the enemy's language). Despite this ban, Rabbi Rubinstein delivered a eulogy in Yiddish at the funeral of his assistant, Rabbi Samuel Schreiber. A senior police official approached the rabbi at the Vilna cemetery and spoke in a hard, dry manner: "Mr. Rabiner, do you not know that it is forbidden to speak Yiddish? Stop your speech." Rubinstein cast a furious glance at the official and, with an angry wave of his hand, said, "Officer, you may write out a citation, but don't dare disturb me now!" And indeed, the officer did not disturb Rabbi Rubinstein further. Abashed, he moved aside, despite the fact that he could have arrested the non-compliant Jew and even turned him over to a military court.

On the whole, Rabbi Rubinstein distinguished himself during World War I and the turbulent postwar period, when governments kept changing and pogroms and other calamities occurred. His interventions with tsarist generals and others in the high command with regard to the edicts, libels, and expulsions of 1915 deserve a separate chapter. Count Tumanov, the commandant for the Vilna-Dvinsk region, assisted by Vilna's governor

Veriovkin, managed to obtain an audience for the rabbi with General Alekseev, the chief officer at the northwestern front.

For Jews, who were the target of incitement from all sides, the entire summer of 1915 was filled with unrest and fear over their fate. The threat of expulsion hung over Vilna's Jewish population. There was talk that the order to drive the Jews out of the city had already been signed; on Shavuot, the Jews had already been expelled from Kovno. At this critical moment, Rabbi Rubinstein appeared at the headquarters of the general staff at the western front.

Going to the headquarters was fraught with danger for the rabbi. He was received by General Alekseev and requested more than the limited time of a few minutes to describe the plight of the Jews in the war zones. The general agreed and Rubinstein spoke freely, accusing the Russian leadership of ill will against the Jewish population. He cited facts concerning the libels and acts of violence perpetrated by Cossacks and soldiers. Finally, Rubinstein requested that the latest expulsion orders be countermanded. The general replied that he had proof there were Jews guilty of espionage and treason.

Rabbi Rubinstein rose and declared in an angry tone, full of conviction, that the general had been misled by false reports, and that a government which treats Jews unjustly cannot win a war: Jewish history demonstrates that those who persecute Jews receive their just punishment from heaven. The general turned pale at those words. Apparently, Rabbi Rubinstein's prophetic stature, piercing glance, and ardent sense of justice made a deep impression on the general and he promised to consider the matter. Alekseev escorted Rubinstein to the door and—to the extent that his position as supreme general in the tsarist forces permitted—behaved cordially to the rabbi and forgave him his bold words. No further expulsions occurred—except for that of the Russian army itself. They were driven out by the Germans, who were victorious over the entire northwest region in September 1915.

When Vilna was evacuated in August 1915, Rabbi Rubinstein did not want to abandon the Jewish community. Those who remained were the poorer folk, who were left virtually without leadership. Thus he, too, experienced all that the martyred city endured under some eight or nine consecutive governments.

During the German occupation, Rabbi Rubinstein was chairman of the central aid committee. At the time, the committee was responsible for numerous social service institutions, schools, and orphanages. In those days of hunger and severe winter weather, there was an infinite number of problems, and the brunt of the burden fell on Rabbi Rubinstein. The rabbi and his remarkable wife, Esther, undertook the establishment of the first modern, strictly religious school for both boys and girls—a new phenomenon for the Jewish communities of the former Russian empire.

Rabbi Rubinstein survived the pogrom carried out by Polish Legionnaries during the siege of Vilna in 1919, in which A. Weiter was killed. Risking their own lives, Rabbi Rubinstein and Dr. Cemach Szabad broke through the rampaging hooligans to reach the Polish commandant. They demanded that he put a stop to the pogrom and immediately release the writers Samuel Niger and Leib Jaffe, who had been arrested along with Weiter.[2] The two were not immediately let go, but their imminent execution by gunfire was halted, and they were later freed.

During their brief period of rule over Vilna in 1920, the Lithuanians demonstrated a high regard for Rabbi Rubinstein and offered him a ministerial post. However, he was unwilling to leave the city's Jewish community council. At a large meeting of Jews, which was also addressed by a Lithuanian minister on behalf of the government, Rabbi Rubinstein delivered a splendid speech on the role of Lithuanian Jewry in the country's history and in that of European Jewry, focusing on the Sages of Zamut.[3] At the time, Jews were inclined to be pro-Lithuanian, and Rabbi Rubinstein expressed this sentiment in full measure.

During the nineteen years of Polish rule, Rabbi Rubinstein did a great deal to protect the rights and honor of the Jewish people. He served first as a deputy to the Polish *Sejm* and later as a senator. In both houses, which were filled with anti-Semites, he delivered speeches in which he spoke candidly about this issue. Once I visited Warsaw with Rabbi Rubinstein on official business concerning attacks by Polish Legionnaries on the Jewish agricultural school run by Help Through Work. When the government decided, for a variety of spurious reasons, to liquidate the school, we turned to Rabbi Rubinstein to appeal the edict. We called on the Commissar of the Eastern Region, Count Kossakowski. I shall never forget how respectfully the rabbi was received by the count. When he was informed that a delegation that included Rabbi Rubinstein had arrived, the count came out of his office and, bowing deeply, exclaimed, "Good morning, Mr. Rabiner!" He took the rabbi by the arm, led him into the office and listened attentively to him. Anyone familiar with the arrogance of the Polish aristocracy and its disdain for an untitled individual, especially a Jew, will understand that only Rabbi Rubinstein, with his proud bearing, could have elicited such deference.

On numerous occasions, when Jews came to him to report unrest in the city's streets, Rabbi Rubinstein telephoned the official in charge to demand that the hooliganism be stopped at once. Rabbi Rubinstein did not humbly request; he insisted with anger and indignation. Polish hooligans picketed Rabbi Rubinstein's home many a time; they shattered windows and otherwise treated him as the symbol of all Polish Jewry. The rabbi was not intimidated. He continued to fight courageously, to demand and to make claims.

As a member of the parliamentary committee of the Cultural Commission of the League of Nations, he spoke before an international forum on the persecution of Jews in Nazi Germany. He warned that Hitler was beginning with Jews in an effort to gauge the measure of humanity among the nations. In the end, not only Jews but others would be harmed as well. Hitler would have to be stopped before it was too late and all of Europe succumbed. Rabbi Rubinstein's words had little effect at the time, but his prophecy was, unfortunately, fulfilled. As a result of World War II, Rabbi Rubinstein was forced to bid farewell to his beloved Vilna congregation and become a refugee.

During the first few years of his life as an émigré, his voice was heard at mass meetings of Jews. He spoke about the great tragedy of the Jewish people, to whom the world was turning a deaf ear. Rabbi Rubinstein poured out his grief and anger in 1944 to thousands of Jews assembled at a mass demonstration at New York City's City Hall. He was gravely ill by then; the Jewish tragedy had broken his health. In the last two years of his life, he was a mere shadow of the great tribune who had spoken not only for religious Jews but for all irrespective of their beliefs. To him every single Jew was precious. Rabbi Rubinstein was only sixty-five when his heart could bear no more. In the history of the Jewish people in the twentieth century, Rabbi Isaac Rubinstein will occupy one of the most honored places.

10

Dr. Cemach Szabad

For forty years, Dr. Cemach Szabad was bound to Vilna and to every individual there by thousands of ties. There were very few people, whether in the city or in the surrounding area, who did not at one time or another turn to this popular physician for medical reasons. Szabad frequently made the definitive diagnosis in difficult cases. Thousands of people were registered in his methodically kept files. Although dozens of years might have elapsed since a patient had last consulted Szabad, the individual's original file was on the doctor's desk whenever the patient visited again.

Szabad strongly advocated that nature was the best doctor, providing that it was not abused by the patient. He favored preventive medicine over the pharmacy and loaded up his patients with optimism and faith. When treating patients with chronic illness, his rule was not to make their lives more difficult by laying down a series of "Thou shalt not's." "Do what is most comfortable for you" was his advice, for he considered negativity a poor physician. Happiness heals and helps a person maintain his equilibrium.

Szabad also employed an optimistic approach in his community activity, which was extensively diverse and productive. One must have faith in everything one does or is about to undertake. His favorite areas of community activism were building a healthy mind and body and creating a strong public culture. In the first area, he initiated the establishment of a number of institutions dealing with preventive medicine. For years he served as their director and then as a consultant. With Dr. Abraham Makower, he established several OZE (an acronym meaning "Society for the Protection of Health of the Jews") facilities, including an orphanage for infants, camps, outpatient clinics, subsidized milk for nursing mothers, consultation services for mothers, and sanatoria for people with tuberculosis, among others. Szabad was involved in public health education, delivering countless lectures on problems of hygiene, various diseases and almost everything related to health. He created a wonderful popular medical journal in Yiddish, called *Folksgezunt,* which found its way into almost every Jewish home and became a handbook for all Jews. Szabad supplied more than half the material for the journal himself. He also wrote a series of scientific articles on problems of social medicine. He continued his medical studies throughout his life and became one of the best informed authorities on medicine in the Vilna area.

In addition to his extensive medical practice and his scientific research activity, Szabad was an indefatigable community leader, concerned about every phase of Jewish life. With Simon Dubnow, he established the *Folkspartey* (Jewish People's Party) and for several years was its leader. In 1919, Dr. Szabad became the first chairman of the Vilna Jewish community council.

Szabad was an outstanding representative of the Russian Jewish intelligentsia of his day. He had absorbed the best ideals of the *Haskalah,*

Sixth grade exercise class at the Dvora Kuperstein School, a Yiddish school in Vilna, 1930.
Courtesy of the YIVO Archives.

Faculty and students in the garden of the I. L. Peretz School, a Yiddish school in Vilna, 1921.
Courtesy of the YIVO Archives.

combined with the finest attributes from such Russian humanitarians as Korolenko, Mikhailovskii, Uspenskii, and the others who fought for human rights.[1] Szabad had adopted the *Haskalah* credo of spreading enlightenment among the Jewish masses. To this end he founded a branch of the once-famous *Mefitsei Haskalah,* serving as the group's chairman and driving force. He helped establish the first Jewish public library and, later, a school, both under the aegis of *Mefitsei Haskalah.* Szabad took part in all the preparations to open these institutions and later became their true founding father.

Szabad remained in Vilna during World War I and became the leader of the Yiddish secular school system, children's homes, kitchens, and other institutions that provided essential aid to the public. During the terrible period of the German occupation, Szabad published the *Vilner zamlbikher* (Vilna Essays), a series of articles and literary sketches that brought to the world's attention the first reports of Vilna's oppression.

After the war, Szabad participated actively in the reconstruction work of EKOPO, ORT, and OZE, serving as their chairman. Relief funds and materials for needy Jews in Vilna and surrounding areas were sent from all over the world to Szabad's address.

When the Central Education Committee was established, Szabad became the custodian of the Yiddish secular school system.[2] In his capacity as honorary chairman, he intervened on the schools' behalf and took part in all essential conferences concerning their activities. Szabad's personal ideal was to make the Jewish masses productive and, in particular, to settle some urban Jews in the country. To this end he helped found special organizations, such as Viltar. He took an active role in other groups seeking to settle Jews on the land, such as the Vilna branch of the Jewish Agricultural Society, which was headquartered in Lwów. From the first day that Help Through Work came into existence, Szabad was an active member in the organization. He never missed an opportunity to strengthen the Jewish economy by creating new vocations in agriculture or craftsmanship.

There was, indeed, no area of community life that did not benefit from Szabad's unassuming and clear reasoning and his optimism. His constant good humor prevented partisan passions or local interests from taking precedence over the common good. The great trust that everyone placed in Szabad and the love they had for him enabled the success of every undertaking with which he was connected. Few such pure, unblemished people as Dr. Szabad remain. His name was known throughout the Jewish world.

11

Dr. Jacob Wygodzki

One of the most discerning thinkers among Vilna's Jewish public figures was Dr. Jacob Wygodzki. He was also one of the most courageous and indefatigable fighters for the rights and status of Jews in Poland. He never thought about his own security and safety. Whenever dealing with Jewish affairs it made no difference to him whether it involved a Russian general, a German colonel, a Polish governor, a government minister or, finally, a Nazi hangman, wearing the uniform of the eternally accursed "field gray," as the Germans called their murderous soldiers.

A chivalrous defender of Jewish honor, Wygodzki was executed because he dared to oppose Nazi cruelty and denigration. The venerable, eighty-five-year-old Wygodzki could not accept the idea that such outrages were to be tolerated. He went to see Murer, chief of the Gestapo, and demanded that he take measures against the wanton violence and do away with the order that Jews wear a yellow badge on the back of their clothing.[1] In response, the old man was pushed down a flight of steps and then tortured in the prison at Łukiszki, where he expired on the stony prison floor as a result of his beating.

Wygodzki truly deserves a place in Jewish history, particularly in the history of Jewish martyrs, our great men and women who sacrificed themselves for the common good and for *kiddush hashem.*

Wygodzki was born in Bobruisk in 1856. It was near the end of the reign of Tsar Nicholas I, when Jews were persecuted and forced to send young men to serve in the Russian army, and on the threshold of the liberal regime of Tsar Alexander II.[2] His parents were fairly well-to-do people from the suburb of Wygoda (thus the family name), near the city of Slutsk. As a child, Wygodzki attended *heder*, where he was both one of the most mischievous and one of the best students. He taught himself to read and understand German from Moses Mendelssohn's translation of the Bible, and he learned Russian in the same manner.[3] The *Haskalah* was gaining momentum at the time and, influenced by the Enlightenment literature written in Hebrew, Wygodzki's father enrolled his son in a gymnasium. Upon graduation, he was awarded a gold medal. In about 1882, he graduated from the famous St. Petersburg Medical-Surgical Academy. By then, the reactionary period that began with the coronation of Tsar Alexander III was in full force. Jacob was arrested for being associated with a revolutionary group. After his release from prison he departed for Vienna, where he specialized in gynecology. He next moved to Vilna, where his parents had already settled, his father having become a supplier of goods to a local military garrison.

Wygodzki practiced in every hospital in Vilna and carried out a variety of research projects in gynecology, publishing a number of papers in Russian and German medical journals. He was one of the few Jewish physicians who, even in tsarist times, had a thorough command of Polish, which enabled him to interact with Polish physicians.

Having always been drawn to politics, Wygodzki withdrew from scientific research, entered the ranks of the Constitutional Democrats (known as Kadets) and became a leader in the Vilna Kadet committee. He participated in every demonstration for freedom that took place in Vilna during the stormy final years of the nineteenth century. His talent as an orator and fluency in all the regional languages soon brought him great popularity. Although he left the Kadets, Wygodzki continued to be active in Vilna's communal life, particularly during the first two years of World War I, when there was often an urgent need to intercede with various Tsarist anti-Semites. The threat of expulsion hung over Vilna, as it did over Kovno. Libelous charges of espionage, as well as ransacking by Cossacks and military personnel, poisoned the atmosphere and threatened the Jewish population. The situation demanded that responsible Jewish leaders, headed by Rabbi Isaac Rubinstein, Dr. Cemach Szabad, and Wygodzki intervene with several anti-Semitic tsarist generals. Thanks to these efforts and those of a group of Jewish community leaders in St. Petersburg, the expulsion of Vilna's Jews was prevented.

In August 1915, most Jewish intellectuals, professionals, and members of the bourgeoisie chose to move to Russia, but Wygodzki did not abandon Vilna. As a member of the local citizens committee and a representative of the principal Jewish charity, he felt it his duty to remain with the "poorest part of the people"[4] to help them withstand the bitter times approaching for the Jerusalem of Lithuania. Following the Germans' occupation of Vilna on the day of Yom Kippur (18 September) 1915, a central relief committee was formed by representatives of the major local Jewish relief organizations.

The German military paralyzed all trade and transportation and, in their usual fashion, began to rob the residents. As one of the most active members of the central relief committee, Wygodzki repeatedly protested to the German authorities, Eichler, the city commander, and the *Oberostkommando* against German plundering. When the Germans ordered the capture and transfer of young people for forced labor, Wygodzki declared that the Jews of Vilna would not go to work voluntarily and called for sabotaging the order. Not content with the forced labor order, the Germans demanded what was ostensibly a loan but was, in reality, a tax meant to drain the municipal coffers. In particular, it targeted the Jewish population, who had always been regarded as people of means. On his own, Wygodzki exhorted Jewish citizens with this brief slogan: "Jews, refuse to pay the tax!"

Finally the patience of the loyal subjects of Hindenburg and Wilhelm ran out. They could endure no more of Wygodzki's constant protests and his "brazen" call to disobey the imperial power. In March 1917, he was arrested and sent to Czersk (in the German part of prewar Poland), the site of their worst prison camp. He was released in April 1918, when it was obvious that the defeat of Germany was imminent.

After the war, Wygodzki joined the Zionist Organization. Always a supporter of cultural autonomy for national minorities, Dr. Wygodzki was named minister for Jewish affairs by the first Lithuanian government. Vilna was soon occupied (on 6 January 1919) by the Red Army, however, which routed the Polish Legionnaries, who had controlled the city for several days. Wygodzki chose not to leave for Kovno, which was under Lithuanian rule, and he remained in Vilna. The Red Army, which did not dare to arrest Wygodzki, was superseded in April 1919 by Piłsudski's Polish troops. The status of Vilna changed several times more. Finally, on 9 October 1920, the Polish government was stabilized, and Vilna was eventually incorporated into Poland. The Jewish population, influenced by Wygodzki and several other Jewish leaders, did not participate in the plebiscite, together with Lithuanians and Belorussians.

In 1922, Wygodzki was elected deputy from Nowogródek to the *Sejm*, and he remained a member of the Polish legislature for a number of years. As a permanent member of the legislature's education committee, he defended the rights of both Yiddish and Hebrew schools.[5] Unlike other Zionist deputies, he voted simultaneously for both.

Following Cemach Szabad's resignation as chairman of Vilna's Jewish community council, Wygodzki was chosen to succeed him. Joseph Czernichow, an attorney, also held the post for a short time. From the middle of 1920, however, Wygodzki headed the council, in which all parties were represented, until the government appointed a Jewish council in about 1937. (This occurred when Piłsudski's successors also did away with elected municipal councils.)

Wygodzki was particularly effective when compulsory Sunday laws, a death knell to Jewish trade and artisans, were enacted. Vilna's Jews heeded Wygodzki's call to keep their stores and workshops open on Sundays. The struggle went on for more than a year, during which Jewish petty merchants and artisans endured all sorts of persecution. Wygodzki gave them encouragement and support. There are still people alive today who recall that struggle, as well as Wygodzki's battle for the rights of "basket women"—street peddlers, who were stationed at the entrance gates of buildings. Harassed by the police, these women ran to Wygodzki for help. "Armed" with his walking stick, he then hurried off to the city administration or the governor to argue with them about the injustice being done to these poor women striving to support their families.

Wygodzki never declined to intervene. When student hooligan disturbances occurred, Wygodzki walked the streets to observe their wild abuse of Jews so that he could then present the authorities with facts.[6] "No one will bother me," he would say to anyone who might be concerned about his safety. Everyone in Vilna, Jew and non-Jew, knew him, and even the hooligans did not dare to lift a hand against the venerable doctor.

During his later years, he could no longer practice medicine. The governing board of the Jewish community council offered him a permanent pension. They considered it an honor to come to the aid of so deserving and beloved a public servant. However, he categorically refused to accept any compensation for his efforts on behalf of his people.

Wygodzki was also a dynamic journalist. He wrote biting political articles attacking the government and Polish reactionaries. Despite the government's policy of tolerating anti-Jewish boycotts, he continued to offer encouragement to the Jewish population. Wygodzki's articles appeared in the Vilna newspaper *Tsayt* and, occasionally, in the *Vilner Tog*, the Warsaw papers *Haynt, Moment, Nasz Przegląd,* and elsewhere.

Dr. Wygodzki wrote three interesting books. *In shturem* (*In the Storm*) concerns the war years and the conduct of the tsarist and German troops. Edited by Moshe Shalit, the book is full of suspense and the writing is lively. The second work, *In gehenem* (*In Hell*), about his experiences in the Czersk prison camp, is a disturbing account of the treatment of prisoners by the Imperial Germans. Wygodzki had, by that time, recognized and described the murderous tendencies of the Germans, to whom other people were merely pigs or only fit to be slaves. His third memoir is titled *In Sambatyon.* Here, Dr. Wygodzki describes the Polish *Sejm* and the Jewish deputies' struggle against the Polish "Black Hundreds." The account contains many historical details of Jewish life in interwar Poland and of the Jewish struggle for human and civic rights. Wygodzki also published important articles in the Vilna *Pinkes* of 1922, in *Pinkes EKOPO,* and elsewhere. His name will remain inscribed in the roster of Yiddish journalists and memoirists.[7]

Wygodzki's oral talents deserve a separate chapter. His keenness of mind and his sayings and quips were well known. Filled with biting satire, they would go from mouth to mouth and were not always printable. When I bade him farewell before leaving for America, I asked Wygodzki how he was faring. He responded, "I've lived for more than eighty years and haven't died once. Long may that last."

At a meeting of the Vilna Yiddish Theater Society, of which Wygodzki was chairman, the actor Abraham Morevski (née Menaker) said he simply could not understand a proposal Wygodzki was making. Wygodzki, who had been the attending physician at Morevski's birth and had had to resort to the use of forceps to take the baby from his mother's womb, instantly responded good-naturedly, "Even when you were being born, Avreml, I saw that you were thick-headed."

This sharp-witted, unblemished community activist would not accept assistance from his prison mates when they wanted to give him their coats to use as a bed. "We shall outlive these torturers," he said. He was mistaken about that, at least in his own case, but he departed from this earth believing firmly that the murderers would receive their just punishment. As we know, they were not truly punished, for their every trace, like that of Amalek, should have been wiped out from under the heavens. Nevertheless, the Jewish people will not forget their martyrs.

12

A. Weiter

I remember A. Weiter (Isaac Meir Devinishsky) from about 1902 and, to a lesser extent, from 1919, when he disappeared like a falling star, having been brutally murdered by Piłsudski's Legionnaries. Weiter was known to working people, the radical intelligentsia, and the young people of Vilna as Comrade Aaron, the name he used in the Bund. His thorough knowledge of the history and methods of the social-democratic movement was impressive, as was his physical appearance. His handsome head, sharp eagle's nose, thick black hair, as well as his aristocratic (in the best sense of that word) manners and warm, pleasant voice all charmed the various groups of people with whom he was involved. From the start, legends about him circulated even in non-radical circles. I recall hearing from well-to-do people about a wonderful speaker in the "Organization" (the name by which people outside of the labor movement referred to the Bund).

People would say that Weiter was a prodigy; he was the very bright son of a rabbi and that his influence in the "Organization" was exceptional. The legend grew during the stormy days of 1905 when he "ruled" Vilna as a leader of that completely revolutionized city. Everyone regarded him as the uncrowned official representative of a force that had come to life against the background of a powerful mass movement. It had emerged courageously from the underground into the open despite the bloodshed by those who fell in the struggle. I recall in particular the imposing funeral of the "victims of the state,"[1] which was led by Weiter. The tsarist authorities went into hiding, and the safety of the city was in Weiter's hands.

The year 1902 was a time of secret revolutionary cells, which had begun to attract the majority of young Jewish students. Intensive propaganda was conducted in underground cells of workers and employees. Participants were instructed in political economy, the history of civilization and revolution, and related subjects. Young students, especially those attending higher academic institutions, soon undertook political activity of their own. They held literary and musical evenings in private "bourgeois" homes of families of some of those who had been drawn into the revolutionary movements. Under various pretexts children persuaded their parents to allow them to "entertain," frequently without the presence of the elders. For the most part, these events occurred in homes where there were grown daughters, whose good Jewish mothers were concerned about finding them husbands. And who could be a more desirable son-in-law than a student—perhaps a future physician, lawyer, or engineer?

One such home was that of the Jewish merchant Waldenberg, whose wife's maiden name was Chwoles. Her industrialist family from the Vilna suburb of Snipiszki owned barracks, public baths, and lumber yards, and worked as contractors. The Waldenbergs had a grown daughter, a pretty socialite. She danced and had a talent for entertaining young men. As was then the custom, such young women spent most of their time in the company of university students, older gymnasium students, and those attending institutes or studying for extern examinations. It was only natural, then, that these young men flocked to Waldenberg's daughter. She was, as people in Vilna would have said, an "empty vessel," who had only a superficial grasp of the movement, but she was indeed beautiful.

Comrade Aaron, the aesthete, could not resist falling in love with her, truly, deeply. And it seems that she was not indifferent to him. Weiter began to frequent the Waldenbergs' home. They lived in a building owned by the Levidov family, which faced the small Safianiki Bridge that spanned the Wilejka River. This neighborhood did not have the best reputation in Vilna. Before World War I, Safianiki Street and the nearby alleys were known for their suspect houses, where "victims of social conditions" and various criminal elements lived. The Levidovs' building, however, stood on a little square that only bordered on this street. One of the Levidovs' sons was a graduate of the Vilna Teachers' Institute and during the first decade of the twentieth century was a well-known correspondent for several major Russian newspapers. Such pursuits seem to have made it acceptable for well-to-do families like the Waldenbergs and Levidovs to reside at the very gate to the street of sin.

Soon, as I recall, an evening was arranged at the Waldenbergs' to "celebrate" Purim. In the event of a police raid, not an uncommon occurrence during such "parties," this would be the reason given for the gathering. The police were usually tipped off by informers or by "good" neighbors. Invitations to the gathering were, of course, delivered by word of mouth. I was among those invited. (I was then lecturing in two secret workers' cells on the history of civilization, the history of revolution, and political economy.) I was told that Comrade Aaron would appear at the gathering along with several guests who were not from Vilna. There would be recitations and the evening would be an intimate, entertaining event. It would be entirely in the spirit of revolution, however, in tune with the tenor of the times. Comrade Aaron was to serve as "master of ceremonies."

Not all the evening's events have remained in my memory. I do, however, recall the impression that Weiter made on all the guests. The large dining room of the Waldenberg home overflowed with students and young intellectuals, male and female, even some "young ladies" from upper bourgeois circles. Weiter opened the evening with a speech in which he described the backward conditions in Russia: the arbitrariness that reigned from the top to the very bottom, the police terror, the miserable situation of workers and peasants, the terrible poverty in the Pale of Settlement, where the Jews were imprisoned, and, finally, how deprived the Jewish population was of its rights. The one thing that all thinking individuals had to do for themselves, their close acquaintances and the nation was to fight against the despised Russian monarchy, or else they should support those engaged in the struggle. Money collected that evening was intended for the secret "Red Cross," to benefit political prisoners and exiles. Weiter spoke softly, smoothly, in intimate, deeply convincing tones. His speech really touched the hearts of his listeners and strengthened their readiness to work for the revolution.

I do not recall whether there were other speeches, but there were many recitations and much singing accompanied on the piano by Miss Waldenberg. Comrade Saveli Gurevich from Gomel' read aloud the famous poem "Sakya Muni."[2] Gurevich, who was very short, was still a student, but he was very expressive and vibrant. When he raised his clenched fists toward the One who holds the fate of man in His hands and shouted, "You are not just!" everyone present was stirred and looked on in wonder.

Next, Weiter, delivered a melodramatic recitation of "Slushai!" (Listen!) by Goltz-Miller.[3] This poem tells of a military guardsman making his rounds outside a prison one dark night, when a political prisoner attempts an escape. He scales the wall to the top and is poised to jump down. Suddenly the crack of the watchman's gun is heard and the prisoner falls, dead. The ominous refrain, *"Slushai!"* is heard again.

The lyric content of the poem, the refrain and the piano accompaniment made a profound impression, the more so because it was performed by two handsome people—Weiter and his bride-to-be. Someone, perhaps Weiter again, recited "Burevestnik" (The Storm Warning) by Maxim Gor'kii. At the time, every progressive person knew this poem. Its bold refrain—"The storm approaches!"— delivered with special emphasis, was an inspiration to young people. The storm did arrive later on, but not in the form in which it was expected.

I should add that Russian was the dominant language that evening. Yiddish had not yet entered the lifeblood of the Jewish intelligentsia. I do not recall that a single recitation or any remarks, including Weiter's, were made in Yiddish. Weiter still breathed the air of Russia's great literature and of its younger representatives: Chekhov, Gor'kii, Skitalets, Andreev, Korolenko, among many others. I soon left Vilna for an extended period. From afar (I was in the south of Russia), I heard about Weiter's exile to Siberia, about his doubts and reconsideration, and about his pessimistic plays.

Weiter returned to Vilna in 1919. The Soviet government's education commissariat, which was then at work in Vilna, had, posing certain conditions, subsumed all Jewish educational institutions under the government school network. Their plans included the publication of a children's magazine. They published one or two issues of a general interest magazine, written entirely in Yiddish. There were a number of prominent Yiddish writers in Vilna at the time, including S. Niger, the Zionist poet Leib Jaffe, and Moishe Taich, among others.[4] By then, Weiter was a respected playwright, and he was writing for the new Yiddish journals. But before anyone realized what was happening, Piłsudski's Legions, abetted by treasonous Polish railroad employees, burst into Vilna on 19 April, and for three days they ransacked, robbed, and murdered.

I was not in Vilna that Passover, having gone to my parents' home for the holiday. On my return, the first news I had was of the deaths of A. Weiter and of Leizer Gurwicz, director of the orphanage. It was reported that, despite the pleading and bitter tears of a Yiddish actress who was Weiter's neighbor (I believe it was Hana Broz), he was dragged into the street by Polish Legionnaries, beaten mercilessly and shot.

His body was left in the street for several days. Jews had been forbidden to go out of doors. Apparently, only a few people attended Weiter on the journey to his eternal resting place. Non-Jewish hooligans, young and old, hurled stones at every Jewish funeral that took place during this period; attending a funeral meant risking one's life.

Weiter's grave, if it is still there, is located to the left of the entrance to the cemetery in Zarechye, back toward the fence.[5] The Vilna Jewish community sponsored a competition for a monument to be placed on the grave. About ten entries were received and the jury chose the design submitted by Daniel Rosenhaus, an architect and sculptor who was a board member of the Taharat Ha-Kodesh synagogue as well as of the S. Ansky Museum.

The monument depicted a mighty eagle with wings outstretched but with the right wing broken. This symbolized Weiter's tragic end in the

The corpse of Isaac Meir Devenishski, also known as A. Weiter, who was murdered in Vilna on 21 April 1919.
Courtesy of the YIVO Archives.

bloom of youth. That was not how the monument was understood by Poles, however, when it was unveiled before a large Jewish audience that included representatives of various organizations and the entire board of the Jewish community council. Naturally, the eulogies mentioned the Polish atrocities and, in general, the chaotic events of the beginning of the Polish reign, the constant harassment inflicted on Jews, and the attacks by hooligans.

Polish authorities resented these speeches. Apparently there were spies who understood Yiddish among the crowd, and there was a series of attacks on the monument. At first, the chauvinist Polish press told its readers that the bird actually represented the two-headed Russian eagle and symbolized the Jewish people's longing for the return of Russian rule. Later on, when the authorities were convinced the eagle was not "Russian," a new incendiary campaign began. The eagle was "Polish,"[6] and the mutilated wing meant that Poland would be cut down and its rule would fall like an eagle that had been shot.

There were other inflammatory exaggerations as well. The result was a repeat of the campaign waged against the Jewish sculptor Antokolsky's proposals for a monument to honor Tsar Alexander II. Local political officials began a formal investigation, which set out to demonstrate that the Vilna Jewish community council had used Weiter's monument to belittle Poland. I believe an order was actually issued to destroy the monument. It required much effort, including the intervention of Jewish members of the Polish parliament in Warsaw, to ensure the retraction of these outrageous accusations and of the order to destroy the memorial. Thus, Weiter was not fated to rest peacefully under the monument, with which Vilna's entire Jewish community had expressed its grief over the premature violent loss of this respected writer and former "Jewish governor of Vilna."

Years later, when I was in New York, I unexpectedly found information concerning Weiter's experiences during his Siberian exile. The YIVO Institute for Jewish Research had announced an essay contest on the subject: "Why I left the Old World and what I accomplished in America." About 200 immigrants submitted autobiographies, most of them in Yiddish, others in Hebrew, English, or German.[7]

I lived in a Jewish neighborhood in Brooklyn, where I made the acquaintance of a seventy-two-year-old neighbor, Louis Feigin, a retired tailor who had come to America from near Minsk. As a poor boy apprenticed to a craftsman, he had been involved in the revolutionary movement. He was eventually arrested and, after a long prison term, was exiled to the interior of Siberia for five years.

Feigin had read a great deal and was well informed about political, social and even literary matters. He spoke both English and Yiddish well. Interested in participating in the YIVO contest, he began writing his autobiography. His written Yiddish was not always correct, and his sentence structure was at times unclear. (He asked that I read his manuscript, give him my opinion of it and, if possible, correct his style.) The contents actually proved most compelling. Moreover, to my great surprise, when Feigin described his life in the terrible Siberian cold with his wife and children, he devoted an entire page to Weiter, who was living in exile in the same village. Feigin also described other revolutionaries, both Jews and non-Jews. In their loneliness, some of them became dissolute, took to drink and womanizing and all but completely descended to the lower depths. Although the number of such cases was minimal among Jewish exiles, some of them did play cards, consume hard liquor, and engage in temporary "love" affairs with low-class Siberian women.

Weiter's life was quite different. He was very meticulous about his clothing, his general appearance, and, especially, his habits. He was a vegetarian, did not play cards or even smoke. At first, his wife was in Siberia with him. Being the spoiled daughter of a bourgeois family, however, she was simply unable to endure the hardships of Siberian exile or the rigorism of her idealistic husband, who tried to emulate the almost reclusive life of Tolstoy. Weiter's wife returned to her parents' home. During the evacuation of Vilna in 1915, they all left for Russia and did not return. It was rumored that she remarried.

A non-Jewish Siberian, the daughter of exiles, worked as the Weiters' housekeeper. According to Feigin, it seemed that Weiter helped her more than she helped him. Frequently, especially on Sundays and holidays, she became drunk and created disturbances, complaining, "Why do I have a master who won't drink and won't . . . ?" (Here she used an unprintable expression, which Feigin repeated to me verbally.) Weiter's wife wanted to dismiss the woman, but Weiter felt that her ignorance and primitive state were not her fault. The rawness of the surroundings, the uncultured Russian environment, and the barbarous government, which treated the exiles and prisoners like cattle, had produced such unfortunate souls as their housekeeper. Weiter also helped the sick and, as a rule, anyone who was in trouble. He wrote appeals for them, refusing to accept payment even when it was offered. He subsisted on the six rubles per month that the government provided to exiles.

Feigin recounts Weiter's life and spirit as though he were surrounded by a halo. Both the peasants and his friends among the political exiles considered him almost holy. He read a great deal and wrote, but he also performed physical labor in the forests, taigas, and fields to supply his domestic needs, and he helped ailing peasants with their chores. He reevaluated his entire life from an ethical and moral standpoint and was apparently one of those penitent individualists who are never content with themselves. To his contemporaries, Weiter was a unique and profoundly interesting person from whom there was much to be learned.

13

ZALMEN REISEN

I first saw Zalmen Reisen at the end of 1915, when the Russians were retreating from Vilna. The period of tsarist persecution had come to an end, and it seemed that it might be possible to manage under the Germans, at least with regard to Yiddish publishing, schools, and culture in general. It should be pointed out that that summer Nikolai Nikolaevich, the dictatorial tsarist commander-in-chief, had prohibited speaking Yiddish in public, closed down Yiddish newspapers, and imposed other restrictions.

The Germans banned Russian as the language of instruction in schools. Each national minority was expected to run its schools in its own mother tongue. Yiddish schools sprang up spontaneously, but the transition to Yiddish as the language of instruction was by no means a simple matter. There were not enough textbooks, and they did not exist on subjects for which there was virtually no Yiddish terminology. Few teachers were really fluent in Yiddish and not all parents were pleased that it was being used as the language of instruction. However, the commandment of the time was: Mother tongue! Yiddish!

Of the semi-assimilated, nationalistically inclined members of Vilna's intelligentsia, only a few remained in the city; the rest had fled to Russia. Those remaining realized that during the difficult days of war, occupation, and volatile national relations they needed to stick together. Several peoples—Poles, Russians, Belorussians, Lithuanians, and Jews—were all struggling for hegemony in Vilna. The Jews were not the least in numbers—they were nearly half of the total population—and certainly were not lowest in cultural development.

Some forty to fifty Jews—including doctors, writers, teachers, actors, artists, and others interested in community activity—gathered in the home of Leib Kadison, located on Great Pohulanka Street. Kadison, an actor, was a refugee from Kovno. Among those present were Dr. Cemach Szabad, S. L. Citron, Moshe Shalit, Don Kaplanowicz, Yasha Rosenbaum (a poet and, later, the director of the Hebrew Immigrant Aid Society in Riga), the publisher Shloyme Shreberk, the attorney Semion Rosenbaum (later a minister in Lithuania), and the actors Azro, Alomis, and Nakhbush, among others.[1]

They all felt the need to be together, to discuss the various problems brought on by their circumstances and to address cultural issues. It was decided to name the home on Great Pohulanka Street "The Jewish Locale." Gatherings took place there virtually every evening. Often there were programs: lectures, lessons, recitations, songs, and piano recitals.

"The Jewish Locale" became a club, so it became necessary to set up a buffet serving tea (with saccharine) and a snack. This was either a slice of black bread or a piece of "potato pie"—a rarity at the time, for most residents of the city were half starved. The main thing is that people enjoyed each other's company in a cultural environment; cultural matters predominated. Most of those who came were young people, but some were middle-aged.

Then, for the first time (at least for me), there appeared on the Vilna horizon a young man with energetic gestures and sparkling eyes. He spoke with feeling, sharply, incisively, attracting everyone's attention. He spoke Yiddish and Yiddish only, no other language. This young man, of whom little was known, was Zalmen Reisen, a younger brother of the poet Abraham Reisen.[2] That alone was reason enough for everyone, including those intellectuals unacquainted with Yiddish, to be interested in Zalmen and pay attention to his message. On the evening in question, Zalmen delivered a lecture about Yiddish. His speech was full of passion. His thesis was as follows: In the daily life of the Jewish masses, Yiddish is the one prevalent language. It lends proper expression to the Jewish people's way of life. No other language has ever expressed the character of the Jewish people as well as Yiddish has. It accompanies the people from the cradle to the grave, as the saying goes. But Yiddish must also be the language of the intelligentsia, not only of the masses. Yiddish must become the language of instruction. There must be schools where Yiddish is taught, and gymnasia, even universities.

Moreover, the current political climate demands that Yiddish be spoken everywhere, that Yiddish must have equal rights. It is high time that we cease being a tool of the majority. To Russify or Germanize is a national crime, and this even has the potential of becoming a mortal danger, given the intensified national attitudes and nationalistic trends.

No one will rebuke us if we do not conform to one nation or another. Enough of being slaves to the gods of others! Don't worry, Yiddish can hold its own, and the Jew who betrays Yiddish is a sinner. The language still lacks much in the areas of standard orthography, terminology, grammar, philological research, and so on. But this will come if we all approach the language with full awareness and with love.

All of this was very new, even for Vilna, which already had an illegal school where Yiddish was taught. It had a Yiddish press and a population that was not linguistically assimilated. Nevertheless, people listened to Reisen. He appeared at meetings of teachers, physicians, attorneys. He railed at the Jewish intelligentsia, charging that most of them were traitors to the most precious possession a people has, its language. Action was especially vital now, because of the other national minorities in the region and the policies of the new German government. Zalmen Reisen's words fell on fertile ground; they stirred people's hearts.

Nationalist sentiments had been building in Vilna, but there had not been anyone to give it form or energize it. Now there was Zalmen Reisen. Although he was not a pedagogue, his perceptive understanding of the masses led him to believe that, if Yiddish culture was to be made strong, it was necessary to begin building from the foundation, with children's education. His primary objective was to establish a modern Yiddish elementary school, which would include all of the best and finest created both by Jews and others. In sum, the Yiddish school ought to be a synthesis of universal human knowledge with historic and modern Jewish treasures.

Both public and private schools were established. Community activity on behalf of these schools centered around the *Mefitsei Haskalah* and involved both Yiddishists and Hebraists. There was dissent in the committees, which carried over into open meetings. After a series of fruitless meetings and heated debates, each faction still maintained its original position—as is usually the case. The meetings of the *Mefitsei Haskalah* committees and of the smaller Yiddishist group were held in the home of Dr. Cemach Szabad. It was finally decided that the two groups must part ways and, instead of debating, get to work. After a great deal of preliminary work, it was decided to begin by opening a school for boys where everything would be taught in Yiddish.

In addition to Szabad, those who advocated for the school included Zalmen Reisen, Sh. Bastomski, Gershon Pludermacher, Moshe Shalit, M. Szur, and a number of other teachers and public figures. Programs were immediately developed. Several teachers worked under Reisen's leadership on a definitive curriculum for teaching Yiddish. A number of committees set about creating terminology, preparing lists of thousands of words so that lessons might proceed unhindered. Reisen was the primary authority for creating or confirming correct terminology in Yiddish. He was also hired to teach in the first school that offered all instruction in Yiddish. Although there were Yiddishists in the *Mefitsei Haskalah,* a number of hours at their school were devoted to teaching traditional Jewish subjects and Hebrew. Somewhat later, classes in Hebrew were introduced at all schools where Yiddish was the language of instruction.

Teaching was not enough for Reisen. Fayvl Margolin, former publisher of *Ha-Zeman,* received permission from the German officials to publish a newspaper, to be called *Letste nays.* Margolin's editorial staff included such writers as S. L. Citron, Moshe Shalit, Zalmen Reisen, and Don Kaplanowicz. They played leading roles on the paper. Despite strict censorship, they endeavored to make the paper as lively as possible by reporting on Jewish meetings, school activities and cultural events. To Reisen's credit, *Letste nays* was the first newspaper in Eastern Europe to introduce modernized Yiddish orthography. He simply would not tolerate the use of old-fashioned spelling. This was reflected in the title of the newspaper—*Letste nays* rather than *Letste nayes.*

At first, many found the new spellings "hard on the eyes," but Reisen and his fellow editors were not intimidated. The new phonetic orthography proved a great success and became widely accepted in Vilna. Most of the Hebrew words used in Yiddish, however, were not phoneticized.[3] The terminology committees of the Yiddish Teachers' Association created and compiled hundreds of Yiddish words for daily use, as well as terms for various subjects taught in the schools. For the most part, these words were approved by Reisen, to whom the committees turned in all doubtful cases.

Thanks to Reisen's influence, the Yiddish language gained respect among the Jews who used it. Doctors conversed with their patients in Yiddish, which had rarely happened before. The first to do so was Cemach Szabad, the great humanitarian and community leader of Vilna. Nearly all Jewish physicians and other professionals followed his example. Among Vilna's Jewish intelligentsia, who had previously spoken in Russian as a matter of habit, an uneasy question would arise: "What would Zalmen Reisen say?" And, indeed, Reisen was a fanatic where Yiddish was concerned.

Not a single Jewish organization used any other language but Yiddish in public. Later on, during the period of Polish rule, a number of Jewish councilmen in the city government made some very courageous attempts to deliver speeches in Yiddish. The Poles shouted and made a commotion, drowning out the speeches. Councilman Boruch Lubocki, a teacher in the Yiddish gymnasium, was distinguished for daring to address the city council (where the majority were Polish nationalists) in Yiddish. The "civilized" Polish councilmen responded by attacking him with their fists. Several meetings were held with the more progressive Polish writers and journalists, at which Reisen and other Yiddish writers spoke in Yiddish (their speeches were translated into Polish by others present). Because of the anti-Semitism prevalent among Poles, however, no closer ties with Polish writers were established.

Following the pogrom by Polish Legionnaries in April 1919, Zalmen Reisen was the first to publish a Yiddish newspaper, the *Vilner tog,* which always offered an aggressive, radical response to both general and Jewish problems. Polish authorities shut down the paper on more than one occasion and imposed a penalty on Reisen. But soon thereafter, the *Tog* would reappear under other names. Reisen attracted all manner of creative and active individuals to the *Tog,* including Cemach Szabad, Joseph Czernichow, and Gershon Pludermacher. The paper was very popular, not only in Vilna but in the surrounding areas. Reisen set its tone. In his editorials and comments, he decried everything in Jewish life that was half-hearted, opportunistic, or even partially assimilationist.

Reisen also solicited articles from people who were not professional writers but had some writing ability and could inject something new and refreshing into any of the various areas of Jewish communal or cultural life. No Jewish intellectual or would-be intellectual could begin the day without the ritual of reading the *Vilner tog.* There were other newspapers in Vilna that had journalistic merit, but none could compare with the *Tog* for its effectiveness and influence. Most workers and young people, too, considered the *Vilner tog* their paper. It had spirit and national feeling, which Reisen sustained consistently. The government authorities could not ignore the *Tog* and, as a result, persecuted Reisen and his newspaper repeatedly.

Reisen did not overlook a single cultural phenomenon in Jewish life. On Fridays he would publish a ten- or twelve-page issue containing articles on literary subjects, as well as Yiddish fiction and poetry. Reisen was the spiritual father of the splendid creative group known as Young Vilna.[4] On one Friday, Reisen devoted a four-page supplement to the group under a bold six-column headline that read, "The entrance of Young Vilna into Yiddish Culture." Almost every member of the group was represented, including Chaim Grade, Abraham Sutzkever, Elkhonen Vogler, Szmerke Kaczerginsky, Leiser Wolf, Moshe Levin, Peretz Miransky, Shimshon Kahan. In subsequent issues, Reisen frequently published works by this noteworthy group, which earned a very fine reputation throughout the Yiddish-speaking world.

Whenever he was present at any kind of Yiddish cultural event, especially those held in Yiddish schools, Reisen's face would light up with joy as he listened to a Yiddish song, recitation, or play. The *Vilner tog* gave much attention and support to Yiddish schools and their problems. Reisen devoted

Jewish writers and journalists in Vilna, 1919. Seated in the center of the group is S. Ansky, author of *The Dybbuk*. Others in the photograph include Zalmen Reisen (front row, second from left), S. L. Citron (second row, third from right), Dr. Cemach Szabad (second row, third from left), Sh. Niger (top row, third from left), Max Weinreich (top row, second from left), Khaykl Lunski (top row, first on left). Courtesy of the YIVO Archives.

generous amounts of space to reports of Yiddish theatrical performances and holiday celebrations at Yiddish schools. He fought against bad taste on the Yiddish stage with all his might, but he had a good word and ample space for all that was artistic, literary, and offered a genuine expression of Jewish folk spirit. He frequently wrote reviews himself, encouraging the actors and producers to continue their artistic journey on the Yiddish stage.

It was only natural that Zalmen Reisen became one of the most active founders of the YIVO Institute. Along with Dr. Max Weinreich and Z. Kalmanowicz, Reisen bore responsibility for the entire work of the Institute and gave it initiative and direction. Reisen devoted virtually every evening, every Saturday—indeed, all his free time—to the Institute. He participated in nearly every committee established by YIVO to further its research and collecting activities.

Reisen was not content with his journalistic, scholarly and communal endeavors alone. He loved everything the Jewish people had created, especially its literature, which he knew thoroughly in all its periods. While I cannot deal comprehensively here with all that Reisen achieved in Yiddish philology, grammar, and literature—that is the task of his biographer— I cannot overlook his famous *Lexicon of Yiddish Literature, Press, and Philology,* which profiled the achievements of Yiddish authors, journalists, scholars, and all other writers.[5]

Even before coming to Vilna, Reisen had published a one-volume lexicon of Yiddish literature. He felt that it was far from exhaustive, however, and decided to prepare a more extensive work. The noted publisher B. Kletzkin offered to issue the lexicon in as many volumes as it required.

Reisen contacted nearly every Yiddish writer by correspondence. One of his requests was for information about deceased writers they had known. Reisen took advantage of every opportunity to question anyone familiar with details about a writer who had passed on. To him, every bit of information, every facet of a writer's life was important. Still, he frequently complained that "no one can be relied on; everything must be validated." He did, indeed, check every bit of information he received with other materials in order to establish the facts. Not everyone responded. Reisen had to repeat his request a second or a third time. He initiated an extended correspondence with people who weren't writers but who were interested in the project. In his international travels, he met with every Yiddish writer he could find, gathering as much material for the lexicon as possible. He traveled to the Soviet Union to collect data about Yiddish writers there, since it was virtually impossible to reach them by mail, and it was certainly unlikely that the mail would bring him their responses.

Reisen's diligence and endurance in completing the four volumes of his lexicon was remarkable. No task connected with it was too difficult for him. The first volume appeared in the early 1920s. It truly was a revelation to all lovers of Yiddish literature and to cultured people in general. Zalmen Reisen strove not to overlook a single Yiddish literary figure. He encouraged people to collect information for the lexicon concerning individuals who at the time were still far from being professional writers but only wrote an occasional article that might qualify as literature or journalism. Reisen considered it sufficient for a person to have had twenty or thirty published articles in order to be classified as a writer. Reisen not only correctly appraised people who were themselves not certain whether or not they belonged in the pantheon of Yiddish writers. With his warm and friendly words, he encouraged them to continue to write and to believe in their abilities. And Reisen was seldom mistaken.

There certainly has never been another author like Zalmen Reisen, who was personally acquainted with all the Yiddish writers who were his contemporaries. He took a bold stand against renegades, those who denigrated Yiddish, or scorned the life and culture of the masses. When he came to Warsaw he strongly condemned those Jewish writers who advocated linguistic assimilation—in this case, by adopting Polish. Reisen was sensitive to all that was creative in Jewish life. He devoted considerable space in his newspaper to pieces about productivity, agrarianism, and rational colonization. He was also sympathetic to the Freeland movement, to the pioneer efforts of the *halutzim*, and to every activity aimed at engaging young people in productive work.

14

MOSHE SHALIT

It would be difficult to name another writer like Moshe Shalit, whose literary and broad-based community activities were so closely paired. He was an idealist in thought, a humanist in feeling, and a positivist in his practical work. In Shalit, these three qualities harmonized in a most felicitous fashion. Shalit was a warm friend to all his countless comrades. In community work, he always kept in mind the welfare of individuals, so that they would not be abused by influential members of society seeking personal aggrandizement, power, or some other, more material, reward.

It is to Vilna's great credit that, as far as I know and can recall, there was never any case of financial fraud, large or small, in any of the city's many Jewish organizations and institutions. I believe that this is due, in no small measure, to the Shalits, Szabads, Wygodzkis, Rubinsteins, Kruks, and the others who were the leaders of Vilna's Jewish communal life.

Moshe Shalit's activities reached far beyond the city's borders, over the extensive province of Vilna to all of Poland. In the Vilna region, Shalit participated in the relief work of EKOPO; in Poland he was involved in the wide-ranging efforts of the vast network of cooperative banks, production and consumer cooperatives, and other public service institutions.

If Shalit was more of a writer and party worker prior to World War I, it was during the interwar period that he achieved full stature as a community leader. There is, regrettably, no authoritative biography of him, nor are there any factual accounts of his colorful life. Indeed, this lack applies to all the Vilna personalities we knew and respected. It is our collective responsibility to gather everything that might possibly pertain to our unforgettable martyrs, so that we may at least know the general course of their lives.

Moshe Shalit was born to a middle-class family in Vilna. When he was three years old his father died. After attending *heder* for a while, Moshe was enrolled at the government school for Jewish children, where he successfully completed the course of study. In Vilna, such schools maintained quite high standards. Shalit did not have the opportunity to continue his education. His "universities," like Gorki's, were books and life itself. His difficult circumstances taught him to observe the world about him with eyes wide open. This, no doubt, accounts for his pragmatism with regard to both Jewish and general problems. The sensitive young Moshe did not escape the anti-tsarist, pro-socialist revolutionary movements in which many Jewish youths were involved. In his case, he encountered it through the Zionist group known as *Vozrozhdenie* (Rebirth).[1]

Shalit was arrested several times and had a taste of tsarist jails and beatings. For a time, he had to take refuge in Germany, settling in Königsberg. At the age of nineteen or twenty, he began writing in Russian. He was drawn spiritually and intellectually to the idealistic students in BILU, who abandoned higher education and went to break the rocky soil of Palestine with their bare hands.[2] Shalit wrote a substantial monograph about them, which was later translated from Russian into Yiddish. In this work, Shalit demonstrated his literary qualities: clarity of content and simplicity of style. He also wrote book reviews. His directness in treating a subject gave him entry to almost every Yiddish journal and newspaper. He became a regular contributor to the Zionist weekly, *Dos yidishe folk,* edited by the St. Petersburg writer Dr. Joseph Lurie.[3]

In 1909, Shalit became a staff member of *Di yidishe tsaytung,* published by Fayvl Margolin, who was also publisher of *Ha-Zeman.* From that time on it was difficult to find a Jewish periodical, whether in Russian or Yiddish, to which Shalit did not contribute. The most important of them are *Razsvet, Dos naye lebn,* edited by Dr. Chaim Zhitlowsky, *Der yidisher kemfer,* and *Dos yidishe folk.*[4]

Despite the fact that Hebrew was not his literary medium, Shalit also contributed to the Hebrew journal *Ha-Olam* and to *Ha-Zeman.* In 1910, Shalit edited the anthology *Folk un land,* which was devoted to philosophical and social enlightenment and to the critique of Zionism. With Boris Goldberg, a prominent Vilna Zionist, Shalit devised the popular Jewish almanac *Kadimah.* Early in 1914 Shalit left for New York, where he became an editor of *Dos naye lebn* and worked on other publications as well. It seemed, however, that he did not particularly care for the atmosphere in New York.

No sooner had Shalit returned to Vilna than the war broke out. He continued to work in the Yiddish press until the summer of 1915, when it was shut down by the Russian military command. Several months later, Vilna was captured by the Germans. *Mefitsei Haskalah* then decided to open its first school for boys, instruction to be conducted in Yiddish. As a member of the organization, Shalit helped prepare a comprehensive curriculum for the school. The directors of *Mefitsei Haskalah* then appointed Shalit to the school faculty. At the same time, Shalit served as director of the People's University established by *Mefitsei Haskalah,* which operated in the great hall of the artisans' school (later known as the Technicum) on Gdańska Street. The People's University was highly successful, some of its lectures drawing audiences of 500 to 600 people.

All this activity was not enough for Shalit, who continued to contribute to Margolin's *Letste nays.* With Szabad, he published the famous two volumes of *Vilner zamlbikher.*[5] Through these anthologies the two editors let the world know, to the extent that the German censor allowed, that Vilna was alive. They explained that the city did not have too much to eat (their euphemism for starving), but was continuing to set up schools, orphanages, kitchens, craftsmen's cooperatives, vocational schools, libraries, outpatient clinics, young people's gardens, and so on. Sections of the *Zamlbikher* were translated into German and aroused the concern of various German-Jewish relief organizations. By clandestine means the books also reached St. Petersburg, and there, too, relief for Vilna was organized. In Moscow, EKOPO was established to provide aid to Jewish war victims, and as soon as Vilna was liberated from German rule, EKOPO extended its activity to Vilna. Shalit took on the task of directing the society's efforts.

In the meantime, S. Ansky arrived in Vilna and created an organization of all its Jewish writers and journalists.[6] Shalit was named vice-chairman. Ansky was its first chairman, followed by S. L. Citron and Zalmen Reisen. Then Shalit became the irreplaceable chairman of the organization's board of directors, serving for a decade and a half with only a few brief interruptions. In 1920, Shalit published *Lebn (Life),* a literary collection dedicated to the memory of Ansky, with essays on his famous play, *The Dybbuk,* and other literary topics. *Lebn* included several pieces by Khaykl Lunski, who offered moving memories of Ansky as a man who had an eye and a compassionate heart for everything in Jewish life. Shalit, too, provided a subtle portrait of Ansky's personality. In addition, Shalit revived the historical-ethnographic society named for S. Ansky and reorganized its museum. He also became a regular contributor to *Literarishe bleter.*

Beginning in the 1920s, Shalit devoted most of his energies to the social work of EKOPO. He organized communal committees in virtually every town in the regions of Vilna, Baranowicze, and Nowogródek. The committees assisted EKOPO in its work of economic reconstruction, which had been entrusted to it by the Joint Distribution Committee. Shalit and his

Weaving class in the shtetl Olszany during the interwar years. The equipment was donated to the town's Jewish community by EKOPO in Vilna.
Courtesy of the YIVO Archives.

closest collaborators, Uri Klionsky, Yitskhok Walk, Mordecai Ewzerow, among others, traveled throughout the provinces to instruct the local activists, who were essentially inexperienced in community work.[7]

The EKOPO conferences that Shalit convened were highly interesting. Participants included rabbis, teachers, artisans, and, to the extent that workers were organized in the region, labor representatives. Proceedings at the conferences were frequently noisy, due to the diversity of those assembled and their opposing viewpoints. For a short time, Szabad was the head of EKOPO. In addition, Rabbi Haim Ozer Grodzinski, famous as the leading figure in Orthodox circles, also exerted considerable influence on the organization, through the rabbinical delegates.

When the work of rehabilitating the towns approached completion, EKOPO—that is to say, Shalit—focused on credit cooperatives, people's banks, free loan societies, the care of orphans, and emigration. I worked with EKOPO on its efforts to care for orphans. Shalit was the leading figure in CENTOS, the central organization for the care of orphans.[8] He saw to it that every orphan who came from a small town and had finished public school was taught a trade. Whenever possible, the orphans were trained in the area where they lived. Otherwise, they went to Vilna and were trained at the trade schools of Help Through Work, at the Association of Jewish Women, or the Vilna Technicum, as well as through the private support of patrons. At one time, there were some fifty war orphans, about ten per cent of the total number of students, studying at Help Through Work schools. At first, a residence for the orphans was set up in the wooded Antokol area; later, they were housed in private homes. Shalit and his assistant for aid to orphans, Motl Ewzerow, constantly attended to all details of the orphans' lives, including their progress in vocational training.

During the period of EKOPO's existence, Shalit published the periodical *Undzer hilf* at regular intervals, which dealt with such matters as the cooperative reconstruction of communities, aid to orphans, and the like. Shalit wrote most of the articles. He was a specialist in statistics and demographics. He edited the book *The Economic Situation of Jews in Poland and the Jewish Cooperative Movement* and the annual almanac *Fun yor tsu yor*, which was published by the orphan's association.[9] These almanacs, which Shalit put together unassisted, contained important statistical tables and information on Jewish life in various countries. Shalit was an excellent editor. Everything that came into his hands was treated professionally and stripped of excess verbiage. From 1937 to 1939 he published the valuable historical journal, *Fun noentn over.*

Board of directors of the Yiddish Writers and Journalists Association (from left to right): A. I. Grodzenski, Moshe Shalit, Hirsz Abramowicz, Chaim Lewin, E. J. Goldschmidt, Shlomo Beilis (last person is not identified). 1936.
Courtesy of the YIVO Archives.

Shalit's participation in the Yiddish Writers and Journalists Association constitutes a separate chapter in the record of his activities. The association was the fortress of the Yiddish written and spoken word. The Jewish Journalists' Syndicate of Warsaw had joined the General Association of Polish Journalists. The members of the syndicate enjoyed certain travel privileges, such as free railroad passes. Nevertheless, the Jewish writers of Vilna refused to accept these privileges because the Polish syndicate would not approve the use of Yiddish on the membership cards of the Jewish syndicate members. Shalit was a member of all three organizations. During his term as president of the Vilna Association of Writers and Journalists, the organization's business was conducted in exemplary fashion, with the cooperation of its secretary, A. I. Grodzenski, and the business manager, B. Terkel. Differences between members or between members and publishers were settled by the organization's administration. The strict neutrality of its presiding officer played a significant role in the resolution of disputes. Everyone knew that Shalit would not show partiality to anyone. Shalit lent stature to the entire organization, for he was known throughout the Jewish world. Thanks to Shalit's extensive connections with the largest Jewish world organizations and the complete trust they placed in him, special grants were made to needy writers who were members of the association.

Very early during Hitler's invasion of Russia, Shalit was transported to the Ponary valley of death. Both his wife, Dvoyrele, who knew Yiddish literature well and read Yiddish poetry aloud beautifully, and their younger daughter perished in the town of Głębokie, where they had been sent to do slave labor.[10]

Glossary

Adar Spring month in the Jewish calendar (March/April).

aggadah The narrative, as opposed to legal, portions of the Talmud; cf. *halakhah*.

aliyah Honorary ritual of being "called up" to recite a blessing and/or to read a portion of the Torah during a synagogue service.

Amtsvorsteher Chief official (title used by German forces occupying Lithuania during World War I).

arendar(n) Lessee of an estate or farm, who manages the property for its owner.

Av Late summer month in the Jewish calendar (July/August).

badkhn Traditional entertainer at Jewish weddings, who performs songs and recites rhymes during the celebration.

bimah Lectern or raised platform in a synagogue, where the Torah is read aloud.

blintze(s) Thin pancake rolled around a filling of cheese. *Blintzes* are traditionally eaten on the holiday of Shavuot.

Bund Abbreviation for the Algemeyner yidisher arbeter-bund (General Jewish Workers' Union). Jewish socialist party established in Russia in 1897. The Bund advocated diaspora Jewish nationalism, secular Yiddish culture, and international socialism.

dardeki-melamed Teacher in an elementary *heder*, in which the youngest students are taught to read the Hebrew alphabet.

eyruv Suspended string or wire used to delineate the boundaries of a Jewish community. The *eyruv* symbolically encloses the space, permitting observant Jews to carry objects within its bounds during the Sabbath.

GLOSSARY

farfl Noodle dough that has been cut, plucked, grated, or chopped into small bits before being cooked.

feldsher(in) Old-time barber-surgeon; *feldsherin* is the feminine form.

Fonye Yiddish slang for Russia or a Russian.

gefilte fish Mincemeat of ground fish, eggs, and meal, sometimes stuffed into fish skin, and then poached or fried.

Gemara Compendium of commentaries on and supplements to the Mishnah, codified by rabbinical academies in Babylon and Jerusalem during the second through sixth centuries of the Common Era (C.E.). The Mishnah and Gemara together make up the Talmud. The term "Gemara" is also sometimes used to refer to both the Mishnah and these commentaries.

gemara-melamed Teacher in an advanced-level *heder,* in which young boys learn to study the Gemara.

haftarah Portion of the Prophets read in the synagogue each week following the weekly reading of a portion of the Torah.

haggadah The text of the seder, the service performed on the first two evenings of Passover, that retells the story of the Israelites' Exodus from Egypt.

halakhah The legal, as opposed to narrative, portions of the Talmud; cf. *aggadah.*

halutz(im) Pioneer, especially a Zionist settler in Palestine or, later, the State of Israel.

Haskalah The Jewish Enlightenment movement, which began in Berlin in the late eighteenth century and spread eastward.

heder School where Jewish children begin their traditional education, learning to read the letters of the Hebrew alphabet, then the Bible and prayer books.

Hevra Kadisha "Sacred Society," traditional name of a Jewish burial society.

Hevrat Mefitsei Haskalah "Society for the Dissemination of Enlightenment" among the Jews of Russia, which, among other things, underwrote modern Jewish educational institutions and supported the publication of *Haskalah* literature. Also known by the Russian acronym OP, this organization was founded in St. Petersburg in 1863 by a group of wealthy Jewish philanthropists.

hopke(s) An East European dance.

Judenrat Jewish council, established by Nazis during World War II. Each Jewish ghetto created by the Nazis in Eastern Europe was administered by a *Judenrat,* which was responsible to German military authorities.

kabbalah Jewish mystical tradition.

Kaddish Prayer praising God, which is recited several times during daily worship. The Kaddish is also recited on special occasions by mourners, hence its association with remembering the dead.

Glossary

Karaites Sect founded in the eighth century C.E., whose followers adhere to Biblical Jewish traditions but reject rabbinic Judaism. Principle areas of Karaite settlement include the Arabian peninsula, Turkey, and Lithuania.

kashrut Practice of following traditional Jewish dietary laws, i.e., "keeping kosher."

kazatske(s) An East European folkdance.

kiddush hashem Jewish martyrdom, in which Jews chose death over renouncing their faith.

kinah (kinot) Hebrew poem of mourning and grief, traditionally recited on the Ninth of Av.

Kol Nidrei Prayer chanted at the beginning of worship on the eve of Yom Kippur, the Day of Atonement. This evening service is also referred to as Kol Nidrei.

Kreishauptmann District chief (title used by German forces occupying Lithuania during World War I).

krepl(ekh) Dumpling made of noodle dough, usually filled with meat.

kugl Baked pudding or casserole, usually of potatoes, noodles, or rice.

litvak(es) Lithuanian Jew.

luftmentsh Person with an insubstantial, inadequate, or unreliable means of making a living.

maskil(im) Follower of the *Haskalah,* the Jewish Enlightenment movement during the eighteenth and nineteenth centuries. *Maskilic* is the adjectival form.

melamed (melamdim) Teacher of young children in a *heder.*

mikvah Ritual bath, in which traditionally observant Jews immerse themselves in rites of purification.

minyan Quorum of ten adult men required for traditional Jewish communal worship.

Mishnah The code of Oral Law compiled by Rabbi Judah Ha-Nasi (ca. 135–217 C.E.) on the basis of previous collections and codified around the year 200 C.E., forming the core of the Talmud; cf. *Gemara.*

mitnaged (mitnagdim) Opponent to hasidism and advocate of traditional rabbinic authority and scholarship. Mitnagdic is the adjectival form.

neilah Prayer recited at the conclusion of worship services on Yom Kippur, the Day of Atonement.

Ninth of Av (Tisha b'Av) Fast day commemorating the destruction of the First and Second Temples in ancient Jerusalem.

Pale of Settlement The eastern half of pre-partition Poland, which was annexed by Russia during the late eighteenth century. As a result of this annexation, the majority of East European Jews came under Russian rule. During most of the period when this region was ruled by tsarist governments, its Jews were forbidden to migrate eastward in the Russian Empire.

Pan Polish title of address, roughly the equivalent of "Mister" or "Sir" in English.

parev(e) Designation for foods that contain neither meat nor dairy products.

progymnasium Preliminary or preparatory gymnasium.

rabiner(s) Rabbi appointed by the Russian government as its official representative to a Jewish community. *Rabiners* were trained in government-sponsored rabbinical academies.

real gymnasium Secondary school in which students studied a curriculum oriented around the sciences.

rosh-yeshiva Head of a traditional rabbinical academy.

Sejm The Polish word for parliament.

Shavuot Late spring harvest holiday, taking place seven weeks after Passover. Shavuot commemorates the divine revelation of the Ten Commandments to Moses on Mt. Sinai.

Seventeenth of Tammuz (Shivah asar b'Tammuz) Fast day commemorating the breaching of the walls of Jerusalem during the Roman siege of 70 C.E.

sheva berachot Series of seven blessings for the bride and groom recited at a traditional Jewish wedding.

Shevat Late winter month in the Jewish calendar (February/March).

shikse Derogatory Yiddish term for a non-Jewish woman.

shtetl(ekh) Small town; market town in Eastern Europe; common name for Jewish settlements in East European towns.

Simhat Torah Fall holiday celebrating God's gift of the Torah to the Jewish people. On this occasion the annual cycle of reading the Torah is renewed.

tallit katan A sleeveless garment worn by traditionally observant Jewish males under their shirts. The *tallit katan* has four corners, onto each of which is attached a knotted fringe. The garment is worn to fulfill the Biblical commandment that Jews wear fringes.

talmud torah Traditional Jewish elementary school where the costs are underwritten by the Jewish community, as opposed to the *heder,* where parents pay tuition.

Tammuz Summer month in the Jewish calendar (June/July).

t'hum shabbat "Sabbath boundary," i.e., the limits beyond which Jews are not permitted to walk from their homes on the Sabbath. The traditional measure—2,000 cubits beyond the town limits—is based on a traditional interpretation of Exodus 16:29.

Tevet Winter month in the Jewish calendar (January/February)

tsimmes Stew, variously made of vegetables such as carrots, dried fruits, or meat.

tsholnt Stew, usually containing meat and beans together with potatoes or barley, prepared on Fridays and, in view of the prohibition on cooking on the Sabbath, kept warm overnight to be served as the main meal on Saturday afternoons.

Wirtschaftsausschuß Commission for economic affairs (established by occupying German forces in Lithuania during World War I).

yeshiva Traditional academy for the training of rabbis.

yortsayt Anniversary of someone's death; ritual observance of that anniversary.

zhid(y) Derogatory Russian term for Jew (not to be confused with the Polish term *żyd*, which, although pronounced the same way, is the proper term for Jew).

ENDNOTES

Introduction

1. The pre–World War II essays were "Rural Jewish Occupations in Lithuania," "A Lithuanian *Shtetl,*" "I. L. Peretz Visits the Jewish Writers in Odessa" (in its original version), "Hirsh Lekert and His Times," "I Join the Militia," "The Germans in World War I," and "April 1919."

2. For comprehensive historical overviews of Lithuanian Jewry, see Masha Greenbaum, *The Jews of Lithuania: A History of a Remarkable Community, 1316–1945* (Jerusalem: Gefen, 1995); and Israel Cohen, *Vilna* (1943; reprint, Philadelphia: Jewish Publication Society, 1992).

3. On the Vilna Gaon and the conflict between Hasidim and *mitnagdim,* see Mordechai Wilensky, "Hasidic-Mitnaggedic Polemics in the Jewish Communities of Eastern Europe: The Hostile Phase," in *Essential Papers on Hasidism,* ed. Gershon Hundert (New York: New York University Press, 1991), 244–71; and Allan L. Nadler, *The Faith of the Mithnagdim: Rabbinic Responses to Hasidic Rapture* (Baltimore: Johns Hopkins University Press, 1997).

4. Yitzhak Isaac Benjacob, "Be-'olam ha-'asiyah," *Ha-Kerem* (Warsaw) 4 (1887): 59.

5. Alexander Zederbaum [pseud: Erez], "Mamlekhet kohanim," *Ha-Melitz* 6, no. 44 (17 November 1866): 667–68. The original Yiddish proverb is: "A poylisher yid zogt: 'Az men ken nit ariber, muz men arunter'; a litvak zogt: 'Az men ken nit ariber, muz men ariber.' "

6. See Arcadius Kahan, "Vilna: The Sociocultural Anatomy of A Jewish Community in Interwar Poland," in *Essays in Jewish Social and Economic History* (Chicago: University of Chicago Press, 1986), 149–60.

My Father's Life and Work

For bibliographical information on the various editions of those essays by Hirsz Abramowicz that are mentioned in this introduction and that appear in this volume, see the prefatory paragraphs to the endnotes for each essay.

333

1. Lithuanian *Žagarė,* Yiddish *Zager.* See Berl Kagan, *Yidishe shtet, shtetlekh un dorfishe yishuvim in Lite* (Jewish Cities, Towns and Villages in Lithuania) (New York[: Berl Kagan], 1991), 448.

2. *Encyclopedia Lituanica* (Boston: Juozas Kapocius, 1978), 6:287.

3. The town's Lithuanian name is Aukštadvaris. The surname Visokidvorer indicates that the Yiddish name of the town was derived from Slavic.

4. On the conflict between the Jews and Karaites in Troki see *Evreiskaia Entsiklopediia* (Jewish Encyclopedia) (1911; reprint, Moscow: Terra, 1991), 15:29–31.

5. Unpublished notes, 17 May 1952, Hirsz Abramowicz Papers, YIVO Archives, RG 446, box 3, folder II.

6. "Hirsz Abramowicz," in *Oyf di khurves fun milkhomes un mehumes* (On the Ruins of Wars and Turmoil), ed. Moshe Shalit (Vilna: EKOPO, 1931), 710–12.

7. The quotation is from the short introduction to the original 1937 version of this essay, which was omitted in the version translated for this volume.

8. See Hirsz Abramowicz, "Vilner froyen un zeyer gezelshaftlekhe arbet" (Vilna Women and Their Social Activities), galley proofs (possibly for a publication by the Women's Division of the Workmen's Circle Vilna Branch), 1948. Hirsz Abramowicz Papers, YIVO Archives, RG 446, box 2, file "Vilna."

9. The Bund (the Yiddish abbreviation for the General Jewish Workers' Union in Lithuania, Poland, and Russia) was a Jewish socialist party founded in Vilna in 1897 and was a major Jewish political force in Eastern Europe before World War II. Opposed to Zionism, Bundism advocated secular Jewish diaspora nationalism and promoted Yiddish culture. See Jonathan Frankel, *Prophecy and Politics: Socialism, Nationalism, and the Russian Jews, 1862–1917* (Cambridge: Cambridge University Press, 1981).

10. Proponents of agrarianism continue to make the same case. See, for example, Richard Critchfield, *Changed Values, Altered Lives: The Closing of the Urban-Rural Gap* (New York: Anchor/Doubleday, 1994); Victor David Hanson, *Fields Without Dreams: Defending the Agrarian Idea* (New York: Free Press, 1996).

11. The Strashun Library, named after its founder, Matthias Strashun (1817–85), a *maskil* and philanthropist, was one of the greatest repositories of books and periodicals produced by Lithuanian Jews (see the essay in this volume titled "Khaykl Lunski"). The Romm family of printers established the first Hebrew printing press in the territory of historical Lithuania.

12. See Hirsz Abramowicz, "A kapitl tsu der geshikhte fun yidisher dertsiung" (A Chapter in the History of Jewish Education), in *Naye Yidishe Shul Y. L. Perets: Yorbukh* (Yearbook of the New Yiddish I. L. Peretz School), ed. Abraham Golomb (Mexico City) 12 (September 1961): 3–11.

13. The footnotes that appeared in the original version of this essay were eliminated in the edition translated in this volume. The following note (p. 214 from the original edition) comments on the method by which Father collected his material: "Unfortunately, I could not utilize the materials and data that I collected. I am writing this particular article from memory and on the basis of personal observations and conversations with people, such as Rabbi Braz from Wysoki Dwór. The materials are on the other side of the border at my parents' home in "Kovno Lithuania" [i.e., Lithuania, whose capital had become Kovno (Kaunas) and was no longer Vilna, where the author resided], which I have not been able to reach for more than a year. Therefore, I ask the reader not to judge me harshly for any small mistakes in dates and chronology."

14. Ch. Sh. Kazdan, ed., *Lerer-yisker-bukh* (Teachers Memorial Book) (New York: Committee to Commemorate Teachers of the TsIShO Schools in Poland who Perished [during

the Holocaust], 1952–54), 2–4. For my reminiscences about Father and Mother, see Dina Abramowicz, "The World of My Parents," *YIVO Annual* 23 (1996): 105–57.

15. Hirsz Abramowicz, "Vegn farshvundene geshtaltn vos darfn fareybikt vern" (On Vanished Images That Ought to Be Memorialized), *Unzer shtime* (Paris), 9 December 1952; clipping, Hirsz Abramowicz Papers, YIVO Archives, RG 446, box 2, file under the same title.

16. Samuel II 20:19.

17. Hirsz Abramowicz, "Di shtot fun undzer benkshaft" (The Town of our Longing), in *Souvenir Journal of the United Vilner Relief Committee, Inc.* (New York, January 1940); Hirsz Abramowicz Papers, YIVO Archives, RG 446, box 2, file "Vilna."

18. Idem, "Vi iz es geven in Vilne" (How It Was in Vilna: Remarks on Sh. Basman's Article about Vilna), *Oyfn shvel* (New York) 8, no. 70 (September 1950): 18.

19. This essay is not included in the present volume. See idem, "Dos baginen fun praktishn yidishizm" (The Dawn of Practical Yiddishism), in *Almanakh fun yidish literatn-un zhurnalistn-fareyn in Vilne* (Almanac of the Yiddish Writers' and Journalists' Association in Vilna), ed. Moshe Shalit, 1 (1938): 156–60. For a bibliography of Father's articles on Yiddish schools, see *Shul-pinkes: finf yor arbet fun tsentraln bildungs-komitet, 1919–1924* (School Chronicle: Five Years of Activities of the Central Education Committee, 1919–1924) (Vilna: Ts.B.K. [Tsentraler bildungs-komitet], 1924). The geographical atlas he coedited was: I. Kadushin, *Geografisher atlas* (Geographical Atlas), ed. Hirsz Abramowicz, E. J. Goldschmidt, and I. Zavels (Vilna: TsIShO, 1922). After World War II, Father contributed over twenty articles to Kazdan, *Lerer-yisker-bukh* (Teacher Memorial Book), and wrote a very informative review of a book about Yiddish schools by Hurwitz-Zalkes (1950). See Hirsz Abramowicz, "Dos baginen fun yidishn shulvezn" (The Dawn of the Yiddish School System), *Kultur un dertsiung* (New York), January 1951, 16–18.

20. The memoirs "Hirsh Lekert and His Times" and "In Tsarist Jails" contain descriptions of critical moments in which these tensions surfaced. They are also discussed in the literature. Cf. Paweł Korzec, "Antisemitism in Poland as an Intellectual, Social and Political Movement," in *Studies on Polish Jewry 1919–1939,* ed. Joshua A. Fishman (New York: YIVO Institute for Jewish Research, 1974), 23; Henry J. Tobias, *The Jewish Bund in Russia from Its Origins to 1905* (Stanford, Calif.: Stanford University Press, 1972), 57, 288; and index under PPS, Piłsudski, Poland.

21. Hirsz Abramowicz, "Dernenterung tsvishn natsyonalitetn" (Rapprochement among Nationalities), *Tog* (Vilna), 3 March 1921, clipping. Hirsz Abramowicz Papers, YIVO Archives, RG 446, box 4, part 2.

22. Not included in the present volume. See idem, "Vilne—a natsyonalitetn-shtot" (Vilna—a Multinational City), in *Vilne: a zamlbukh gevidmet der shtot Vilne* (Vilna: A Book Dedicated to the City of Vilna), ed. Ephim H. Jeshurin (New York: Workmen's Circle Vilna Branch 367, 1935), 267–72.

23. Idem, "Jak Żyć" (How to Live), *Nasza Trybuna* (New York), 31 October, 1941; clipping, Hirsz Abramowicz Papers, YIVO Archives, RG 446, box 4, part 2. *Nasza Trybuna* (Our Tribune) was a weekly Polish-language publication for Jewish war refugees from Poland in the United States.

24. For clippings of his articles on agriculture and vocational education from *Oyfn shvel,* see Hirsz Abramowicz Papers, YIVO Archives, RG 446, box 2, part 2.

25. See I. Charlasz, "Hirsz Abramowicz," *Unzer tsayt* (New York), January–February 1960, 50.

26. See Hirsz Abramowicz, "Regyonale oysgabes" (Regional Publications), *Der frayer gedank* (Paris) 14 (November 1950): 15; clipping. Hirsz Abramowicz Papers, YIVO Archives, RG 446, box 2, part 2.

Rural Jewish Occupations in Lithuania

The anthropological study was first published in the quarterly *Fun noentn over* I & III (Warsaw 1937): 45–51, 212–25, titled "Farshvundene yidishe parnoses" (Vanished Jewish Occupations). It was preceded by a short introduction in which the author explained the purpose of his work. The second part of the work appeared in *Yivo-bleter* XXII, no. 2 (New York, Nov.–Dec. 1943): 178–200, with an introduction which was changed for the post-Holocaust period and the American reader. The author did not have to elaborate on the need to leave a record for posterity—it was evident without explanation. But the American reader needed some information on the general agrarian picture of Eastern Europe and the role of rural Jews in that area. The concluding statement was that "The Jews complemented the ethnographic landscape of Lithuania . . . that on the whole they lived on friendly terms with the surrounding Christian population, which needed them for their economy" (76).

The book edition (Buenos Aires, 1958) included both parts of the work without any changes. For general historical background, see Salo Baron, *The Russian Jew under the Tsars and Soviets* (New York: MacMillan, 1964), 90–119.

1. On the geographic extent of "Lithuania" in the Jewish context, see Greenbaum, *The Jews of Lithuania*, 51–53. See also David E. Fishman, "Introduction," pp. 10–12.

2. A reference to a Talmudic expression (Avoda Zara 35b), used in everyday Yiddish speech.

3. A pood is 36 pounds avoirdupois.

4. The Platers were an old noble family that owned large estates in Lithuania. See *Encyclopedia Lituanica*, 6:295.

5. The first nine days of Av are a period of mourning for the destruction of the Temple in ancient Jerusalem. During this period, it is customary to refrain from eating meat.

6. A verst is about two thirds of a mile.

7. Polish sources often presented the Jewish innkeeper as a very negative character. He was made responsible for the drunkenness of the peasant. The picture emerging from Abramowicz's description differs from these biased stereotypes. On Jewish innkeepers, see also Simon Dubnow, *History of the Jews in Russia and Poland* (1920; reprint, New York: Ktav, 1975), 1:93, 265; Teodor Jeske-Choinski, *Historja Żydów w Polsce* (History of the Jews in Poland) (Warsaw: Gebethner and Wolff, 1919), 183–87; Magdalena Opalski, *The Jewish Tavern-Keeper and His Tavern in Nineteenth-Century Polish Literature*, vol. 4 of *Studies on Polish Jewry* (Jerusalem: Zalman Shazar Center for the Furtherance of the Study of Jewish History, 1988).

8. A reference to Proverbs 31:1–3.

9. In 1897, Russian law placed the sale of alcoholic beverages under a government monopoly. This legislation drove many Jews out of the business of producing and selling liquor. See Greenbaum, *The Jews of Lithuania*, 192; Nachum Gross, ed., *Economic History of the Jews* (New York: Schocken, 1975), 137–38.

10. *Maskil* and philosopher Solomon Maimon (1754–1800) was the son of a Lithuanian village innkeeper. His memoirs offer a vivid picture of Jewish rural life in his native country. See *Solomon Maimon: An Autobiography*, ed. Moses Hadas (New York: Schocken, 1947).

11. This humorous dialogue between the innkeeper and her guest resembles a similar exchange in the short story "Kasrilevker restoranen" (1901) by Yiddish writer Sholem Aleichem (the pen name of Sholem Rabinovitsh, 1859–1916), a major prose writer and champion of Yiddish as a modern literary language. See "Kosher Restaurant" in Sholem Aleichem, *Inside Kasrilevke* (New York: Schocken, 1965), 45–56.

Notes to Lithuanian Jewish Traditions

12. The character Tevye the Dairyman appeared in a series of monologues by Sholem Aleichem written between 1894 and 1914. The ill-fated marriage of one of Tevye's daughters to a non-Jew is decribed in "Chava." See Sholem Aleichem, *Tevye the Dairyman and the Railroad Stories,* trans. Hillel Halkin (New York: Schocken, 1987), 69–81.

13. The YIVO Institute for Jewish Research, an academic center for the study of East European Jewish culture, was founded in Vilna in 1925. Since 1940, YIVO has been headquartered in New York.

14. On Jewish criminals in pre–World War I Russia, see Saul M. Ginsburg, *Historishe verk* (Historical Works) (New York: Saul M. Ginsburg Testimonial Committee, 1937), 1:266–84. For statistics on Jewish criminal activity during this period, see *Evreiskaia Entsiklopediia,* 12:907–10.

15. On the Sabbath, the traditional day of rest, Jews are permitted to walk only within the *t'hum shabbat,* a limited area around their homes. Jews living at a considerable distance from each other must obtain permission from a local rabbi to extend this distance, which is usually established by creating an *eyruv,* a fictitious center of habitation, symbolized by the presence of food.

16. Unless they are specially prepared by an authorized kosher butcher, the hindquarters of a "kosher" animal are not eaten; the meat is usually sold to non-kosher butchers.

17. A hectare equals 2.471 acres.

A Lithuanian *Shtetl*

Originally published in *Oyf di khurves fun milkhomes un mehumes* (On the Ruins of Wars and Turmoil), ed. Moshe Shalit (Vilna: EKOPO, 1931), 361–84. It was reprinted in the book edition without any significant changes, except that the present tense was replaced by the past in the short introduction and a humorous footnote referring to the fondness for "a drink of whiskey" among the elderly was eliminated as no longer fitting the mood of the post-Holocaust narrative. On interwar *shtetl* life, see Samuel Kassow, "Community and Identity in the Interwar *Shtetl,*" in Yisrael Gutman, Ezra Mendelsohn, Jehuda Reinharz, eds., *The Jews of Poland between Two World Wars* (Hanover N.H., and London: University Press of New England, 1989), 198–222. On the conceptualization of the term *shtetl,* see Barbara Kirshenblatt-Gimblett's introduction to Mark Zborowski and Elizabeth Herzog, *Life is with People: The Culture of the Shtetl* (1952; reprint, New York: Schocken, 1995), ix–xlviii.

1. The diminutive in Yiddish can be used either as a sign of endearment or, as is the case here, a pejorative.

2. Often rabbis and other Jewish community officials were not given a salary. Instead, the community paid them indirectly, through a tax on yeast or other goods. This frequently failed to provide the officials with an adequate income.

3. The anti-Semitic measures of the tsarist government limiting Jews' access to land were known as the Temporary Rules of 3 May 1882. See Dubnow, *History of the Jews in Russia and Poland,* 2:312ff; Greenbaum, *The Jews of Lithuania,* 191.

4. Agrarian reforms introduced by the Lithuanian government in the early 1920s favored the peasant class. The government promoted peasant cooperatives, which monopolized the export of agricultural products and thereby excluded the participation of Jews who often served as middlemen, purchasing farm products from peasants. Jewish landowners were often denied their legal rights to own land. See Greenbaum, *The Jews of Lithuania,* 272–74.

5. The practice of an individual interrupting the synagogue service to address a grievance against another member of the Jewish community in a public forum dates back to

the Middle Ages. See Israel Abrahams, *Jewish Life in the Middle Ages* (New York, Meridian Books, 1958), 7.

6. It is customary to offer a man observing the anniversary of the death of a close relative the honor of participating in the Torah reading service.

7. In Eastern Europe, throwing burrs or thistles at other members of the congregation, as an act of mortification, was a traditional part of the observance of this day of mourning.

8. Jewish tradition requires men to cover their heads as a sign of reverence to God.

9. The laws of refraining from work on the Sabbath prohibit lighting fires or carrying anything in public.

10. The remark is a play on the Yiddish word *trogn,* which can mean either "to carry" or "to be pregnant."

11. The Maccabi World Union is an international organization promoting sport activities among Jewish youth. Established in 1895, it later became affiliated with the Zionist movement. In 1939, there were over 200,000 members of the movement, located in 38 countries.

12. Polish Tatars are descendants of Tatars who took service with Lithuanian nobles and the Polish crown. Although they adopted Polish culture and language, they retained their Islamic faith.

13. Jewish law requires a corpse to be buried promptly, usually within twenty-four hours of death.

14. EKOPO, a relief organization for Jewish victims of World War I, was founded in Moscow in 1915 (the name is an acronym meaning "Jewish Relief Committee"). During the interwar years, it was active in Poland, working with the American Jewish Joint Distribution Committee and other American relief organizations.

15. On traditional *heder* instruction, such as that described here, see Yekhiel Shtern, "A *Kheyder* in Tyszowce," *YIVO Annual of Jewish Social Science* 5 (1950): 152–71; Diane Roskies, "Alphabet Instruction in the East European Heder: Some Comparative and Historical Notes," *YIVO Annual of Jewish Social Science* 17 (1978): 21–53.

16. The Christian Democrats were a chauvinistic and anti-Semitic political party in interwar Lithuania.

17. This epithet may have been derived from the term "havelock," a cloth covering for a cap with a back flap that shields the wearer's neck from the sun, named after Sir Henry Havelock (1795–1857), an English general in India.

The Diet of Lithuanian Jews

Originally published in Mendl Sudarsky, et al., eds. *Lite* (Lithuania) (New York: Jewish-Lithuanian Cultural Society "Lite," 1951). For further discussion of Jewish foodways, see *Jewish Folklore and Ethnology Review* 1987.

1. A reference to the popular Yiddish folksong "Zuntik bulbes, montik bulbes" (Sunday, Potatoes; Monday, Potatoes). See Ruth Rubin, *Voices of a People: The Story of Yiddish Folksongs* (New York: McGraw-Hill, 1973), 279.

2. Eliakum Zunser (1836–1913) was a Yiddish folk poet and *badkhn.* The text and music of "Di sokhe," which extolls the hard work of Jewish agricultural workers, appears in Elyokum Tsunzer, *Elyokum Tsunzers verk* (The Works of Eliakum Zunser), ed. Mordkhe Schaechter (New York: YIVO Institute for Jewish Research, 1964) 1:352, 2:895. M. Aronson's "Der tsien-marsh" appears in *Kvutsat shirim* (Collection of Songs) (New York: Hebrew

Publishing Co., 1915), 224. "Shtey oyf, mayn folk" by Abraham Goldfaden appears in *Hasomir's Sangbog* (Hasomir's Songbook) (Copenhagen: Hasomir, 1937), 224–25.

Healing the Mentally Ill

Originally published in *Byalistoker lebn* (Białystok Life) (New York), February 1946.

1. Tsar Nicholas I ruled Russia from 1825 to 1855. Beginning in 1835, the Russian government encouraged the establishment of Jewish agricultural colonies in the northwestern territories of the Russian Empire. See Gross, *Economic History of Jews,* 115–16, 284.

2. The Jewish Colonization Association (JCA) was a philanthropic organization founded in 1891 by Baron Maurice de Hirsch. The JCA provided financial aid and vocational training to impoverished and unemployed Jews in Eastern Europe and also assisted them in efforts to emigrate.

3. See Hans Walter Schmuhl, *Rassenhygiene, Nationalismus, Euthanasie: von der Verhütung zur Vernichtung "lebensunwerten Lebens," 1880–1945* (Racial Health, Nationalism, Euthanasia: From the Protection to the Annihilation of "Lives Not Worthy of Life," 1880–1945) (Göttingen: Vanenjek und Ruprecht, 1987).

4. Dr. Abraham Wirszubski (1869–1943) was a prominent psychiatrist in interwar Vilna. For his study of the treatment of the mentally ill in these rural colonies, see Abraham Wirszubski, "Community Care of Mentally Sick in the Vilna Region" (Polish), in *Nowiny Lekarskie* (Poznań) 39, no. 2 (1927): 30–31.

5. Ormuzd and Ahriman, gods of light and darkness in Persian mythology, are mentioned in the Talmud (Sanhedrin 39a).

Joshua Steinberg

Originally published in *Byalistoker shtime* (Białystok Voice) (New York), September 1952.

1. The Vilna Rabbinical School and a similar school in Zhitomir (both of which were opened in 1847) were the first academies for training *rabiners* and modern Jewish pedagogues in Russia. In 1873, they became the Vilna and Zhitomir teachers institutes, where teachers were trained to educate Jewish children in both government and private elementary schools. See Michael Stanislawski, *Tsar Nicholas I and the Jews: The Transformation of Jewish Society in Russia 1825–1855* (Philadelphia: Jewish Publication Society, 1983), 97ff.; *Evreiskaia Entsiklopediia*, 13:257–63, 15:149–50. The YIVO Archives possess extensive documents on the Vilna Jewish Teachers Institute (RG 24).

2. Isaac Baer Levinsohn (1788–1860) was a Russian-Jewish writer and *Haskalah* pioneer. Adam Ha-Kohen Lebensohn (1794–1878), a Hebrew poet, was a central figure in the Lithuanian *Haskalah*. Samuel Joseph Fuenn (1818–90), a Hebrew scholar, *maskil,* and wealthy philanthropist was superintendent of Jewish schools in the Vilna region. Abraham Baer Gottlober (1810–99), a Hebrew and Yiddish writer, was one of the first adherents of the *Haskalah* in Ukraine.

3. See A. Sh. Hershberg, *Pinkes Byalistok* (A Chronicle of Białystok) (New York: Białystok Jewish Historical Association, 1949), 1:411.

4. Eliezer David Lieberman (1819–95) was a *maskil,* writer, and journalist. References to Mordecai Zabludovski and I. B. Volkovyski appear in ibid.

5. In Slavic cultures, bread and salt are traditional gifts presented to guests on their arrival.

6. Asher Lazarevich Wohl, an educator, biblical scholar and writer, was a graduate of the Vilna Rabbinical School. He was appointed to its faculty, where he remained until his retirement.

7. Externs were students who did not attend gymnasia, but who studied independently to obtain their diplomas by passing external examinations given by the Ministry of Education.

8. Joshua Steinberg, *Mishpat ha-urim: otsar ha milim le-mikra'e ha-kodesh . . . meturgam russit ve-ashkenazit* (Judgement of the Urim: Hebrew-German-Russian Lexicon to the Bible), 8th ed, (Vilna: I. Pirozhnikov, 1902); Idem, *Otsar milim russi . . . meturgam ivrit ve-ashkenazit.* (Russian-Hebrew-German Dictionary), 20th ed. (Vilna: I. Pirozhnikov, 1903).

9. Abraham Mapu (1808–67) was the author of the first modern Hebrew novel, *Ahavat Zion* (Love of Zion, 1853). The *sheva* is a Hebrew vowel sign that indicates either the absence of any vowel sound (quiescent *sheva*) or a very short vowel (mobile *sheva;* cf. English "schwa").

10. Gordon's "For Whom Do I Toil?" first appeared in *Ha-Shahar* 2, no. 8 (1870–71), 353–54. See Michael Stanislawski, *For Whom Do I Toil?: Judah Leib Gordon and the Crisis of Russian Jewry* (New York: Oxford University Press, 1988), 104–5.

11. Yiddish playwright and novelist Peretz Hirschbein (1880–1948) was active in Warsaw and Odessa in the early 1900s, before moving to the United States. On his encounter with Steinberg, see Peretz Hirschbein, *In gang fun lebn: zikhroynes* (In the Course of Life: Memoirs) (New York: CYCO, 1948), 66–69.

12. Zalman Shneour (1887–1959), a Hebrew and Yiddish poet and novelist, was known for introducing sensual motifs into Hebrew poetry and for describing Russian Jewish life in his prose.

13. For the text of "Miriam," see Peretz Hirschbein, *Ha-Zeman* (Vilna), nos.1–4 (1905): 1–25, 161–69, 415–22. Fayvl Margolin (1870?–1943) was a publisher who played a major role in Hebrew publishing during the first quarter of the twentieth century. See Hirsz Abramowicz, *Farshvundene geshtaltn: zikhroynes un siluetn* (Vanished Figures: Memoirs and Silhouettes) (Buenos Aires: Central Association of Polish Jews in Argentina, 1958), 106–11.

14. For the text of the poem, see M. M. Dolitzki, *Kol shirei M. M. Dolitski* (Collected Verse of M. M. Dolitzki) (New York, 1895), 46–52. A. Bernstein was cantor of Vilna's Taharat Ha-Kodesh synagogue.

15. Maksimilian Ovseevich Steinberg (1883–1947), a composer, conductor, and educator, was recognized as a "Distinguished Worker in Art of the USSR" in 1934.

16. Shmarya Levin (1867–1935), a Yiddish and Hebrew writer and Zionist leader, served as *rabiner* in Vilna in the early 1900s.

17. Isaac Pirozhnikov (1859–1933) was a conductor and music teacher in the Vilna Jewish Teachers Institute. In 1900, he established a publishing house in Vilna. He emigrated to the United States in 1912.

18. The famous yeshiva of Wołożyn, a small town in Lithuania, was founded in 1802. It was closed by Russian authorities in 1892 and reopened in 1899.

19. Joshua Steinberg, *Mishle Yehoshu'a le-ha'ir or la-yesharim . . .* (Joshua's Proverbs: Anthology for the Mind and for the Heart . . .), 2nd enl. ed (Vilna: Widow and Brothers Romm, 1871).

20. Sholem Yankev Abramovitsh (1835–1917), known to his readers as "Mendele" or "Mendele Moykher-Sforim" (Mendele the Bookseller), was a major founding figure of modern Yiddish and Hebrew prose fiction. I. L. Peretz (1852–1915), author of short stories,

plays, and essays, was a leading Yiddish literary modernist. Together with Sholem Aleichem, Mendele and Peretz are considered the three *klasikers,* or "classic" modern Yiddish writers. See Ken Frieden, *Classic Yiddish Fiction: Abramovitsh, Sholem Aleichem, and Peretz* (New York: SUNY Press, 1995). David Pinsky (1872–1959) was an American Yiddish playwright, novelist, and author, whose works were also popular in Europe.

21. Prominent Russian orientalist Daniel Chwolson (1819–1911) was born in Vilna and trained in Breslau. In 1855, Chwolson converted to the Russian Orthodox Church, after which he was appointed professor of Hebrew, Syriac, and Chaldean philology at the University of St. Petersburg. Chwolson maintained close ties to the Russian Jewish community throughout his career.

Samuel Gozhanski

Originally published in *Unzer shtime,* 18 July 1951.

1. Samuel Gozhanski (ca. 1867–?), a teacher in Vilna, graduated from the Vilna Jewish Teachers Institute in 1888. His early revolutionary activity was in the Bund, for which he wrote a number of propaganda pamphlets in Yiddish. He was exiled by the tsarist government, but then pardoned. After the 1917 Revolution, Gozhanski went to the USSR, where he joined the Communist Party. The cause and circumstances of his death are unknown.

Chaim Fialkov

Original publication unknown.

1. Moshe Hacohen Reicherson, ed., *Maslul bedikduk lashon ha-kodesh* (Path to the Grammar of the Holy Tongue) (Vilna: Finn, Rosenkrantz, and Schriftsetzer, 1879).

2. Johann Heinrich Pestalozzi (1746–1827), an educational reformer, introduced innovative ideas about child development and learning through understanding rather than memory. Maria Montessori (1870–1952) developed a popular method of preschool and elementary education that emphasized initiative, sense perception, and self-help among young children.

3. *Hevrat Mefitsei Haskalah,* the Society for the Dissemination of Enlightenment among the Jews of Russia (also known by the Russian acronym OP), was founded in St. Petersburg in 1863 by a group of wealthy Jewish philanthropists. The society assisted *maskilim* in provincial towns, underwrote modern Jewish educational institutions, and supported the publication of *Haskalah* literature.

4. Vera Matveevna Kuperstein, a renowned blind educator, was active in organizing Jewish schools for girls in pre–World War I Russia. One such school, opened in Vilna in 1912, was renamed in her honor during World War I. See Gershon Pludermacher, "Folkshul oyfn nomen fun Dvoyre Kupershteyn" (Elementary School named for Dvora Kuperstein), in *Shul-pinkes,* 167–81.

5. Dr. Arkadii (Azriel) Ratner, a prominent Jewish educator in Gomel', was founder and director of the city's gymnasium for Jewish boys.

6. Kasrilevke and Kabtsansk are invented names of archetypal impoverished Ukrainian *shtetlekh* that appeared repeatedly in these authors' satirical works.

7. Baron David Guenzburg (1857–1910), a member of a renowned family of Russian-Jewish philanthropists and communal activists, was also a prominent scholar of Judaic and Oriental studies.

Hirsh Lekert and His Times

Originally published in *Royter pinkes* (Warsaw) 2 (1924). About Hirsh Lekert in English, see Tobias, *The Jewish Bund in Russia,* 150–51.

1. Viacheslav Konstantinovich von Plehve (1846–1904) was a reactionary statesman, active in the suppression of revolutionary and liberal movements in Russia.
2. Hermann Sudermann (1857–1928) was one of the leading writers of the German naturalist movement. His famous play *Heimat* (known in English as *Magda*) was first performed in Berlin in 1893. It dealt with a conflict between a famous opera star and the narrow, provincial citizens of her hometown.

Anna Lifshits

Originally published in *Unzer shtime* (Paris), 3, 4, 5 June 1953.

1. Anna Lifshits (1881–1926) was active in the Social-Democratic Party's underground in pre–World War I Russia. In the post-revolutionary years, she continued her political affiliation with the party abroad, living in Copenhagen and Riga. She died in Riga following an accident at a railroad station. See Jacob Sholem Hertz, ed., *Doyres bundistn* (Generations of Bundists) (New York: Unzer Tsayt, 1956), 1:363–65. On the mutiny aboard the Potemkin, see J. N. Westwood, *Endurance and Endeavor: Russian History 1812–1992,* 4th ed. (Oxford: Oxford University Press, 1993), 156–57.
2. Eduard Bernstein (1850–1932), a German Social Democrat, attacked the orthodox Marxist doctrine that socialism could be achieved only by means of a violent revolution.
3. *Nashi Raznoglasiia* (Our Differences) is the treatise by Marxist Georgii Valentinovich Plekhanov (1856–1918) attacking the Russian Populist movement. See Georgii Valentinovich Plekhanov, *Nashi Raznoglasiia* (Our Differences) (Geneva: Tip[ografia] Gruppy Osvobozhdenie Truda, 1884). Populism, the movement led by Nikolai Konstantinovich Mikhailovskii (1842–1904), attempted to eradicate social injustice by establishing peasant communes and by fostering cooperation between peasants and the intelligentsia.
4. August Bebel (1840–1913) and Wilhelm Liebknecht (1826–1900) were leaders of the German Social Democratic Labor party, founded in Eisenach in 1869. Franz Mehring, Palmar, and Paul Singer were prominent members of the party, known in revolutionary circles abroad. See August Bebel, *Woman under Socialism,* trans. Daniel De Leon (New York: Schocken Books, 1971); Koppel Pinson, *Modern Germany,* 2nd ed. (New York: Macmillan, 1966), 194–219.
5. Ponary, located on the outskirts of Vilna, was the site where German soldiers executed the local Jewish population during World War II. See Yitzhak Arad, *Ghetto in Flames: The Struggle and Destruction of the Jews in Vilna in the Holocaust* (Jerusalem: Yad Vashem, 1980).

In Tsarist Jails

Originally published in *Lebns-fragn,* June–July 1954.

1. Yiddish poet and revolutionary Moshe Bassin (1889–1963) was arrested by the tsarist government, but he managed to escape. He emigrated to America in 1907.

2. For a detailed description of the pogrom in Iuzevka, see *Die Judenpogrome in Russland* (The Jewish Pogroms in Russia) (Cologne and Leipzig: Jüdischer Verlag, 1910), 2:210–21.

3. See L. Melshin (Petr Filipovich Iakubovich), "V Mire Otverzhennykh" (In the World of Outcasts: Notes of a Former Labor Camp Inmate), in *Russkoe Bogatstvo* (Moscow-St. Petersburg), 1895–98.

4. Black Hundreds (Russian: *Chernaia Sotnia*) was the name popularly given to local branches of Soiuz Russkogo Naroda, an antiliberal Russian nationalist organization that came into being after the 1905 revolution. Violently anti-Semitic, they played a leading role in staging pogroms against Jewish communities.

5. An allusion to Esther 1:12.

Jewish Gymnasia without Quotas

Originally published in *Lebns-fragn,* April–May 1953.

1. During the reign of Tsar Alexander II (1855–81), Jews were allowed to enroll in non-Jewish schools without any restrictive quotas. But under the reactionary reign of Tsar Alexander III, a law was passed in 1887 limiting the number of Jewish children permitted to enroll in non-Jewish schools. Only ten percent of Jewish children living within the Pale of Settlement, and only five percent of those outside this region, could be admitted to gymnasia. Universities were permitted to accept only three percent of Jewish applicants. See Dubnow, *History of the Jews in Russia and Poland,* 2:349–51.

I. L. Peretz Visits the Jewish Writers in Odessa

First published as "Perets in Odes" (Peretz in Odessa) in *Ringen* III–IV (Warsaw, 1921); revised version titled "I. L. Perets tsvishn odeser shrayber" (I. L. Peretz Among the Odessa Writers) appeared in *Fraye arbeter-shtime* (New York), Oct. 8 & 15, 1946. For the difference between the two versions, see the author's footnote to the memoir on pp. 163–64, and Dina Abramowicz's "My Father's Life and Work," pp. 28, 29.

1. Elhanan Leib Lewinsky (1857–1910), whose pen name was Reb Korev, was a Zionist leader and Hebrew writer best known for popular, humorous essays.

2. Generally considered the greatest modern Hebrew-language poet, Hayyim Nahman Bialik (1873–1934) also wrote essays and short stories, and he worked as an editor, and translator. Bialik was based in Odessa from 1891 to 1921, when he left for Berlin and then Palestine.

3. Hebrew essayist and philosopher Ahad Ha-Am (pen name of Asher Ginsburg, 1856–1927) was a leading Zionist ideologist who championed "cultural" rather than "political" Zionism. Historian, editor, and literary critic Joseph Gedaliah Klausner (1874–1958) lived in Odessa before emigrating to Palestine in 1919. Hebrew journalist and publisher Yehoshua Hana Rawnitzki (1859–1944) cofounded the Moriah publishing house with Bialik. He emigrated to Palestine in 1922, where he helped found the Dvir press.

4. The citation from Ruth (1:16) alludes to ideological differences between Zionism and Hebraism, represented by Ahad Ha-Am, and Yiddishism, represented by Peretz.

5. An allusion to Peretz's story "Oyb nisht nokh hekher" (If Not Higher, 1900). See I. L. Peretz, *The I. L. Peretz Reader,* ed. Ruth R. Wisse (New York: Schocken, 1990), 178–81.

6. Allusions are made here to two stories by Peretz: "Bontshe shvayg" (Bontshe the Silent, 1894) and "Di frume kats" (The Pious Cat, 1893). See Peretz, *The I. L. Peretz Reader,* 129–30, 146–52.

7. Humorist Khayim Chemerinsky (1862–1917), who wrote under the pen name Mordkhele, was one of the best translators into Hebrew of the classic fables by Russian writer Ivan Krylov (1769–1844).

8. Hebrew journalist Abraham Ludvipol (1865–1921) was active in the Zionist movement in Odessa before settling in Israel in 1907. S. Ben-Zion (pen name of Simhah Alter Guttmann, 1870–1932) was a Hebrew writer, editor, and translator who emigrated to Palestine in 1905.

9. Zionist leader Alter Druyanow (1870–1938) was a Hebrew writer and anthologist who lived in Palestine from 1906 to 1909 and then from 1921 until his death.

10. The Bessarabian city of Kishinev was the site of a major anti-Semitic pogrom in 1903, in which forty-seven Jews were killed and ninety-two injured. This event provoked an international outcry and was a watershed in Jewish national consciousness throughout Eastern Europe. See John D. Klier and Shlomo Lambroza, *Pogroms: Anti-Jewish Violence in Modern Russian History* (Cambridge: Cambridge University Press, 1992), 191–94.

11. Polish playwright and artist Stanisław Wyspiański (1869–1907), a member of the "Young Poland" literary movement, wrote surrealistic, deeply symbolic plays. His play *Wesele* (The Wedding, 1901) is said to have influenced Peretz's 1907 drama *Bay nakht oyfn altn mark* (At Night in the Old Market Place).

12. Simon Dubnow (1860–1941) was a prominent Jewish historian and a founder of the *Folkspartey*, a diaspora nationalist Jewish political party. Peretz's satirical poem "Monish" (first version, 1888) marked his literary debut and is considered a landmark work of modern Yiddish poetry. See Peretz, *The I. L. Peretz Reader,* 1–15.

13. Isaak Il'ich Levitan (1861–1906), born in a small town in Lithuania, was one of the most famous Russian landscape painters.

14. A reference to *Di goldene keyt* (The Golden Chain, 1907), Peretz's drama about a hasidic dynasty. The "golden chain" is, more generally, a symbol of Jewish continuity.

Chaim Weizmann and Kolia Tepper Debate

Originally published on 24 August 1952 (title of publication unknown).

1. Poalei Zion (Labor Zionist party, established ca. 1900) advocated the creation of a Jewish state that would be governed by socialist principles. General Zionists' call for a Jewish state was not linked with socialist ideology, and many were opposed to socialism.

2. Zionist leader Chaim Weizmann (1874–1952) was the first president of the State of Israel. A scientist, he also headed the Weizmann Institute of Science (established in 1949). See Jehuda Reinharz, *Chaim Weizmann: the Making of a Zionist Leader* (Oxford: University Press, 1985).

3. Zionist activist Vladimir (Ze'ev) Jabotinsky (1880–1940) was the founder of the Jewish Legion, which fought in Palestine during World War I, and of the World Union of Zionist Revisionists in 1925.

4. The song "One bottle of beer . . ." counts the bottles from one to twelve and then reverses the order. See Rubin, *Voices of a People,* 194.

5. French writer Bernard Lazare (1865–1903) was active in Jewish affairs, and he participated in the second Zionist Congress in 1898. However, his socialist and anarchist sympathies prompted him to break with Herzl over the latter's policy to create the Jewish Colonial Trust (the first Zionist bank and, therefore, a capitalist undertaking).

6. Grigorii Lourie was a member of a prominent family that developed various industries in Pińsk. See Wolf (Zeev) Rabinowitsch, ed., *Pinsk . . . History of the Jews of Pinsk 1506–1941* (Tel-Aviv-Haifa: Association of Jews of Pinsk in Israel, 1973), 7.

7. Belaia Tserkov (literally, "White Church") is a town in Ukraine. In referring to the town, pious Jews, who were reluctant to use words related to Christianity, replaced the Russian word *tserkov* with the Yiddish word *tume* (literally "impurity," the word is used to denote a non-Jewish house of worship). They also changed the adjective "white" to "black." As this name change suggests, the town had a bad reputation in Jewish history, beginning with pogroms committed there in 1648 by Bohdan Chmielnicki's Cossacks.

8. Arnadski was a government spy who infiltrated the Bund. He informed on many of the party's members, leading to their arrest. Arnadski's murder on 18 October 1903 led to more arrests and exiles to Siberia. See Rabinowitsch, *Pinsk,* 53–54.

I Join the Militia

Originally published in A. I. Grodzenski, ed., *Vilner almanakh* (Vilna Almanac) (Vilna: Ovnt-kuryer, 1939).

1. Chronicles I 21:23.
2. Some of these regulations are almost identical to those instituted throughout German-occupied Poland from October 1939 onward.

The Germans in World War I

This is one of the two earliest essays. It was first published in 1922 in Zalmen Reisen, ed., *Pinkes far der geshikhte fun Vilne in di yorn fun milkhome un fun okupatsye* (Register for the History of Vilna in the Years of War and Occupation) (Vilna: S. Ansky Historical-Ethnographic Society, 1922), and republished in the author's collected volume of 1958. The changes introduced by the editor were minimal: the original title "Di daytshn oyf di erter" (The Germans Among Us) became more specific, and one footnote dealing with the author's methodology was removed (see endnote 13 to "My Father's Life and Work" in this volume). Another short footnote was restored to the text, see p. 205.

The following two essays cited the author's account of the Jewish situation in the region in the period 1914–1919: Louis Stein, "Der geyresh fun di litvishe yidn in fayer fun der ershter velt-milkhome" (The Exile of Lithuanian Jews in the Conflagration of World War I), in Sudarsky et al., *Lite,* 89–119; Azriel Shohat, "The Beginning of Anti-Semitism in Independent Lithuania," in *Yad Vashem Studies on the European Jewish Catastrophe and Resistance,* ed. Saul Esh (Jerusalem: Yad Vashem, 1958), 2:9–10, 67.

1. Joel 3:3.
2. Esther 4:14.
3. The western territories of the Polish Commonwealth, acquired by Prussia during the partition of the country at the end of the eighteenth century, were inhabited by ethnic Poles. This region had a relatively small Jewish population compared to areas of Poland under Austrian and Russian rule (due to early Jewish emancipation by Prussian authorities). This led to the creation of a sizable (for Poland) Polish middle class—the group in Polish society most directly in economic competition with Jews. Due to its anti-Semitic and anti-German stance, the National Democratic Party (Endecja) had its power base in this region.

4. Junkers were members of the Prussian landed aristocracy, generally known to be politically reactionary and militaristic.

5. Blood libel is the false accusation that Jews use the blood of Christians, especially children, in the preparation of matzah. Such accusations, which date back to the Middle Ages, have been made sporadically throughout European Jewish history into the twentieth century.

6. *Ostgelt* (literally, "Eastern money") is money that the Germans printed for use in the eastern territories they occupied during World War I and which had very little actual value.

7. The status of Yiddish has been controversial throughout the modern period. Many *maskilim* considered it essential that Jews abandon Yiddish and adopt German or another official European language in order to modernize. Others championed Hebrew as a more appropriate modern Jewish language than Yiddish.

8. The Yiddish idiom *a lange tsung* (a long tongue) is used to describe someone who talks too much (cf. English "a big mouth").

April 1919

This is one of the two earliest essays. It was first published in 1922 in *Pinkes far der geshikhte fun Vilne in di yorn fun milkhome un fun okupatsye* (Register for the History of Vilna in the Years of War and Occupation), ed. Zalmen Reisen, and republished in the author's collected volume of 1958.

The dedication to the memory of the author's father is the only addition to the memoir "April 1919" in the reprinted book version.

1. The term *kerenki* referred to worthless paper money, named after Alexander Kerensky, Russia's prime minister from July to November 1917.

2. Bestuzhev courses were academic classes for women offered in prerevolutionary Russia.

3. The Yiddish term *gdoylim* (big ones) is used here as a play on the Russian word *bolsheviki,* which is derived from *bolshoi* (big).

4. The outbreak of World War I contributed greatly to the deterioration of the Jewish situation in Poland. Pogroms erupted in several larger and some smaller cities of the country. The situation was even worse in the northeastern territories, where three nations were contending for control over Vilna and the surrounding area: Poles, Lithuanians, and Soviets.

The events of the last day of Passover, April 19, 1919, are the background of two chapters in this book, "April 1919" and "The Jewish Agricultural School in Wieluciany," and are also mentioned in the sketches of Eliezer Kruk, A. Weiter, Dr. Jacob Wygodzki, and Rabbi Isaac Rubinstein. Historical sources dealing with them directly are Cohen, *Vilna,* 376–79; Samuel Kassow, "Jewish Communal Politics in Transition: The Vilna *Kehile,* 1919–1920," *YIVO Annual* 20 (1991): 72; Korzec, "Antisemitism in Poland as an Intellectual, Social and Political Movement," 37*ff., 50*.

Some of the primary sources are: Official protest of the Jewish community published in the Yiddish daily *Yidishe tsaytung,* no. 1, May 9, 1919, and the account of A. Weiter's death, published a few days later in the same newspaper and republished in his collected works: A. Weiter, *Ksovim* (Writings), ed. E. J. Goldschmidt (Vilna: B. A. Kleckin, 1923), clv–clix. All these materials are available at the Library of the YIVO Institute for Jewish Research, New York.

Notes to Jewish Vocational Education

The Vilna "Help Through Work" Society

Originally published in *Unzer shtime* (Paris), 29–30 June, 1–2 July, 15–16 September 1953. See also Hirsz Abramowicz, *Yubiley-oysgabe "Hilf durkh arbet" 1903–1923 . . .* (Anniversary edition of "Help Through Work," 1903–1923 . . .) (Vilna, 1923); Abraham Klebanow, "Di profesyonele shuln bay 'Hilf durkh arbet' " (The Professional Schools at "Help Through Work"), in Jeshurin, *Vilne,* 288–95; Idem, "Problemen fun 'Hilf durkh arbet' " (Problems of "Help Through Work") and "Zeks un draysik yor 'Hilf durhk arbet' "(Thirty-Six Years of "Help Through Work"), in Grodzenski, *Vilner almanakh,* 263–70.

    1. Hebrew writers Abraham-Dov Lebensohn (also known as Adam Ha-Kohen, 1794–1878), Mordecai-Aaron Gunzburg (1795–1846), Kalman Schulman (1819–99), and Yiddish writer Isaac Meir Dick (1807–93) were all *maskilim* who championed modern education as a means of improving Jewish economic and social conditions.
    2. Isaac Benjacob (1801–63) was a *maskil* and the first modern Hebrew bibliographer. See Isaac Benjacob, *Ozar Ha-Sefarim* (Inventory of Books) (Vilna: Jacob Benjacob, 1880).
    3. I. M. Berman (pseud. Leybetshke), *Di tishler-arbet: vikhtige yedies far yudishe stolyares* (Carpentry: Important Information for Jewish Carpenters) (St. Petersburg: Jewish Colonization Association, 1913).
    4. The library of YIVO Institute for Jewish Research has the reports of the conferences. The title is: Trudy S'ezdov po Evreiskomu Professional'nomu Obrazovaniiu: 1. Deiatelei po Zhenskomu Evreiskomu Professional'nomu Obrazovaniiu v Dekabre 1909 g. - 2. Zaveduishchikh Evreiskimi Muzhskimi remeslennymi klassami, Dekabr' 1908 g. (Proceedings of the Conferences on Jewish Vocational Education: 1. Workers on Women's Jewish Vocational Education, December 1909. - 2. Administrators of Jewish Vocational Courses for Men, December 1908), 2 vols. (St. Petersburg: Jewish Colonization Association, 1911).
    5. The Hebrew Immigrant Aid Society (HIAS, originally the United Hebrew Sheltering and Immigrant Aid Society) was an agency established in New York in 1909 to assist Jewish immigrants from Eastern Europe.

Jewish Agricultural School in Wieluciany

Originally published in *Yidisher kemfer* (New York), 15 and 22 April 1955. A pre–World War II history of the school in Wieluciany by Abraham Klebanow appeared in Grodzenski, *Vilner almanakh,* 183–87.

    1. The Hilfsverein der Deutschen Juden was a German-Jewish charitable organization established in 1901 to assist Jews living in Eastern Europe and in the Middle East.
    2. Jewish religious law forbids working on the Sabbath. An exception is made for chores that involve the welfare of farm animals.
    3. The Workers Council was a local communist group that tried to take control of Vilna after the retreat of the German occupying forces on 30 December 1918.
    4. General Mokrzecki was one of two Polish officers who led local Polish forces in seizing control of the city on January 2, 1919. They attacked the Communist Party house during the night. In the battle, four communists were killed, five committed suicide, and seventy-six surrendered. See Norman Davies, *White Eagle, Red Star: The Polish-Soviet War of 1919–1920* (London: MacDonald, 1972), 25–26. Accurate information on the rapidly changing events of the period was hard to get. The Poles were driven from the city four days

after they liquidated the Council. The Bolsheviks who took over may have contributed to the rumor of the collective suicide. The available sources differ in detail. The events of the period were so hard to trace correctly that even Davies, the historian of the Polish-Soviet war, confused the activities of two generals in the war, the brothers Stefan and Adam Mokrzecki. See ibid., index. The biographies of the two generals are included in Piotr Stawicki, *Słownik Biograficzny Generałów Wojska Polskiego 1918–1939* (Biographical Dictionary of Generals of the Polish Military 1918–1939) (Warsaw: Bellona, 1994), 224–25.

Other sources are *Istoriia Grazhdanskoi Voiny v SSSR* (History of the Civil War in the U.S.S.R.), vol. 3 (Moscow: Gosudarstvennoe Izdatel'stvo Politicheskoi Literatury, 1957), 294, and Władysław Wejtko, *Samoobrona Litwy i Białorusi* (Self-Defense in Lithuania and Belorussia) (Warsaw: Warszawska Oficyna Wydawnicza Gryf, 1992), 86–87, 90. These sources give a much greater number of people killed during the siege.

5. Józef Piłsudski was the Commander-in-Chief of the Polish army. He arrived at the frontlines of the Polish-Soviet War (near Lida) on April 15 and on April 21 was already in the conquered city (see Davies, *White Eagle, Red Star,* 49–50). The author's use of the term "Legionnaries" refers to a core group of Piłsudski's supporters within the Polish army and is meant here as a general term for all Polish troops. The expressions "white Polish armies" and "Polish white legionnaries" are the equivalents of the Russian term "belopoliaki."

6. The American Jewish Joint Distribution Committee (also known as the JDC and the "Joint") is an organization established in New York in 1914 to provide relief and other forms of aid to Central and East European Jewry.

7. Cf. "The Wilno Problem," in *Cambridge History of Poland from Augustus II to Piłsudski* (New York: Octagon Books, 1971), 530.

The Białystok Vocational School

Originally published in *Byalistoker lebn,* February 1945.

1. The American Relief Administration was an agency of the United States government administered by Herbert Hoover. It was established in the wake of World War I to bring economic relief to Europeans.
2. ORT (Russian acronym for "Society for Manual Work") was established in 1880 to provide vocational training for Jews living under tsarist rule. Later, the organization also supported Jewish agricultural settlements. See Leon Shapiro, *The History of ORT: A Jewish Movement for Social Change* (New York: Schocken, 1980).

Matthias Schreiber

Originally published in *Kultur un dertsiung,* November 1946. Schreiber wrote two articles on the vocational school; see Jeshurin, *Vilne,* 313–21; Grodzenski, *Vilner almanakh,* 251–54. See also Dina Abramowicz "The World of My Parents," 148–51; Shapiro, *The History of ORT,* 182–83.

1. Sofia Markovna Gurewicz (1880–1942) was an educator and founder of a Yiddish gymnasium in Vilna during the interwar years.
2. Gershon Pludermacher (1876–1942), an educator, was one of the founders of the Yiddish school system in Vilna. He died in the Vilna Ghetto.
3. In September 1941, German occupying forces confined Vilna's Jews in a ghetto, as a step toward their eventual annihilation. The Vilna Ghetto was liquidated on 23 September

1943. See Arad, *Ghetto in Flames.* On the technical school in the Ghetto, see Mark Dworzecki, *Yerusholayim d'Lite in kamf un umkum* (Jerusalem of Lithuania in Struggle and Destruction) (Paris: Folksfarband in Frankraykh, 1948), 234. Anna Simaite's correspondence with the author is included in Hirsz Abramowicz's papers at YIVO, RG 446, box 1, separate file.

4. During the last years of its existence, the Vilna Jewish Technicum, in recognition of its excellent record, was granted the status of a college by the Polish educational authorities. Its name was changed to "Vilna Jewish Technical Lyceum."

Mark Antokolsky

Originally published in *Der tog* (New York), December 1952; *Unzer shtime* (Paris), 17–31 July, 1953.

1. Vladimir Vasil'evich Stasov (1824–1906), Russian art and music critic, was an honorary member of the St. Petersburg Art Academy. He is the author of Antokolsky's biography, *Mark Matveevich Antokolskii: ego zhizn', tvoreniia, pis'ma i stat'i* (Mark Matveevich Antokolsky: His Life, Work, Letters and Articles) (St. Petersburg-Moscow: M. O. Volf, 1905). Il'ia Yefimovich Repin (1844–1930), a painter of historical subjects, was known for his powerful and dramatic works.

2. Semen Iakovlevich Nadson (1862–87) was a Russian poet of Jewish descent. Victor Petrovich Burenin (1841–1926), reactionary Russian journalist, was the editor of *Novoe Vremia* (New Times).

3. This museum of Jewish art and artifacts was first established in Vilna in 1913 by the Friends of Jewish Antiquities. After World War I, S. Ansky reestablished the organization as the Jewish Historical-Ethnographic Society of Lithuania and Belorussia. It was renamed the S. Ansky Historical-Ethnographic Society when Ansky died in 1920. On the museum's history, see Cohen, *Vilna,* 412; A. I. Goldschmidt, "The Vilna Historical-Ethnographic Society and Its Museum," in *Vilner almanakh,* 189–94.

4. Mikhail Nikolaevich Muraviov (1794–1866), a senior tsarist official, was known for his reactionary views, his severe persecution of peasants who were remiss in paying their taxes, and his brutal oppression of Polish uprisings. Muraviov was named governor general of six Lithuanian provinces in 1863.

5. Claude Joseph Goldsmid Montefiore (1858–1938) was a liberal English Jewish leader and scholar. The Sforzas were a prominent family in Italy since the fifteenth century.

6. The reference is to the Gaon of Vilna, the popular name of renowned Talmudic authority Elijah ben Solomon Zalman (1720–97).

7. Il'ia Muromets is a mythological Russian hero, the personification of Russian patriotism and heroic defense against Russia's enemies.

8. Hirsz Abramowicz incorrectly attributed this critique of Antokolsky to Peretz Smolenskin. According to Zeitlin, the critique was made by the Hebrew writer Ahad Ha-Am. See Aaron Zeitlin, "Ahad un Antokolsky" (Ahad and Antokolsky) *Der tog* (New York), 1 May 1959. Ahad Ha-Am's remarks on Antokolsky appear in English translation in the essay "The Spiritual Revival" in his *Selected Essays,* trans. Leon Simon (Philadephia: Jewish Publication Society, 1936), 269–72.

Khaykl Lunski

Original publication information unknown. For Lunski's brief history of the Strashun Library, see Jeshurin, *Vilne,* 273–87.

1. Leon Moiseevich Rubinov (1873–?), a writer of short stories about Jewish life in Russia, was appointed to prepare the catalog of the Strashun Library.

2. The Synagogue Courtyard (known as the *Shulhoyf*) was the center of traditional Jewish life in Vilna. It was the site of the central synagogue known as the *Groyse shul* (the Great Synagogue), as well as a number of smaller prayer houses, among them the *Alte kloyz* (the Old Synagogue). See Carol Herselle Krinsky, *Synagogues of Europe: Architecture, History, Meaning* (New York: Architectural History Foundation/Cambridge: MIT Press, 1985), 223–25; Leizer Ran, ed., *Jerusalem of Lithuania: Illustrated and Documented* (New York: Vilna Album Committee, 1971) 1:104–13; M. Vorobeichic, *Ein Ghetto im Osten: Vilna 65 Bilder von M. Vorobeichic* (The Ghetto Lane in Vilna: 65 Pictures by M. Vorobeichic) (Berlin: Edition Hentrich, Frolich and Kaufman, 1984).

3. Khaykl Lunski, *Fun vilner geto: geshtaltn un bilder, geshribn in shvere tsaytn* (From the Vilna Ghetto: Images and Scenes, Written during Difficult Times) (Vilna: Fareyn fun di yidishe literatn un zhurnalistn in Vilne, 1920), 109–32.

4. See Reisen, *Pinkes far der geshikhte fun Vilne in di yorn fun milkhome un okupatsye*.

5. Judah ben Eliezer (also known as The Yesod, ?–1762), a Lithuanian Talmudist, communal worker, and philanthropist, was the rabbi of Vilna. His successor in 1750 was his son-in-law, Samuel ben Avigdor (1720–83), Vilna's last official rabbi. *Hayye Adam* (Life of Man), by Rabbi Abraham ben Jehiel Michael Danzig (1748–1820), is a popular Hebrew-language treatise on Jewish law. Danzig was often referred to by the title of his most famous work. Abraham ben Abraham Solomon, known as Reb Abele Posvoler (1764–1836), was a Talmudic scholar and the head of the Vilna rabbinical court. Reb Ayzele Harif of Słonim was the nickname of Reb Joshua Isaac Shapira, born in 1803 in the Belorussian town of Głębokie. A Talmudic scholar and Chief Rabbi of Słonim, he was known for his sharp wit.

6. Lunski's writings on Słonim were serialized in the Yiddish newspaper *Slonimer vort* in 1938–39. Excerpts appear in *Pinkas Slonim* (Chronicle of Słonim), ed. Kalman Lichtenstein (Tel Aviv: Association of Slonim Jews in Israel, 1962–79), vols. 3–4.

7. See Szmerke Kaczerginski, *Khurbn Vilne* (Destruction of Vilna) (New York: CYCO, 1947), 198.

Samuel Hurwicz

Originally published in *Lebns-fragn,* September–October 1954. Samuel Hurwicz described his activities in a pamphlet titled *30 yor bay der antviklung un organizirung fun dem yidishn hantverker in Vilne* (Thirty Years of Developing and Organizing the Jewish Artisan in Vilna) (Vilna: Central Union of the Jewish Craftsman in Vilna, 1933).

1. *Shulhan Arukh* (1565) is a code of Jewish law compiled by Joseph Caro (1488–1575). It is recognized as an authoritative source by Orthodox Jews throughout the world. *En Ya'akov* (1516) is an annotated compilation of Talmudic lore by Jacob Ibn-Haviv (1460–1516). It became very popular in Yiddish translation.

2. Il'ia Iakovlevich Guenzburg (1859–1939) was a sculptor and a protegé of Mark Antokolsky. Leopold Bernstein-Sinaeff (1867–1944) was a sculptor. A native of Vilna, he was awarded the Order of the Legion of Honor by France.

3. Avenir Grilikhes and his son Abraham were engravers to the Tsars Alexander III and Nicholas II.

4. "Opener of gates" is a reference to the benediction at the opening of the daily evening prayer. It is a paraphrase of the biblical verse, "Open to me the gates of righteousness" (Psalms 118:19).

5. The Shimen Frug School was a Yiddish elementary school for girls in Vilna from 1908 to 1940. It was named after the Yiddish poet Shimen Frug (1860–1916).

6. Mendele's novel *Dos kleyne mentshele* (The Parasite), first published in Odessa in 1865, is a bitter satire on Jewish communal life of the time. See Dan Miron, *A Traveler Disguised: A Study in the Rise of Modern Yiddish Fiction in the Nineteenth Century* (New York: Schocken, 1973).

7. According to the Talmud (Bezah 16), Jews receive a second soul on the eve of Sabbath, and at the end of the Sabbath it returns to Heaven.

8. The New Economic Policy (NEP) was initiated by Lenin in the 1920s to mitigate the opposition of the peasant class to the Soviet regime. Its main features were the cessation of grain requisitions from the peasants and the readmission of private enterprise to industry.

Eliezer Kruk

Originally published in *Kium* (Paris), no. 64 (October) and no. 65 (December), 1954. On Jewish trades in Vilna, see Leizer Ran, *Jerusalem of Lithuania* (New York: Vilna Album Committee, 1971), 3:338–41. On the Vilna Jewish community council, See Samuel Kassow, "Jewish Communal Politics in Transition: The Vilna *Kehile* 1919–1920," *YIVO Annual* 20 (1991): 61–92.

1. B. Michalewicz (1876–1928), pseudonym of Joseph Izbicki, was an active member of the Bund, a popular labor leader, and a journalist.

2. Moshe Żabinski, a printer and engraver, was active in Vilna's Yiddish schools. Szymon Lichtmacher, a printer, was involved in Jewish trade organizations and served as chair of the Society for the Jewish Deaf and Dumb. Both men perished in the Holocaust.

3. In interwar Poland, when Władysław Grabski (1873–1938) was secretary of the treasury, "Grabski's hearse" was the nickname for the tax collector's wagon.

4. Moshe Lejbowski, Ber Zalkind, and Jacob Szer were artists who also taught art in Vilna's Yiddish schools during the interwar period. All of them perished in the Holocaust. See Kaczerginski, *Khurbn Vilne;* Kazdan, *Lerer-yisker-bukh;* Kazimierz Brakoniecki, *Wilenskie Środowisko Artystczne: Wystawa 1919–1945* (Wilno Artistic Circle Exhibition, 1919–1945) (Olsztyn: Biuro Wystaw Artystycznych w Olsztynie, 1989).

5. The city government consisted of a city council, whose members were elected, and a city administration ("magistrat"), with a president, three vice-presidents, and four alderman ("ławnik"), nominated by the council. See *Miasta Polskie w Tysiącleciu* (Polish Cities in the Millenium) (Wrocław: Zakład Narodowy im Ossolińskich), vol. 1 (1965), 151. There were several Jewish members of the city council, but only one Jewish alderman.

6. The National Democratic Party (Endecja) was founded in 1897 by Roman Dmowski (1864–1939) and espoused an exclusive brand of Polish nationalism. It was an anti-Semitic, anti-German party whose main rival was Józef Piłsudski's Polish Socialist Party.

7. "City and mother in Israel" is a biblical phrase (2 Samuel 20:19) originally applied to Jerusalem.

B. Kahan-Wirgili

Originally published in *Unzer shtime* (Paris), 17–18 May, 1951. *B. Kahan-Virgili: zamlbukh tsu zayn biografye un kharakteristik* (B. Kahan-Wirgili: Collected Essays on his Biography and Character) (Vilna: YIVO, 1938) was published on the first anniversary of his death.

1. See Kadushin, *Geografisher atlas.*

Joseph Jaszunski

Originally published in *Forverts*, 3 March 1946.

1. Menashe ben Joseph of Ilye (1767–1831), a rabbinical writer and philosopher, was an early Russiah Jewish reformer and an early *maskil.*
2. Dr. Moses Silberfarb, Leon Bramson, and Dr. Aaron Syngalowski were active in many Russian Jewish social organizations. Leon Bramson was the head of the ORT in Russia beginning in 1908, and of the World ORT Union after it moved its headquarters to Berlin in 1920. Following Bramson's death in 1941, Dr. Syngalowski became the organization's director.
3. Vladimir Dmitrievich Nabokov (1869–1922) and Iosif Vladimirovich Gessen (1869–1922) were members of the Kadets (the acronym for the Constitutional Democratic Party, founded in 1905) and editors of the Russian legal weekly *Pravo* (1897–1917) in St. Petersburg.
4. *Izvestiia Vserossiiskoi po Delam o Vyborakh v Uchreditel'noe Sobranie Kommissii* (Bulletin of the All-Russian Electoral Commission) was an organ of the Provisional Government. It was abruptly terminated with the issue [25] of December 20, 1917. It is mentioned as an extremely rare document in "Bibliographical Note" in Oliver Henry Radkey, *The Election to the Russian Constituent Assembly 1917* (Cambridge: Harvard University Press, 1950), 81. Jaszunski was one of fifteen members of the All-Russian Commission on Elections [to the Constitutional Assembly] on August 1, 1917. See Mark Vishniac, *Vserossiiskoe Uchreditel'noe Sobranie* (All-Russian Constitutional Assembly) (Paris: Sovremennye Zapiski, 1932), 86.
5. WUZET is a Polish acronym for the Association for the Dissemination of Vocational Education among Jews in Little Poland. The organization was active in southern Poland during the interwar years.
6. On this convention, see *Baratung far profesyoneler bildung, Bialystok 20–23 februar 1922: rezolutsyes un tezisn* (Conference on Vocational Education, Białystok, February 20–23, 1922: Resolutions and Theses) (Vilna: 1922).
7. For Joseph Jaszunski's activities in Warsaw in the 1930s, see Leon Shapiro, *The History of ORT* (New York: Schocken, 1980), 180–83.

Joseph Czernichow (Danieli)

Originally published in *Frayland* (Paris), December 1951. On the Freeland movement, see Michael Astour, *Geshikhte fun der frayland-lige un funem teritoryalistishn gedank* (History of the Freeland League and the Territorialist Idea) (Buenos Aires-New York: Freeland League, 1967). Danieli was Czernichow's pen name.

1. Joseph Czernichow, *In revtribunal: zikhroynes fun a farteydiker* (In the Revolutionary Tribunal: Reminiscences of a Defense Lawyer) (Vilna: J. Czernichow, 1932).
2. See Czernichow's introductory essay in *Arbet: zamlbukh far di oyfgabn fun Ort* (Work: Symposium on the Goals of Ort) (Kaunas: Lithuanian Committee of the Society for the Propagation of Trades and Agricultural Occupations among Jews—Ort, 1924), 5–16.
3. The Hawks (Yiddish: *Shparbers*) was a Socialist-Territorialist youth organization, connected with the Freeland League. Organized in the late 1930s, the Hawks concentrated

on training young people in agricultural work, which would be their main occupation in the new Jewish colonies to be established by the Freeland League.

4. A number of prominent Yiddish literary personalities participated in the Paris Congress of 1937, which was held in order to unify and strengthen international Yiddish cultural activities. However, because the conference was sponsored by the Yidisher kulturfarband, which was clearly pro-Communist and pro-Soviet, others in the Yiddishist community did not participate.

5. Joseph Opatoshu (1886–1954) was an American Yiddish novelist and journalist. Sh[loyme] Bastomski (1891–1941) was a prominent Yiddish educator and writer in Vilna. H. Leivick (pen name of Leivick Halpern, 1888–1962) was a major American Yiddish poet and playwright.

6. Yiddish poet and journalist Daniel Charney (1888–1959) was active in Eastern Europe before World War II and later lived in the United States.

Gershon Malakiewicz

Originally published in *Frayland,* October 1952.

1. Fayvl Trupianski, a follower of the Freeland movement, was the editor of its organ, *Fraye shriftn,* and administrator of the Yiddish publishing house Tomor. He was deported from Vilna at the liquidation of the Vilna Ghetto in 1943. Jeremiah Szapiro was a philanthropist and supporter of the YIVO Institute for Jewish Research.

2. See Kaczerginski, *Khurbn Vilne,* 253.

3. According to Talmudic legend (Sanhedrin 97b; Sukkah 45b), thirty-six righteous men live in every generation; their presence insures the continued existence of the world.

Chief Rabbi Isaac Rubinstein

Originally published in *Litvisher yid,* April–May, 1946; revised version in *Morgn-zhurnal,* 30 December 1951.

1. Jacob Mazeh (1859–1924), a prominent *maskil* and Zionist, was appointed *rabiner* of Moscow in 1893. Mendl Beilis (1874–1934) was accused of a ritual murder of a young Christian boy in 1911. Beilis's trial, which attracted international attention, led to an acquittal after the defendant spent two years in prison. Rabbi Moses Eliezer Eisenstadt (1869–1943), scholar and author, was *rabiner* of St. Petersburg from 1911 to 1923. Shmarya Levin (1867–1935) was a Zionist leader and a writer in both Yiddish and Hebrew who was also elected to the first Russian Duma in 1906. Judah Leib Kantor (1849–1915), Hebrew author and journalist, was *rabiner* in the cities of Libava, Vilna, and Riga.

2. Samuel Niger (pseudonym of Samuel Charney, 1883–1956), Yiddish journalist, editor, and literary critic, emigrated to the United States in 1920. Leib Jaffe (1876–1946), poet and Zionist leader, was a native of Lithuania who emigrated to Palestine in 1920.

3. Zamut is a region of Lithuania (also known as Żmudź, Samogitia) that was an important center of the *Haskalah.* See Jacob Shatzky, "Kultur-geshikhte fun der haskole in Lite" (The Cultural History of the Haskalah of Lithuanian Jews), in Sudarsky, *Lite,* 691–758; Hermann Frank, "Di khokhmey Zager" (The Sages of Zhagare), ibid., 775ff.

Dr. Cemach Szabad

Originally published in *Tsayt* (Vilna), 22 January 1935. See also Cemach Szabad, *Oytobiografye* (Autobiography) (Vilna: YIVO, 1935); Hirsz Matz, *Dr. Tsemakh Shabad* (Dr. Cemach Szabad) (Warsaw: TOZ, 1937).

1. Vladimir Korolenko (1853–1921) and Gleb Ivanovich Uspenskii (1843–1902) were Russian writers known for their humanitarian and democratic ideals, as well as their compassionate portrayal of Russia's poor. Nikolai Konstantinovich Mikhailovskii (1842–1904), a Russian sociologist and political writer, was a leader of the populist movement during the reign of Tsar Alexander II.

2. The Central Education Committee was established in May 1919 to supervise Vilna's Yiddish school system. See *Shul-pinkes*.

Dr. Jacob Wygodzki

Originally published in *Kium* (Paris) no. 3–4, March–April 1952.

1. Franz Murer was the German commander of the Vilna Ghetto during the years 1941–42. He had power over the life and death of the Ghetto's residents.

2. During the reign of Tsars Alexander I and Nicholas I, young Jews were drafted into the Russian Army at an early age. This practice had a profoundly disruptive impact on Jewish communities under tsarist rule. See Stanislawski, *Tsar Nicholas I and the Jews*.

3. Moses Mendelssohn (1729–86) is known as the father of the *Haskalah*. His *Biur*, a translation of the first five books of the Bible into German (printed in Hebrew characters) with commentaries in Hebrew, was published in 1780–83.

4. Jeremiah 52:15.

5. The two main political systems among Jews in interwar Poland—Bundism and Zionism—each developed their own school networks, which promoted different ideologies and languages. Bundists championed diaspora nationalism and Yiddish, while Zionists advocated creating a Jewish state in Palestine and the cultivation of Hebrew as a modern language. See Miriam Eisenstein, *Jewish Schools in Poland, 1919–1939* (New York: Columbia University Press, 1950), 6–17.

6. Student-led anti-Semitic disturbances occurred in Vilna after 10 November 1931 when Stanisław Wacławski, a Polish student, died as a result of clashes between Polish and Jewish students at Vilna University. See Cohen, *Vilna*, 418.

7. For Wygodzki's memoirs, see Jacob Wygodzki, *In shturm* (In the Storm) (Vilna: Kleckin, 1926); Idem, *In gehenem* (In Hell) (Vilna: Kleckin, 1927); Idem, *In Sambatyon* (Vilna: Kleckin, 1931). See also his essays on Vilna Jewry during World War I in Reisen, *Pinkes far der geshikhte fun Vilne in di yorn fun milkhome un okupatsye*, 41–66, 67–80.

A. Weiter

Originally published in *Unzer shtime* (Paris), 24–28 November 1951. See also Zorakh Nanes, "Vilne in di revolutsyonere teg fun 1905" (Vilna in the Revolutionary Days of October 1905), in Jeshurin, *Vilne*, 176–90. On Weiter's death, see A. Weiter, *Ksovim*, 157–60.

1. The term "victims of the state" (Hebrew: *harugei malkhut*) is a metaphor derived from the "Ten Martyrs" who, according to Talmudic tradition, were executed by the Roman government for defying the prohibition on Jewish observances and religious teaching.

2. "Sakya Muni," an epithet applied to Buddha, is the title of a poem by the Russian poet Dmitri Sergeevich Merezhkovskii (1865–1941). In the poem, Buddha accepts with humility the protest of a beggar, who shames Buddha for his hypocrisy and rejects his divine superiority over suffering humanity.

3. "Slushai!" was written by Ivan Ivanovich Golts-Miller (1842–71), a Russian poet and revolutionary. "*Slushai!*" was the customary call of Russian prison guards to signal their presence. This six-stanza poem became famous as a symbol of revolutionary struggle against the prison system in tsarist Russia.

4. Moishe Taich (1882–1935), Yiddish poet, novelist, and journalist, also composed poems and stories for children.

5. The cemetery was liquidated in the 1960s. See G. Agranovskii and I. Gruzenberg, *Litovskii Ierusalim* (Jerusalem of Lithuania) (Vilnius: Litanus, 1992), 64 (there is no mention of the Weiter monument being preserved). A picture of the monument appears in Jeshurin, *Vilne,* 502.

6. The emblem of the new Polish state was a single-headed eagle.

7. In 1942, YIVO held a public autobiography contest on the theme "Why I Left Europe and What I Have Accomplished in America," which elicted some 250 entries from immigrant Jews. See YIVO Archives, New York, RG 102.

Zalmen Reisen

Originally published in *Di tsukunft* (New York), May–June, 1952; *Di yidishe tsaytung* (Buenos Aires), 24 February, 3 March 1953. On Reisen and his argument for Yiddish as a public language in Vilna, see Kassow, "Jewish Communal Politics in Transition."

1. S. L. Citron (1860–1930) was a Hebrew and Yiddish writer and literary historian. Don Kaplanowicz (1880–1932) was a Yiddish short-story writer and journalist. Shloyme Shreberk (1866–1944) was a publisher of Hebrew and Yiddish books in both Vilna and Warsaw. Semion Rosenbaum (1860–1934) was a jurist and Zionist leader. Active in Lithuanian politics during and after World War I, he emigrated to Palestine in 1924. Leib Kadison, A. Azro, Sonia Alomis, and Noah Nakhbush were all members of the Vilna Troupe, a Yiddish theatrical group. See A. Azro, "Der onheyb" (In the Beginning), in Itsik Manger, Jonas Turkow, and Moshe Perenson, eds., *Yidisher teater in Eyrope: Poyln* (Yiddish Theater in Europe: Poland) (New York: World Congress for Yiddish Culture, 1968), 23–34; Nahma Sandrow, *Vagabond Stars* (New York: Harper and Row, 1977), 213–21.

2. Abraham Reisen (1876–1953), Yiddish poet and short-story writer, was active both in Europe and the United States.

3. During the early twentieth century, there were a number of efforts made in Eastern Europe, the United States, and the Soviet Union to standardize and modernize Yiddish spelling. A major issue of debate was whether Yiddish words of Hebrew origin should retain their traditional spelling or be rendered in the same phonetic orthography used for all other Yiddish words.

4. Young Vilna (Yiddish: *Yung-Vilne*) was the name of a circle of young modernist Yiddish writers and artists active during the interwar years. See Irving Howe, Ruth R. Wisse, and Khone Shmeruk, eds., *The Penguin Book of Modern Yiddish Verse* (New York: Viking Penguin, 1987), 40ff; Sol Liptzin, *A History of Yiddish Literature* (Middle Village, N.Y.: Jonathan David Publishers, 1985), ch., 21.

5. Zalmen Reisen, *Leksikon fun der yidisher literatur un prese* (Lexicon of Yiddish Literature and Press), ed. Sh. Niger (Warsaw: Central, 1914); Idem, *Leksikon fun der yidisher literatur, prese un filologye* (Lexicon of Yiddish Literature, Press and Philology) (Vilna: B. Kleckin, 1926–29).

Moshe Shalit

Originally published in *Di tsukunft,* March 1954.

1. *Vozrozhdenie* was a Jewish nationalist and socialist group in Russia during the years 1903–1905.

2. BILU, a group of young Russian Jews who pioneered modern Jewish settlement in Palestine, was founded in 1882.

3. Joseph Lurie (1871–1937) was a Zionist leader and Hebrew educator.

4. Chaim Zhitlowsky (1865–1943) was a leading ideologist of Diaspora nationalism and champion of secular Yiddishism.

5. Cemach Szabad, ed., *Vilner zamlbikher* (Vilna Anthologies) (Vilna, 1916–17).

6. The Association of Yiddish Writers and Journalists in Vilna (Yidisher literatn- un zhurnalistn-fareyn in Vilne) was formed at the initiative of writer S. Ansky, the author of the famous drama *The Dybbuk*. Ansky arrived in Vilna in 1918, fleeing the Bolshevik revolution.

7. Shalit, ed., *Oyf di khurves fun milkhomes un mehumes,* 741, 760, 828.

8. CENTOS is the Polish acronym for the Society for the Care of Orphans. This organization was founded by EKOPO to care for Jewish children whose parents died in the aftermath of World War I.

9. Moshe Shalit, ed. *Di ekonomishe lage fun di yidn in poyln un di yidishe kooperatsye* (The Economic Situation of the Jews in Poland and the Jewish Cooperative Movement) (Vilna: Association of Jewish Cooperative Societies in Poland, 1926).

10. On Shalit's tragic death at the hands of the Nazis, see Kaczerginski, *Khurbn Vilne,* 215–16.

Place-names

For an explanation of use, see the Note from the Editors (pp. 72–73).

Form Used in Text	Alternate Forms
Baranowicze (Pol.)	Baranovichi (Rus.)
Brześć (Pol.)	Brest (Rus.)
Butrymańce (Pol.)	Butrymonis (Lith.)
Chernigov (Rus.)	Chernihiv (Ukr.)
Constanţa (Rom.)	Constantsa (Rus.)
Datnów (Pol.)	Dotnuva (Lith.)
Deksznie (Pol.)	Deksnys (Lith.)
Dukszty (Pol.)	Dūkštas (Lith.)
Dvinsk (Rus.)	Daugavpils (Latv.)
Głębokie (Pol.)	Glubokoe (Rus.)
Janów (Pol.)	Jonava (Lith.)
Jewje (Pol.)	Vievis (Lith.)
Jezno (Pol.)	Jieznas (Lith.)
Kiejdany (Pol.)	Kedainiai (Lith.)
Kishinev (Rus.)	Chişinău (Rom.)
Kovno (Rus.)	Kaunas (Lith.)
Kozłowa-Ruda (Pol.)	Kazlu Ruda (Lith.)
Landwarów (Pol.)	Lentvaris (Lith.)
Lejpuny (Pol.)	Leipalingės (Lith.)
Libava (Rus.)	Liepāja (Latv.)
Lwów (Pol.)	L'viv (Ukr.)
Mogilev (Rus.)	Mahileu (Belor.)
Niemen (Pol.)	Nemunas (Lith.)

Form Used in Text	Alternate Forms
Nowogródek (Pol.)	Novogrudok (Rus.)
Onikszty (Pol.)	Anykščiai (Lith.)
Pińsk (Pol.)	Pinsk (Rus.)
Ponevezh (Rus.)	Panevėžys (Lith.), Poniewież (Pol.)
Popilva (Rus.)	Popiłwa (Pol.), Papilys (Lith.)
Poznań (Pol.)	Posen (German)
Prużana or Prużany (Pol.)	Pruzhany (Belor., Rus.)
Rudziszki (Pol.)	Rūdiškės (Lith.)
Samogitia (Eng.)	Żmudź (Pol.), Žemaičiai (Lith.)
Słonim (Pol.)	Slonim (Rus.)
Sołoki (Pol.)	Sālakas (Lith.)
Stokliszki (Pol.)	Stakliškės (Lith.)
Sumiliszki (Pol.)	Semeliškės (Lith.)
Święciany (Pol.)	Švenčionys (Lith.)
Szyrwinty (Pol.)	Širvintos (Lith.)
Telsze (Pol.)	Telšiai (Lith.), Tel'shi (Rus.)
Troki (Pol.)	Trakai (Lith.)
Uciana (Pol.)	Utena (Lith.)
Vilna (Eng.)	Vilnius (Lith.), Wilno (Pol.)
Widze (Pol.)	Vidžiai (Lith.)
Wierzbołowo (Pol.)	Virbalis (Lith.)
Wołożyn (Pol.)	Volozhin (Rus.)
Wyłkowyszki (Pol.)	Vilkaviškis (Lith.)
Wysoki Dwór (Pol.)	Aukštadvaris (Lith.)
Żagory (Pol.)	Zhagory (Rus.), Žagarė (Lith.)

Periodicals mentioned in the text

Yiddish

Baginen (Dawn) 1932, 1934–35, 1936, Vilna, monthly
Bikher-velt (Book World) 1922, Warsaw
Bikher-velt (Book World) 1928–29, Warsaw
Folks-blat 1908, Vilna, only one issue published
Folksgezunt (Popular Health) 1923–37, Vilna-Warsaw, varying frequency
Folkstsaytung (People's Newspaper) 1906–07, Vilna, daily
Folkstsaytung (also *Naye folkstsaytung* [New People's Newspaper]) 1921–39, Warsaw, daily
Folk un land (People and Land) 1910, Vilna, only one issue published
Forverts (Jewish Daily Forward) 1897–present, New York, daily (weekly since 1987)
Fraye shriftn farn yidishn sotsialistishn gedank (Free Writings for Jewish Socialist Thought) 1926–37, Warsaw, irregular
Frayer gedank (Free Thought) 1926–27, Vilna-Warsaw, biweekly
Der fraynd (The Friend) 1903–08, St. Petersburg; 1909–13, Warsaw, daily
Frimorgn (Morning) 1920–33, Riga daily
Fun noentn over (From the Recent Past) 1937–38, Warsaw, quarterly
Fun yor tsu yor (From Year to Year) 1926–29, Warsaw, annual
Haynt (Today) 1919–39, Warsaw daily
Di yidishe tsaytung (The Yiddish Newspaper) 1914–73, Buenos Aires daily
Der klasn-kamf (The Class Struggle) 1898–1901, Vilna, irregular
Lebn (Life) 1920–21, Vilna, monthly
Letste nays (Latest News) 1916–19, Vilna, daily
Literarishe bleter (Literary Pages) 1924–39, Warsaw, weekly
Der litivisher yid (The Lithuanian Jew) 1934–37, New York, irregular
Luakh "Kadimah" (Calendar "Forward") 1909–12, Vilna-St. Petersburg, annual
Moment (Moment) 1910–39, Warsaw, daily

Dos naye lebn (The New Life) 1908–15; 1922–23, New York, monthly
Oyfn shvel (On the Threshold) 1941–present, New York, varying frequency
Slonimer vort (The Słonim Word) 1929–39, Słonim, daily
Tog (Day) [also *Der vilner tog* (The Vilna Day)] 1920–39, Vilna, daily
Di tsayt (The Times) 1921–39, Vilna, daily
Unzer hilf (Our Help) 1921–23, Vilna, biweekly
Unzer shtime (Our Voice) 1935–95, Paris, daily
Vilner zamlbikher (Vilna Essays) 1916–17, Vilna
Dos vort (The Word) 1924–39, Vilna, weekly
Dos yidishe folk (The Jewish People) 1906–08, Vilna; 1914, Warsaw, weekly
Yidishe tsaytung (Yiddish Newspaper) May–December 1919, Vilna daily
Di yidishe tsaytung (The Yiddish Newspaper) 1909, Vilna, daily
Der yidisher hantverker (The Jewish Craftsman) 1916–26, Vilna, jubilee edition
Der yidisher kemfer (The Jewish Frontier) 1907–present, New York, weekly

Hebrew

Ha-Maggid (The Preacher) 1856–1903, Lyck-Berlin-Cracow, weekly
Ha-Melitz (The Advocate) 1860–1904, Odessa-St. Petersburg, weekly (daily from 1886)
Ha-Olam (The World) 1907–50, various European cities and Jerusalem, weekly (in Vilna, 1908–12)
Ha-Shahar (The Morning) 1868–85, Vienna, monthly
Ha-Tsefirah (The Dawn) 1862–1931, Warsaw, daily
Ha-Zeman (The Time) 1905, Vilna, daily with quarterly supplements

Russian

Budushchnost' (Future) 1899–1904, St. Petersburg, weekly with annual supplements (1900–04)
Izvestiia Vserossiiskoi po Delam o Vyborakh v Uchreditol'noe Sobranie Kommissii (Bulletin of the All-Russian Electoral Commission)
Knizhki Voskhoda (Books of the Sunrise) 1899–1906, St. Petersburg, monthly
Nedel'naia Khronika Voskhoda (Weekly Chronicle of the Sunrise) (also *Khronika Voskhoda*) 1882–1906, St. Petersburg, weekly
Novoe Vremia (New Times) 1868–1917, St. Petersburg, daily
Posledniia Izvestia (Latest News) 1901–06, London-Geneva, irregular
Pravo (The Law) 1897–1917, St. Petersburg
Razsvet (Dawn) 1860–61, Odessa, weekly; 1879–84, St. Petersburg, weekly; 1907–15, St. Petersburg, weekly
Russkii Evrei (The Russian Jew) 1879–84, St. Petersburg, weekly
Voskhod (Sunrise) 1881–99, St. Petersburg, monthly; see also *Knizhki Voskhoda, Nedel'naia Khronika Voskhoda*

Polish

Nasz Przegląd (Our Survey) 1922–39, Warsaw, daily
Nasza Trybuna (Our Tribune) 1940–1951, New York, biweekly

Bibliography

The bibliography includes books, pamphlets, and a selection of articles published in journals and collective volumes. The listing of articles by the author contains contributions that were not included in his Yiddish collected volume, but were mentioned by his daughter in her biographical essay.

Hirsz Abramowicz Papers, YIVO Institute for Jewish Research, New York

Papers, 1920s–1960. ca. 1 ft. 5 in. (RG446).
Contains correspondence with Yiddish literary figures, letters to his daughter Dina Abramowicz, manuscripts of Abramowicz's articles about personalities and about literary and social questions, clippings of articles by and about Abramowicz, and personal documents.

Abrahams, Israel. *Jewish Life in the Middle Ages.* New York: Meridian Books, 1958.
Abramowicz, Dina. "The World of My Parents." *YIVO Annual* 23 (1996): 105–57.
[Abramowicz, Hirsz.] *Yubiley-oysgabe "Hilf durkh arbet" 1903–1923 . . .* (Anniversary edition of "Help Through Work," 1903–1923 . . .). Vilna, 1923.
Abramowicz, Hirsz. "Vilne di natsyonalitetn-shtot" (Vilna the City of Many Nationalities). In *Vilne: a zamlbukh gevidmet der shtot Vilne* (Vilna: A Book Dedicated to the City of Vilna), ed. Ephim H. Jeshurin, 267–72. New York: Workmen's Circle Vilna Branch 367, 1935.
———. "Der baginen fun praktishn yidishizm in Vilne" (The Beginnings of Practical Yiddishism in Vilna). In *Almanakh fun yidishn literatn- un zhurnalistn-fareyn in Vilne* (Almanac of the Yiddish Writers' and Journalists' Association in Vilna), ed. Moshe Shalit, 1:156–60. Vilna, 1938.
———. "Vi iz es geven in Vilne?" (How was it in Vilna?: Remarks on Sh. Basman's Article about Vilna). *Oyfn shvel* (New York) 8, no. 70 (September 1950): 18–19.
———. "Der kayor fun yidishn shulvezn" (The Dawn of the Yiddish School System). *Kultur un dertsiung* (New York) (January 1951): 16–18.

———. *Farshvundene geshtaltn: zikhroynes un siluetn* (Vanished Figures: Memoirs and Silhouettes). Buenos Aires: Central Association of Polish Jews in Argentina, 1958.

———. "A kapitl geshikhte fun yidisher dertsiung" (A Chapter in the History of Jewish Education). In *Naye yidishe shul I. L. Peretz, yorbukh* 12 (Twelfth Yearbook of the New I. L. Peretz Yiddish School), ed. Abraham Golomb, 3–11. Mexico City, 1961.

Agranovskii, G., and I. Gruezenberg. *Litovskii Ierusalim* (Jerusalem of Lithuania). Vilnius: Lituanus, 1992.

Ahad Ha-am. *Selected Essays*. Translated by Leon Simon. Philadephia: Jewish Publication Society, 1936.

Arad, Yitzhak. *Ghetto in Flames: The Struggle and Destruction of the Jews in Vilna in the Holocaust*. Jerusalem: Yad Vashem, 1980.

Arbet: zamlbukh far di oyfgabn fun Ort (Work: Symposium on the Goals of Ort). Kaunas: Lithuanian Committee of the Society for the Propagation of Trades and Agricultural Occupations among Jews—Ort, 1924.

Astour, Michael. *Geshikhte fun der frayland-lige un funem teritoryalistishn gedank* (History of the Freeland League and the Territorialist Idea). 2 vols. Buenos Aires, New York: Freeland League, 1967.

Baratung far profesioneler bildung, Bialystok 20–23 februar 1922: rezolutsyes un tezis. (Conference on Vocational Education, Białystok, February 20–23, 1922: Resolutions and Theses). Vilna, 1922.

B. Kahan-Virgili: zamlbukh tsu zayn biografye un kharakteristik (B. Kahan-Wirgili: Collected Essays on his Biography and Character). Vilna: YIVO, 1938.

Baron, Salo. *The Russian Jew under the Tsars and Soviets*. New York: Macmillan, 1964.

Bebel, August. *Woman under Socialism*. Translated by Daniel De Leon. New York: Schocken Books, 1971.

Benjacob, Yitzhak Isaac. "Be-'olam ha-asiyah." *Ha-Kerem* (Warsaw) 4 (1887): 41–62.

Benjacob, Isaac. *Ozar Ha-Sefarim* (Inventory of Books). Vilna: Jacob Benjacob, 1880.

Berman, I. M. (pseud. Leybetshke), *Di tishler-arbet: vikhtige yedies far yudishe stolyares* (Carpentry: Important Information for Jewish Carpenters). St. Petersburg: Jewish Colonization Association, 1913.

Brakoniecki, Kazimierz. *Wileńskie Środowisko Artystczne: Wystawa 1919–1945* (Wilno Artistic Circle Exhibition, 1919–1945). Olsztyn: Biuro Wystaw Artystycznych w Olsztynie, 1989.

Charlasz, I. "Hirsz Abramowicz." *Unzer tsayt* (New York), January–February 1960, 50.

Cohen, Israel. *Vilna*. 1943. Reprint, Philadelphia: Jewish Publication Society, 1992.

Critchfield, Richard. *Changed Values, Altered Lives: The Closing of the Urban-Rural Gap*. New York: Anchor/Doubleday, 1994.

Czernichow, Joseph. *In revtribunal: zikhroynes fun a farteydiker* (In the Revolutionary Tribunal: Reminiscences of a Defense Lawyer). Vilna: J. Czernichow, 1932.

Davies, Norman. *White Eagle, Red Star: The Polish-Soviet War, 1919–1920*. London: MacDonald, 1972.

———. *God's Playground: A History of Poland*. New York: Columbia University Press, 1984.

Dolitzki, M. M. *Kol shirei M. M. Dolitski* (Collected Verse of M. M. Dolitzki). New York, 1895.

Dubnow, Simon. *History of the Jews in Russia and Poland*. 3 vols. 1920. New York: Ktav, 1975.

Dworzecki, Mark. *Yerusholayim d'Lite in kamf un umkum* (Jerusalem of Lithuania in Struggle and Destruction). Paris: Folksfarband in Frankraykh, 1948.

Bibliography

Eisenstein, Miriam. *Jewish Schools in Poland, 1919–1939.* New York: Columbia University Press, 1950.
Encyclopedia Lituanica. 6 vols. Boston: Juozas Kapocius, 1978.
Esh, Saul, ed. *Yad Vashem Studies on the European Jewish Catastrophe and Resistance.* Vol. 2. Jerusalem: Yad Vashem, 1958.
Evreiskaia Entsiklopediia (Jewish Encyclopedia). 1911. Reprint, Moscow: Terra, 1991.
Frankel, Jonathan. *Prophecy and Politics: Socialism, Nationalism, and the Russian Jews, 1862–1917.* Cambridge: Cambridge University Press, 1981.
Frieden, Ken. *Classic Yiddish Fiction: Abramovitsh, Sholem Aleichem, and Peretz.* New York: SUNY Press, 1995.
Ginsburg, Saul M. *Historishe verk* (Historical Works). 3 vols. New York: Saul M. Ginsburg Testimonial Committee, 1937.
Greenbaum, Masha. *The Jews of Lithuania: A History of a Remarkable Community, 1316–1945.* Jerusalem: Gefen, 1995.
Grodzenski, A. I., ed. *Vilner almanakh* (Vilna Almanac). Vilna: Ovnt-kuryer, 1939; Reprint: Brooklyn, N.Y.: Moriah Offset Co., 1992.
Gross, Nachum, ed. *Economic History of the Jews.* New York: Schocken, 1975.
Gutman, Yisrael, Ezra Mendelsohn, Jehuda Reinharz, eds. *The Jews of Poland between Two World Wars.* Hanover, N.H., and London: University Press of New England, 1989.
Hanson, Victor David. *Fields Without Dreams: Defending the Agrarian Idea.* New York: Free Press, 1996.
Hasomir's Sangbog (Hasomir's Songbook). Copenhagen: Hasomir, 1937.
Hershberg, A. Sh. *Pinkes Byalistok* (A Chronicle of Białystok). 2 vols. New York: Bialystok Jewish Historical Association, 1949.
Hertz, Jacob Sholem, ed. *Doyres bundistn* (Generations of Bundists). 3 vols. New York: Unzer Tsait, 1956.
Hirschbein, Peretz. "Miriam." *Ha-Zeman* (Vilna), nos. 1–4 (1905): 1–25, 161–69, 415–22.
———. *In gang fun lebn: zikhroynes* (In the Course of Life: Memoirs). New York: CYCO, 1948.
Howe, Irving, Ruth R. Wisse, and Khone Shmeruk, eds. *The Penguin Book of Modern Yiddish Verse.* New York: Viking Penguin, 1987.
Hurwicz, Samuel. *30 yor bay der antviklung un organizirung fun dem yidishn hantverker in Vilne* (Thirty Years of Developing and Organizing the Jewish Artisan in Vilna). Vilna: Central Union of the Jewish Craftsman in Vilna, 1933.
Hurwitz-Zalkes, S. *Zikhroynes vegn der nayer yidiser shul* (Reminiscences about the New Yiddish School). New York: R. I. Novak, 1950.
Istoriia Grazhdanskoi Voiny v SSSR (History of the Civil War in the U.S.S.R.). 3 vols. Moscow: Gosudarstvennoe Izdatel'stvo Politicheskoi Literatury, 1957.
Jaszunski, Joseph. "Di yidishe prese zint 1917 biz 1919 in Rusland" (The Yiddish Press between 1917 and 1919 in Russia). In *Bikher-velt* 1–4 (1922).
Jeshurin, Ephim H., ed. *Vilne: a zamlbukh gevidmet der shtot Vilne* (Vilna: A Book Dedicated to the City of Vilna). New York: Workmen's Circle Vilna Branch 367, 1935.
Jeske-Choinski, Teodor. *Historja Żydów w Polsce* (History of the Jews in Poland). Warsaw: Gebethner and Wolff, 1919.
Jewish Folklore and Ethnography Review 9, no. 1 (1987).
Die Judenpogrome in Russland (The Jewish Pogroms in Russia). 2 vols. Cologne and Leipzig: Jüdischer Verlag, 1910.
Kaczerginski, Szmerke. *Khurbn Vilne* (Destruction of Vilna). New York: CYCO, 1947.

Kadushin, I. *Geografisher atlas* (Geographical Atlas). Edited by Hirsz Abramowicz, E. J. Goldschmidt and I. Zavels. Vilna: Tsisho, 1922.

Kagan, Berl. *Yidishe shtet, shtetlekh un dorfishe yishuvim in Lite* (Jewish Cities, Towns and Villages in Lithuania). New York[: Berl Kagan], 1991.

Kahan, Arcadius. *Essays in Jewish Social and Economic History*. Chicago: University of Chicago Press, 1986.

Kassow, Samuel. "Jewish Communal Politics in Transition: The Vilna *Kehile*, 1919–1920." *YIVO Annual* 20 (1991): 61–92.

Kazdan, Ch. Sh., ed. *Lerer-yisker-bukh* (Teachers Memorial Book). New York: Committee to Commemorate Teachers of the TsIShO Schools in Poland who Perished [during the Holocaust], 1952–54.

Klier, John D., and Shlomo Lambroza. *Pogroms: Anti-Jewish Violence in Modern Russian History*. Cambridge: Cambridge University Press, 1992.

Korzec, Paweł. "Antisemitism in Poland as an Intellectual, Social and Political Movement." *Studies on Polish Jewry 1919–1939*. Edited by Joshua A. Fishman. New York: YIVO Institute for Jewish Research, 1974, 12*–104*.

Krinsky, Carol Herselle. *Synagogues of Europe: Architecture, History, Meaning*. New York: Architectural History Foundation; Cambridge: MIT Press, 1985.

Kvutsat shirim (Collection of Songs; Contains Zion- and Folksongs with Music). New York: Hebrew Publishing Co., 1915.

Leksikon fun der nayer yidisher literatur (Biographical Dictionary of Modern Yiddish Literature), vols. 1–8. New York: Congress for Jewish Culture, 1956–81.

Lichtenstein, Kalman, ed. *Pinkas Slonim* (Chronicle of Słonim). 4. vols. Tel Aviv: Association of Slonim Jews in Israel, 1962–79.

Liptzin, Sol. *A History of Yiddish Literature*. Middle Village, N.Y.: Jonathan David Publishers, 1985.

Lunski, Khaykl. *Fun vilner geto: geshtaltn un bilder, geshribn in shvere tsaytn* (From the Vilna Ghetto: Images and Scenes, Written during Difficult Times). Vilna: Fareyn fun di yidishe literatn un zhurnalistn in Vilne, 1920.

Maimon, Solomon. *Solomon Maimon: An Autobiography*. Edited by Moses Hadas. New York: Schocken, 1947.

Manger, Itsik, Jonas Turkow and Moshe Perenson, eds. *Yidisher teater in Eyrope: Poyln* (Yiddish Theater in Europe: Poland). New York: World Congress for Yiddish Culture, 1968.

Matz, Hirsz. *Dr. Tsemakh Shabad* (Dr. Cemach Szabad). Warsaw: TOZ, 1937.

Melshin, L. (Petr Filipovich Iakubovich). "V Mire Otverzhennykh . . ." (In the World of Outcasts: Notes of a Former Labor Camp Inmate). In *Russkoe Bogatstvo* (Moscow–St. Petersburg), 1895–98.

Miasta Polskie w Tysiącleciu (Polish Cities in the Millenium). 2 vols. Wrocław: Zakład Narodowy im Ossolińskich, 1965.

Miron, Dan. *A Traveler Disguised: A Study in the Rise of Modern Yiddish Fiction in the Nineteenth Century*. New York: Schocken, 1973.

Nadler, Allan L. *The Faith of the Mithnagdim: Rabbinic Responses to Hasidic Rapture*. Baltimore: Johns Hopkins University Press, 1997.

Opalski, Magdalena. *The Jewish Tavern-Keeper and His Tavern in Nineteenth-Century Polish Literature*. Vol. 2 of *Studies on Polish Jewry*. Jerusalem: Zalman Shazar Center for the Furtherance of the Study of Jewish History, 1988.

Peretz, I. L. *The I. L. Peretz Reader*. Edited by Ruth R. Wisse. New York: Schocken, 1990.

Bibliography

Pinson, Koppel. *Modern Germany.* 2nd ed. New York: Macmillan, 1966.

Plekhanov, Georgii Valentinovich. *Nashi Raznoglasiia* (Our Differences). Geneva: Tip. Gruppy Osvobozhdenie Truda, 1884.

Rabinowitsch, Wolf (Zeev), ed. *Pinsk . . . History of the Jews of Pinsk 1506–1941.* Tel-Aviv-Haifa: Association of Jews of Pinsk in Israel, 1973.

Radkey, Oliver Henry. *The Election to the Russian Constituent Assembly 1917.* Cambridge: Harvard University Press, 1950.

Ran, Leizer, ed. *Jerusalem of Lithuania: Illustrated and Documented.* 3 vols. New York: Vilna Album Committee, 1971.

Reicherson, Moshe Hacohen, ed. *Maslel bedikduk lashon ha-kodesh* (Path to the Grammar of the Holy Tongue). Vilna: Finn, Rosenkrantz, and Schriftsetzer, 1879.

Reinharz, Jehuda. *Chaim Weizmann: The Making of a Zionist Leader.* Oxford: Oxford University Press, 1985.

Reisen, Zalmen, ed. *Pinkes far der geshikhte fun Vilne in di yorn fun milkhome un okupatsye* (Register for the History of Vilna in the Years of War and Occupation). Vilna: S. Ansky Historical-Ethnographic Society, 1922.

Reisen, Zalmen. *Leksikon fun der yidisher literatur un prese* (Lexicon of Yiddish Literature and Press). Edited by Sh. Niger. Warsaw: Central, 1914.

———. *Leksikon fun der yidisher literatur, prese un filologye* (Lexicon of Yiddish Literature, Press and Philology). 2nd rev. ed. 4 vols. Vilna: B. Kleckin, 1926–29.

Roskies, Diane. "Alphabet Instruction in the East European Heder: Some Comparative and Historical Notes." *YIVO Annual of Jewish Social Science* 17 (1978): 21–53.

Rubin, Ruth. *Voices of a People: The Story of Yiddish Folksongs.* 2nd ed. New York: McGraw-Hill, 1973.

Sandrow, Nahma. *Vagabond Stars.* New York: Harper and Row, 1977.

Schmuhl, Hans Walter. *Rassenhygiene, Nationalismus, Euthanasie: von der Verhütung zur Vernichtung "lebensunwerten Lebens," 1880–1945* (Racial Health, Nationalism, Euthanasia: From the Protection to the Annihilation of "Lives Not Worthy of Life," 1880–1945). Göttingen: Vanenjek und Ruprecht, 1987.

Shalit, Moshe, ed. *Di ekonomishe lage fun di yidn in poyln un di yidishe kooperatsye* (The Economic Situation of the Jews in Poland and the Jewish Cooperative Movement). Vilna: Association of Jewish Cooperative Societies in Poland, 1926.

———. *Oyf di khurves fun milkhomes un mehumes* (On the Ruins of Wars and Turmoil). Vilna: EKOPO, 1931.

Shapiro, Leon. *The History of ORT: A Jewish Movement for Social Change.* New York: Schocken, 1980.

Sholem Aleichem. *Inside Kasrilevke.* New York: Schocken, 1965.

———. *Tevye the Dairyman and the Railroad Stories.* Translated by Hillel Halkin. New York: Schocken, 1987.

Shtern, Yekhiel. "A *Kheyder* in Tyszowce." *YIVO Annual of Jewish Social Science* 5 (1950): 152–71.

Shul-pinkes: finf yor arbet fun tsentraln bildungs-komitet, 1919–1924 (School Chronicle: Five Years of Activities of the Central Education Committee, 1919–1924). Vilna: Ts.B.K. [Tsentraler bildungs-komitet], 1924.

Stanislawski, Michael. *Tsar Nicholas I and the Jews: The Transformation of Jewish Society in Russia 1825–1855.* Philadelphia: Jewish Publication Society, 1983.

———. *For Whom Do I Toil?: Judah Leib Gordon and the Crisis of Russian Jewry.* New York: Oxford University Press, 1988.

Stasov, Vladimir Vasil'evich. *Mark Matveevich Antokolskii: ego zhizn', tvoreniia, pis'ma i stat'i* (Mark Matveevich Antokolsky: His Life, Work, Letters and Articles). 2 vols. St. Petersburg and Moscow: M. O. Volf, 1905.

Stawicki, Piotr. *Słownik Biograficzny Generałów Wojska Polskiego 1918–1939* (Biographical Dictionary of Generals of the Polish Military 1918–1939). Warsaw: Bellona, 1994.

Steinberg, Joshua. *Mishle Yehoshu'a le-ha'ir or la-yesharim* . . . (Joshua's Proverbs: Anthology for the Mind and for the Heart . . .). 2nd enl. ed. Vilna: Widow and Brothers Romm, 1871 [1861].

———. *Otsar milim russi . . . meturgam ivrit ve-ashkenazit.* (Russian-Hebrew-German Dictionary). 20th ed. Vilna: I. Pirozhnikov, 1903 [1880].

———. *Mishpat ha-urim: otsar ha milim le-mikra'e ha-kodesh . . . meturgam russit ve-ashkenazit* (Judgement of the Urim: Hebrew-German-Russian Lexicon to the Bible). 8th ed. Vilna: I. Pirozhnikov, 1902 [1896].

Sudarsky, Mendl, et al., eds. *Lite* (Lithuania). New York: Jewish-Lithuanian Cultural Society "Lite," 1951.

Szabad, Cemach. *Oytobiografye* (Autobiography). Vilna: YIVO, 1935.

Szabad, Cemach, ed. *Vilner zamlbikher* (Vilna Anthologies). Vols. 1–2. Vilna, 1916–17.

Tobias, Henry J. *The Jewish Bund in Russia from Its Origins to 1905.* Stanford, Calif.: Stanford University Press, 1972.

Tsunzer, Elyokum. *Elyokum Tsunzers verk* (The Works of Eliakum Zunser). 2 vols. Edited by Mordkhe Schaechter. New York: YIVO Institute for Jewish Research, 1964.

Vishniac, Mark. *Vserossiiskoe Uchreditel'noe Sobranie* (All-Russian Constitutional Assembly). Paris: Sovremennye Zapiski, 1932.

Vorobeichic, M. *Ein Ghetto im Osten: Vilna 65 Bilder von M. Vorobeichic* (The Ghetto Lane in Vilna: 65 Pictures by M. Vorobeichic). Berlin: Edition Hentrich, Frolich, and Kaufman, 1984 [1931].

Weiter, A. *Ksovim* (Writings). Edited by E. J. Goldschmidt. Vilna, B. A. Kleckin, 1923.

Wejtko, Władysław. *Samoobrona Litwy i Białorusi* (Self-Defense in Lithuania and Belorussia). Warsaw: Warszawska Oficyna Wydawnicza Gryf, 1992.

Westwood, J. N. *Endurance and Endeavor: Russian History 1812–1992.* 4th ed. Oxford: Oxford University Press, 1993.

Wilensky, Mordechai. "Hasidic-Mitnaggedic Polemics in the Jewish Communities of Eastern Europe: The Hostile Phase." In *Essential Papers on Hasidism,* edited by Gershon Hundert, 244–71. New York: New York University Press, 1991.

"The Wilno Problem." *The Cambridge History of Poland.* Vol. 2: From Augustus II to Piłsudski. New York: Octagon Books, 1971, 530–34.

Wirszubski, Abraham. "Community Care of Mentally Sick in the Vilna Region" (Polish). *Nowiny Lekarskie* (Poznań) 39, no. 2 (1927): 30–31.

Wygodzki, Jacob. *In shturem* (In the Storm). Vilna: Kleckin, 1926.

———. *In gehenem* (In Hell). Vilna: Kleckin, 1927.

———. *In Sambatyen.* Vilna: Kleckin, 1931.

Zborowski, Mark and Elizabeth Herzog. *Life is with People: The Culture of the Shtetl.* Foreword by Margaret Mead, Introduction by Barbara Kirshenblatt-Gimblett. New York: Schocken, 1995 [1952].

Zederbaum, Alexander [pseud: Erez]. "Mamlekhet kohanim." *Ha-Melitz* 6, no. 44 (17 November 1866): 667–68.

Zeitlin, Aaron. "Ahad un Antokolsky" (Ahad and Antokolsky). *Der tog* (New York), 1 May 1959.

INDEX

Aaron, Comrade. *See* Weiter, A.
Abele Posvoler (Abraham ben Abraham Solomon), 263, 340n. 5
Abramovitsh, Sholem Yankev. *See* Mendele
Abramowicz, Abram, 18–19
Abramowicz, Anna Schreiber, 30, 162
Abramowicz, Hirsz, 325; and agricultural school in Wieluciany, 231, 234, 236; April 1919 trip to Vilna region, 209–11; arrest for involvement in Bund, 23; arrest in Vilna May Day demonstrations, 135–39; association with Bund, 21, 23, 143–44, 147–48; and Białystok conference on vocational education, 241–42, 282–83; and Białystok gymnasia, 160–61; birth, 18; and Bolshevik occupation, 209–13; and Bolshevik retreat, 213–16; correspondent for Yiddish newspapers, 28; death, 34; and death of Antokolsky, 256; as educator, 15, 22–23, 27, 147–48; efforts for reinstatement at Gomel', 159–60; and family farm, 19–20; and Freeland League, 21; German lessons with Anna Lifshits, 143, 145; at Gomel' gymnasium, 158–59; heart attack in 1942, 29, 34; interest in Jewish agriculture, 20, 290; interest in Russian culture, 32; interest in writing, 28; and Jewish Teachers Institute, 15; literary manifesto for the post-Holocaust period, 30; loss of position in Yekaterinoslav, 154–55; love of land, 20; OP offer, 129–30; parents, 18, 19, 20–21; photograph of family, 25; photograph with family in Wysoki Dwór, 81; portraits of figures among Vilna Jewry, 30–32; prison experiences in Yekaterinoslav, 23–24, 148–54; refugee in U.S. during WWII, 28–30, 33–34; as regional historian, 34–35; secular education, 22–23; travels, 28–29; on Vilna, 30–31; and Vilna militia, 177–81; and Vilna pogrom, 214, 216–18; and Vilna as a multinational city, 32–33; vocational education work, 27–28, 112; Yiddish geographic atlas, 277–78; Zionism, 21
Abramowicz, Mera (Miriam) Zagor. *See* Zagor, Mera
Abramowicz, Tamara. *See* Gotman, Tamara
Abramowicz, Witold, 273
Abramowicz, Yankev, 81
Abramowicz, Zelig bar Avrom, 18, 209, 211–12, 216–17

367

INDEX

Adam Ha-Kohen. *See* Lebensohn, Abraham Dov
Adar, 53
Adler, Irving (Itskhok Yankev Abramovich), 29
Agrarianism, 287
Agrarian reforms, 337n. 4
Agricultural training, 229–39
Agriculture, 47–51, 72–74, 109–10
Ahad Ha-Am (Asher Ginsberg), 163–64, 165, 343nn. 3, 4 (bottom)
Ahavat Zion (Love of Zion) (Mapu), 119, 340n. 9
Ahiezer ("Kinship is Help"), 269
Alcoholic beverages, 61–63
Aleksandrovsk, 149
Alekseev, General, 294
Alexander II, 118, 251, 258, 301, 343n. 1 (top)
Alexander III, 76, 251, 302, 343n. 1 (top), 350n. 3 (bottom)
Alfes (May Day demonstrator), 139
Algemeyner yidisher arbeter-bund (General Jewish Workers' Union). *See* Bund
Alomis, Sonia, 314, 355n. 1
Alte kloyz (Old Synagogue), 262, 350n. 2
American Jewish Joint Distribution Committee (JDC or "Joint"), 338n. 14, 348n. 6; aid to agricultural school at Wieluciany, 236, 237
American Red Cross, 240
American Relief Administration (ARA), 240, 348n. 1(middle)
Amtsvorsteher (Ger.), 187, 190, 196, 197, 200, 201
Anarchists, 147, 233
Andreev, L., 309
Ansky, S., 28, 263, 268, 318, 323, 349n. 3, 356n. 6
Anti-Semitism, 20; Polish, 26, 317; Russian, 23, 32, 183, 251–52, 337n. 3; in Vilna, 354n. 6; in Wysoki Dwór, 95, 96
Antokolsky, Leontii, 267
Antokolsky, Mark, 251–59, 267, 350n. 2 (bottom); death and funeral, 255–56; design of monument to Alexander II, 251–52, 310; house in Vilna, 252–53; Paris life, 254; Repin's portrait of, 252; sculpture of Catherine II, 254–55

Arbet (Work) (Czernichow), 286
Arendarn (Yid.), 21, 46, 50, 68, 72–75, 82
Arnadski (Russian government spy), 173, 345n. 8
Artistic Industrial Society, 226–27
Association of Jewish Women, 324
Association of Yiddish Writers and Journalists in Vilna, 28, 356n. 6
"Astour," 288
At Twilight (Kulwianski), 267
Av, 55, 336n. 5
Avigdor, Samuel ben, 350n. 5
Ayzele Harif of Słonim, Reb (Reb Joshua Isaac Shapira), 263, 350n. 5
Azro, A., 314, 355n. 1

Badkhn (Yid.), 87
Baginen (journal), 289
Baliasny, Vice-Governor, 141
Banditry, during German occupation, 205–8, 210–11, 212, 233
Baranowicze, EKOPO committee in region of, 323
Barrel making, 225
Barter, 71
"Basket women," 304
Bassin, Moshe, 148, 342n. 1 (bottom)
Bastomski, Sh[loyme], 288, 315, 353n. 5
Bathhouses, 84, 89
Bay nakht oyfn altn mark (At Night in the Old Market Place) (Peretz), 344n. 11
Bebel, August, 145, 342n. 4
Beilis, Mendl, 292, 353n. 1 (bottom)
Beilis, Shlomo, 325
Belaia Tserkov, 345n. 7; "Georgia," 171
Belorussia, 11, 147; Jewish farmers in, 229; relations between Jews and non-Jews, 61
Belorussian Soviet Socialist Republic, 16
Belorussian-Yiddish expressions, 69
"Ben Chaim." *See* Jaszunski, Joseph
Benjacob, Isaac, 347n. 2 (top)
Ben-Zion, S. (Simhah Alter Guttmann), 165, 344n. 8
Ber, Mrs., 222
Bercovich, Liza, 127
Berman, I. M., 226
Bernstein, A., 121, 340n. 14
Bernstein, Eduard, 342n. 2 (middle); Bernsteinism ("revisionism"), 144, 169

368

Index

Bernstein, M., 66
Bernstein-Sinaeff, Leopold, 265, 350n. 2 (bottom)
Bestuzhev courses, 210, 346n. 2
Białystok, 240; conference on Jewish vocational education, 240–42, 282–83; gymnasium, 159, 161; industrial productivity, 240; Jews of, 159; "Nowolipie" (New Linden Street), 241; *rabiners* of, 117–18
Białystok Vocational School, 27, 241–42
Bialik, Hayyim Nahman, 163, 164–65, 167–68, 343n. 2 (bottom)
Bibliography, Jewish, 261
Di bikher-velt (journal), 281
Biletsky (minister of the interior), 160
BILU, 322, 356n. 2
Birobidzhan, 246
Black Hundreds, 154, 158, 166, 304
Blacksmiths, 43–44
Blood libel, 201, 346n. 5
Boke (Antokolsky), 258
Bolotin (engineer), 222
Bolshevik-Lithuanian front, 211, 212–13
Bolsheviks, 207, 210, 211, 212, 214–15, 347n. 4 (bottom); bandits, 207; defeat by Poles, 235; defeat of Polish forces in Vilna, 233; programs for children, 213
"Bontshe the Silent," 165
Botvinik (May Day demonstrator), 135
Bramson, Leon, 281, 283, 352n. 2 (top)
Brasław, fishing in, 52
Braz, Rabbi, 334n. 13
Bream, 53
Bribes, 76, 95, 195
Brockhaus-Efron Encyclopedias, 282
Broides, Y., 263
Broido, Alexander, 223
Bronzburg (school administrator), 222
Broz, Hana, 309
Brumberg, Arye ("Ari"), 143, 144, 145, 146
Brustein, *Rabiner,* 156–57
Brześć, 11
Budushchnosť (journal), 281
Bund (General Jewish Workers' Union), 21, 30, 169, 306, 334n. 9; activities in Vilna, 14–15, 23, 143–44; Central Committee, 148; commitment to Yiddish, 125; defined, 327; ideology, 172, 354n. 5; influence of Kahan-Wirgili on, 276; May Day demonstration in Vilna, 133–35; in Pale of Settlement, 171, 223; in Poland, 269; protest of von Wahl as Vilna governor, 132; in Ukraine, 147–48
Burenin, Victor Petrovich, 252, 349n. 2
"Burevestnik" (The Storm Warning) (Gor'kii), 308–9
Burial, under Jewish law, 338n. 13
Burial society, 91
Butrymańce, 110, 201
Butter making, 51
Butter tax, 190

Calends, 55
Calfskins, 71
Caro, Joseph, 350n. 1 (bottom)
Carpenters, 46, 81, 272
Casso (minister of education), 158
Catherine II, sculpture of, 254–55
Catholicism, 224
Catholic press, 236
Caucasus, 128
Cemeteries, German, 204, 205
Censorship, 120–21
CENTOS (Society for the Care of Orphans), 324, 356n. 8
Central Association of Polish Jews in Argentina, 36
Central Education Committee, Vilna, 300, 354n. 2 (top)
Central Yiddish School Organization (TsIShO), 30, 277
Charney, Daniel, 288, 353n. 6
Charney, Samuel. *See* Niger, Samuel
Cheese making, 51
Chekhov, Anton, 255–56, 309
Chemerinsky, Khayim (Mordkhele), 165, 344n. 7
Children, Bolshevik programs for, 213
Chmielnicki, Bohdan, 345n. 7
Christian cooperatives, 94
Christian Democrats, 338n. 16
Chronicle of Vilna in the Years of War and Occupation (Reisen), 263
Chwolson, Daniel, 123, 341n. 21
Citron, S. L., 314, 316, 318, 323, 355n. 1

369

INDEX

Ha-Cohen, Mordecai ben Hillel, 276
Colonial Bank, 170
Compulsory Sunday laws, 304
Constanța, *Potemkin* in, 145
Constitutional Democratic Party. *See* Kadets
Conversion, 65–66; of Steinberg's son, 122
Cooperatives, 45–46, 76, 269–70, 321, 324
Coopers, 225
Cossacks, 178, 183, 184, 345n. 7
Council of Four Lands *(Va'ad Arba Aratsot)*, 12
Council of Lithuanian Jewish Communities *(Va'ad Medinat Lita)*, 11–12
Courland, 18, 122
Czernichow (Danieli), Joseph, 21, 278, 285–88, 289, 303, 317
Czernichow, Michael, 288, 289
Czernichow, Rachel, 288
Czersk prison camp, 303, 304

Dairy workers, 50–51
Dances, 87, 98
Danzig, Abraham ben Jehiel Michael (Hayye Adam), 263, 350n. 5
Datnów, hometown of Isaac Rubinstein, 293
"Dawn of Practical Yiddishism, The" (Abramowicz), 32
Deksznie: "home cure," 20, 110–13
"Delousing centers," 203
Destruction of Vilna (Kaczerginski), 264, 290
Diaspora nationalism, 334n. 9, 354n. 5, 356n. 4
Dick, Isaac Meir, 223, 347n. 1 (top)
Dictionaries, 119, 123
Diet. *See* Lithuanian Jewish community—Diet
Disease, during German occupation, 203–4
Distilleries, 62–63
Dmowski, Roman, 351n. 6 (bottom)
Dolitski, M., 121
Domestic service, 72
Dowry, 86
Drivers, 59–60
Druyanow, Alter, 166, 344n. 9
Dubnow, Simon, 166–67, 298, 344n. 12
Dukszty, fishnets made in, 57

Dvinsk, 215
Dybbuk, The (Ansky), 28, 318, 323, 356n. 6

East European Jews, 10, 26
Economic self-help, 15
The Economic Situation of Jews in Poland and the Jewish Cooperative Movement (Shalit), 325
Education: agricultural, 230–40, 295; under German occupation, 203; *heders*, 68, 75, 92, 302; private Jewish gymnasia, 158; progymnasia, 92; real gymnasia, 281, 283, 288; of rural children, 75; in tsarist Russia, 21–22, 124–25, 127–31, 158; vocational, 15, 26, 27–28, 221–28, 240–48, 266–67, 282–83; in Wysoki Dwór, 92; yeshiva, 12, 92, 122, 340n. 18; Yiddish schools in Vilna, 32, 299, 300, 315–16
Eichler (city commander of Vilna), 303
Einstein, Albert: theory of relativity, 281
Eisenstadt, Rabbi Moses Eliezer, 292, 353n. 1 (bottom)
EKOPO, 91, 237, 299, 303, 321, 323–25, 338n. 14, 356n. 8
EKOPO bank, Vilna, 146
Elijah of Vilna, Rabbi (Vilna Gaon), 12–13, 223, 256, 264, 349n. 6
Embroidery, 227
Emigration, 89, 324
Engravers, 265–66, 272
En Ya'akov (Ibn-Haviv), 265, 350n. 1 (bottom)
The Essence of Mathematics (Jaszunski, trans.), 282
Evil eye, 56–57, 90
Ewzerow, Mordecai/Motl, 324, 325
Exorcism, 90
Externs, 119, 340n. 7
Eyruv (Heb.), 68, 337n. 15
Ezras-ahim ("Brotherly Help"), 269

Fairs, 50
Farshvundene geshtaltn: zikhroynes un siluetn (Vanished Figures: Memoirs and Silhouettes) (Abramowicz), 10, 36
Feather plucking, 103
February revolution, 285
Feigin, Louis, 311–12

370

Index

Feinberg (May Day demonstrator), 135
Feldsher(in) (Yid.), 90, 97, 203
Fialkov, Chaim, 22; command of Hebrew, 127; as school inspector for OP, 128–29, 130–31; study in Switzerland, 127; as teacher in Nikolayev, 127; at Vilna Teachers Institute, 126–27
Fichman, Nehemiah, 148, 149, 150
Fire brigades, 205
Fishermen, 53–57
Fish merchants, 52–58
Fishing cooperatives, 58
Fishing industry, 52–58
Fishmongers, 57, 58
Fish supply, management of during German occupation, 192–94
Folkist-Democratic Party. See *Folkspartey*
Folksgezunt (journal), 298
Folksongs, 103
Folkspartey (Jewish People's Party, Folkist-Democratic Party), 287, 298, 344n. 12
Di folkstsaytung (newspaper), 148, 276
Folkstsaytung (Naye) (newspaper), 280, 281
Folk un land (Shalit), 322
Food. See Lithuanian Jewish community—DIET
Foresters *(Förster)*, 196–97
Forests, reduction of during German occupation, 197
For Whom Do I Toil? (Gordon), 119
Frankenfeld, B., 166
Die Frau und der Sozialismus (Woman and Socialism) (Bebel), 145
Der frayer gedank (journal), 287
Fraye shriftn (journal), 289, 353n. 1 (bottom)
Der fraynd (newspaper), 162, 265, 281, 282
Freeland League, 21, 34, 287, 289–90, 320, 352, 352n. 3 (bottom)
Free loan societies, 324
Frenkel, Lev, 222, 223, 226–27, 267, 268
Friends of Jewish Antiquities, 349n. 3
Frimorgn (newspaper), 28, 254
From the Vilna Ghetto: Written during Bad Times (Lunski), 263
Frug, Shimen, 351n. 5 (top)

Fuenn, B., 224–25
Fuenn, Samuel Joseph, 16–17, 117, 223–24, 260, 293, 339n. 2 (bottom)
Fun noentn over (journal), 325
Fun yor tsu yor (annual), 325
Fur, 272

Galpern (Privy Counselor, Ministry of Justice), 128
Gaon of Vilna. See Elijah of Vilna, Rabbi (Vilna Gaon)
Gardeners, 47–48
Gardens, 47–48, 103–4
Geese, 71
Gefilte fish, 55
Gendarmes, German, 196, 200
General Association of Polish Journalists, 326
The General History of Philosophy (Jaszunski, trans.), 282
General Jewish Workers' Union (Algemeyner yidisher arbeter-bund). See Bund
General Zionists. See Zionism
Genichesk, 292, 293
German Social Democratic Labor Party, 342n. 4
German Tenth Army, 230
Germany, occupation of Lithuania. See Lithuania, German occupation
Gessen, Iosif Vladimirovich, 281, 352n. 3 (top)
Gestapo, 301, 354n. 1 (middle)
Getselter (school administrator), 127
Getz, Fayvl Bentselevich, 144
Ginsberg, Asher. See Ahad Ha-Am
Głębokie, 326, 350n. 5
Goldberg, Boris, 322
Goldberg, Grigory Abramovich, 129
Goldberg, I. L., 224
Di goldene keyt (The Golden Chain) (Peretz), 344n. 14
Goldschmidt, E. J., 277, 325
Golts-Miller, Ivan Ivanovich, 355n. 3 (top)
Gomel', 23, 129, 130; "Ditch," 171; gymnasium, 158, 160
Gordon, Abraham, 266
Gordon, Adolf, 222, 267
Gordon, Judah Leib, 119, 340n. 10

371

INDEX

Gor'kii, Maxim, 121, 308, 309
Gotman, Tamara, 30, 34
Gottlober, Abraham Baer, 117, 339n. 2 (bottom)
Gozhanski, Samuel Isakovich ("Lonu"), 22, 124–25, 341n. 1 (top)
Grabski, Władysław, 271, 351n. 3
Grade, Chaim, 317
Grajewo, nets imported via, 58
"Grandfather of Yiddish literature" (Mendele), 163
Great Synagogue, Vilna, 293, 350n. 2 (top)
Grilikhes, Abraham, 265–66, 350n. 3 (bottom)
Grilikhes, Avenir, 350n. 3 (bottom)
Grishkes (Rus.), 61
Grodno, 11, 41, 281, 286
Grodno gymnasium, 281
Grodzenski, A. I., 325, 326
Grodzinski, Haim Ozer, 324
Groyse shul. *See* Great Synagogue
Gruenbaum, Y., 239
Guensburg, M. A., 223
Guenzburg, Baron David, 22, 129–30, 341n. 7
Guenzburg, Il'ia Iakovlevich, 265, 350n. 2 (bottom)
"Guild law," 275
Gunzburg, Mordecai-Aaron, 347n. 1 (top)
Gurevich, Saveli, 308
Gurewicz, Sofia Markovna, 245, 348n. 1 (bottom)
Gurovich, Anatolii Saadievich, 158–59, 160–61
Gurwicz, Leizer, 309
Gymnasia, 130, 158–59, 160–61, 281
"Gypsies," 102

Haftarah (Heb.-Yid.), 68
Haggadah (Heb.-Yid.), 69
Halakhah (Heb.-Yid.), 165
Halpern, Leivick. *See* Leivick, H.
Halutz(im) (Heb.), 93, 229, 236, 320
Hartglas, A., 239
Harvests, 74
Haskalah (Jewish Enlightenment), 13, 16, 258, 264, 298, 302, 353n. 3 (bottom); father of the, 354n. 3 (bottom); Lithuanian, 339n. 2 (bottom); Vilna as center of in Lithuania, 21; and vocationalism, 280. *See also* Hevrat Mefitsei Haskalah (Society of the Dissemination of Enlightenment among the Jews of Russia—OP)
Haskalah literature, 262, 302, 341n. 3
Hawks, 287, 352n. 3
Haynt (newspaper), 304
Hayye Adam (Life of Man) (Danzig), 13, 350n. 5
Hayyim, Rabbi, 12
Hebrew Immigrant Aid Society (HIAS), 228, 314, 347n. 5
Heder (Yid.), 68, 75, 92, 302
Heimat (Magda) (Sudermann), 342n. 2 (top)
Help Through Work, 27, 221–28, 267, 270, 300, 324–25; conferences of vocational schools, 226, 228; emigration offices, 228; exhibition of 1920, 272–73; founding of, 223, 224–25; goal of, 226; school for tailors, 227; school of needle trades, 226, 227; and vocational school conference in Białystok, 241; and Wieluciany agricultural school, 230, 231, 232, 235, 236–37, 238–39, 295
Herzl, Theodor, 170, 344n. 5
Hevrat Mefitsei Haskalah (Society for the Dissemination of Enlightenment among the Jews of Russia—OP), 15, 22, 128, 129, 341n. 3; orphanages for Jewish refugees, 131; St. Petersburg committee, 129–30; Vilna branch, 299, 315, 316, 323
High Holy Days, 68; synagogue attendance, 75
Hilfsverein der Deutschen Juden, 230, 347n. 1 (bottom)
Hirsch, Baron Maurice de, 339n. 2 (top)
Hirschbein, Peretz, 120–21, 340n. 11
Hitler, Adolf, 283, 284, 296
Hoover, Herbert, 348n. 1 (top)
Horses, 82; requisitioning of by occupying Germans, 191
Horse traders, 67
Hospitals, 203
Humorous anecdotes and songs: about "gourmets," 59, 99, 101; about housewives, 100; about inns, 64, 65; about non-conforming Jews, 66–67;

about townspeople, 70; about village Jews, 68–70, 83, 99; other, 51, 57
"Hunger and High Prices in Vilna during the German Occupation" (Lunski), 263
Hurwicz, Samuel, 28, 227, 265–68, 270
Hygiene, 84

I. L. Peretz School (Vilna), 299
Iakubovich, P. (L. Melshin), 153
Ibn-Haviv, Jacob, 350n. 1 (bottom)
The Image of the World According to the Theory of Relativity (Schmidt), 281
"Images of a Lost World" (Abramowicz), 30
Industrial Art Society, 267
In gehenem (In Hell) (Wygodzki), 304
Innkeepers, 60, 76; leasing of inns, 61; observance of Sabbath, 62; piety and honesty, 67; propination system, 61–62; relations with non-Jewish community, 70; and whiskey inspectors, 62
Inns: construction and amenities, 63–64; number of, 60–61; parties at, 65; role in the history of transportation, 60; stables, 63–64
Inquisition (Antokolsky), 258
In Sambatyon (Wygodzki), 304–5
In shturem (In the Storm) (Wygodzki), 304
Intermarriage, 65
"In the Snakes' Nest" (Dolitski), 121
In the World of Outcasts (Melshin), 153
Iuzovka, pogrom in, 152–53
Ivan the Terrible (Antokolsky), 251, 257, 258
Izbicki, Joseph (B. Michalewicz), 351n. 1
Izvestiia Vserossiiskoi po Delam o Vyborakh v Uchreditel'noe Sobranie Kommissii (Bulletin of the All-Russian Electoral Commission), 352n. 4

Jabotinsky, Vladimir (Ze'ev), 170, 172, 344n. 3
Jacob ben Jacob, 225
Jaffe, Leib, 295, 309, 353n. 2 (bottom)
Jagiełło, Grand Duke, 11
Jagodziński (Polish agronomist), 235, 236
Janów, 46, 81
Jaszunski, Joseph, 27–28, 280–84
"Jerusalem of Lithuania," 9, 31, 256, 260, 265, 268

Jewish Agricultural Society, Vilna branch, 300
Jewish Artisans' Union, 270–71
Jewish bibliography, 261
Jewish Colonial Trust, 344n. 5
Jewish Colonization Association (JCA), 26, 109, 112, 236, 282, 339n. 2 (top); aid to farmers, 229; emigration offices, 228; joint vocational conventions with ORT, 278, 283; support for Jewish vocational education in Poland, 242, 246; vocational school conferences with Help Through Work, 226, 266; vocational training programs for Jews in Russia, 221–22, 227
Jewish Daily Forward, 122
Jewish diaspora nationalism, 334n. 9, 354n. 5, 356n. 4
Jewish economic self-help, 15
Jewish Enlightenment. *See Haskalah* (Jewish Enlightenment)
Jewish Historical-Ethnographic Society of Lithuania and Belorussia, 349n. 3
Jewish Journalists' Syndicate of Warsaw, 326
Jewish Labor Bund (Poland): socialist artisans' section, 269
Jewish Legion, 344n. 3
Jewish Mutual Credit Society, 160
Jewish People's Party. *See Folkspartey*
Jewish Relief Committee for War Victims. *See* EKOPO
Jewish religious law: burial, 338n. 13; working on the Sabbath, 347n. 2 (bottom); writing on the Sabbath, 262–63
Jewish Tailor, A (Antokolsky), 258
Jewish Teachers Institute. *See* Vilna Jewish Teachers Institute
Jewje, retreat of Red Army via, 215
Jezno, in Yiddish idiom, 60
Judah ben Eliezer. *See* Yesod, The
Judenrat (Ger.), 275, 284

Kaczerginski, Szmerke, 264, 290, 317
Kadets (Constitutional Democratic Party), 281, 302, 352n. 3 (top)
Kadimah (almanac), 322
Kadison, Leib, 314, 355n. 1

INDEX

Kadushin, I., 277
Kahan, Arcadius, 16
Kahan, Shimshon, 317
Kahan, Sofia Stupel-, 277
Kahan-Wirgili, B., 27–28, 243, 271, 276–79, 281, 282
Kalabanovskii (provincial school administrator), 22–23, 154–56
Kalmanowicz, Z., 318
Kamenetsky, S., 129
Kamichau works, 240
Kantor, Judah Leib, 292, 353n. 1 (bottom)
Kaplanowicz, Don, 314, 316, 355n. 1
Karaites, 18, 41, 48, 130
Kerenki (Rus.), 210, 346n. 1
Kerensky, Alexander, 346n. 1
Kharef (Antokolsky), 258
Kharkov, 22, 285–86
Kharkov, University of, 148, 159
Kherson province, 127, 147
Kiejdany, cultivation of cucumbers in, 48
Kiev, in grand duchy of Lithuania, 10
Kinah (Kinot), 85
Kiryah ne'emanah (Faithful City) (Fuenn), 16–17
Kishinev pogrom, 21, 148, 164, 166, 173, 261, 344n. 10
Klachko, Shepsl, 132–33
Klasn-kamf (Class Struggle), 133
Klausner, Joseph Gedaliah, 163, 165–66, 343n. 3 (bottom)
Klebanov, Abraham (Vilna engineer), 270
Kletzkin, B., 319
Klionsky, Uri, 324
Klooga concentration camp, 248
Korev, Reb. *See* Lewinsky, Elhanan Leib
Korolenko, Vladimir, 299, 309, 354n. 1 (top)
"Kosher Restaurant" (Sholem Aleichem), 336n. 11
Kossakowski, Count, 295
Koszedary district, 193
Kovno, 11, 16, 41, 286; expulsion of Jews in 1915, 294; fall of, 182; fish market of, 57; loggers, 46
"Kovno Lithuania," 334n. 13
Kozłowa-Ruda, slave labor in, 197
Kreinin, Miron Naumovich, 129

Kremenchug, evacuation of Vilna vocational school to, 267
Kremer, Arkady, 243
Kruk, Eliezer, 28, 227, 269–75
Krunciki, World War I atrocity in, 200
Krylov, Ivan, 165, 344n. 7
Kulwianski, A., 267
Kuperstein, Vera Matveevna, 128, 341n. 4
Dvora Kuperstein School, 298
Kvutsah (Heb.), 86

Labor Zionism. *See* Zionism
La Ferme tobacco factory, 132
Lancers, 98
Landsberg, Prussia, nets made by machine in, 58
Landsmanshaftn (Yid.), 34
Landwarów, 201, 210, 217, 290
Lazare, Bernard, 170, 344n. 5
Lazarev, Il'ia, 253, 254
Lazarev-Rakovitsky, Sofia, 254
League of Nations, Cultural Commission, 296
Learned Jew, 223
Lebensohn, Abraham-Dov (Adam Ha-Kohen), 117, 118, 223, 339n. 2 (bottom), 347n. 1 (top)
Lebn (Life) (Shalit), 263, 323
Leivick, H., 288, 353n. 5
Lejbowski, Moshe, 227, 267, 272, 351n. 4
Lejpuny, 20, 110, 111
Lekert, Hirsh, 23, 141–42
Lerer-yisker-bukh (Teachers Memorial Book), 30
Letste nays (newspaper), 230, 316, 323
Levi, Sali, 230–31
Levidov family, 307
Levin, Mendl, 28, 31, 162–63, 165
Levin, Moshe, 317
Levin, Shmarya, 122, 292, 340n. 16, 353n. 1 (bottom)
Levin (Vilna merchant), 160–61
Levinsohn, Isaac Baer, 117, 280, 339n. 2 (bottom)
Levitan, Isaak Il'ich, 167, 344n. 13
Lewin, Chaim, 325
Lewinsky, Elhanan Leib (Reb Korev), 162, 163, 165, 343n. 1 (bottom)
Lexicon of Yiddish Literature, Press, and Philology (Reisen), 319–20

374

Libava, 111, 277
Lichtmacher, Szymon, 270, 351n. 2
Lida, Yeshiva in, 262
Lieberman, Eliezer David, 118, 339n. 4 (bottom)
Liebknecht, Wilhelm, 145, 342n. 4
Lifshits, Anna, 143–46, 342n. 1 (middle)
Lime burners, 44–45
Liquor monopoly, 62, 76, 336n. 9
Literarishe bleter (journal), 281, 323
Lithuania, 10–11; agrarian reforms, 76, 83; Catholicism, 11; Jewish counterculture, 14; German cemeteries, 204, 205; "Golden Age," 11; Grand Duchy of, 10, 11; Haskalah, 21, 339n. 2 (bottom); lakes, 52; national cultural autonomy, 286; partition of, 16; Polish and Russian influence and domination, 11; Talmudic academies, 12–13
Lithuania, German occupation: and agricultural school at Wieluciany, 230–32; assistance to Lithuanians against Bolsheviks, 212–13; banditry during, 205–8; battle with contagious disease, 203–4; child labor, 190, 202; confiscation of millstones, 189; demoralization of occupying forces, 196–97; exploitation of estates and fields, 191–92; extermination of mentally ill, 111; German attitude toward Jews, 201–2; German attitude toward local population, 199–201; Jewish refugees, 183–86; liquidation, 208, 232–33; livestock, confiscation of, 190; management of fish supply, 192–94; occupation of Vilna, 179–81; organization of new authority, 187–88; positive aspects of, 204–5; reduction of forests, 196–97; requisitioning of foodstuffs, 189–91; requisitioning of horses, 191; retreat of Russians, 182–86; schools under, 203, 294–95; slave labor edict, 197–99; smuggling during, 194–96; taking of farm produce from peasants, 187–89; wealthy peasants, 202–3
Lithuanian Jewish community, 295; agricultural colonies in tsarist Russia, 109, 229; conditions of during German occupation, 201–2; divergence from Polish Jews, 11–12; formation of, 10–12; impact of Vilna Gaon on, 12–13; *maskilim,* 14, 15, 21, 22; partition of after World War I, 16; speech patterns, 12; townspeople's ridicule of village people, 69–70; Zionists, 13, 16
———. DIET, 42, 54, 64, 71, 74, 84, 99–108, 110; black rye bread, 99, 104–5; *farfl,* 106; herring, 104; lack of regularity of meals, 84, 99–100; main meal, 99–100; midday meal, 106; pancakes, 105; peas, 106–7; pickled beets and cabbage, 100–101; potatoes, 99, 101–4; Sabbath meals, 84, 107–8; sour soup, 99–100, 106; supper, 106–7
———. RURAL, 20–21, 99; blacksmiths, 43–44; dairy workers, 50–51; decline of, 75–76; distillers, 62–63; drivers, 59–60; education of children, 75; effect on World War I on, 76; efforts to ward off conversion of children, 66; emigration, 76; fisherman, 52–58; gardeners, 47–48; household servants, 72–75; innkeepers, 60–70; lack of education, 68–70; language use, 69; lime burners, 44–45; and liquor monopoly, 76; lumberman and loggers, 46–47; merchants and peddlers, 71–72; millers, 51–52; nonconformists among, 66–67; orchard keepers, 48–50; pitch burners, 45; prayer services, 68; ridicule of town Jews and Yeshiva students, 70; shoemakers, 43; tailors, 42–43; wheelwrights, shinglers, and carpenters, 45–46
"Little Manchester" (Białystok), 27, 240
Litvak(es) (Yid.), 10, 11, 12; image of, 13–14
Der litvisher yid (journal), 29
Locksmiths, 266
Loggers, 46–47
London Social Democratic Conference, 159
"Lonu." *See* Gozhanski, Samuel Isakovich ("Lonu")
Lourie, Grigorii, 171, 345n. 6
Lubocki, Boruch, 274, 316
Ludvipol, Abraham, 165, 344n. 8
Luftmentsh (Yid.), 71, 79, 80

INDEX

Lumbermen, 46–47
Lunski, Hana, 264
Lunski, Khaykl, 17, 260–64, 268, 318
Luria, Rabbi Solomon, 11
Lurie, Joseph, 322, 356n. 3
Lwów, Jewish Agricultural Society headquarters in, 300

Maccabi World Union, 85–86, 338n. 11
Magda (Heimat) (Sudermann), 342n. 2 (top)
Ha-Maggid (newspaper), 118
Maids, 72
Maimon, Solomon, 64, 336n. 10
Majdanek, 30, 162, 248
Makower, Abraham, 237–38, 297
Maksimov (education official), 159
Malakiewicz, Gershon ("the Convict"), 21, 287, 289–91
Malbish erumim ("Clothing the Naked"), 269
Mapu, Abraham, 119, 340n. 9
Margolin, Fayvl, 121, 316, 322, 340n. 13
Markets, 50, 55, 57
Maskil(im) (Heb.-Yid.), 13, 14, 59, 64, 122, 164, 347n. 1 (top); early loyalty to Russian government, 117, 118, 120; of Słonim, 263; view of Yiddish, 203, 346n. 7; of Vilna, 260; workhouses, 223
May Day demonstrations, Vilna, 133–35
Mazeh, Rabbi Jacob, 292, 353n. 1 (bottom)
Medical care in the *shtetl*, 90
Mefitsei Haskalah. See *Hevrat Mefitsei Haskalah* (Society for the Dissemination of Enlightenment among the Jews of Russia) (OP)
Mehring, Franz, 145, 342n. 4
Melamed (melamdim) (Yid.), 70, 75, 81, 91, 92
Ha-Melits (newspaper), 261
Melshin, L. *See* Iakubovich, P.
Menashe ben Joseph of Ilye, 280, 352n. 1 (middle)
Mendele (Mendele Moykher-Sforim), 123, 129, 162, 163, 165, 168, 266, 340n. 20; *The Parasite*, 266, 275
Mendelssohn, Moses, 302, 354n. 3
Mental illness: healing of, 109–13; nature treatment, 20

Mephistopheles (Antokolsky), 258
Merchants, 71
Merezhkovskii, Dmitri Sergeevich, 354n. 2 (bottom)
Michalewicz, B., 270
"Middle Lithuania," 238, 273
Mikhailov, Dr., 137, 140
Mikhailovskii, Nikolai Konstantinovich, 144, 299, 342n. 3, 354n. 1 (top)
Mikvah (Heb.-Yid.), 71, 84, 89
Militias: under German occupation, 177–81; after German withdrawal, 211, 212
Milk quotas, 189–90
Mills and millers, 51–52; during German occupation, 189
Minsk, 11, 286
Minyan (Heb.-Yid.), 46, 68, 82, 262
Miransky, Peretz, 317
Miriam (Hirschbein), 121
The Miser (Antokolsky), 258
Mishlei Yehoshua (Proverbs of Joshua) (Steinberg), 123
Mokrzecki, Stefan, 233, 347n. 4 (bottom)
Moment (newspaper), 304
"Monish" (Peretz), 167, 344n. 12
Montefiore, Claude Joseph Goldsmid, 255, 349n. 5
Mordkhele (Khayim Chemerinsky), 165, 344n. 7
Morevski, Abraham (née Menaker), 305
Motol, home of Weizmann family, 126
Muraviov, Mikhail Nikolaevich, 255, 349n. 4
Murer, Franz, 301, 354n. 1 (middle)
Muromets, Il'ia, 258, 349n. 7

Nabokov, Vladimir Dmitrievich, 281, 352n. 3 (top)
Nadson, Semen Iakovlevich, 252, 349n. 2
Nakhbush, Noah, 314, 355n. 1
Nashi Raznoglasiia (Our Difference) (Plekhanov), 342n. 3
Nasz Przegląd, 304
Nasza Trybuna (journal), 335n. 23
Nathan the Wise (Antokolsky), 258
National Democratic Party (Endecja), 274, 345n. 3, 351n. 6 (bottom)
Natur un kultur (Jaszunski), 281

376

Index

Naye folkstsaytung (newspaper), 280, 281
Dos naye lebn (journal), 322
Nazi Germany, 262, 296
Nazimov, Police Chief, 132, 134
Needle trades, 226, 227
Nets, fishing, 53, 56, 57; machine-made, 58
Neuschul, Arye, 224
New Economic Policy (NEP), 268, 351n. 8
Nikolaevich, Nikolai, 313
Nicholas I, 18, 109, 301, 339n. 1 (top)
Nicholas II, 76, 154, 350n. 3 (bottom)
Nicknames: for Bolsheviks, 215; for Germans, 179, 184, 205, 301; for Jews as "gourmets," 59, 99, 102; for Polish tax collectors, 271, 351n. 3; for Russian officials, 124; in Wysoki Dwór, 85, 96–97
Niemen River, logging on, 46
Niger, Samuel (Charney, Samuel), 295, 309, 318, 353n. 2 (bottom)
Nikolayev, government Jewish school in, 127
Ninth of Av (Tisha b'Av), 47, 85, 103
Nizhnii Novgorod: M. Schreiber in, 244
Nomberg, Hirsz-Dovid, 287
"Northwest Provinces," 11
Novoe Vremia (newspaper), 252, 255–56, 349n. 2
Novoseltses (Rus.), 75–76
Nowogródek, 303, 323

Oberostkommando (Ger.), 303
October Revolution: of 1905, 143, 144, 146; of 1917, 289
Odessa, 13, 143, 144, 162; educational district, 129; Jewish writers, 162–68; "Moldavanka" district, 171
Okun, Israel, 243
Ha-Olam (newspaper), 322
Old Believers, 41
Old Synagogue *(Alte kloyz)*, 262, 350n. 2 (top)
Olkieniki, 110, 112
Olszany, weaving school in, 324
Onikszty, logging in, 46
"Only Tears Can Help Us" (Abramowicz), 29
Opatoshu, Joseph, 287–88, 353n. 5
Opatov, Yudl, 253–54

Opatov-Antokolsky, Genya, 253, 254
Orchard keepers, 48–50
Orphans, 72, 324–25
Orthodox Church, 11
ORT (Society for Manual/Skilled Work), 279, 282–83, 286, 348n. 2 (top); joint vocational conventions with JCA, 278, 283; relief work after World War I, 299; support for Jewish vocational education, 26–27, 242, 243, 245–46, 266, 280; training courses for vocational instructors, 284; in Warsaw Ghetto, 284
Osmolowski, M. S.(?), Chief Commissar, 237
Ostgelt (Bons, or "Eastern money"), 202, 212, 346n. 6
Ostpaß, 197
Ostroumov (director of education in Vilna), 159–61
Outhouses, 204
Ovens, medical functions of, 63
Oyfn shvel (journals), 34
OZE (Society for the Protection of Health of the Jews), 297–98, 299

Pack carriers, 194, 195
Pale of Settlement, 129, 276; Bund activity in, 171, 223; condition of Jews in, 308; Jewish education under Alexander III, 343n. 1 (top); private Jewish gymnasia in, 129
Palmar, 145, 342n. 4
Parasite, The (Mendele), 266, 275
Paris Congress for Yiddish Culture of 1937, 287, 288, 353n. 4
Parnes, Yakov, 253
Participant observation, 24
Passover, 88, 101; meals, 106
Paupers, 90
Pavlograd, 22, 147
Peasants: agreements with blacksmith, 44; Christian holidays, 65; cooperatives, 337n. 4; fishing, 52; footwear, 43; increased standard of living, 76; interdependency with Jewish community, 41–42, 65, 103–4; lack of cultural activity, 61; lime purchases, 44; orchards, 48; production of fishing nets, 57; use of "Jewish waste," 104; use of

377

miller's services, 51–52; wealthy, under German occupation, 202–3
Peddlers, 71–72
People's banks, 324
People's University, 323
Peretz, I. L., 15, 28, 123, 162–68, 340n. 20, 343n. 4 (bottom); address to the Jewish writers, 166–67; Hasidic tales, 164–65
Peter the Great (Antokolsky), 258
Phonetic orthography, Yiddish, 316, 355n. 3 (bottom)
Piłsudski, Józef, 235, 272, 274, 303, 348n. 5, 351n. 6 (bottom)
Piłsudski's Legionnaries, 306, 309
Pińsk, 126, 169; as center of Jewish labor movement, 171; demonstrations of 1903, 173; industrialization, 170–71; Jewish intelligentsia of, 169–70; "Linishches," 171
Pinsky, David, 123, 340n. 20
Pirozhnikov, Isaac, 122, 340n. 17
Pitch burners, 45
Plater, Count, 52, 336n. 4
Plekhanov, Georgii Valentinovich, 144, 342n. 3
Plows, 73
Pludermacher, Gershon, 247, 315, 317, 348n. 2 (bottom)
Poalei Zion (Labor Zionist party), 147, 169, 344n. 1
Podworańce, World War I death sentence in, 200
"Pogrom money," 164n.
Pogroms, 96, 152–53, 158; in Kishinev, 21, 148, 164, 166, 173, 261, 344n. 10; in Mogilev, 154–55; in Vilna (April 19, 1919), 16, 33, 214, 216–18, 235, 272–73, 295, 317, 346n. 4
Poland: anti-Semitism, 201, 317; Belorussian territories of, 286; edict against use of Yiddish in public, 316–17; Jewish artisans' unions in, 271; landed gentry, 72–73; nationalism, 224; occupation of Vilna, 213–14; partitions of, 11, 303, 345n. 3; *Sejm*, 95, 275, 295, 303, 304; Vilna pogrom of April 19, 1919, 16, 33, 214, 216–18, 235, 272–73, 295, 317, 346n. 4
Polish Chamber of Commerce, 274

Polish Commonwealth, 345n. 3
Polish Jews: settlement in Lithuania, 11; view of Lithuanian Jews, 14
Polish Legionnaries, 111, 235, 238, 306, 309, 317, 348n. 5
Polish-Lithuanian Commonwealth, 11
Polish Republic: anti-Semitism, 26; Jewish vocational schools, 240–42
Polish Socialist Party, 23, 351n. 6 (bottom)
Polish-Soviet war, 347n. 4 (bottom), 348n. 5
Polish Tatars, 90, 338n. 12
Political prisoners, 149, 153
Poltava, evacuation of Vilna trade school to, 243
Ponary, 146, 275, 290, 326, 342n. 5
Popilva: slave labor during German occupation, 197–99
Posledniia Izvestiia (newspaper), 144
"Postal service," 253
Postawy, fishing in, 52
Potemkin, mutiny of, 143–44, 145–46
Poznań, Poles from, 201
Pravo (journal), 281, 352n. 3 (top)
Prisoners of war, 205–6
Productivization, 20–21, 221–48, 287, 289–90
Progymnasium, 92
Propination, 61, 62–63
Prussian Junkers, 201
Pulovnik(i) (Rus.), 73
Purim, 307

Quota system, 158

Rabbi and His Pupil, A (Kulwianski), 267
Rabiner(s) (Yid.), 117, 156–57, 292, 293; training, 117, 339n. 1 (bottom)
Racial genocide, 25
Rafts, 46
Railroad strike of 1905, 152
Rationing, during German occupation, 194
Ratner, Arkadii (Azriel), 129, 158, 341n. 5
Ratner gymnasium, 130
Rawnitzki, Yehoshua Hana, 163, 165, 343n. 3 (bottom)
Razsvet (journal), 261, 281, 322
Red Army, 15, 210, 213, 214, 237; defeat in the battle outside Warsaw, 238;

Index

reoccupation of Vilna, 238; retreat from Lithuania, 215–16
Reisen, Abraham, 314, 355n. 2
Reisen, Zalmen, 16, 32, 287, 313–20, 323; *Chronicle of Vilna in the Years of War and Occupation,* 263; a founder of the YIVO Institute, 318–19; as publisher of *Vilner tog,* 317–18; support for Yiddish culture, 288, 314–15; as writer for *Letste nays,* 316
Rekhes (May Day demonstrator), 139
Rennenkampf, Baron, 133
Repin, Il'ia Yefimovich, 251, 349n. 1; portrait of Antokolsky, 252
A Report on National Elections to the Founding Assembly (Jaszunski), 282
Revcoms (revolutionary committees), 212, 234
Revolutionary movements in Tsarist Russia, 306–7
Rickets, 104
Rimsky-Korsakov, Nikolai, 122
"The Role of Teachers in Establishing Normal Relations among Nationalities" (Abramowicz), 33
Romanov dynasty tercentennial, 266
Romm press, 13, 21, 334n. 11
Romny, 277
Rosenbaum, Semion, 314, 355n. 1
Rosenbaum, Yasha, 314
Rosenhaus, Daniel, 309
Rosh Hashanah, 75, 103
Royal Hermitage Museum, 257–58
Rubenchik, Abraham (Aba), 170, 171, 172
Rubinov, Leon Moiseevich, 260, 350n. 1
Rubinstein, Chief Rabbi Isaac, 17, 236, 239, 292–96, 302
Rubinstein, Esther, 294–95
Rudziszki, World War I atrocity in, 200
Rumpl (Yid.), 87
Rural Jewish community. *See* Lithuanian Jewish community—RURAL
Russia: annexation of Lithuania, 11; anti-Semitism, 23, 32, 337n. 3; defeat by Germans, 294; executions of revolutionaries, 157; Jewish colonies in Vilna-Grodno region, 109; Jewish community schools, 21–22, 124–25, 127–31; liberalization of Jewish education system, 158; mutiny of *Potemkin,* 143–44, 145–46; October 1905 revolution, 133, 149, 152–53, 158; oppression of Jews of Vilna, 132–42; prison conditions, 148–53; refugees during World War I, 182–86; retreat from Lithuania, 182–86; retreat from Vilna, 177–79; St. Nicholas Day, 154. *See also* Bolsheviks; Red Army
Russian bandits: in German-occupied Lithuania, 205–8
Russian Duma, 353n. 1 (bottom)
"Russian *habeas corpus,*" 76
Russian Jewish intelligentsia, 255, 258–59, 298–99
Russian Jewish liberalism, 15
Russian Jewish press, 28
Russian Populist Party (*Narodniki*), 144
Russkii Evrei (journal), 261
Russo-Japanese War, 154, 171, 225

S. Ansky Historical-Ethnographic Society, 349n. 3
S. Ansky Museum, 252, 309, 349n. 3
Sabbath, 337n. 15, 338n. 9, 351n. 7 (top); meals, 55, 107–8; observance of among *arendarn,* 74; observance of among innkeepers, 62; prohibition against working on, 347n. 2 (bottom); prohibition against writing on, 262–63; rural peddlers' observance of, 71–72
Sages of Zamut, 295, 353n. 3 (bottom)
"Sakya Muni" (Merezhkovskii), 308, 354n. 2 (bottom)
Samoobrona (Pol.), 15
Sarna (contractor), 244
Sawmills, 46
Schmidt, H., 281
Schmidt, Lieutenant (of *Potemkin*), 145, 146
Schools. *See* Education
School tax, 203
Schreiber, Matthias (Matvei Samoilovich), 24, 27, 243–48, 278; photograph of in 1935, 247
Schreiber, Samuel, 244, 253, 256, 263, 285; funeral, 293; photograph of, 257
Schreiber, Sulamit, 248
Schreiber, Valentina, 248

379

Schulman, Kalman, 223, 347n. 1 (top)
Schwartz (Russian education minister), 158
Seamstresses, 43
Secular Yiddishism, 356n. 4
Seder, 69, 231
Sejm (Pol.), 95, 275, 295, 303, 304
Sejmists, 147, 169
Servants, 72
Seventeenth of Tammuz (Shivah asar b'Tammuz), 47, 103
Sforza, Count, 255
Shalit, Dvoyrele, 326
Shalit, Moshe: communal spirit, 31–32; death, 356n. 10; and EKOPO, 323–25; and *Letste nays,* 316; literary activity, 263, 304, 322–23, 325–26; and museum of Jewish history, 268; and "The Jewish Locale," 314; and Yiddish boys' school, 315, 323
Shapira, Reb Joshua Isaac. *See* Reb Ayzele Harif of Słonim
Shavuot, 51, 88, 105
Shenkerke (female tavernkeeper), 67
Sheva (vowel point), 119, 340n. 9
Shevat, 104
Shimen Frug School, 266, 351n. 5 (top)
Shinglers, 45–46
Shmuel, Reb, 263
Shneour, Zalman, 121, 340n. 12
Shneur Zalman of Lyadi, Rabbi, 12
Shoemaking, 43, 226
Sholem Aleichem, 66, 129, 336nn. 11, 12, 340n. 20
Shreberk, Shloyme, 314, 355n. 1
Shtetl(ekh) (Yid.), 15; as economic basis of East European Jewish life, 77. *See also* Wysoki Dwór
"Shtey oyf, mayn folk" (Arise, My People) (Goldfaden), 103
Shulhan Arukh (Heb.), 265, 350n. 1 (bottom)
Shvarts-tume ("Black Impurity"), 171, 345n. 7
Silberfarb, Moses, 281, 352n. 2 (top)
Šimaite, Anna, 248
Simhat Torah, 68
Singer, Paul, 145, 342n. 4
Skitalets, S., 309
Slaughterers, 78, 81, 107

Slave labor, 197–99, 205
Slonimer vort (newspaper), 350n. 6
"Slushai!" (Listen!) (Goltz-Miller), 308, 355n. 3 (top)
Smallpox vaccination, during World War I, 204
Smigelski, Joseph, 241
Smolenskin, Peretz, 258
Smolny Institute, 132
Smuggling, during German occupation, 194–96
Snipiszki, 142, 307
Snitko (police officer), 136, 137
Sołoki, fishnets made in, 57
Soccer, in Wysoki Dwór, 85–86
Social-Democratic Party, 144, 145
Socialism, 169, 170
Socialist Zionists. *See* Zionism
Social-Revolutionary Party, 244, 289
Society for the Dissemination of Enlightenment among the Jews of Russia (OP). *See Hevrat Mefitsei Haskalah*
Society for the Jewish Deaf and Dumb, 351n. 2
Society for Manual/Skilled Work. *See* ORT
Society for the Protection of Health of the Jews. *See* OZE
Socrates (Antokolsky), 258
Soiuz Russkogo Naroda (Union of the Russian People), 154
"Di sokhe" (the Hook Plow) (Zunser), 103
Songs, multilingual Yiddish-Lithuanian-Belorussian, 42–43
Soup kitchens, 270
Soviet communism, 21
Sparrows, 289, 290
St. Petersburg, 255
St. Petersburg, University of, 244, 281
St. Petersburg Art Academy, 349n. 1
St. Petersburg Institute of Technology, 244
St. Petersburg Medical-Surgical Academy, 302
Stachowicz (gendarme), 200
Stasov, Vladimir Vasil'evich, 251, 256–58, 349n. 1
Steinberg, I. N., 21, 289
Steinberg, Joshua, 22, 254, 293; befriending of Chaim Fialkov, 126–27; as censor, 120–21; evaluation of yeshiva of

Wołożyn, 122; first graduating class of Vilna Rabbinical School, 117; loyalty to tsarist regime, 118, 120–21; marriages, 122; negative assessments of, 117; official uniform, 118–19; portrait, 120; as *rabiner* in Białystok, 117; as *rabiner* in Vilna, 118; scholarly work, 119, 122–23; as teacher, 118–19
Steinberg, Maksimilian Ovseevich, 122, 340n. 15
Steinbok, Katya, 227
Stirrer (fishing tool), 53
"Stolypin's neckerchief," 157
Strashun, Isaac, 260, 263
Strashun, Matthias, 223, 260, 334n. 11
Strashun Library, 21, 260–63, 334n. 11
Strazh, Zalmen, 267–68
Street Vendor, The (Antokolsky), 258
Sudermann, Hermann, 342n. 2 (top)
Sukkot, 88, 100, 237, 290
Sumiliszki, retreat of Red Army via, 215
Sutzkever, Abraham, 317
Suwałki, 41, 238
Święciany, 52, 210
Symbolism, 121
Symbolists, 166
Synagogue caretaker, 81, 92
Synagogue Courtyard *(Shulhoyf),* 262–63, 350n. 2 (top)
Synagogues, 89: *Groyse shul* (the Great Synagogue), 262, 293, 349n. 2; Old Synagogue *(Alte kloyz),* 262, 350n. 2 (top); Taharat Ha-Kodesh, 14, 293, 309, 340n. 14
Syngalowski, Aaron, 281, 283, 352n. 2 (top)
Syrkin, Isaac, 231
Szabad, Dr. Cemach, 177, 218, 270, 277, 297–300, 302, 323; and establishment of Yiddish schools, 315; and *Folkspartey,* 287, 298; photographs of, 278, 318; and 1919 pogrom, 295; and "The Jewish Locale," 314; use of Yiddish, 316; *Vilna Anthologies,* 263; and *Vilner Tog,* 317
Szapiro, Jeremiah, 290, 353n. 1 (top)
Szapiro, Reuven, 289–90
Szer, Jacob, 272, 351n. 4
Szur, M., 315
Szyrwinty, retreat of Red Army via, 215

Taharat Ha-Kodesh Synagogue, 14, 293, 309, 340n. 14
Taich, Moishe, 309, 355n. 4 (top)
Tailors, 42–43, 227
"Talks on Natural Science and Technology" (Jaszunski), 280, 281
Tallit Katan, 169
Talmud, 339n. 5 (top), 351n. 7 (top), 353n. 3 (top); Romm edition of *(Vilner shas),* 13; teaching of in schools, 130
The Talmudic Argument (Antokolsky), 258
The Talmudists (Kulwianski), 267
Talmud torah (Heb.-Yid.), 221; of Vilna, 222, 266
Tanner *(baltushnik),* 42
Taryba (Lith.: Council of Lithuania), 15
Tatars, 41, 42, 90; healing of mentally ill, 110
Taverns, 67
Taxes: school, 203; yeast, 337n. 2
Tcherikower, Elias, 260
Teachers: *heder*, 92; rural, 75
Technical education, 245–48
Technicum, 323, 325
Telsze, 12, 45
Tenant farmers, 73
"Ten Martyrs," 354n. 1 (bottom)
Tepper, Kolia, 21, 170; debate with Chaim Weizmann, 171–72
Terkel, B., 326
Tevet, 104
Tevye the Dairyman (Sholem Aleichem), 66, 340n. 12
Textile weaving, 242
Thirty-six righteous men, 353n. 3 (top)
T'hum shabbat (Heb.), 68, 337n. 15
Tinsmiths, 272
Tkachenko-Petrenko (prisoner), 151
Tog. See *Vilna Tog*
Tomor, 353n. 1 (top)
Tomashevo, 18
Torah scroll, 68
Torture, 206, 207, 211, 212
Trade unions, 270
Treaty of Versailles, 33
Treblinka, 264, 284
Triwush, Joseph Eliyahu, 281
Troki, 18, 41, 48, 52, 217; expulsion edict, 18; Jewish fishermen in, 53

Troki County, 41
Trupianski, Fayvl, 290, 353n. 1 (top)
Di Tsayt (newspaper), 262, 268, 304
Ha-Tsefirah (newspaper), 261
Tseylem-kop (Yid.), 14
"Der tsion-marsh" (the Zionist March) (Aronson), 103
Tumanov, Count, 293
Turgenev, Ivan, 257
Turners, 270, 272
Turpentine distilleries, 45
Typhus, during World War I, 203

Uciana, shinglers' cooperative in region of, 45
Ukraine, 10, 147
Ukrainian Jewish community, 147; economic prosperity, 147; political activity in early 1900s, 147, 157
Unzer hilf (journal), 325
Union of Lublin, 11
University of Kharkov. *See* Kharkov, University of
University of St. Petersburg. *See* St. Petersburg, University of
University of Warsaw. *See* Warsaw, University of
Unzer shtime (newspaper), 30
Urbanowicz (Christian from Rudziszki), 200
Urban poverty, 26
Uspenskii, Gleb Ivanovich, 299, 354n. 1 (top)

Va'ad Medinat Lita (Council of Lithuanian Jewish Communities), 11–12
Vanished Figures: Memoirs and Silhouettes *(Farshvundene geshtaltn: zikhroynes un siluetn)* (Abramowicz), 10, 36
Veriovkin, Governor, 293–94
Verst, 336n. 6
Verwertungsanstalt (Ger.: conversion plant), 191
"Victims of the state," 354n. 1 (bottom)
Victor Emmanuel, King, 255
Vilna, 9, 10, 11; April 1919 pogrom, 16, 33, 214, 216–18, 235, 272–73, 295, 317, 346n. 4; assassination attempt on von Wahl, 140–42; Bund in, 14–15; central aid committee, 294; Central Education Committee, 300; changes in political control over, 15–16, 32, 233; committee of ORT, 271; Department of Education, 128, 159–60; fish market, 57; German military cemetery, 204; German occupation, 15, 23, 24, 25, 33, 179–81, 193, 270, 302–3; government rabbinical appointees, 292–93; incorporation into Poland, 303; Jewish artists in, 272; Jewish communal life, 16, 31–32; Jewish craftsmen and artisans, 269–75; as Jewish intellectual center, 13, 16, 21, 265, 313–14, 316; Jewish poverty, 26–27; Jewish refugees during World War I, 185–86; Jewish writers and journalists, 318; kitchen at Zawalna 60, 270; Lithuanian rule in 1920, 238, 295; Łukiszki Square, 185; May Day demonstrations, 133–35, 133–1135; municipal militia, 177–81; municipal theater, 135; nationalist sentiments, 315; "Novigorod," 171; occupation by Red Army, 238, 303; opening of Jewish community schools in, 128; Polish rule, 16, 20, 33, 235, 238; relations between Poles and Jews, 33; Russian schools of 1890s, 22; Russian-speaking, 32; shoemaking, 226; *talmud torah,* 222, 266; 1915 threat of expulsion, 294, 302; vocational education, 222–23, 243–48, 266–67; woodworking industry, 225; Yiddish real gymnasium, 283, 288; Yiddish schools, 32; Yiddish-speaking, 16; Zawalna 66, 143
"Vilna—a Multinational City" (Abramowicz), 33
Vilna Artistic Industrial Association, 223
Vilna Association of Craftsmen, 227
Vilna Essays. See Vilner zamlbikher
Vilna Gaon. *See* Elijah of Vilna, Rabbi (Vilna Gaon)
Vilna Ghetto, 30, 248, 264, 287, 290, 348n. 3, 354n. 1 (middle)
Vilna-Grodno region, Jewish colonies, 109–13; care for mentally ill, 109–13; hardships during German occupation, 111
Vilna Jewish Community Council, 227, 256, 267, 271, 273, 274, 287, 290, 303–4

Index

Vilna Jewish Teachers Institute, 15, 22, 117, 118, 126, 254
Vilna Jewish Technical School, 27, 245–48
Vilna Jewry: Antokolsky, Mark, 251–59; Czernichow (Danieli), Joseph, 285–88; Hurwicz, Samuel, 265–68; intelligensia, 313–14, 316; Jaszunski, Joseph, 280–84; Kahan-Wirgili, B., 276–79; Kruk, Eliezer, 269–75; Lunski, Khaykl 260–64; Malakiewicz, Gershon, 289–91; Reisen, Zalmen, 313–20; Rubinstein, Isaac, 292–96; Schreiber, Matthias, 243–48; Shalit, Moshe, 321–26; Szabad, Cemach, 297–300; Weiter, A., 306–12; Wygodzki, Jacob, 301–5. *See also* Lithuanian Jewish community; Vilna
Vilna Kadet committee, 302
Vilna Rabbinical School, 14, 15, 117, 118, 339n. 1 (bottom), 340n. 6
"Vilna Synagogues in the *Shulhoyf*" (Lunski), 263
Vilna Technicum, 323, 324
Vilna Troupe, 355n. 1
Vilna Yiddish Theater Society, 305
Vilner shas (edition of Talmud), 13
Vilner tog (newspaper), 16, 304, 317
Vilner zamlbikher (Shalit and Szabad), 263, 299, 323
Viltar, 300
Visokidvorer, Hirshl, 18
Vitaut, Duke, 11
Vocational education, 15, 26, 27–28, 221–28, 240–48, 266–67, 282–83; in Vilna, 222–23, 243–48, 266–67
Volkovysky, I. B., 118, 339n. 4
von Hindenburg, Paul, 203
von Klingenberg (governor of Yekaterinoslav), 154–55
von Minn, Baron, 133
von Plehve, Viacheslav Konstantinovich, 132, 141, 342n. 1 (top)
von Riman, Baron, 133
von Wahl, Victor, 132–33, 135, 137, 142; assassination attempt upon, 140–42
Dos vort (newspaper), 263
Voskhod (journal), 130, 162, 261, 265, 281
Vozrozhdenie (Rebirth), 322, 356n. 1

Wacławski, Stanisław, 354n. 6

Wagon drivers, 59–60
Waka River, destruction of railroad bridge over, 210
Waldenbergs, 307–8
Walk, Yitskhok, 324
Warsaw, Jewish community council of, 284
Warsaw, University of, 237
Warsaw Ghetto, 284
Wedding celebrations, 87, 112
Weinreich, Max, 34, 318
Weiter, A. (Devinishsky, Isaac Meir), 33, 295, 306–12; experiences during Siberian exile, 311–12; monument controversy, 309–11
Weizmann, Chaim, 21, 22, 126, 169–72, 344n. 2; debate with Kolia Tepper, 171–72
Weizmann Institute of Science, 344n. 2
Wesele (The Wedding) (Wyspiański), 344n. 11
Wheelwrights, 45
Whiskey: monopoly, 70; as principal commodity of inns, 62; production of, 62–63
White Legionnaries (Polish), 111, 235, 238, 295, 306, 309, 317, 348n. 5
White Poles, 233
Widze, fishnets made in, 57
Wieluciany, 20; colony for juvenile offenders, 229; German military economic administration at, 230; Jewish agricultural school in, 230–39, 295
Wierzbołowo, border station at, 255
Wilensky (lawyer), 231
Wilhelm, Kaiser, 200
Wilia River, 10, 46, 288
Windmills, 52
Winter Palace, 265
Wirszubski, Abraham, 111, 268, 339n. 4 (top)
Wirtschaftsausschuß (Ger.), 188, 189–90, 191, 233
Wogler, Elhanan, 317
Wohl, Asher Lazarevich, 118, 340n. 6
Wójt (village headman), 112
Wolf, Leiser, 317
Wołożyn, 12, 340n. 18
Women: in arendar's household, 73–74; "basket women," 304; dairy workers, 51;

fishmongers, 58; maids, 72; seamstresses, 43; *shenkerke* (tavernkeeper), 67
Woodlands, 109
Woodworkers, 45–46
Woodworking industry, 225–26
Wool, 52
"Workers' and peasants' government," 212
Workers Council, 233, 347n. 3 (bottom)
Workhouses, 223
Workmen's Circle: Home for the Aged, 34; Vilna branch, 34
World ORT Union, 352n. 2 (top)
World Union of Zionist Revisionists, 344n. 3
World War I: plight of Jewish refugees, 183–84; Russian refugees, 182–83; Russian retreat from Lithuania, 182–85; suffering of Lithuanian Jews during, 15, 24, 25–26. *See also* Lithuania, German occupation
WUZET (Pol.: acronym for "Wykształcenie Zawodowe" [Vocational Education]), 246, 282
Wygodzki, Dr. Jacob, 17, 237, 270, 301–5
Wysocki, Kalman Zev, 240
Wysoki Dwór: agriculture, 82; anti-semitism, 95, 96; behavior of young people, 85; burial society, 91; charity, 90, 91; community institutions, 89–91; controversy in synagogue on Sabbath, 84–85; education, 91–93; emigration, 86–87, 89; family feuds, 93–94; financial assistance from relations abroad, 89; food, 84; friendliness toward visitors, 88; government officials, 95, 96; graveyard, 77–78; housing, 83–84; hygiene, 84; innkeeper, 78; Jewish population after World War I, 79; Jews of in 1915, 183–84; library, 86; livestock, 81–82; location, 18, 77; love of children, 94; marriage in, 86–87; medical care, 90–91; merchants, 80–81; nicknames, 96–97; Ninth of Av, 85; obsession with soccer, 85–86; occupations, 79–80; paupers, 90; prices for goods, 89; rabbi, 78; relations between Jews and Christians, 94–96; religious spirit, 84; rural Jews on High Holy Days, 88; rural population, 82–83; wedding celebrations, 87–88; wise men and philosophers, 97–98; workmanship, 81; during World War I, 78, 183–84; Zionism, 86
Wyspiański, Stanisław, 166, 344n. 11

Yam shel Shlomo (The Sea of Solomon) (Luria), 11
Yehuda, Eliezer Ben, 277
Yekaterinoslav (Dnepropetrovsk), 23, 153
Yekaterinoslav province, 129, 147, 152–53
Yermak Timofeyevich (Antokolsky), 258
Yeshiva, 12, 92
Yeshiva students, 70
Yesod, the (Judah ben Eliezer), 263, 350n. 5
Yiddish Culture, Paris Congress of 1937, 287, 288
Yiddish language: avoidance in government-run Jewish schools, 124–25; cryptic terms, 66; distinct Lithuanian dialect of, 12; German attitudes toward, 203; increasing use of among Jewish intelligentsia, 316–17; as language of instruction of Vilna Jewish Technical School, 247; Jewish cultural renaissance in, 14–15, 16, 125, 162; lack of interest in, 123; as language of instruction under Germans, 313; medical journal in, 298; prohibition against speaking in public, 293, 313; role in Vilna's Jewish communal life, 31–32; status of, 346n. 7; technology textbooks in, 245; use in government offices, 285
Yiddish literature, 163–65, 258
Yiddish orthography, 316, 355n. 3 (bottom)
"Yiddish Press since 1917, The" (Jaszunski), 281
Yiddish schools, 32, 299, 300, 315–16
Yiddish Teachers' Association, 316
Yiddish Writers and Journalists Association, 31–32, 325, 326
Dos yidishe folk (journal), 322
Di yidishe tsaytung (newspaper), 28, 322
Der yidisher hantverker (jubilee edition), 268, 271
Der yidisher kemfer (journal), 322
Yidisher kultur-farband (YKUF), 287–88, 353n. 4
Yishuvim (Yid.), 82

YIVO Institute for Jewish Research, 16, 66, 311, 318–19, 337n. 13; autobiography contest, 355n. 7
Yokes, carried by dairymen, 50
Yortsayt (Yid.), 84
Young Vilna, 317, 355n. 4 (bottom)

Żabinski, Moshe, 270, 351n. 2
Zabludovski, Mordecai, 118, 339n. 4 (bottom)
Żagory, 18
Zagor, Mera (Miriam), 18, 20–21, 81, 209, 211–12, 216–17
Zakheim, Leivik ("Dmitri"), 143, 144, 145, 146
Zalkind, Ber, 272, 351n. 4
Zalkind, Doctor (Iakov?), 129
Zalman, Elijah ben Solomon. *See* Elijah of Vilna, Rabbi (Vilna Gaon)
Zamość, 13

Zarechye, 252, 309
Zavels, J., 277
Zawalna 66, Vilna, 143
Zazdrość, 205
Zederbaum, Alexander, 13–14
Żeligowski, General Lucjan ("Conqueror of Vilna"), 15, 238, 272, 273
Ha-Zeman (Margolin), 121, 316, 322
Zhid(y) (Rus., pej.), 183, 233, 256
Zhitlowsky, Chaim, 322, 356n. 4
Zhitomir, 117, 339n. 1 (bottom)
Zionism, 13, 21, 166, 171, 338n. 11, 354n. 5; General, 170, 344n. 1; Labor, 147, 169, 170, 172, 344n. 1; Russian, 169, 170; Socialist, 288; in Wysoki Dwór, 86
Zionist Congresses, 170, 280, 344n. 5
Zunser, Eliakum, 103
Zwilling (attorney), 153
"Żydowskie komisary" (Pol.: vulgar term for Jewish Bolshevik commissars), 217

385

INDEX

**Books in the Raphael Patai Series in
Jewish Folklore and Anthropology**

The Myth of the Jewish Race, revised edition, by Raphael Patai and Jennifer Patai, 1989

The Hebrew Goddess, third enlarged edition, by Raphael Patai, 1990

Robert Graves and the Hebrew Myths: A Collaboration, by Raphael Patai, 1991

Jewish Musical Traditions, by Amnon Shiloah, 1992

The Jews of Kurdistan, by Erich Brauer, completed and edited by Raphael Patai, 1993

Jewish Moroccan Folk Narratives from Israel, by Haya Bar-Itzhak and Aliza Shenhar, 1993

For Our Soul: The Ethiopian Jews in Israel, by Teshome G. Wagaw, 1993

Book of Fables: The Yiddish Fable Collection of Reb Moshe Wallich Frankfurt am Main, 1697, translated and edited by Eli Katz, 1994

From Sofia to Jaffa: The Jews of Bulgaria and Israel, by Guy H. Haskell, 1994

Jadıd al-Islām: The Jewish "New Muslims" of Meshhed, by Raphael Patai, 1997

Saint Veneration among the Jews in Morocco, by Issachar Ben-Ami, 1997

Arab Folktales from Palestine and Israel, introduction, translation, and annotation by Raphel Patai, 1998

Profiles of a Lost World: Memoirs of East European Jewish Life before World War II, by Hirsz Abramowicz, translated by Eva Zeitlin Dobkin, edited by Dina Abramowicz and Jeffrey Shandler, 1998